NATIONS OF THE MODERN WORLD

ARGENTINA   H. S. Ferns
Professor of Political Science,
University of Birmingham

AUSTRALIA   O. H. K. Spate
Director, Research School of Pacific Studies,
Australian National University, Canberra

BELGIUM   Vernon Mallinson
Professor of Comparative Education,
University of Reading

BURMA   F. S. V. Donnison
Formerly Chief Secretary to the Government of Burma
Historian, Cabinet Office, Historical Section 1949–66

CEYLON   S. A. Pakeman
Formerly Professor of Modern History, Ceylon University
College; Appointed Member, House of Representatives, Ceylon,
1949–52

CYPRUS   H. D. Purcell
Lecturer in English Literature, the Queen's
University, Belfast

DENMARK   W. Glyn Jones
Reader in Danish, University College London

MODERN EGYPT   Tom Little
Managing Director and General Manager of Regional News
Services (Middle East) Ltd, London

ENGLAND   John Bowle
Professor of Political Theory, Collège d'Europe
Bruges

FINLAND   W. R. Mead
Professor of Geography, University College London

EAST GERMANY   David Childs
Lecturer in Politics, University of Nottingham

WEST GERMANY	Michael Balfour *Reader in European History, University of East Anglia*
MODERN GREECE	John Campbell *Fellow of St Antony's College, Oxford*
	Philip Sherrard *Assistant Director, British School of Archaeology, Athens, 1958–62*
MODERN INDIA	Sir Percival Griffiths *President India, Pakistan and Burma Association*
MODERN IRAN	Peter Avery *Lecturer in Persian and Fellow of King's College, Cambridge*
ITALY	Muriel Grindrod *Formerly Editor of* International Affairs *and* The World Today *Assistant Editor* The Annual Register
KENYA	A. Marshall MacPhee *Formerly Managing Editor with the* East African Standard *Group*
LIBYA	John Wright *Formerly of the* Sunday Ghibli, *Tripoli*
MALAYSIA	J. M. Gullick *Formerly of the Malayan Civil Service*
MOROCCO	Mark I. Cohen *Director of Taxation, American Express*
	Lorna Hahn *Professor of African Studies, American University*
NEW ZEALAND	James W. Rowe *Director of New Zealand Institute of Economic Research*
	Margaret A. Rowe *Tutor in English at Victoria University, Wellington*
NIGERIA	Sir Rex Niven *Administration Service of Nigeria, 1921–54 Member, President and Speaker of Northern House of Assembly, 1947–59*

PAKISTAN   Ian Stephens,
                    Formerly Editor of The Statesman
                    Calcutta and Delhi, 1942–51
                    Fellow, King's College, Cambridge, 1952–58

PERU   Sir Robert Marett,
                    H.M. Ambassador in Lima, 1963–67

POLAND   Václav L. Beneš
                    Professor of Political Science,
                    Indiana University

                    Norman J. G. Pounds
                    Professor of History and Geography,
                    Indiana University

SOUTH AFRICA   John Cope
                    Formerly Editor-in-Chief of The Forum *and South*
                    Africa Correspondent of The Guardian

SPAIN   George Hills
                    Formerly Correspondent and Spanish Programme Organizer,
                    British Broadcasting Corporation

SUDAN   K. D. D. Henderson
    REPUBLIC   *Formerly of the Sudan Political Service and Governor of Darfur*
                    Province, 1949–53

TURKEY   Geoffrey Lewis
                    Senior Lecturer in Islamic Studies, Oxford

YUGOSLAVIA   Muriel Heppell
                        and
                    F. B. Singleton

POLAND

POLAND

VÁCLAV L. BENEŠ
and
NORMAN J. G. POUNDS

PRAEGER PUBLISHERS

New York · Washington

BOOKS THAT MATTER

*Published in the United States of America in 1970
by Praeger Publishers, Inc., 111 Fourth Avenue,
New York, N.Y. 10003*

*Copyright 1970 in London, England, by
Václav L. Beneš and Norman J. G. Pounds*

Library of Congress Catalog Card Number: 74-77306

Printed in Great Britain

Preface

Poland has been fully treated if not always well served in the literature of western Europe and America. This is easy to explain. Poland has for so long been near the centre of European diplomacy that the relationship between Polish affairs and European affairs has always been close. The political importance of Poland derives in large measure from the country's location, in the North European Plain, with Germany to the west, Russia and later the Soviet Union to the east, and, for much of its history, the Austro-Hungarian state to the south. The diplomatic and military game between these three had necessarily to be played across the body of Poland. The misfortunes of Poland are not in question; what one may ask is whether Poland herself contributed significantly through her own internal weaknesses to her own disasters. In their answers to this question scholars have differed widely, with, all too often, their political bias influencing their scholarly judgement. The authors of this book, while admitting the grave internal weaknesses that have allowed Poland to be raided and partitioned so many times, are convinced that the existence of a strong and independent Poland best serves the interests of Europe as a whole. They would further assert that Poland has had a noble and distinguished history, possesses a deep and rich cultural heritage, and has greatly enriched the culture of all of Europe.

This book is the work of two authors who differ in their training and interests; the one a political scientist and international lawyer, the other an historian with an interest in the history of material culture and resource management. The latter has written the first four chapters; the former the rest of the book.

Professor Beneš wishes to thank his friend, Professor Piotr S. Wandycz, of Yale University, who has read critically those passages dealing with post-1863 and inter-war developments. Also, he is greatly indebted to a number of other scholars, both at Indiana University and in Poland, whose opinions, views, and advice were of invaluable help in his effort. Professor Pounds is deeply grateful to very many friends in Poland for their kindness and help to him during his explorations of their country and to his colleagues at Indiana University for assistance in many ways. Both are grateful to Mr Daniel Dull who printed the lettering on the maps and graphs.

Bloomington, Indiana
In die constitutionis   Václav L. Beneš
3 May 1970   Norman J. G. Pounds

9

Contents

List of Illustrations

Maps

Acknowledgements

ACKNOWLEDGEMENT for kind permission to reproduce illustrations is made to the following, to whom the copyright of the illustrations belongs :

Camera Press, London : 9, 18, 19, 22, 23, 24, 25, 26

The National Museum, Warsaw : 1, 2

Paul Popper Ltd : 13, 14, 20

United Press International (UK) Ltd : 21

Numbers 3, 4, 5, 6, 7, 8, 10, 11, and 12 are from Professor Pounds's own collection

Numbers 15, 16, and 17 are from Peter Supf, *Der Luftkrieg in Polen* (Berlin, 1941)

Abbreviations

AK   (Armia Krajowa) – Home Army : the non-communist underground resistance movement during the Second World War

BBWR   (Bezpartyjny Blok Współpracy z Rządem) – Non-Party Bloc of Co-operation with the Government : organization of different pro-Piłsudski groups founded in 1928

CPSU   Communist Party of the Soviet Union

GDR   German Democratic Republic

KPP   (Komunistyczna Partia Polski) – Communist Party of Poland : the new name of the Communist Party adopted after its 'Bolshevization' in 1924

KPRP   (Komunistyczna Partia Robotnicza Polski) – Communist Workers' Party of Poland : the first Polish communist organization founded in December 1918

KRN   (Krajowa Rada Narodowa) – National Council of Poland : communist-controlled Popular Front-type legislative and executive organization founded in December 1944

NKN   (Naczelny Komitet Narodowy) – Supreme National Committee : military and political organization founded in Galicia in 1914 in co-operation with Austrian authorities

NKVD   (Narodnyi Komissariat Vnutrennikh Del) – People's Commissariat of Internal Affairs (USSR)

ORMO   (Ochotnicza Rezerwa Milicji Obywatelskiej) – Voluntary Reserve of the Citizens' Militia : an auxiliary police organization founded in early 1946

OWP   (Obóz Wielkiej Polski) – Camp of Great Poland : right-wing organization founded by Roman Dmowski in 1926

Ozon   (Obóz Zjednoczenia Narodowego) – Camp of National Unity : government party created along military lines in 1937

PKWN	(Polski Komitet Wyzwolenia Narodowego) – Polish Committee of National Liberation : pro-Soviet organization of several political parties referred to as 'Lublin Committee'
PPR	(Polska Partia Robotnicza) – Polish Workers' Party : Communist Party as reconstructed in 1942
PPS	(Polska Partia Socjalistyczna) – Polish Socialist Party
PSL	(Polskie Stronnictwo Ludowe) – Polish People's (Peasant) Party : name of the first Polish peasant party, abandoned in 1931, and returned to in 1945
PZPR	(Polska Zjednoczona Partia Robotnicza) – Polish United Workers' Party (PUWP); result of the 1948 merger of the PPR and the PPS
SDKPiL	(Socjaldemokracja Królestwa Polskiego i Litwy) – Social Democracy of the Kingdom of Poland and Lithuania
SL	(Stronnictwo Ludowe) – The Populist (Peasant) Party : emerged from the merger of the three peasant opposition parties under Wincenty Witos in 1931; after 1944 the same name chosen by the pro-communist wing of the Peasant Party
SND	(Stronnictwo Narodowo-Demokratyczne) – National Democratic Party : right-wing party founded by Roman Dmowski
Wici	(Związek Młodzieży Wieskiej Rzeczypospolitej Polskiej) – Union of Village Youth of the Polish Republic; rural youth organization associated with SL
ZBOWID	(Związek Bojowników o Wolność i Demokrajcę) – Union of Fighters for Freedom and Democracy : organization of veterans and former members of underground resistance
ZLN	(Związek Ludowo-Narodowy) – National People's Union : organization of rightist political parties founded in 1919
ZNR	(Związek Naprawy Rzeczypospolitej) – Association for the Reform of the Republic : organization of the younger members of the pro-Piłsudski intelligentsia.

PART ONE

History

Chapter 1

The Beginning of the Polish State

Panno święta, co Jasnej bronisz Częstochowy
I w Ostrej świecisz Bramie! Ty, co gród zamkowy
Nowogródzki ochraniasz z jego wiernym ludem!
(Adam Mickiewicz, *Pan Tadeusz*[1])

THE POLISH STATE came into being a thousand years ago. It was born amid the lakes and marshy valleys which stretch from the Odra to the Vistula. Its earliest capitals were the cities of Gniezno and Poznań, and it was from these centres that the earliest Polish kings extended their authority westward to the Odra river; northward to the Baltic Sea; southward to the mountains that ring Bohemia; and eastward into the forests of White Russia and the steppes of the Ukraine. It was a vast territory that Poland thus came for at least a period of her history to occupy, larger indeed than she could control or effectively administer. For part of her history she was territorially the largest state in Europe west of Russia, and at the same time one of the most populous. For another period, lasting considerably more than a century, she disappeared from the map of Europe, partitioned by the empires which surrounded her. No European country has known such contrasts in its fortunes. None has met adversity with greater courage, nor forged from its most bitter experiences so unique a spirit of patriotism.

Throughout her changes Poland remained a country of the plain, lying always between the shores of the Baltic Sea and the mountains which border this plain on the south. Some have seen in this situation astride the great plain of northern Europe a reason for the sharp vicissitudes in Poland's history and for the fluctuations of her boundaries during the past thousand years. Nature, it has been said, provided no natural barriers to movement across the plain between west and east, and Poland, thus deprived of protection, succumbed to onslaughts from both directions. Nothing could be farther from the truth. The medieval chroniclers were unanimous in representing

---

[1] 'Holy Virgin, who protectest bright Czestochowa and shinest above the Ostra [Narrow] Gate in Wilno! Thou who dost shelter the castle of Nowogrodek with its faithful folk.' (G. R. Noyes (tr.), in the Everyman edition.)

Poland as unusually well defended by nature. They saw in the lesser facets of the terrain : the marshy flood-plains of the rivers; the lakes, with their fringe of reed-covered swamp; the steep bluffs which rose from the river banks; and the vast extent of the forest itself, the strongest of natural barriers. Otto of Freising, writing at the end of the twelfth century, described Poland as 'particularly well fortified by natural defences', and praised the Emperor Frederick I Barbarossa for his penetration of Polish territory 'although it is strongly fortified by nature and art, so that previous kings and emperors had with great difficulty barely reached the river Odra. . . .'[2]

Contemporary thought is not wholly free from the teleological view that what nature allegedly failed to make adequate provision to protect is in fact not worth preserving. The tragic history of Poland was not written in her geography; what history, indeed, ever was? Throughout the Middle Ages Poland had her own important and respected place in European history, and one chronicler after another commented on the natural strength of her location. It was only in the seventeenth and eighteenth centuries that the political weakness of Poland, due in part to the over-extension of her boundaries and the weaknesses of an elective monarchy, coincided with the rise of strong and vigorous rulers in Prussia and Russia. Poland was then crushed, as if between the upper and the nether millstones.

The population and resources of both Germany and Russia have always been greater than those of Poland. When both were weak or divided Poland could expand her boundaries. When one or the other was strong and united the tendency was for Poland to pull in her boundaries on this side and to expand on the other. Only when both have been both strong and allied with one another has the security of Poland been really endangered.

This conjunction has occurred twice in the long history of Poland : in the eighteenth century when it culminated in the partitions of Poland; and in the late 1930s, when an unholy alliance of Nazi Germany and Stalinist Russia again led to the partition and destruction of the state. The revived Poland of 1945 has been shifted physically westward by her eastern neighbour, the Soviet Union. If the lessons of history mean anything in the context of the twentieth century, the future of Poland is secure as long as there is no united and aggressive Germany to the west. An aggressive Germany, in alliance with the Soviet Union, could again spell the destruction of Poland, and perhaps also of much of Europe. It is to Europe's advantage to maintain, to guarantee, a viable and strong Poland.

Polish history did not begin when, in 966, both the country and its king, Mieszko, appeared in the pages of the documents. The Slav

2 *Gesta Frederici*, III, 1–3; the translation is that of C. C. Mirow.

tribe of the Poljane, who thus emerged into the light of history, occupied an extensive area in central Poland. This territory lay within the bend of the river Warta. To the north was the marshy valley of the Noteć, and beyond it the maritime region of Pomorze, or Pomerania. On the east lay the valley of the Vistula. The Poljane are generally considered to have taken their name, which they in turn passed on to the state which they created, from the *pola*, the fields or plains of this region. The Poles were both etymologically and in reality the people of the plains.

The Slav language which they spoke was the source from which modern Polish has derived; it was also one of a close family of languages which had its origin here in the northern plain of Europe. The diffusion of the Slavs is one of the most remarkable features in the ethnic history of Europe. At the time when the Roman legions held the line of the Rhine and the Danube against the Germanic tribes, the Slavs lived probably in the forests of Poland and of western Russia. Their present linguistic subdivisions were not yet differentiated, and they cannot at this time have been particularly numerous. Polish archaeologists have identified the proto-Slavs with the bearers of the Lusatian culture which was distributed in the late Bronze Age over approximately the valleys of the lower Odra and Vistula. Others place their origin farther to the east and nearer the headwaters of the great Russian rivers, the Dnestr and Dnepr.

Their expansion from this homeland in the Great Northern Plain had begun by the early years of our era. The numbers of the Slavs must have increased greatly in a short period of time. They spread southwards into Bohemia and Moravia, which had previously been inhabited by Celtic peoples, across the Danube and into the Balkans. They besieged Thessaloníki in the seventh century, and for a long period during the Middle Ages the population of southern Greece was more Slav than it was Greek. In the northern plain itself the Slav peoples spread westwards until their villages reached beyond the river Elbe, and eastwards to the river Volga. Most of the present East Germany was Slavic at the time when the Polish state appeared, and the sites of Brandenburg, Leipzig, and Berlin – all of them names of Slav origin – were occupied by the fortified *grody*, or cities of the Slavs.

For several centuries the Slav tribes of east Germany bore the brunt of the Germans' political and military expansion towards the east. They never achieved any degree of political unity partly on this account, but their existence allowed the Polish state to develop, comparatively free from interference from the west. In time they were absorbed by the Germans who settled among them, with the exception of the Sorbs who continue to live in small and diminishing numbers in the Spreewald of Lusatia.

Along the Baltic coast there were also Slav tribes, the Pomeranians and Kaszubs. Their relative isolation from the Poljane allowed them to develop dialects different from the latter, which their descendants in some measure still retain. To the north-east, however, was a sharp ethnic divide, which ran very roughly from west to east across East Prussia. Beyond lived Baltic peoples, ancestors of the later Lithuanians and Latvians. The Borussi – the original Prussians – were the Baltic people nearest geographically to the Poles. They were more primitive than the Poles, or at least were so regarded by early Polish writers, and were slower to adopt any form of urban life. They resisted the attempts of early missionaries to christianize them, and their raids into Polish territory ultimately led to the unfortunate association of the Poles with the Germans in an attempt to subjugate them.

Eastward, beyond the Vistula, stretched the forest, merging southward, in the Ukraine, into wooded steppe and then into the grasslands which extended to the Black Sea. There the population was sparse. The names of the local Slavic tribes were preserved by the author of the Primary Russian Chronicle, and are referred to in Polish and Byzantine sources, but it is impossible to relate them with any certainty to the Polish, Belorussian, Great Russian, or Ukrainian branches of the great Slav family. They lived in small village communities, widely scattered through the forests, and hunted, fished, and practised a rudimentary form of agriculture. Contemporary writers recognized the broad cultural uniformity of this northern Slav region which extended from the Elbe far into Russia. Adam of Bremen, who wrote a history of the dioceses of Bremen and Hamburg, described *Slavia* as a vast and little-known region, which extended 'from our diocese . . . toward the east and . . . in boundless expanses reach[es] clear to . . . Hungary and Greece'.[3] Helmold, his younger contemporary, who was a priest in Holstein, knew of Poland as 'a large province' which reached to Russia.[4]

Within this cultural region the Poles themselves – the Poljane – had developed a somewhat more sophisticated culture when they first appeared in the light of history. They inhabited a clay-covered plain, surrounded by wide, deep, and in places impassable valleys. It thus had the advantages of natural protection in a troubled age, and yet was not so completely cut off from surrounding areas that commercial and cultural interchange was impossible. Though not an area of

---

[3] Adam of Bremen, *History of the Archbishops of Hamburg-Bremen,* trans. Francis J. Tschan (New York, 1959), p. 65.

[4] Helmold the Priest, *The Chronicle of the Slavs,* trans. Francis J. Tschan (New York, 1935), pp. 47–8.

outstanding fertility, it was nevertheless cleared and settled at a relatively early date. Its waterways were narrow and probably difficult to navigate, yet it became the focus of trade routes, and the coin hoards that have been found here, dating from as early as classical times, are evidence of both the antiquity and the continuity of long-distance trade in the Polish plain.

The Poljanian tribes in the tenth century probably lived still in small and shifting communities, yet a network of more permanent settlements had been established. These were *grody*, well fortified and often occupying an island or peninsula in a lake or river. Within their wooden walls and palisades lay the buildings of a small town, as well as the dwelling of a tribal chieftain or prince. Their functions were still primarily agricultural, but recent excavations have revealed abundant evidence that crafts were pursued and trade carried on. A network of such *grody* covered the area of early Poland. At its centre lay Gniezno; on its western margin, beside the Warta, was Ostrów Tumski, predecessor of the city of Poznań. The approaches to Gniezno can be thought of as protected by a ring of such *grody*, while an outer ring guarded the passages across the marshy valleys which ringed the early state. Many of these settlements are a great deal older than the first appearance of the Polish state in the tenth century. Their development is part of the process of economic growth and capital accumulation, of which the actual formation of a united state is only the culmination.

About the middle of the tenth century the district of Gniezno and, indeed, much of the province which later came to be known as Wielkopolska, or Great Poland, fell under the authority of the family of Piast. The earliest authentic member of this dynasty was Mieszko, who first appeared in history in 963, when he was defeated in a struggle with other Slavs for control of lands near the lower Odra. The chroniclers recorded – or invented – the names of his ancestors back through four generations to Piast, of whom we know nothing but his name, one nevertheless that has never ceased to echo through Polish history.

This sudden appearance of the Polish state and its almost meteoric rise to importance in Europe are not easy to understand, and some writers have assumed that it must have been leadership from outside the Slav peoples which thus fashioned the Poljane into a state. Both the Avars, a Ural-Altaic people from the Russian steppe, and the Norse have been credited with this role. For neither is there a shred of historical evidence in this regard; on the contrary, the archaeological record demonstrates a gradual accumulation of wealth and political experience which culminated in the tenth century in the emergence of the Polish state. The latter was the creation of the

Poljane from whom it derived its name. Unknown leaders of the Poljane must first have united their own tribe and then brought the neighbouring tribes of Kujawy, Mazowsze, Lubusz, and Kalisz under their control. They were helped by the broad cultural and linguistic uniformity of these areas, though they must have been plagued, as were their successors in the historical period, by the strength of local and tribal feeling.

Poland's early relations with Germany resembled those of the Slavic tribes between the Odra and the Elbe at this time. Mieszko accepted some kind of German suzerainty, which probably meant little to him and not much to the Germans who recorded the fact. His distance from the frontier of German settlement gave him protection and, for further assurance, he accepted Christianity and placed his state directly under the authority of the Papacy. It was this event which was in fact commemorated in the millenary celebrations of the Polish state. The instrument by which Mieszko performed this act has been preserved in a later copy, and has come to be one of the most important as well as controversial sources in Polish history. It purports to define the limits of the Polish state. In it Dagome *Judex,* usually assumed to have been Mieszko himself,

> presented to St Peter an entire city [*civitas,* i.e. state or territory] called Schinesne with all its territory as enclosed within the following frontiers : starting first from the long sea shore as far as *Pruzze,* running thence to a country called *Russe* and extending as far as *Graccoa* [Kraków], thence to the river *Odere* [Odra] and straight on to a place called *Alemure,* and from *Cracow* to the land of *Milze;* and from *Milze* right on to the Oder and along its banks as far as *Schinesne,* mentioned previously.

'Schinesne' can be none other than Szczecin, or Stettin, the present port-city at the mouth of the Odra. On the east the state was bordered by the lands of the Prussians and Russians. The southern boundary was defined less clearly, but it certainly included Kraków and the Mura river, if that is intended by the term 'Alemure'. The Milze were a Slav tribe then inhabiting Lower Silesia, while on the west, the Odra formed the boundary as it does today. This tenth-century record appears to delineate the boundaries of a state which occupied, as nearly as one can judge, an area corresponding closely with that of modern Poland.

Mieszko died in 992, and was succeeded by his son, Bolesław Chrobry, 'the Brave', as he has since been called, who ruled until 1025. This was a period of territorial expansion, during which Poland reached what may be regarded as her historical boundaries. Bolesław enjoyed the friendship of the German emperor, Otto III,

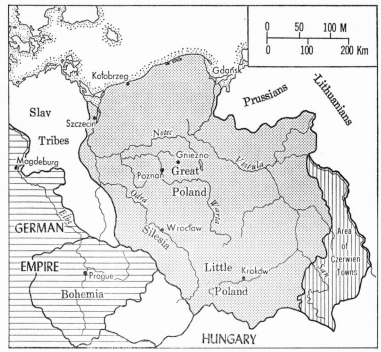

1. Poland at the time of Bolesław Chrobry (*c*. A.D. 1000)

who not only released him from the subordinate status in which Mieszko had been placed, but also recognized him as 'king'. He also acquiesced in the establishment at Gniezno of an archiepiscopal see, dependent directly on the Papacy and thus free from obligations to the German archdiocese of Magdeburg, which had claimed a general jurisdiction over Central Europe.

Bolesław extended the boundaries of Mieszko's state in some directions and consolidated them in others. The attachment of Pomerania to the Polish state was probably loose because of the barrier of forest and marsh which separated it from the core-area of the latter. Nevertheless, the episcopal see established at Kołobrzeg (Kolberg), near the Baltic coast, was made tributary to Gniezno. The Pomeranian coast was at this time the centre of an important nexus of trade routes, and, in addition to Szczecin and Kołobrzeg, Wolin, near the Odra mouth, was 'a most noble city . . . a very widely known trading centre for the barbarians and Greeks . . . there live in it Slavs and many other peoples, Greeks and barbarians. For even alien Saxons also have the other right to reside there on equal terms with the others. . . .'[5] The arrival of Germans in Pomerania, thus recorded in the early eleventh century by Adam of Bremen, was the beginning of a pressure that was later to detach Pomerania from the Polish state.

The Poland of Bolesław was bounded on the west by the wide, marshy valley of the lower Odra. From the bend of the river above Frankfurt-on-Oder the boundary ran southwards to the mountains of Bohemia. Today this boundary follows the course of the Nysa (German : Neisse). In the tenth and eleventh centuries it was not defined with such precision. It was a frontier rather than a boundary, a zone of sparsely populated and little-developed land over which neither side asserted its sovereignty. Within this zone, the valleys of the Kwisa and Bóbr, lying to the east of the Nysa, and of the Spree to the west all constituted obstacles to movement and hindrances to settlement. The natural barriers were intermittently reinforced along the Bóbr valley by artificial banks and ditches and by forts established to guard the crossings of the rivers. It was at one of these that Bolesław, in the year 1000, met his guest, the Emperor Otto III, and conducted him to his capital at Gniezno.

The southern boundary was less definite than the western, and remained so throughout much of Poland's history. The ninth-century state of Great Moravia had probably extended into southern Poland before it was destroyed by the invading Magyars at the beginning of the tenth century, and an early description of the boundaries of the diocese of Prague would appear to have embraced much of Silesia, as well as Kraków and part of southern Poland. Ecclesiastical jurisdiction commonly paralleled closely that of the secular arm, and it is likely that Poland's claim to at least the more southerly parts of the area defined in the *Dagome Index* did not go altogether unchallenged by the Czechs of Bohemia and Moravia. It was probably to make good his claim to these areas that Bolesław invaded Bohemia and actually established himself for a time in Prague. Thereafter contemporary writers appear to have regarded the Sudeten mountains as a frontier zone between the Polish and the Czech states.

Farther to the east, the authority of the Polish king probably extended into the Carpathian mountains but is unlikely to have extended beyond them into the Hungarian Plain. The chroniclers frequently described the Poles as bordered on the east by the Russians, and the Primary Russian chronicle described the attacks made by the princes of Kiev on the territory of Poland. These conflicts largely took place along the southern part of their mutual frontier, where the forest thinned and merged gradually into the steppe. To the north lay the wide tract of marshes which bordered the Prypeć river and beyond it lay the forests inhabited by the Baltic peoples, especi-

[5] Adam of Bremen, op. cit., pp. 66–7.

ally the Prussians (*Borussi*), the Jaćwież, and the Lithuanians. It is uncertain how far to the south-east the rule of Mieszko had extended, and when in the closing years of the tenth century Bolesław extended his authority in this direction, he probably occupied territory that had hitherto been loosely held either by the Přemyslid kings of Bohemia or the princes of Kievan Russia.

The boundary of Poland was thus advanced by the early years of the eleventh century to the line of the river Bug and to the 'Volhynian Gate', between the marshes and the mountains, where the steppe road passed from Poland into the Ukraine. Except in the north-east, where the boundary of the state was quite indefinite, Poland had by this date assumed a geographical shape that is very close to that of the present day. It is not without some historical justification that the Poles today refer to their boundaries of 'a thousand years'.

If the original boundaries have in large measure been restored, the intervening years witnessed changes in them that were both violent and extreme. Polish writers of the present day have stressed that the boundary changes which resulted from the Second World War constituted a return to the traditional limits, the recovery of ancient lands, and the abandonment of imperialism in the east. A theme of this and subsequent chapters will be the 'distortions' of the geographical framework of the early Polish state. The considerable space given to a consideration of the boundaries of the earliest Poland can be justified because these conditions greatly influence current Polish thinking and constitute, at least in a very small degree, some justification for the new western boundary.

More is known of the boundaries of Poland at this time than of the tribal groups of which the state was composed. A national sentiment was very far from appearing. If outlying tribes recognized the suzerainty of the king, his real authority among them was little more than nominal. The authority of the Piasts was firmly anchored in the soil of Wielkopolska. They had no capital in the modern sense, but they were to be found most often in the region of Gniezno, which was their principal seat. Here were preserved the relics of Poland's national saint, St Adalbert, who had been martyred by the Prussians a few years earlier, and here too was established the archdiocese of Poland, the ecclesiastical expression of Poland's independence of German control. The role of capital of Wielkopolska was later shifted to the more accessible and commercially more important city of Poznań, and that of national capital about 1300 to Kraków, but the seat of the archbishop remained in Gniezno until the nineteenth century.

In the tenth and eleventh centuries Wielkopolska was a focus of trade-routes, which linked it not only with the ports of the Baltic coast, but also with western Europe, Russia, and the Black Sea. It became a region of considerable wealth, as measured by the building activity and the crafts which were carried on in the cities at this time. This cultural and economic development was somewhat premature. Poland's commercial role was later undermined by piracy in the Baltic Sea and by Tatars on the steppe. German occupation of lands east of the Elbe and the foundation of Lübeck in the twelfth century drew off trade in this direction and the economic basis of the Polish state began to weaken.

The monarchy, to outward appearances so strong under Bolesław, also weakened under his successors. It was the practice of the Polish king, as also of the French, to make provision for his younger sons by granting them territorial *apanages*, within which they enjoyed quasi-royal dignities and privileges. There were likely at any one time to be several Piast dynasties, each ruling in effective independence some part of the country. Dependence on the titular king of Poland was at times merely nominal. Rivalries between the descendants of Piast were reinforced by the individuality of the provinces which they ruled. The concept of a unified Poland was even weaker than that of the unity of France during the early Middle Ages. Kingship rested with the descendants of Piast, but it mattered little which of them wore the crown. At any one time the rival Piast families fought for its possession, and in doing so only intensified the individualism of the duchies which they ruled.

Given the high mortality and short expectation of life even of princely families, it could be expected that one Piast line after another would become extinct. Its titles, possessions, and pretensions would thus revert to the principal or royal line, just as the *apanages* of France one after another reverted to the king. Thus at intervals the duchies were, at least in part, brought together again by a 're-storer', who for a short period embodied the unity of the Polish lands, only to be dispersed again amongst his successors.

At the same time the pressure of the Germans, both political and economic, was growing in the west, and the majority of the Polish kings had neither the wisdom to appreciate it nor the ability to resist. Thus began a Polish retreat in the west, with the loss first of Pomerania and of the lands along the middle Odra and then of Silesia. These losses were to some extent compensated by conquests in the east, but the extension of Polish rule in this direction was blocked by the vast, sprawling state of Lithuania. It was not until the Piast dynasty had, in 1386, been succeeded by that of Jagiełło that eastward expansion became an important factor in Polish history.

In these trends lay, at least in germ, two contrasted policies which have since been associated with the two dynasties, the Piasts and their successors, the Jagiełło, which ruled Poland from the tenth until the death of Zygmunt II in 1572. To the Piast kings has been ascribed the policy of holding fast in the west and of resisting the pressure of the Germans; to the Jagiełło, that of expanding to the east. This is to oversimplify the course of Polish history and to devise a contrast in policy that did not exist. None, except perhaps the earliest of the Piast kings, ever conceived of themselves as dedicated to holding a western line, nor did the Jagiełło kings consciously abandon this policy in favour of eastward conquest. By a series of mischances, of errors of judgement, and of human failures the Polish rulers lost lands that had been historically theirs and acquired others of greater extent but probably of smaller intrinsic value, which served only to embroil them with the rulers of Russia.

The successors of Bolesław were unequal to the task of holding the territories that their predecessor had put together. Kievan Russia, exposed to the attacks of the Pechenegs, ceased to trouble Poland, but to the west the Germans were expanding their rule, and, to the south-west, the Bohemian kings sought again to incorporate Silesia. Within Poland itself the tribal rivalries were perpetuated in the jealousies of the duchies and provinces.

In the middle years of the twelfth century, Kazimierz I (1038–58), nicknamed *Odnowiciel,* the 'Restorer', the great-grandson of the first Mieszko, temporarily reasserted the authority of the king over the wayward provinces, and drove the Czechs from Silesia. His successor, Bolesław II (1058–79), worked to secure the borders of Poland; made some slight territorial advances in the east; and shifted his capital from Wielkopolska to Kraków in Małopolska, or Little Poland.

This change signalled a new direction in Polish policy. The Carpathian mountains along Poland's southern boundary constituted no impenetrable barrier. On the contrary, the routes across the ranges were numerous and easy, and the Polish king had every encouragement to meddle in the affairs of the Hungarian Plain. He may have been motivated by a desire to check the spread of the German settlers. But, whatever its origin, association with Hungary became a recurring theme in the policy of Poland. This short and active period was brought to a close when internal revolt ended the career of Bolesław himself.

His successor, Władysław Herman, not only failed to claim the royal title, but actually divided the country between himself and two of his numerous progeny. Their successor, the third Bolesław (1102–38), known as *Krzywousty,* or 'Wry-mouthed', recognized the centrifugal tendencies, and tried before his death to regulate and control them. He provided for the division of the provinces between his sons and their descendants, but enacted that the senior among them should bear the title of 'Duke of Poland' and should hold sway in the capital city of Kraków and the surrounding province of Małopolska. This scheme worked badly. The letter of Krzywoústy's testament was rarely observed; its spirit, never. Poland broke up into a number of competing and, for practical purposes, sovereign and independent principalities, reminiscent of the confusion of Merovingian France. Even the name of Poland – *Polonia* – came to be restricted to Wiel-kopolska, and only one institution, the Church, preserved any kind of functional unity over Poland in the larger sense of that term. Though the Catholic dioceses corresponded roughly with the pro-vinces, all were subject to the Polish metropolitan, the archbishop of Gniezno. For the first time, though not for the last, the Polish Church was to be the chief instrument in perpetuating the concept of a single, united Polish state.

A fatal consequence of political division was the failure of Poland as a whole to assume responsibility for, or even to recognize, external dangers to the nation. Defence against Germans, Czechs, Prussians, and Russians was left to the provinces immediately and directly threatened. It was Konrad of Mazowsze, ruler of the Mazovian province along the middle Vistula valley, who called in the German knights to assist him against the Prussians, expecting them to hold the lands they conquered as a dependency of himself. In this he was mistaken. Hermann von Salza, leader of the knights, at once (1226) secured the formal incorporation of Prussia in the German Empire.

A few years later Poland was faced with another danger, that of the Tatars. The princes of Halicz, who controlled the steppe-road between the marshes of the Prypeć and the Carpathian mountains, were unable to restrain them. In 1241, their bands broke across southern Poland, and had reached Lower Silesia before, at the battle of Legnica,[6] they were intercepted and defeated. The great Tatar invasion had left a train of destruction, comparable with that to be found in Hungary. This was in time repaired. There were no re-newed invasions on the scale of that of 1241, but for many centuries Poland lived under the shadow of the Tatars. Energies were con-sumed and lives lost in the defence of Poland – and of Central Europe – that could well have been used in political and economic development within Poland.

A direct consequence of the Tatar inroad was the death of Henry II of Silesia. He was a Piast, and son and successor to Henry I, the 'Bearded', who had unified the province of Silesia around himself and occupied the titular capital, Kraków. The death of the younger

---

[6] Correctly Legnickie Pole, a village nearby, where the battle was actually fought.

Henry was followed by renewed tension and rivalry within Poland. The attempt of the Silesian Piasts to unify the Polish state around themselves foundered on the hostility of the Piasts of Great Poland. Silesia itself passed under the control of the Bohemian kings. Pomerania was occupied by the Danish king, and, after his expulsion, lapsed into virtual independence until it was settled and absorbed by the Germans. Prussians, Lithuanians, Ukrainians, and Russians threatened the eastern borders, and to the west was the ever-present danger from the Germans.

The latter had long been extending their political control by the formation of 'march' states between the Elbe and the Odra. The peoples thus subjugated were mainly Slav but not, in general, Polish. At the same time there occurred both an economic and a demographic penetration of Poland. The number of Germans who participated in the eastward migration has been exaggerated. But communities of Germans moved into thinly populated Slav territory. A thirteenth-century land register of the lordship of Zary (Sorau)[7] in western Poland represents Germans and Slavs as each living in their own villages, which lay intermixed in a vast clearing in the forest.

The economic penetration was felt most strongly in the towns. The Polish princes were eager to stimulate the economic growth of their provinces and to develop urban life, craft industries, and trade. Many of them invited Germans to take the initiative. The number who responded was small, because in the aggregate the urban population of Germany was itself not large. But they did introduce German institutions into countless towns and laid out the regular ground-plan of many of them. The Germans did not introduce urban life to Poland – it had been there for centuries. They intensified it, and gave it new architectural and institutional forms. The economic growth of each of the principalities of Poland seemed for a time to preoccupy the princes to the exclusion of dreams of Polish unity.

The accident of birth and death, which had done much to produce this political division, itself contributed to its remedy. The number of contenders for the Polish crown was considerably reduced during the thirteenth century; a number of territories were merged, and the way was prepared for Władysław I, Łokietek, or the 'Short' (1296–1333), to unite most of the country and to be crowned as its king in 1320. With most of Poland united under his rule – he never regained control of Silesia, and even Mazowsze acknowledged Czech rule – he could adopt a more positive policy towards his neighbours. He married his daughter, Elisabeth (Elżbieta), to Charles Robert, the Angevin

---

[7] *Das Landregister der Herrschaft Sorau von 1381*, ed. Johannes Schultze, Veröffentlichungen der Historischen Kommission für die Provinz Brandenburg und die Hauptstadt Berlin, 1936.

king of Hungary, and his son and heir, Kazimierz, to the daughter of the prince of Lithuania. These marriages, whose purpose was to increase the security and enhance the prestige of Poland and the Piast dynasty, were to have important consequences.

Władysław was succeeded by his only son, Kazimierz III, to whom posterity gave the name of *Wielki*, the 'Great'. Under his rule (1333–70) medieval Poland reached the peak of her prosperity and political success. Kazimierz III is chiefly known for his administrative reforms, his codification of Polish law, and his foundation of the first Polish university at Kraków, and his encouragement of art, culture, and economic development. All this helped to cement the newly-found Polish unity. He raised Poland again to an equality with other states of Europe. He also stabilized the boundaries, though not without compromising on some issues of vital concern to the welfare of the Polish state. He gained political control over Mazowsze, but was obliged to acknowledge Bohemian rule over Silesia. To the south-east, however, he succeeded in annexing the principality of Halicz, and thus initiated the Polish policy, continued so disastrously in later centuries, of expanding through the Russian steppe towards the Black Sea. On the other hand, he acquiesced in the loss of Pomerania and made no effort to dislodge the German knights from their castles on the lower Vistula and in Prussia.

The Polish claim to the province of Silesia had never gone un-challenged, and, with the disintegration of the Polish state during the twelfth and thirteenth centuries, the Piast dukes in Silesia entered into ever-closer relationships with the Přemyslids of Bohemia. By the end of the thirteenth century Silesia had become merely an append-age of Bohemia, and was itself being used as a base from which the later Přemyslids attempted to establish themselves in southern Poland. Łokietek had failed to shake Czech control of Silesia, and Kazimierz recognized it as a fact which his statesmanship could not alter. In 1335 he agreed with John of Luxembourg, who had succeeded the last of the Přemyslids on the Czech throne, to recognize Bohemian sovereignty over Silesia in return for John renouncing all Bohemian claims in Poland.

Thus was Silesia lost to Poland for over six hundred years. It passed, along with the Bohemian crown, to the Habsburgs, and was snatched from the latter by Frederick the Great of Prussia in the war of 1740. In 1919–22, a small part of the traditional province of Silesia was included within the restored Polish state, but the greater part of the territory remained German until, in 1945, the Polish boundary was advanced again to the line of the Odra and Nysa.

The attachment of Pomerania to Poland was even looser than that of Silesia. It was separated from Wielkopolska by a formidable barrier of marsh and forest, and its most populous areas lay along the coast, exposed to raids and invasion by the Danes and other seafaring peoples of the Baltic. Western Pomerania thus fell under the influence of Saxon and Danish princes, and circumstances within Poland were such that no help could come from this quarter. By the end of the twelfth century western Pomerania had become tributary to Brandenburg and the German Empire. The settlement of German towns-folk and peasants in this region had already begun, and during the later Middle Ages it spread towards eastern Pomerania. The movement was in general peaceful, and the Slav peasantry were gradually assimilated to the language and culture of the Germans. But this was a long process, and not until the nineteenth century was it even nearly complete. A number of cities was established, with their urban government based upon the German model, but in many rural areas German settlers were few. Many of those to be met with in the four-teenth century had been introduced by the monastic orders, par-ticularly the Cistercians and Norbertines, who, here as elsewhere in Central Europe, played a prominent role in land settlement, and by the military orders such as the Templars.

Pomerania was lost to the Polish crown when its local rulers trans-ferred their allegiance from the Polish king to a Saxon duke. The fact that for a considerable period there was no crowned king in Poland, and that primacy among the Piast princes was by no means easy to establish, made this process all the easier. The juridical, as dis-tinct from the social, Germanization of Pomerania, thus took place during the thirteenth century.

Between western Pomerania and Lower Silesia lay the *Ziemia Lubuska,* the Lubusz Lands, the 'Achilles heel', as the Polish historian Kaczmarczyk called them, of Piast Poland. This province was bor-dered on the west by the Odra, on the north and east by the Warta. It had little agricultural value, but could be entered easily from the west, and from its geographical position could command routes from Wielkopolska into western Pomerania as well as into Lower Silesia. German settlement in the Lubusz province can only have weakened the ties which bound Silesia and Pomerania to Wielkopolska.

In the process of Germanization there were three distinct phases, of which only two were accomplished during the Middle Ages. The first consisted in the transfer of sovereignty from Poland to the German Empire. This was done by a symbolic act, an oath of allegi-ance or a declaration of loyalty. It was essentially a feudal act, and carried with it no necessary social or economic overtones, because, as a general rule, it left unaltered the authority of the local rulers within their own lands.

The second phase was the establishment of German settlers. This was of greater importance. It could not happen without the prior invitation or at least consent of the Polish ruler, and it implied that there was on his part a desire to take advantage of German commercial and technical skills, or perhaps merely to develop lands which had hitherto been waste. Nor were all such settlers of German origin. Many Netherlanders were settled in the marshy lands of northern Poland and were given the task of reclaiming them. A number of Czechs also moved into Silesia.

The process of Germanizing the mass of the local population was the last and the slowest of these processes, and in some areas was scarcely complete when, in the present century, German authority ended in these territories. Evidence for the progress of Germanization in this cultural sense is scanty. It does not appear that the Germans brought pressure to bear on the Poles to make this cultural change before the eighteenth century, and in many areas before the nineteenth. Perhaps the most effective step in the Germanization of the Polish peasant was taken in the sixteenth century, when the Hohenzollern or Brandenburg lands became Lutheran. This in itself permitted church services to be conducted in Polish, but it also cut the rural communities off from the Catholic Church, whose priests have always been the strongest apostles of Polish national feeling.

German settlement in these western lands of Poland was independent of the transfer of sovereignty over them, but it is doubtful whether it would have been on the same scale without it. It is even possible that most of the German settlers would have been absorbed into the Polish masses if the territory had remained under ultimate Polish jurisdiction. It cannot be questioned that the forcible establishment of Lutheranism and the Germanization of the Slavic population stem from the transfer of sovereignty. In the last resort the latter was made possible by the divisions and dissensions which followed the death of Krzywousty and by the feeble power of the central government, and even on occasion its total absence. The German absorption of Poland's Western Territories was the unforeseen but cumulative result of countless political and economic acts, each one of which may have seemed reasonable and proper at the time.

The conditions were, however, entirely different along the northeastern borders of Poland. German settlement and colonization here were, in the first instance, at the expense of a people, the Prussians, who were as much the enemies of the Poles as of the Germans, and the latter first came in response to an appeal for help against them made by a Polish duke.

In 1226, as has been noted, Konrad, the Piast duke of Mazowsze, invited the Knights of the Teutonic Order to undertake missionary work among the Prussians and, at the same time, to take their pressure off himself. Konrad's lands lay along the right bank of the middle Vistula, and stretched north into the lake-region of Mazuria, or East Prussia. There the poverty and difficulty of the land combined with the ferocity of the local Baltic or Prussian peoples to deter Polish settlement. The Prussians were uncomfortable neighbours, and in the manner of poorer and more primitive peoples living alongside richer and more developed, they not infrequently raided the lands of the latter.

In the thirteenth century the peripheral provinces were left to guard their boundaries as best they could and to obtain aid from whatever source they could get it. In return for their help Konrad was obliged to make concessions to the knights, which in retrospect seem excessive. They occupied Chełmno, on the lower Vistula, and built castles in the chief towns, such as Gdańsk, Grudziąż, and Toruń. The knights undertook to hold the lands which they might conquer from the Prussians as vassals of the duke of Mazowsze, but in fact accepted the sovereignty of the German emperor over them.

In the course of the century they defeated the Prussians, who were in reality numerically small and militarily weak, and then made good their conquest by settling Germans on the lands of Prussia. The settlement of East Prussia was probably the best organized and the most intensive of all the German population movements in eastern Europe. Military bases along the Vistula were accessible by boat, and were supplemented by others along the Baltic coast: Elbing (Elbląg), Königsberg, Memel. By 1300 the Baltic coast from the Vistula to Königsberg had been settled by Germans, but inland where the soil was less fertile, the Prussians were expelled and Germans took their place. This area continued in fact to be known as the 'Wilderness', an empty region separating the Poles of the Vistula basin from the Germans of the Baltic coast and the Lithuanians of the Niemen valley.

Medieval German settlement reached its peak in the fourteenth century, when, it is said, there were 1,400 German villages in Prussia alone. The north-western part of East Prussia was the most effectively Germanized, and the English traveller Fynes Moryson described it at the beginning of the seventeenth century as 'German in language and manners'.[8]

The German knights also occupied the lands to the west of the lower Vistula, known either as West Prussia or eastern Pomerania. The population here was either Polish or belonged to the closely related Kaszubs, and the territory fell within the Polish diocese of Wrocławek. Here there were no pagan peoples deserving the attentions of the knights; the local population was not uprooted, and few

[8] Fynes Moryson, *An Itinerary* (Glasgow, 1907), vol. IV, p. 68.

German communities were settled. The region remained predominantly Slav into the twentieth century.

Such was the situation when Kazimierz Wielki came to the Polish throne. He was no less eager to stabilize his relationship with his uncomfortable neighbours to the north-east than with those to the south-west. His demands that the knights retrocede their lands along the lower Vistula and hold the rest as a fief of Poland, though supported by the Papacy, were more than the latter would accept. In the end, he was obliged to compromise, and by the Treaty of Kalisz of 1343 he left West Prussia and the lower Vistula lands in the hands of the knights.

In the meanwhile, however, the Teutonic Knights had extended their authority eastward and then northward along the Baltic coast, and had joined hands with the Knights of the Sword, another German order which had established a field of far from peaceful missionary activity in Courland and Livonia. In 1237 the two orders were merged.

Beyond the Prussians and the related Jaćwież tribes lived the Lithuanians, a related people whose tribes were now becoming more closely united in the face of the danger from the Germans. The Lithuanians were reinforced at this time by fugitive elements from the Prussians and Jaćwież. The Russians, who had previously been a threat to the Lithuanians, were now preoccupied with Tatars and Pechenegs. In the fourteenth century Tatar power in the steppe was itself weakening, and the field was left open for Lithuanian expansion in this direction. The rapid unification and growth of the Lithuanian state during the fourteenth century was as remarkable as that of the Polish state had been four centuries earlier.

Within a few years the Lithuanian prince Gedymin succeeded in extending his political control south-eastwards to the upper Dnepr valley and had even seized Kiev. Advancing southwards into the steppe, he quickly found himself involved in a three-way struggle for the lands which the Tatars were slowly relinquishing. The Polish boundary had advanced very little in this direction since the times of Bolesław Chrobry. Beyond the formal boundary which he had established the frontier principality of Wołyń and Halicz had grown up, with its capital in the city of Lwów. Its historic role had been to protect the approaches to Poland from the south-east. Now that its mission had been completed and the last of the princes of Lwów killed in battle with the Tatars, the lands were waiting to be taken over by a more powerful neighbour. The Hungarian claim to them was not pressed, and Kazimierz Wielki obtained Halicz, leaving Wołyń, or Volhynia, to Lithuania. This partition of the Lwów-Halicz lands prepared the way for the collaboration and ultimately

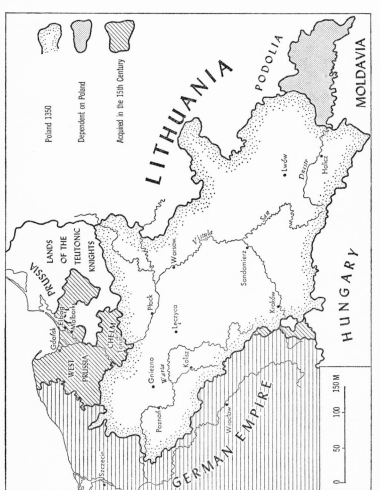

2. Poland at the time of Kazimierz the Great (Wielki) *c.* 1350

the union of Poland and Lithuania, which was to continue until the Partitions put an end to both.

The themes of the Lithuanian alliance and eastward expansion were to remain dominant in Polish policy for several centuries. Kazimierz Wielki died in 1370, leaving no direct heir. At his own desire the Polish crown passed to King Lewis of Hungary, son of his sister Elisabeth, and for the first, but not the last, time, the two countries were linked in a personal union. Such an association had much to recommend it. The Carpathian mountains constituted only a feeble barrier between the two countries; both were exposed to the danger of German invasion from the west and of Tatar or Turkish from the east.

Lewis accepted the Polish crown, neglected his new realm, and reduced its territory by transferring Galicia from Poland to Hungary. Furthermore, he had only daughters, and to secure the succession of the youngest of them, Jadwiga, to the Polish throne, he made concessions to the Polish nobility that were excessive and unwise. By an agreement reached in 1374 at the Slovak town of Košice, in Polish Koszyce, Lewis exempted the Polish *szlachta*, or nobles, from all taxes, and assured them that all territorial offices in Poland should be filled exclusively from among their number.

A short interregnum followed the death of Lewis, while elements of the many Piast families struggled to capture the crown of Poland. But in 1384 Jadwiga was crowned 'king' of Poland at Kraków. At the same time the marriage was proposed between Jadwiga and Yagaylo or, as he is more familiarly known, Jagiełło, Grand Prince of Lithuania.

The Lithuanian prince found himself at this time in difficult circumstances. His extensive lands, which extended from the Baltic Sea to the steppe, were still largely pagan. The German knights had overrun Samogitia and Courland, and were threatening the central parts of the Lithuanian state in the Niemen valley. Furthermore, dissensions within Lithuania were weakening its power to resist the knights. Jagiełło had everything to gain from union with Poland. From the Polish point of view the marriage also had its advantages. The conversion of the Lithuanians to Catholicism would add to the prestige of the Poles and at the same time remove the pretext for the activities of the Teutonic Knights in the Baltic region. The great reserves of Lithuanian manpower might, with Polish leadership and military skill, be used to stem the German advance, and even to regain lands lost in Mazuria and Pomerania.

The marriage took place, and in 1386 Jagiełło was crowned king of Poland as Władysław II. The union of Lithuania and Poland was for almost two centuries only a personal one. Jagiełło ruled in Poland,

and his viceroy, the Grand Prince, who was for much of his long reign his able and ambitious cousin Witold, ruled in Lithuania. This dual monarchy faced from the outset two problems, each of which threatened its existence. The first was the continued danger from the German knights; the other, the disruptive forces within the joint state.

The first Jagiełło king died in 1434 after a reign of forty-eight years, the longest in Polish history. His firmness and prudence had done much to ensure the success of the personal union of Poland with Lithuania. His son, Władysław III, succeeded while still a child, and died on a fruitless crusade against the Turks before he had attained manhood. His younger brother succeeded him as Kazimierz IV (1447–92). Both their reigns were occupied by intermittent war with the German knights. In 1409 the German seizure of a Polish border town marked its beginning. A year later the Polish-Lithuanian forces gained an overwhelming victory over the order at Grunwald, or Tannenberg. They demonstrated that their manpower and resources were fully adequate to resist the Germans, but they could not demonstrate enough political skill to profit fully from their victory and to bring the war to an end. Punctuated by truces and a temporary peace, the war dragged on until 1466, when, by the Treaty of Toruń, the Poles regained West Prussia and the Vistula lands, together with the port of Elbląg, and Malbork (Marienburg), the former capital of the German order. Even before the Northern War had ended, the bishop of Warmia, or Ermland, had placed himself under the protection of the Polish crown and thereby recognized that his lands formed an integral part of the Polish state. This is the origin of the peculiar Polish enclave in East Prussia, which existed until the time of the Partitions. Furthermore, the Grand Master of the Teutonic Order himself did homage to the king of Poland for his lands in Prussia.

Poland experienced no more difficulties with the Teutonic Order. Its day had already passed. It lingered on as an ineffectual religious organization until the time of the Reformation, when its last Grand Master, Albrecht of Ansbach, secularized it and made it into a lay fief hereditary in his own family. In 1605 it passed by succession to the Hohenzollern family of Brandenburg. This event, so fraught with political consequences, passed almost unnoticed at the time.

The German order had failed in the face of joint Polish and Lithuanian opposition. But its collapse must also be associated with contemporary economic change in Central and western Europe. The Black Death of the mid-fourteenth century sharpened a population decline which had begun perhaps a generation earlier. Land in the west was passing out of cultivation; there was no longer a flow of peasants towards the east, and landless nobles could find adequate and even more rewarding employment on the battlefields of France and England, without journeying all the way to the eastern Baltic. Chaucer's knight had fought in Prussia, but he must have been one of the last Englishmen to do so. The pools of humanity from which the eastward migration had flowed were drying up, but at the same time population was increasing in Poland and settlements were becoming larger and more numerous. Polish settlers, moving northwards from Mazowsze, met the frontier of German colonization, overwhelmed, and absorbed it. The language boundary between Slav and German was pushed back during the closing decades of the Middle Ages, and the southern borderland of East Prussia became and remained Polish.

The fatal campaign of Władysław III marked the appearance of a new danger upon the Polish horizon : the Turks. After the successful conclusion of the war with the knights, Kazimierz IV found himself deeply involved with the Turks in the extreme south-east of the Polish-Lithuanian state, but, by and large, succeeded in holding his frontier against them.

At his death there was a short-lived separation of Lithuania from Poland, each state being ruled by a prince of the house of Jagiełło. In 1501, the death of one of them led to a renewed union of the two states. The short experiment in separatism was not successful; Poland and Lithuania had become weaker militarily during the previous century, and at the same time both the Turks and the princes of Muscovy were growing stronger; union was in the interests of both.

The renewed union was stronger than that which had existed up to 1492. In 1506 Zygmunt I, the last Jagiełło in the male line, succeeded to the rule over both states. He was an able and energetic ruler at a time which called for all his abilities and energies. His reign saw the beginning of a clear policy to protect the frontiers of the state. He created the nucleus of a standing army, built fortresses to protect the state, and held the line against Turks and Russians.

Poland under the Jagiełło kings was on a rising tide of prosperity. While in western and Central Europe cropland was being abandoned to pasture and replaced by sheep-runs, in eastern Europe new land was coming under the plough. Great estates were being created at the same time that in western Europe they were beginning to disintegrate. The East was becoming a market for the West's manufactures and was, in turn, beginning to ship its grain and lumber westwards. The river Vistula played an important role in both the grain- and the timber-trade of Poland. The formation of great estates and the reduction to serfdom of the once free peasantry was most strongly marked along its banks and those of its major tributaries. Granaries for storing the grain, many of which still survive, were built along the banks of the river, and the need for an outlet to the sea gave point to the Poles' struggle to recapture West Prussia and the ports of the Vistula mouth.

Despite the rising level of wealth, the problem of internal unity remained as intractable as ever. Before the reign of Kazimierz Wielki some parts of Poland, notably Mazowsze, had fragmented into a number of small and effectively independent principalities, each under a ruler of the Piast family. Kazimierz was able to restore some degree of order and bring a number of these areas back to their earlier dependence on the Polish crown. But his work was undone by the foolishness of his successor, Lewis of Hungary. Despite repeated efforts by the Jagiełło kings to reincorporate the Mazovian principalities, it was not until the sixteenth century that the last of them finally returned to Poland.

There was some reason for the independence of Mazowsze. It had been, until the union with Lithuania, a march or frontier province, exposed to the raids of the Prussians and the Jaćwież. Long after these had been replaced by the Germans, it continued to be a frontier province in the triangular struggle between Poles, Germans, and Lithuanians, and thus acquired a greater independence of action than other provinces.

The effect of the union with Lithuania was to increase the divisions within Poland. The Jagiełło kings found it difficult to bridge the gap between the two nations, and in doing so made concessions to Polish provincialism that were in the end fatal to the Polish state. Foremost among the contrasts between Poland and Lithuania were their different levels of social and economic development. Lithuania was still, as Poland had been until the twelfth century, a congeries of tribes, whose tribal leaders were slowly turning themselves into feudal princes. Poland was already moderately urbanized, while towns in the Western sense were almost non-existent in Lithuania. Even at the end of the sixteenth century Fynes Moryson wrote of Lithuania that 'it hath very few Townes and the Villages are commonly distant 20 German miles one from the other'. The Lithuanian economy was primitive, a 'natural' economy in which the use of money was little known and each community was in most respects self-sufficing.

Fortunately the two peoples were not brought together in the same state for nearly two centuries after the formation of the personal union. This gave some time, though far from enough, for the levelling-up of the Lithuanian economy. The Lithuanian leaders themselves had the local outlook which had characterized the Poles themselves a century or two earlier. In the north-west they were fighting to

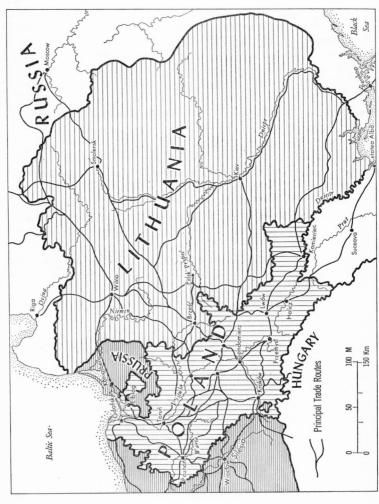

3. Poland and Lithuania in the fifteenth century: routes, ports, and commercial towns

resist the German orders; to the south-east, they were moving into the steppe, recently vacated by the Tatars; to the east they were in conflict with the Russians of Muscovy and Novgorod. It is difficult to speak of a dichotomy in something as inchoate as the policy of Lithuania. It is nevertheless clear that those who lived nearest the Baltic Sea regarded resistance to the Germans as their primary obligation and solidarity with Poland as a necessary means of achieving it. Those lying farther to the east saw their opportunities in expansion to the east and south-east, where vast estates were to be had at the price of a minor frontier war. Witold, Grand Prince of Lithuania and cousin of Jagiełło, took part in both, at one time leading his army against the Germans; at another, turning to his eastern marches, where richer pickings were to be had at a smaller price. These eastern ventures help to explain the long drawn-out character of the war against the knights. In effect, Lithuania sacrificed the small and strategically placed province of Żmudź, or Samogitia, for the limitless horizons of the Ukraine. The eastward advance in the fifteenth and later centuries was as much the work of the nobility as of their rulers, and Polish nobles played as active a role as Lithuanian.

Despite the separateness of Poland and Lithuania and the dual nature of the monarchy, the landed aristocracy of the two states began to draw more and more close to one another. In the so-called Union of Horodło of 1413 the Polish nobility, the *szlachta*, incorporated the Lithuanian boyars among their number, extending to them the right to bear their own coats-of-arms. This peculiar 'blood-brotherhood' did far more than the personal union of their rulers to bring the two countries together, to unify their policies and merge their cultures. *Szlachta* and boyar met with increasing frequency on the hunting field and around the council table, and these associations led to co-operation on the battlefield and in the settlement of the Ukraine. The aristocracies of the two countries intermarried and merged, so that a century or two later only their names betrayed whether their origin was Polish or Lithuanian. It is an interesting reflection on society that heraldry rather than kingship became its cement.

The Union of Horodło provided also for the extension to Lithuania of the Polish system of administrative units, the *województwa* and *kasztelany*. In the course of the following century, not only Lithuania proper but also parts of Belorussia and the Ukraine were divided into such administrative units and governed by officers with Polish-sounding names.

By the terms of the first union of Poland and Lithuania, the latter had accepted Catholicism, and the Lithuanian aristocracy quickly became stalwart defenders of their new faith. Their eastward and south-eastward conquests, however, took them into areas of Russian speech and Orthodox religion, where the local magnates claimed descent from Rurik rather than kinship with Gedymin, and where the religious orientation was towards Byzantium rather than Rome.

Good relations between Catholic and Orthodox were essential if some kind of unity was to emerge in the amorphous Polish-Lithuanian state. The Union of Horodło had been between Catholic Poles and Catholic Lithuanians, and did nothing to conciliate the Orthodox. At the same time, however, the Catholic Church was anxious to end the schism with the Eastern Church, which had lasted since the eleventh century. The Union of Florence of 1439, which resulted from the attempts of the Papacy to bring the Orthodox back into the fold of the Church, was short-lived and ineffectual. In Lithuania it received little support and contributed nothing to relieving the most serious threat to the internal unity of at least the more easterly provinces of this dual monarchy.

The Lithuanian rulers were obliged to deal more gently with their Orthodox subjects than the Church approved, if they hoped to maintain the unity and extend the boundaries of their state. But Catholic boyars surrounded the Grand Prince, and Catholic bishops were among his advisers; the Orthodox played no part in ruling the country. Nevertheless, the rights of non-Catholics were protected, in marked contrast with the practice of Catholic rulers in western Europe. In 1432, Jagiełło himself addressed a charter to the 'prelates, boyars, and nobles of the land of Łuck, whether in the faith of the Holy Catholic Church, or [in that] of the East', in which he promised that 'we will neither cause nor permit either Ruthenian or Greek rite churches either to be destroyed or to be made over into churches of the Roman Church, and we will not force with violence any person of the aforementioned Greek rite of whatever sex or station into the faith of the Roman Church'. Freedom to practise their religion did not, however, carry with it complete equality of the Orthodox with the Catholics. Lithuanian nobles enjoyed the same privileges as Polish, but a similar equality with their Polish counterparts was not extended to the Orthodox bishops and clergy. In general, the policy of the Polish-Lithuanian state was the unrealistic one of restricting the freedom of the Orthodox Church while giving full rein to the Orthodox nobility, a policy which was to bear bitter fruit in the eighteenth century and to contribute materially to the destruction of the Polish state.

The display of toleration manifested by the Jagiełło rulers was made necessary not only by the internal divisions of their state, but also by the growing power of the princes of Muscovy. The latter were slowly expanding their territory within the forests of the upper Volga basin. Many Lithuanian nobles defected and went over to

Muscovy. The religious issue, coupled with a certain jealousy of Polish cultural and political preponderance, may help to explain this phenomenon.[9] The defection was not merely a transfer of loyalties; it was a physical migration of Lithuanian nobles out of Lithuania and into Russia. They left a thinly populated land even less populous, and thus all the more vulnerable to the encroachment of the Muscovites.

The joint Polish-Lithuanian state of the Jagiełło reached its greatest geographical extent in the late fifteenth century. In the west, Pomerania, Silesia, and Lubusz had been lost beyond recall, but some small gains were nevertheless made. The principality of Oświęcim, a name corrupted by the Germans into the notorious Auschwitz, was obtained from Bohemia, and the neighbouring territory of Zator was acquired a few years later. The 'thirteen cities' of Spiš in the Carpathian mountains were obtained from Hungary, and with them some of the silver-mines, developed by the Fuggers, of this region.

Even before the personal union with Lithuania the Poles had begun to reach out towards the south-east. The steppe, which extended from Galicia to the Black Sea and had provided an open invasion route for the Tatars, provided no less clear a route for Polish expansion. During the intervals between the Tatar raids, trade moved along the steppe road, and fairs grew up at Lwów and other towns. Oriental goods were brought from the Black Sea ports along the *Droga Tatarska* (Tatar Road) to Polish territory. Polish influence extended in this direction far beyond the limits of Polish rule. The Hungarian king relinquished his claim to sovereignty over territory beyond the great curve of the Carpathian mountains, and in 1387 Peter, prince of Moldavia, did homage to Jagiełło for his lands, and was followed by the rulers of Bessarabia and Wallachia. These symbolic acts meant little, beyond demonstrating the paramountcy of Poland in eastern Europe.

At the opposite extremity of the Polish-Lithuanian state, Żmudź was regained from the knights and the boundary stabilized between Lithuania on the one hand and Livonia and Novgorod on the other. Thus for a time the Polish-Lithuanian state reached from the Baltic to the Black Sea, *od morza do morza* as the Poles liked to repeat; and from the borders of Silesia almost to the gates of Moscow. Across this vast area – the largest political unit in contemporary Europe – ran trade routes from Hungary through Kraków and Poznań to the Baltic coast, and from the Black Sea through Lwów and Lublin to Gdańsk. Poland became the chief intermediary in the

---

[9] Oswald P. Backus, *Motives of the West Russian Nobles in Deserting Lithuania for Moscow* (Lawrence, Kansas, 1957).

overland trade between western Europe and the Orient. Hanseatic merchants frequented her northern ports, and the Genoese, those in the south-east. Polish merchants, profiting from their role as middlemen, began to work up the raw materials that crossed their land into finished goods. Crafts developed in the towns of Great and Little Poland, and Kraków became an emporium of the cloth trade.

Poland was on her way to becoming one of Europe's richest commercial countries when these prospects were cut short by both internal and external developments. Commerce and crafts can flourish only in a social and political atmosphere that encourages the entrepreneur, allows him to innovate, and rewards him when he is successful. Such a climate of opinion did not develop in late medieval and Renaissance Poland. Perhaps it was the baleful influence of the more backward and conservative Lithuanian aristocracy which restricted the intellectual growth of the Polish. It is certain that the Polish kings never had the wisdom to encourage the growth of a commercial and middle class to balance the power of the gentry. Instead, concession after concession to the greed and ambition of the latter gradually reduced the kings to the role of puppets in their hands. At the same time the peasants were becoming ever more closely bound to the soil; local markets contracted; and local crafts became less important. More and more of the land passed into great estates, and the middle class, which had begun to appear in the void between the *szlachta* and the peasant, was gradually squeezed out. Commerce continued, and even grew in volume, but it consisted largely in the sale of grain and lumber from the great estates. Thus the vision of an Amsterdam or of an Antwerp at the mouth of the Vistula vanished.

The external dangers may in any event have made the realization of such a vision impossible, but in the fifteenth century these were remote and their import was not clearly perceived. The Turks had reached the Danube, and King Władysław III lost his life leading a futile crusade against them. They were later to spread through Moldavia and Bessarabia, to threaten the kingdom and cut its commercial routes to the Black Sea. The princes of Muscovy might nibble at the boundaries of Lithuania, but at this time they constituted no threat to its integrity. The knights were in decline, and scarcely able to recruit members for their anachronistic order, and to the west the Hohenzollern family, amid the marshes and heaths of Brandenburg, were only a cloud on the horizon, no bigger than a man's hand.

Chapter 2

The Decline of the Kingdom

O Zbarażu! O szańcu
Kamieniecki, który
Niez bodyty ulatasz!
O wieżo Jasnej Góry!
Hel padnie, i Westerplatte
Ukradną zbójcy,
Ty przetrwasz, święty Okopie
Poetów Trójcy!

(M. Hemar, *Inwokacja*)[1]

THE POLISH-LITHUANIAN state achieved its greatest geographical extent in the later years of the fifteenth century, but already it contained the seeds of its own decay. The political division, which kept the kingdom of Poland apart from the principality of Lithuania, was healed by the Union of Lublin of 1569; the nobles of Lithuania came increasingly to assume the culture of those of Poland, and the union between them was cemented on countless battlefields where they fought side by side against the Tatars, the Turks, and the Russians. But these successes were achieved only at the expense of opening new wounds. The rift between the Catholic and the non-Catholic populations of the dual state grew wider, and was gradually reinforced by a linguistic and cultural antipathy.

The virtual extinction of the middle class left the nation divided between the nobility, or *szlachta,* and the peasant masses. The nobles had already excused themselves from the obligation to pay taxes; industry and trade, which could have provided a tax base, had been reduced to negligible proportions, and there was no economic foundation, even if the leadership were present, for a strong central government.

1 'Thou Zbaraż! Thou rampart of Kamieniec, ever delivered from the conqueror! Thou tower of Jasna Góra! Hel falls and assassins steal our Westerplatte; but thou endurest, Holy Rampart of our Poets Three!' M. A. Michael (tr.), in *A Polish Anthology,* ed. T. M. Filip and M. A. Michael (London, 1944). The poem was written after the Fall of Poland (September 1939). The Westerplatte and Hel Peninsula were defended against the Germans. The 'Poets Three' are Mickiewicz, Słowacki, and Krasiński.

The Union of Lublin

From the Union of Krevo in 1386 to that of Lublin in 1569, a period of almost two centuries, Poland and Lithuania had in a legal sense been linked only by the person of their common ruler. This was a precarious bond, even though their respective aristocracies had become increasingly closely associated with one another. The Polish monarchy had, since the election of the first Jagiełło, become in theory elective, though it was a custom of the constitution that only a Piast or a Jagiełło might be chosen. In Lithuania, however, the princely title was hereditary in the family of Jagiełło, although its descent had not become fixed. There was thus an element of choice in Lithuania also in the selection of the ruler. In both countries the choice was made by their respective *Sejm,* or parliament, and it was fortunate that from the time of Jagiełło onwards until 1572, there was an obvious and acceptable candidate from the family of Jagiełło, and that both parliaments agreed in selecting him. There was no assurance that this state of affairs would continue.

Despite the 'blood-brotherhood' which had grown up between the higher aristocracies of Poland and Lithuania, the social structures of the two countries differed radically. Poland was itself a land of gentry, the true *szlachta,* rather than of nobles. The gentry of each locality met at their provincial *sejmiki,* dietines, or 'little' parliaments, and acquired a preponderant political role in their provinces. By a series of concessions, exacted from successive kings from the time of Lewis of Hungary, the *szlachta* had acquired a judicial as well as a fiscal immunity, that permitted them in effect to become a law to themselves. On the other hand, most of them were poor. A few were lords of a handful of villages; most possessed only single villages or even fractions of a village. In some parts of Poland there were whole villages of 'gentry', who lived like peasants and thought like nobles. Enlightened leadership was not to be expected from persons as parochial in outlook as the *szlachta.* They would cheerfully sacrifice what middle class there was to their immediate interests, place the whole burden of taxation on the shoulders of a few, and wonder why the tax income gradually diminished. Many of them were boors, licentious, stupid, irascible, and jealous of their privileges, compared with whom Squire Western was a model of elegance and progress.

The strengthening of the position of the *szlachta* brought with it inevitably the further depression of the peasantry. Gradually these lost their free status and became *adscripti glebae,* bound to the soil. They lost their right of appeal to the king's courts against capricious demands of their lords and the burden of field-work that was placed upon them steadily increased.

Developments in Lithuania were in some respects different. The landowning class there had a stronger social structure; there was a considerable range of wealth and political power between the magnates and the lesser gentry. The tenurial system was dominated by great estates, whose owners, the Radziwiłł, Gasztold, Holszański, and others, wielded immense power and influence. Indeed, the Radziwiłł had aspirations to become the Grand Princes of Lithuania in the place of the Jagiełło. The Lithuanian *Sejm* was not the egalitarian affair that the Polish *Sejm* had become, and there were no dietines at which every petty owner of a few acres could make himself heard and obstruct the actions of the whole.

These differences in social structure influenced the ways in which the nobles of Poland and Lithuania viewed the question of a closer union of their two countries. The lesser nobility of Lithuania desired it, on the assumption that it would improve their own social standing. The greater nobility, the Radziwiłł in particular, opposed it as tending to reduce their own prestige and importance. In Poland itself a closer union was on the whole preferred, by the *szlachta* on the sentimental grounds of the brotherhood of the nobility of the two states, and by the king because his higher standing in Lithuania was calculated to strengthen his position in Poland.

Yet it was not these domestic considerations that did most to bring about the Union of Lublin, but the urgent need for a closer union in the face of the growing power of Muscovy. The immediate question was that of Inflanty, or Livonia, the territory which lay on both sides of the Gulf of Riga. It was outside the limits of Lithuania, and had been settled in the thirteenth century by the Knights of the Sword[2], who later merged with the Teutonic Knights. Though controlled in theory from Malbork and later from Königsberg, the Livonian section of the order enjoyed a considerable degree of independence in virtue of its remoteness. Furthermore, the order did not possess in Livonia the lion's share of the land, as it did in Prussia, and large areas were controlled by the archbishop of Riga and his suffragans, and by the Hanseatic cities of Riga, Reval, and Dorpat. A triangular struggle developed in Livonia, when the order and the cities accepted the Reformation, and the archbishop called for help from outside to maintain his position.

The Protestant elements made similar appeals, and Livonia became the battleground of neighbouring states, each intent on preventing the others from annexing some part of the area without adequate

[2] See above, p. 38.

compensation for themselves. The chaotic situation which developed in Livonia led the Tsar Ivan IV to intervene. His armies devastated the eastern part of the territory and threatened Riga. A combination of greed and fear led the kings of Sweden and Denmark to intervene, and the Polish-Lithuanian state entered the struggle to protect itself. In 1561 a settlement was reached. All parties gained something, though the princes of Muscovy were barred from access to the sea, which they appear to have particularly desired. Courland was made into a duchy for the last Grand Master of the Order; the Swedes got much of Estonia; the Danes, the islands off the Gulf of Riga; and the Polish-Lithuanian state the southern part of Livonia.

In the event the Russians came out of the struggle poorly, but the Lithuanian nobles were well aware of their danger from a renewed Russian advance. As Russian bands entered Livonia and Lithuania, the nobles in the latter called upon the Poles for help and pointed to the wisdom of a political union that would spread more evenly the burden of resisting the Russians. When the Russian invaders had been defeated and forced back, the Lithuanian nobles tended to regret their earlier overtures to the Poles. But the brunt of the fighting had been borne by the lesser Lithuanian nobles, and their political weight had increased with their military importance. In the end they overcame the reluctance of the greater nobles, and negotiations were begun at Lublin in 1569 between Polish and Lithuanian representatives.

The Union which resulted consisted essentially of a common *Sejm* for both Poland and Lithuania, with the resulting increase in the political significance of the minor Lithuanian gentry. Zygmunt II had himself been crowned king of Poland in the Wawel Cathedral at Kraków and also inducted as Grand Duke of Lithuania in Wilno. His successor would be crowned once as king of the united Commonwealth, or *Rzeczpospolita*. Lithuania retained, however, some of the appurtenances of its former independent status. It continued to have its own Treasurer, a separate hetman to command its army, and a chancellor to speak as the king's local representative. These titles became increasingly honorific, and the attempts of the Radziwiłł family to use them as a means of re-establishing an independent Lithuania failed disastrously.[3]

Lithuania was by now so much a part of Poland that changes in their mutual boundary were of little consequence. There was some historical justification for transferring to Poland the provinces of Wołyń (Volhynia), Podlasie, and Bracław, which had in part been

[3] The romantic novel of H. Sienkiewicz, *With Fire and Sword (Ogniem i Mieczem)*, is woven around the ambitions of the Radziwiłł family at this time.

occupied by Bolesław at the beginning of the eleventh century; lost to the Tatars; and regained by the Lithuanians. They were historically Polish and contained a sprinkling of Polish population. This, however, was not true of parts of the Ukraine which were also transferred to the Poles, in order to involve them more deeply in this region.

The Reformation in Poland coincided with that in Germany, and made rapid headway in Gdańsk and other cities of northern Poland, where it assumed a social and economic, as well as a strictly theological, form. It was strenuously but vainly resisted by the king, Zygmunt I, and the ecclesiastical hierarchy. The *szlachta*, increasingly jealous of the rights and privileges which they had obtained from successive kings, were in no mood, whatever their religious inclination, to accept dictation by the king. And this spirit of independence, which owed nothing to the Reformation as such, was equally opposed to control by the bishops. It thus became necessary for the authorities first to tolerate the activities of the reformers and then, in 1573, to accept religious toleration as the law of the land.

This practice was in fact only the extension to the Lutheran and Calvinist gentry and burgesses of a principle that had long been adopted towards the Orthodox of Lithuania. But the Reformation had little depth in Poland. It was a class movement; its protagonists were the lesser gentry, many of whom appear to have supported it primarily because it gave them the opportunity to defy authority and assert their so-called 'liberties' before the world. The Reformation made no impression whatever upon the peasantry, and its most sincere supporters, the burgesses of the cities, were few in number and of little political importance. The Reform movement was itself divided. Lutherans and Calvinists, normally jealous of one another, were prepared to join forces only against the Anabaptists, the Bohemian Brethren, and the Unitarians, and in the end all failed before the monolithic strength of Roman Catholicism.

Not so, however, the Orthodox Church. The lesser boyars of Lithuania and many of the peasantry remained faithful to the Eastern Church, and attempts to convert them to Catholicism, or to absorb them into the intermediate Uniate Church, failed. The Polish gentry, which was becoming increasingly intolerant, was nevertheless obliged to tolerate the schism. The geographical boundary between the predominantly Catholic west and the mainly Orthodox east is difficult to establish with precision. The jurisdictions of the Catholic bishops and of the Orthodox metropolitans overlapped. All except the south-east of Poland had become by the end of the sixteenth century almost exclusively Catholic; all except the more northerly and north-westerly parts of Lithuania remained Orthodox, with, however, a sprinkling of Polish and Lithuanian Catholics who had moved into the region.

Poland's failure to solve, or even to face up to, the problem of the Dissidents, as the non-Catholic population was called, was a major factor in the events which led up to the Partitions. The liberal and tolerant Poland of the sixteenth century gave place to one that was fiercely intolerant.

> That instinct for national unity which was grotesquely frustrated by the Polish State, seemed to seek appeasement in the Polish church ... the Polish masses now believed ... that fellow-country-men outside the national church were untrustworthy and even wicked, and that connivance at dissent imperilled their own salvation.[4]

The Orthodoxy of the Russian Tsars and the Lutheranism of the Brandenburg electors served merely to intensify the fanaticism of the Polish gentry until it led to violence and war in the eighteenth century.

The Deluge

For two centuries after the Union of Lublin the Polish state was outwardly stable. Its boundaries retreated somewhat in the east and in Livonia, but remained unchanged in other directions. In all other respects, however, this was a period of decline. Three years after the union of Poland and Lithuania, Zygmunt II, the last king of the house of Jagiełło, died. With no candidate available from either of the only two reigning families that Poland had known, the field was wide open, and the *szlachta* prepared to increase the price of their support to any candidate rash enough to enter the competition.

The mechanism of election was fluid. The gentry were intent only on preventing the election of any king who might trim their precious liberties. After an interval of many months they chose, as successor to Zygmunt, the feckless French prince, Henri de Valois, the pampered son of Catherine de Medici. Henri was forced to accept in advance every limitation on his sovereignty that the *szlachta* could devise. His relationship to the magnates became merely a contractual one. The latter remained free to break their bargain whenever it seemed opportune to do so, while the new king lacked the force of character necessary to extract the little which they owed him. Within six months Henri de Valois was disillusioned and defeated, and had fled back to France, where his subsequent career as Henri III was as undistinguished as his short rule over Poland.

4 W. F. Reddaway, in *Cambridge History of Poland* (Cambridge, 1951), vol. 2, p. 95.

His successor, who was not chosen until eighteen months had passed after Henri's flight, was Stefan Batory, prince of Transylvania (1575–86). He was the conspicuous – and only – exception to the generalization that the elective principle produced only nonentities. He was the strongest ruler to have occupied the Polish throne in modern times, but by the time of his death the *szlachta* had had their fill of strong rulers who threatened their liberties and conducted costly, if successful, military campaigns. Their next choice fell on Sigismund of Sweden, a relative of the last Jagiełło, who became Zygmunt III of Poland in 1587. He was suitably ineffectual and during his long reign 'royalty lost, to a great extent, the moral prestige it had enjoyed in the time of the Jagiełłos, which alone could compensate for all the constitutional limitations of its power'.[5]

Zygmunt III intervened ineffectively in the affairs of Russia during the 'Time of Troubles'; fought sporadically with the Swedes in Livonia and Estonia; but succeeded in preserving Poland from embroilment in the Thirty Years' War. And yet Poland lost on every front. The Swedes occupied Livonia; Prussia, under her Hohenzollern rulers, became effectively independent of Poland; and the Swedes succeeded in establishing their *dominium maris Baltici,* which they were to retain for a century. Indeed, the only positive achievement for which he was remembered by later generations was the transfer of the capital and seat of the government from Kraków to Warsaw. Kraków had served well enough during the Middle Ages, when the focus of economic power had lain in western Poland and the chief dangers had threatened from Bohemia and Germany. But it was ill-suited to the needs of the Commonwealth which extended into the Ukraine. Warsaw was more centrally placed and more accessible, and grew rapidly in the seventeenth century, and more especially the eighteenth, into a city of great beauty and not inconsiderable size.

The quiet decadence of Poland was then rudely interrupted. Zygmunt III died in 1632, and was succeeded by his son, an ex-cleric and ex-Cardinal, who became Władysław IV. At the same time problems began to multiply. The Russians had by now set their own house in order, and the new Tsar, Michael Romanoff, invaded Poland. The Tatars were again becoming troublesome in the steppe; the Turks were threatening; and a new danger appeared in the form of the Cossacks.

These were the frontiersmen of the Polish-Lithuanian state. The steppe, long the scene only of raid and counter-raid, had been pacified in the sixteenth century, and settlers had filtered into this wilderness, trappers and hunters, soldiers of fortune, runaway serfs from the great estates, and criminals and peasants who hoped to settle and

[5] Oskar Halecki, *A History of Poland* (New York, 1961), p. 144.

cultivate it. These were the Cossacks. In the middle years of the sixteenth century they acquired a kind of organization and were encouraged to serve as guardians of Poland against Tatars and Turks. In fact, they soon learned how easy it was to play Pole off against Russian, and to profit from the hostility of both towards Tatar and Turk.

The Union of Lublin had transferred part of the steppe, and with it the Cossacks, from the jurisdiction of the Lithuanians to that of the Poles. Cossack units were recruited for the Polish army, and the so-called 'Registered Cossacks' were formed, a privileged cadre of soldiers responsible directly to the Polish king. The rest, the so-called 'Independent Cossacks', increased in numbers as more and more people moved into the steppe. At the same time, however, members of the Polish and Lithuanian aristocracies either pre-empted or received by direct grant from the king large areas of the fertile steppe, on which Cossacks were already settled. But serfs and others had not fled to the Ukraine merely to remain under the heel of a new master who differed in no significant respect from the old. The resistance of the Cossacks increased as their numbers grew. The attempts of the magnates to reduce them again to a servile status provoked rebellions even before the end of the sixteenth century.

The problem, however, was not entirely a social one. By and large, the Cossacks were members of the Orthodox Church, in so far as they can be said to have belonged to any. To some degree they were supported by what remained of the Tatars and, in the background, but casting its shadow over the whole region, was the growing might of Tsarist Russia. In 1648 matters came to a head, when Bogdan Chmielnicki, a prominent Cossack, was dispossessed of his lands by Poles to whom they had been allocated, rallied the Cossack malcontents, and won over the Registered Cossacks to his side. He defeated the Polish army, and advanced to within 150 miles of Warsaw. He failed, however, to hold either the lands which he had overrun or the loyalty of his turbulent Cossack followers. The Tatars deserted him and the Russians held back, until Chmielnicki formally transferred his allegiance to the Russian Tsar Alexis. The latter was then quick to accept; sent armies to support the Cossacks, overran Belorussia and part of Lithuania, and even sacked Wilno.

The second act of this tragedy then began. There had been peace between Poland and Sweden since the short war in the sixteenth century, in the course of which the Swedes had occupied part of Livonia. Now Charles X of Sweden, successor to Queen Christina who had abdicated, saw in Poland's embroilment the opportunity to extend yet farther his control of the Baltic littoral. He was assisted by the deep-rooted antagonisms which existed within the state. The Lithuanian magnates, unreconciled to the secondary role which they were now called upon to play in the united Commonwealth, hoped to find more power for themselves in alliance with Sweden. The Protestants, few in number though they were, added to the dissensions within Poland, and looked upon the Lutheran king of Sweden as a potential saviour.

In 1655, Charles X invaded Poland with a trained army made up largely of veterans of the Thirty Years' War. The hetman of Lithuania, Janusz Radziwiłł, who represented the Lithuanian grievances against Poland and had, furthermore, aspirations to the Polish throne, joined him. The pampered gentry of Wielkopolska offered no resistance, and the Swedes took Warsaw and Kraków and overran the whole country.

The king, Jan Kazimierz, fled to Silesia, now a province of Austria, and for a time only the fortified monastery of the Paulicians, built on the summit of a low hill, the Jasna Góra, outside the town of Częstochowa, continued to offer resistance. The story of this defence has been so obscured by legend that it is difficult to disentangle the true record of events. Allegedly the defenders were assisted by the intervention of the 'Black Madonna', a stylized portrait which still hangs within the walls of the abbey church. In any event, the Swedes suffered their first reverse; the Poles were profoundly encouraged; the king returned from his exile; and the Polish army, now confident that a miracle had been wrought in its favour, carried all before it.

The Swedes were forced back to their coastal bases in Prussia. The Elector of Brandenburg, who at this time was Frederick William, the so-called 'Great Elector', was induced to desert them by the promise of complete sovereignty over East Prussia, together with the cession by Poland of certain territories along the Vistula which the Poles had won back from the German knights two centuries earlier. In 1660, a general peace was concluded at a conference held in the monastery of Oliva, near Gdańsk. Poland was at last freed of invaders, but at the price of Livonia which the Swedes retained, and of East Prussia and Malbork, which became the personal and sovereign possession of the Hohenzollerns of Brandenburg.

Poland might have gained less onerous terms if renewed danger from the east had not made the conclusion of peace with Sweden and Brandenburg an urgent necessity. For several years the situation in the Ukraine and along the eastern border of Lithuania had been quiescent. But already the Russian Tsar had begun to intervene in the affairs of the Ukraine. The personal animosity which had marked Bogdan Chmielnicki's relations with Poland ended with his death, and his successors amongst the Cossack leadership began to think that membership of the Polish state might in fact be preferable to being within Russia. The Polish king was thus able to reach an agreement with the Cossacks in 1659 by which the Ukraine, divided into the *województwa* of Kiev, Bracław, and Czernichów, became a separate duchy of Ruthenia, linked to Poland and Lithuania in exactly the same way that these two were themselves joined. The Cossacks were conciliated by the grant of privileges and honours, and many among them were ennobled.

Russian armies, sent to prevent the defection of the Ukraine, were defeated by the Poles, Lithuanians, and Cossacks. But the friendship of the fickle Cossacks for Poland did not last. The honours handed out by the Poles aroused jealousies amongst them. The old Chmielnicki faction revived and encouraged fears amongst the Cossacks that, once the Russian threat had passed, the Polish magnates would again try to force serfdom upon them. The Ukraine became divided in its loyalties. West of the Dnepr Polish rule was recognized; to the east, it was ignored. At this point, worn out by the long contest and threatened by the revival of the power of the Turks, Jan Kazimierz and Tsar Alexis concluded the Truce of Andruszów (1667). Poland, so often victorious in the field, seemed fated to lose at the conference table. This time the Turkish danger led her to conclude a precipitate agreement and to yield to the Tsar more than the strength and successes of Russia warranted. Poland lost all her territory to the east of the Dnepr, including the cities of Smoleńsk, Seversk, and Czernichów, and the city of Kiev, lying to the west of the river, was to be garrisoned by the Russians, an occupation that proved to be permanent.

The Cossack problem was not, however, settled. The mantle of Chmielnicki had fallen upon Dorošenko, who with his Cossacks, in alliance with both Tatars and Turks, invaded Poland itself. Held for a time by the Polish hetman, Jan Sobieski, they were then reinforced by fresh Turkish armies; overwhelmed the Polish fortress of Kamieniec Podolsk on the Dnestr; and advanced to the siege of Lwów. Again the tide was stemmed by Sobieski, but in the Treaty of Buczacz he obtained peace only at the price of ceding Podolia and sovereignty over the Ukraine to the Turkish Sultan. The war was soon renewed. Fresh Turkish armies emerged from Moldavia, and Lwów was again besieged. Sobieski's generalship, however, enabled him to divide the Turkish army, and to defeat it piecemeal. Defence against the Turks took precedence in Sobieski's mind over recovering East Prussia and his whole policy was shaped to this end.

The Turkish danger was probably exaggerated. The Ottoman Empire was more decadent than Sobieski could have realized, and had only been galvanized into this show of vigour and activity by the Kiuprili family, which retained the office of Grand Vizier for most of the second half of the seventeenth century. But to the Polish gentry the Turkish threat seemed real enough, and they followed Sobieski beyond the boundaries of their own country, when in 1683 he led them to the relief of the beleaguered city of Vienna.

The siege of Vienna marked the high tide of Turkish conquest. From this point onwards the Turks ebbed slowly and haltingly back to Buda, then to Beograd and the Balkans. Defeat on their left front led to retreat on their right. While the Austrians were advancing into the Hungarian plain, Sobieski led the Polish armies towards Moldavia, which he hoped to recover from the Turks and attach again to the Polish crown. He got as far as Iaşi, was defeated by the Turks, and obliged to retreat, his army broken, the Moldavians alienated, and himself worn out by his continuous campaigning.

This was, in fact, the end of the last truly heroic king of Poland. Only a few months after the disaster at Iaşi, he reaffirmed the terms of the Truce of Andruszów of 1667, and the city of Kiev together with all the lands east of the Dnepr passed formally into the possession of the Tsar. As for the Turks, despite their victory at Iaşi, they were in reality a defeated people. They retained a nominal sovereignty over Moldavia until the nineteenth century, but they ceased to trouble the Commonwealth.

The Eighteenth Century

The last act in the drama of the Polish Commonwealth began with the death of Sobieski in 1696. He had failed to found a dynasty, as he had hoped to do; indeed, he left no obvious successor, and the choice of the *szlachta* fell on Augustus 'the Strong', king of Saxony. His strength, unfortunately, was entirely physical. No foreign king of Poland, not even the unfortunate Henri de Valois, ever identified himself less with the interests of his adopted country. His successes, such as the reoccupation of Podolia from the Turks in 1699, were in reality the posthumous victories of his predecessor. His failures were conspicuously his own. Through a foolish alliance with the Tsar he was dragged into war with the Swedes in Livonia. His policy of trying to strengthen his own position by setting the magnates against one another was easy to pursue, but disastrous in its consequences. His territory became a battleground between Charles XII of Sweden and Tsar Peter the Great of Russia, while Augustus found a quiet refuge back in his palace at Dresden. The Poles were adept at keeping out of a struggle that did not directly concern them, but they could not prevent the renewed devastation and impoverishment of their land. After the final defeat of the Swedes at Poltawa (1709), Augustus was brought back to Warsaw, a mere dependent henceforward of Peter the Great. This time Poland had lost something even more important than territory.

During the Swedish war, a faction within Poland had renounced its allegiance to Augustus and chosen a Polish nobleman, Stanisław Leszczyński, as king. His candidature was defeated with the defeat of the Swedes, but at least he could not be identified with the interests of the House of Saxony. On the death of Augustus II in 1733, his name was again brought forward, and he was elected king by a *Sejm* that was united by dislike of the Saxons. But a native Polish ruler did not suit the interests of the Russian ruler, now the Tsarina Anne, and a Russian army came to Warsaw to secure the election of Augustus III, the yet more odious son of Augustus II. The lukewarm supporters of the younger Augustus were mainly drawn from the Lithuanian nobles, whose estates, lying close to the Russian border, would be likely to suffer most from renewed war with the Tsar.

Poland was ruled by the agents of Augustus III, who himself lived in Saxony, where he amused himself with the rebuilding of Dresden. Poland herself remained at peace, but not inviolate, during his reign. Factions began to form within Poland, two of which came to dominate the scene for the rest of the century. One, in general pro-Russian in its sympathies, was headed by the 'Family' of Czartoryski and its dependents. The other, less clear-cut and generally anti-Russian, was led by the Potocki family. The Russian question dominated political thinking in Poland as the Turkish danger had done in the time of Sobieski. The threat posed by Brandenburg-Prussia was almost ignored, and Frederick the Great's conquest of the former Polish province of Silesia in 1741 passed almost unnoticed. There was no foreign policy except that which was dictated by the self-interest of the Saxon king or the ambitions of the Russian Tsar. There was talk of reform, but Augustus would do nothing that would endanger his position, and the *szlachta* were determined at all cost to protect their 'golden anarchy'.

The second Saxon king died in 1763, unwept, and indeed unknown, by his subjects. His successor was Stanisław Poniatowski, a member of the 'Family' and the nominee of the Tsarina Catherine the Great, whose lover he had once been. He was expected by all concerned to identify himself fully with the interests of the Russians, and it was his failure to live up to these expectations that embroiled him with the Tsarina and brought about the Partitions.

Despite the losses of territory that Poland had sustained since the Truce of Andruszów, the Commonwealth continued to cover an immense area, larger in fact than that of any other European country except Russia. It covered an area of considerably more than a quarter of a million square miles, and its population has been put at about

11 million, more than that of any European country except France. But the distribution of population, like the level of economic development, was uneven. Both were greatest west of the Vistula, especially in Wielkopolska and the more westerly parts of Małopolska. East of Warsaw the density of population diminished rapidly, and parts of Podlasie and Polesie were marsh and forest, virtually without inhabitants. Nevertheless, the population was growing rapidly during the eighteenth century, and the calculations made by Korzon and others suggest that over the Commonwealth as a whole it increased by some 2½ million in the space of twenty-five years, a rate of increase probably greater than that which is taking place in Poland today.

It is difficult to form any clear estimate of the division of this population on the basis of language and religion. Approximate figures are, however, available for the year 1791, just before the Second Partition. At this time, 8,790,000 were recorded as living in Poland; 53 per cent of them were Roman Catholics, and almost all were ethnic Poles or Lithuanians. Rather less than 30 per cent were described as members of the Uniate Church, which was Orthodox in ritual, but accepting the supremacy of the Pope and the doctrines of the Catholic Church. There were small numbers of Protestants and Jews, and even fewer Moslems and Armenians. The rest were members of the Orthodox Church.

But by 1791 Poland had already lost about a fifth of her territory in the First Partition, together with a population of up to 4 million. Among the areas lost were the lower Vistula valley and West Prussia and Galicia from the Silesian border to the Moldavian. These were relatively densely populated, with ethnic Poles predominating in all except eastern Galicia. The area taken by the Russians lay mainly to the east of the upper Dnepr and of the Dvina, and was thinly peopled by Orthodox Belorussians. The proportion of Roman Catholics in the whole country before the Partitions was probably higher than in 1791, but it would have included a large proportion of the Lithuanians. It thus seems that the statement of R. H. Lord that 'the Poles can scarcely have formed more than fifty per cent . . . at most'[6] of the population is an over- rather than an under-estimate of their numbers.

This population was largely rural. Cities and towns were numerous, especially in western Poland, but most were very small and served only the market needs of the surrounding villages. More than 1,400 such towns were listed in 1789, of which almost two-thirds had each less than 300 inhabitants. Only about fifty could be described as even of moderate size. Foremost among these was Warsaw, which at this

[6] R. H. Lord, *The Second Partition of Poland* (Cambridge, Mass., 1915), p. 26.

time was growing rapidly. From about 30,000 inhabitants at the time of the death of the last Saxon king, it grew to about 60,000 after the First Partition, and to 120,000 at the time of the Second. Its population was undoubtedly swollen by an influx of refugees from territory lost in the Partitions, but a more important reason for the city's growth was probably the building there of the city palaces of the wealthier members of the aristocracy and the establishment by each of them of a little court of his own. In 1794 there were no less than 117 such palaces in and around the city, most of them built, or at least enlarged, during the eighteenth century.

Gdańsk, with a population of about 36,700 in 1793, and considerably more than this before the beginning of the Swedish wars in the seventeenth century, was the second largest city. Poznań and Kraków had each about 20,000 persons; Lublin, about 12,000; and Toruń, some 9,000. In the eastern provinces, only Wilno, with perhaps 24,000, appeared to be of even moderate size. No others, in either Poland or Lithuania, exceeded 5 or 6,000 inhabitants, and most had a great deal less. The urban population in all probability did not greatly exceed a million. Up to half a million of these were Jews, whose numbers had in recent years been increasing rapidly with immigration from the Austrian and Russian empires. Much of the small town business was already in their hands.

The rest of the population was made up of the nobility, the peasants, and the clergy. The nobility and gentry, or *szlachta*, were estimated in 1791 to have numbered about 725,000 or about 8 per cent of the total population. They included 'every grade of wealth, education and social position, from great magnates to the *pauperes nobiles* who worked on their own lands or served at the court of a lord.'[7] The wealthiest were among the richest people in Europe. Many of these were of Lithuanian or Ruthenian origin, and in the veins of some there flowed the blood of the Tatars.[8] Their great estates had been carved out of the forests of Belorussia or the steppe of Podolia or the Ukraine. Individually many of them were wealthier than the king; they raised private armies, and pursued their dynastic policies with greater vigour and purpose than the national policy had ever been guided. In 1770 Stanisław Lubomirski, perhaps the richest of them all, owned almost 10,000 square miles of territory, with thirty-one towns and 738 villages. Several such families had become extinct; some were impoverished by the loss of their territory to Russia; the rest – the Potocki, Czartoryski, Lubomirski, Radziwiłł, and others – gathered around themselves the swarms of impecunious gentry and

[7] *Polish Encyclopedia*, vol. II, part 2, p. 116.
[8] It was held against King Michał Wiśniowiecki (1669–74) that he was partly Tatar; his home had been in the Ukraine.

divided the country into hostile camps, whose feuds the king was powerless to halt or even restrain.

The clergy made up only about a half of one per cent of the population. They were drawn from the ranks of the gentry, especially from the more educated and patriotic 'middle' gentry. The more enlightened among them were prominent in the reform movement and, during the dark years that lay ahead, they were to serve as repositories of Polish tradition and culture. Not all the clergy, however, were as forward-looking. All too many shared the worst of the prejudices and superstitions of the gentry, and some played their part in stirring up hostility to the Dissidents, or Orthodox, and in provoking the intervention of the Russians.

The peasantry, lastly, made up almost three-quarters of the population. Their position in society was abject, but there were, as amongst the peasantry of medieval Europe, 'degrees of unfreedom'. A small minority were legally free. Though landless, they were not bound to the soil, and could, in fact, pack their belongings and move, making their own conditions with the noble on whose lands they chose to settle. The remainder, about 85 per cent of the total, were serfs. The minority, who lived on royal or ecclesiastical estates, were not worse off than serfs in Germany or France, but the rest, who lived and worked on the lands of the magnates, were in a more unfortunate position. No attempt was made to give them any legal protection against their lords before the reforms of the Four-year *Sejm* (1788–92), and none to enlist them in the national cause until Kościuszko held out to them the prospect of a happier future in a free and independent Poland.

After the invasions of the seventeenth century trade and industry had languished in Poland. An important reason for the reoccupation of Gdańsk in the fifteenth century had been to provide an outlet to the sea for Poland's commerce. This trade continued through the eighteenth; over half the roughly built, wooden boats that sailed down the Vistula in the 1780s, headed for Gdańsk, were laden with rye, wheat, and lumber, but the volume of this commerce had for many years been diminishing. The exports of Poland were primary goods, the products of the fields and forests; scarcely any came from factories and workshops.

By the First Partition Poland lost her access to the sea as well as the salt-mines of Galicia and the forests of the Carpathians, both of which had provided materials for export. Yet these years, perhaps because of the restrictions placed on foreign trade, saw a rebirth of domestic industries. It was not a large-scale renaissance, and it tended to concentrate on luxury goods for the magnates who alone had the purchasing power to acquire them. The cloth industry revived in

Wielkopolska; the iron industry was extended in Małopolska; and the manufacture was established of a number of luxury goods, such as pottery and porcelain, silks and fine clothing, paper and jewellery. Stanisław Poniatowski encouraged this modest industrial growth, but it was ill-conceived and in the end unsuccessful. It concentrated too much on the manufacture of highly priced goods for a very small section of the community. The workers were in many instances recruited – or rather conscripted – from the servile labour force on the great estates and had neither the aptitude for the work nor the desire to learn. The few craftsmen of the towns, who could have supplied a skilled direction, were ignored, and the capital made available for industry by the aristocracy which was promoting it was totally inadequate.

An extraordinary feature of these years was the attempt to further industry and trade by the construction of canals. Between 1765 and 1784, Ogiński, the *wojewoda* (provincial governor) of Wilno, had a canal cut from the upper Dnepr to the Niemen. By the time that it was completed, much of the territory which it was designed to serve had passed under Russian rule, and its western outlet was dominated by Prussia. During the same years, another canal, the Królewski, was cut from the Bug, a tributary of the Vistula, to Prypeć and thus created a link with the Dnepr and the Black Sea. It also came too late, and, even if it had been in service before the Partitions, it is doubtful whether it could have contributed much to Poland's economic growth.

Economic decline accompanied the political decay of the seventeenth and eighteenth centuries. The period as a whole was marked by the triumph of the *szlachta* over both the Crown and the middle class. The former they had deprived of all real power by the price which they had exacted at the election of each successive ruler. The decline of the cities and of the middle class was not entirely the fault of the *szlachta,* though they must bear much of the responsibility. To some extent it was due to the changes which took place in the sixteenth century in the geographical pattern of the world's trade. In the fifteenth century the policy of expanding 'from sea to sea' and of canalizing across Poland much of the overland trade between the Middle East and north-west Europe made good sense. In the sixteenth it had ceased to do so. Not only did Turks and Tatars obstruct the routes, but a sea route to the East had been opened up. Under these conditions trade inevitably declined.

The *szlachta* made its decline more rapid by their attempts to profit from it. Cities gradually lost their power to govern themselves; the lands beyond their walls passed into the possession of the *szlachta* and the latter proceeded to regulate to their own advantage the price of merchandise. The sources of long-distance trade dried up, and towns were reduced to the status of local markets.

If the middle class could put up little resistance to the pretensions of the *szlachta*, the peasantry could offer none. They were reduced to serfdom at the same time that in western Europe they were gaining personal freedom and economic independence. In Poland they could escape their lot only by flight, and the fact that the Cossacks were in part recruited from runaway serfs helps to explain the extreme bitterness which they felt towards the magnates.

The *szlachta* was a huge and nondescript body. At its head was a handful of wealthy and illustrious families. Below them were the 'middle' gentry, not rich or well-connected enough to play a part in international politics, but educated after a fashion, usually well travelled and with some cultural sophistication. From this class came most of the writers and reformers and the most enlightened of Polish leaders in the eighteenth and nineteenth centuries. But the bulk of the *szlachta* were individually the owners of only a few acres. As their wealth diminished their pride increased. They were the 'barefoot' *szlachta*, ignorant and often illiterate. Lacking the means to travel to the national Diet, they assembled at intervals in the rowdy *sejmiki*, or local dietines. The enactments of the national Diet had to pass their scrutiny, and they could be counted upon to approve nothing that infringed in the slightest degree their pretended rights and privileges. They came to the *sejmiki* prepared to sell their sword or their vote, always ready to join some 'Confederation', or armed rising to correct some imagined wrong, and certain to oppose any change that savoured of reform.

Such was the *demokracja szlachecka*, the 'gentlemen's democracy', which had nothing democratic about it, and whose devotion to the *Rzeczpospolita*, or Commonwealth, took no account of the common weal. Poland, in the words of R. H. Lord, 'had no effective government whatever. The nation lived in an anarchy thinly concealed under the forms of an elaborate republican constitution. It is in the unfortunate historic evolution of that constitution that the explanation of the decline of Poland is to be sought.'[9]

The Partitions

The events of the years 1772 to 1796 are well known. They saw the disappearance of the Polish Commonwealth from the map of Europe. In 1769 there occurred a kind of curtain-raiser to the Partitions : Austria reoccupied the territory of Spiš, or Zips, which Poland had obtained from the king of Hungary in the sixteenth century as

[9] Lord, op. cit., p. 7.

surety for the repayment of a loan. This minor aggression passed without protest and almost without notice. Already a more drastic dismemberment of Poland had been suggested. Its origin lay in that religious question which has already been discussed and which remained in the eighteenth century even farther from solution than in the sixteenth. The chief difference now was that the Dissidents had found a champion in the person of the Russian Tsarina.

In 1768, the *Sejm*, under Russian dictation, had made far-reaching concessions to the Dissidents. It was always difficult for the Poles to distinguish clearly between loyalty to Church and to state. The Confederation of Bar, formed away in Podolia by a group of Polish nobles and churchmen, with the active participation of the bishop of Kamieniec, was outwardly a protest against this betrayal of Catholicism by the *Sejm*. But it was at the same time a protest against Russian influence in the affairs of Poland. A Russian army was sent into Poland to suppress the Confederates, and war spread through the Ukraine, and the Ottoman Empire, nervous of Russia's intentions, joined in.

Catherine the Great was not yet secure enough on the throne to which she, a Baltic German, had by chance succeeded, to welcome a war with the Turks. At the same time Frederick the Great of Brandenburg-Prussia had set his eyes on Gdańsk and West Prussia, and dropped a hint into the ear of the Russian ambassador that if they could only agree amongst themselves they might help themselves to those parts of Poland which each desired. Austria had already shown how easily it could be done; the only question was for the great powers to consult and agree on method and timing. The Austrians were brought in, and the three powers bargained in secret regarding their individual shares of Polish territory. Only when agreement had been reached were the conditions announced to the incredulous Poles and three separate treaties imposed on their king who was impotent to resist.

By the treaties of 1772, which together make up the First Partition, Prussia annexed Warmia, or Ermland, and West Prussia. The treaty had specified that Frederick should take the territory as far south as the Noteć river, but he, acting both as claimant and as judge in his own case, took the whole basin of the Noteć. Austria, with a similarly generous interpretation of the treaty her Ministers had drawn up, annexed the whole of Galicia, from the border of Silesia eastwards to Tarnopol and Halicz. Russia's claims were relatively modest; she took as her western boundary the 'line of the rivers', the Dnepr, Drut, and Dvina, thus acquiring only relatively small areas of Belorussia and Livonia.

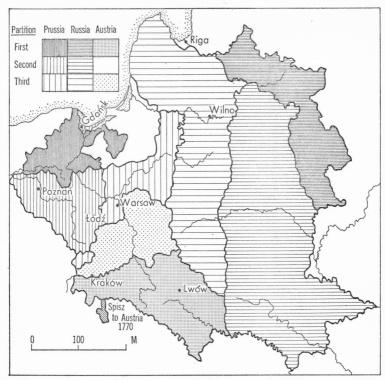

Partition	Prussia	Russia	Austria
First			
Second			
Third			

Riga

Gdańsk

Wilno

Poznań

Warsaw

Łódź

Kraków

Lwów

Spisz
to Austria
1770

0   100   M

4. The Partitions of Poland, 1772–95

There had been some signs of a movement directed towards the reform of society and of the constitution even before the First Partition. The shock of the events of 1772 hastened the movement for political reform, for ameliorating the lot of the peasantry, and for economic development. Grief over the Partition and the mistakes which had made it possible assumed an almost religious character. The fervour of the songs of the Confederates of Bar and of some of the writings of Krasiński have a mysticism equalled only by certain of the nineteenth-century works of Słowacki and Mickiewicz. Was a new Poland, purged by her ordeals, reborn and revitalized, to emerge from the struggles with the Prussian king and Russian Tsarina? Such was the hope and the expectation of the advocates of reform, the noblest of whom had unfortunately more of the visionary and prophet than of the practical politician.

The twenty years that passed between the First Partition and the Second were years of economic growth. Population increased sharply, and, despite the disadvantageous position in which Poland had been placed by the First Partition, industry and trade showed signs of reviving. It may, perhaps, be too much to say, with the *Cambridge History of Poland*, that 'Poland thus joined in the progressive movement of Enlightened Europe'. But there was at least a break in the dark clouds that had been gathering for over a century.

Yet it was the very success of the reform movement that brought on the Second Partition. Since his coronation in 1764 Stanisław had been the tool of the Russian Tsarina. The Polish constitution in its existing form had been shaped by the Russians; the Russian ambassador at Warsaw had an altogether excessive influence, not to mention far too much money with which to buy votes and influence people. The Germans were disliked in Poland, but the Russians were despised and detested as enemies both of the Poles and of their faith. So it was that the earliest attempts at reform took on a markedly anti-Russian character.

It was not, however, until 1788 that the *Sejm* met in Warsaw. From the first it dedicated itself to reform. One of its first decisions, to maintain a large standing army, was quite unrealistic and out of keeping with the country's resources. On the other hand, the delegates pursued with vigour and intelligence the proposals for constitutional reform. In these discussions Stanisław himself participated. Much was done behind the back of the Russian ambassador, who had no alternative but to oppose and resist reforms that would tend to give the Polish government a broader public support and a greater degree of independence of Russia. The constitution of 3 May 1791, which emerged from the deliberations of the Four-Year *Sejm*, was, for its time, a liberal and politically intelligent document. It was confirmed by king and *Sejm* amid public rejoicing. It regulated the legislative process; it abolished the *liberum veto* (the right of *any* member of the *Sejm* to veto legislation); created a stronger executive, and a hereditary monarchy; and held out to the mass of the people the prospect of greater personal liberties.

Yet the constitution was not to the liking of all Poles and, needless to say, was strongly opposed by the Russians. There were those who clung to their 'golden anarchy', and regarded any concession to constitutional government as revolutionary and subversive. Such were the gentry from the Ukraine, who in 1792 formed the Confederation of Targowica, with the object of resisting the new constitution and of accepting, if necessary, the help of the Russians. The Treaty of Iaşi had just ended the war between Russia and the Turks, and the Russian army was thus free to support the Confederation. The latter appealed for aid; the Tsarina Catherine gave it; and Suvorov led her armies on Warsaw. The Prussian king, Frederick William II, hastened to ally himself with Catherine, so that he would not be left out from any division of the spoils that might take place. Between them they dictated the terms of the Second Partition of Poland. This time the Tsarina bit deeply into Poland. Podolia and the Ukraine, much of Wołyń, a large part of the Polesian marshes, and the remainder of Belorussia were added to her empire. The new boundary ran from the Dvina south to the Dnestr at Choczim. The *Sejm* resisted the demands of Prussia for several weeks, but ultimately yielded to the demand for the cession of Gdańsk, which had since the First Partition constituted a small Polish enclave in West Prussia, and the whole of Wielkopolska. The boundary between Poland and Prussia now ran southwards from the East Prussian border, crossed the Vistula to the west of Warsaw, and thence ran almost direct to the meeting-point of Silesia and Galicia.

The Poland that remained covered little more than a third of her extent before the Partitions. Deprived of her ancient nucleus in Wielkopolska, she was now more Lithuanian than Polish. Warsaw lay close to her western boundary, and Wilno dangerously near her eastern. Courland, which still remained legally within Poland, was for practical purposes independent and the geographical core of the rump state was made up of the almost uninhabited provinces of Podlasie and Polesie.

The Third Partition followed quickly on the Second. Military resistance to the Russian and Prussian troops had collapsed when the feckless Stanisław himself adhered to the Confederation of Targowica, thus joining the opposition to his own policies. Plans were quickly laid for a national uprising against the occupying powers. It was led by Tadeusz Kościuszko, and among its supporters, in addition to members of the 'middle' gentry, were many from the middle class. The social breadth of the army of Kościuszko showed how successfully the latter, and even the peasantry, had been drawn into the national movement.

The insurrection, despite early successes and the occupation of Warsaw, collapsed before the larger, better-equipped, and more fully trained armies of Russia and Prussia. Suvorov again attacked Warsaw, and, not for the last time, Russian troops occupied and despoiled the east-bank suburb of Praga. Resistance ended, and the Tsarina decided once and for all to end the Polish question by liquidating Poland. Her allies, the Prussian king and the Austrian emperor, agreed, and the Third Partition followed. The act which delimited their respective spheres took almost a year to prepare, and was not completed until 1797. Russia took most of Lithuania and all of Polesie and Wołyń as far as the river Bug. Prussia took a broad belt of territory which enveloped East Prussia on the east and south and included Warsaw itself. Austria, which had abstained at the time of the Second Partition, made up for her restraint, and took the whole of Małopolska as far to the north and east as the river Bug.

Poland disappeared from the political map after a continuous existence of over eight centuries. The white eagle, as the Poles are represented heraldically, had fallen a prey to the three black eagles by which it was surrounded. And, but for the brief interlude of Napoleon's Grand Duchy of Warsaw, Poland was to remain divided until the three black eagles, or the empires which they represented, all met defeat during the First World War.

The Nineteenth Century

A number of Polish soldiers and patriots escaped from their partitioned country, and sought service with France, the only power which at this time could have done anything to assist them. Napoleon used to the full the valour and the fighting qualities of the Polish soldiery, but in the cause of Poland herself he was lukewarm. For political reasons he did not wish to antagonize all the partitioning powers at the same time, and for this reason, when he did re-establish a Polish state, it was from the Prussian and Austrian shares alone that he took the territory.

The armies of Russia and Prussia were both defeated at Friedland, in June 1807, and by the Treaty of Tilsit, which followed a month later, the king of Prussia was obliged to cede all the territory that had been gained in the Second and Third Partitions, together with part, including the city of Bydgoszcz (Bromberg), which had been acquired in the First. The whole of this area, with the exception only of the Białystok region in the east, which was incorporated into Russia, was constituted the Grand Duchy of Warsaw. At the same time Gdańsk became a 'Free City', and freedom of navigation on the Vistula between the Grand Duchy and the port was guaranteed. Two years later, the Austrians were defeated at Wagram, and Napoleon took the opportunity in the Treaty of Schönbrunn which followed to add to the Grand Duchy the territory which Austria had acquired at the Third Partition.

The king of Saxony became hereditary ruler of the new state. Its constitution was to be liberalized, and the serfs freed. The 'Continental System', the naval blockade, the occupation of the territory by French troops, and the control of its government by French officials left little scope for the resumption of the political and economic development which had been interrupted by the last Partitions.

Many Poles regarded the Grand Duchy as the nucleus from which the old Poland might be rebuilt. Others, including Kościuszko him-

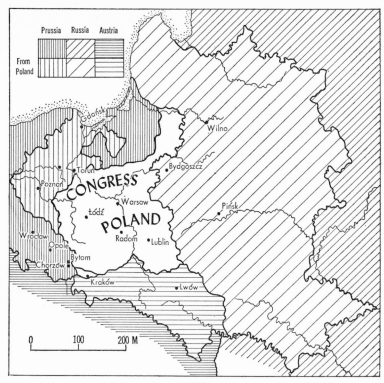

5. The territory of Poland, 1815–1918

self, distrusted Napoleon, and regarded his policy towards Poland as merely opportunist, to be abandoned when he ceased to derive personal advantage from it. The latter were proved right. Napoleon showed no real attachment to the Polish cause, and exerted himself for it only when such a course fitted his general policy. Yet the French experience had a deep influence on the development of Polish nationalism. The ideas and ideals of the French Revolution gave it a clearer shape, endowed it with a programme, and infused it with ideals of toleration and liberal democracy. The survival of Polish nationalism through the nineteenth century owed much to French influence, and it was to France that the Polish leaders fled after the suppression of the 1830 rising.

The new ideas, however, did not go unopposed. Those members of the *szlachta* who had resisted the constitution of 3 May were no less opposed to the egalitarian ideals of the French Revolution. Even before the tragedy of Napoleon's retreat from Moscow in the autumn of 1812, their leaders, among them Adam Czartoryski, had raised the question of an autonomous Poland under the protection of the Tsar. This proposal was bitterly attacked by the liberals, including Kościuszko, but gained widespread support among the aristocracy. The defeat of Napoleon, the invasion of the Grand Duchy by the armies of the Tsar, and the disintegration of the Polish legion which had fought heroically, and with little recognition, for Napoleon, left no room for any alternative policy. Spokesmen for Poland welcomed the incorporation of their country into Russia, hoping only that they might be guaranteed some degree of liberty and local autonomy.

Polish interests were represented at the Congress of Vienna by Adam Czartoryski. It was widely believed that he enjoyed the confidence of Tsar Alexander I, and it was hoped that he would prevail upon the Tsar to establish an independent Polish state, with a Habsburg, or a Romanoff, or even himself as king. Such hopes were doomed to disappointment. The Prussian and Austrian representatives strenuously opposed the perpetuation of the Grand Duchy in any form, and demanded that it again be broken up. The Tsar made a show of resistance, but came round to their view. Only the British Foreign Minister, Lord Castlereagh, among the representatives of the powers, supported the proposal to re-create an independent Polish state. But Alexander had already made up his mind to include as much as possible of the Grand Duchy within Russia. He agreed to the return to Prussia of the so-called Duchy of Posen, the more westerly part of Wielkopolska, as compensation for Prussia's failure to retain Saxony. At the same time Austria regained some small territories which she had lost by the Treaty of Schönbrunn, and the city of Kraków and its surrounding region was constituted a free and independent city-state.

The treaties embodying these territorial changes were signed at Vienna in May 1815. The political geography which they established differed significantly from that laid down by Napoleon. Toruń and Poznań were included within Prussia, and that part of the Grand Duchy which remained – about two-thirds of its former extent – became the kingdom of Poland hereditary in the Romanoff family. A constitution was drawn up by a committee of Poles, including Adam Czartoryski, and Russians. It was, as might have been expected, significantly less liberal than that of 1791. It made little attempt to limit the autocracy of the king and none to protect the rights of the peasants and religious minorities. The foreign policy of the new state was, in effect, to be brought into line with that of Russia, but it was permitted to pursue its own economic policy, subject, of course, to the very considerable personal influence of its Tsar-king.

Even if the conditions of the Treaty of Vienna had been faithfully carried out, they would have fallen short of the aspirations of many of the Poles. They were, in fact, implemented neither honestly nor efficiently. The Tsar's representatives in Warsaw were his brother, the Grand Duke Constantine, and his Minister, Novosiltsov, neither of whom felt any partiality towards the Poles or any obligation to govern the country in the interests of its inhabitants. They were as autocratic as Tsar Alexander, but without sharing his bizarre streak of enlightenment. The government of Poland was reactionary, at a time when the seeds of liberalism, planted in the eighteenth century and fertilized by the French, were beginning to grow and to mature into political movements. The rigours of serfdom were revived; the press was controlled; and all societies which savoured of liberalism, freemasonry, or free-thought were suppressed.

But not all the servants of the Tsar were reactionary and ignorant. Several in lesser governmental positions were highly competent. Though necessarily strongly Russophile, they did their utmost to make a bad system work. Foremost among them were Stanisław Lubecki, the arrogant, competent Finance Minister, and Stanisław Staszic, who had the supervision of mining and related industries. The industrial growth which these two promoted within the span of a few years was little short of miraculous. Poland, which had previously been an exporter only of the raw materials produced from her fields and forests, now began to export textiles, minerals, and metal goods. This industrial expansion owed something to the foundations laid during the latter part of the eighteenth century, but it was better conceived and more wisely directed, and was based on the manufacture of capital goods and of consumer goods in wide demand.

Such progress, however, did not dispel the widespread hostility to the regime. The 1820s were filled with plots, conspiracies, and secret societies, which increased in number and boldness, and culminated in the November Rising of 1830. Unrest was no less marked in other parts of the former Polish state, and with more reason. The Lithuanian provinces, which had not formed part of the Grand Duchy, had been promised a Polish-Lithuanian administration by the Tsar. Alexander died, however, in 1825, and his good intentions perished with him. His successor, Nicholas I, assimilated the Lithuanian provinces completely into the Russian system. Meanwhile there was never any suggestion that Podolia and the Ukraine should have any special privileges. These were merged with the Russian system of administration, where they remained until the Communist Revolution.

The Austrian share of Poland consisted still of the territory acquired in the First Partition, less the Zamość district, which had been ceded to the Grand Duchy in 1809 and subsequently incorporated into the 'Congress' Kingdom. Austria was obliged by the Vienna treaty to provide some kind of autonomous government in Galicia, but this condition was observed in only the most perfunctory fashion. The administration was, in fact, highly centralized, and was closely controlled by the Austrian bureaucracy. Polish language and culture were penalized in the public educational system, and the Austrian governor deliberately embittered the relations between the Poles and the Uniate Ruthenes of eastern Galicia.

The republic of Kraków was, relatively at least, an island of freedom amid a sea of reaction. Its small area and about 30,000 inhabitants continued to observe the Napoleonic Civil Code, which had been introduced into the Grand Duchy by the French. The peasants were not only free but even enjoyed a degree of political representation. But Kraków was too liberal for its neighbours, which were represented in it by Commissioners and possessed furthermore the duty to 'protect' the city. In 1828, these Commissioners nullified the acts of the city chamber, and henceforward, until the city-state of Kraków was liquidated in 1846, its liberal constitution was replaced by a committee which ruled in accordance with the wishes of the Tsar.

Prussia fared better territorially than Austria had done, and recovered in 1815 not only all the Polish territory that had been lost when the Grand Duchy was established, but also the Poznań region. Warmia had been absorbed into East Prussia; the rest of the territory obtained from Poland was organized as the provinces of West Prussia and Posen. The Prussian government set out to observe the conditions imposed by the Treaty of V.enna with greater regularity than either of the other powers, and for a few years Polish culture received far more protection and encouragement from the Hohenzollerns than it ever did from the Habsburgs and the Romanoffs.

The accumulated discontents in Russian Poland broke out in the ill-planned, ill-conceived rising of November 1830. Badly led, the Polish army was defeated in the field, and part of it crossed into Prussia, where it surrendered and went into exile. A stream of refugees crossed Germany to France, whose rising in the previous July had provided the spark which ignited the Polish revolution. Only those who were strongly pro-Russian among the Polish élite remained in Poland. The leaders of the nationalist movement, not only the politicians and soldiers, but also the poets, writers, and musicians, gathered in Paris. Some obtained employment and merged as best they could with French society; most waited and hoped for a turn in Poland's fortunes that would offer them a homeland to which to return. In this they were disappointed. Yet the group of exiles who gathered round the Hôtel Lambert succeeded by the intensity of their patriotism not only in keeping the flame alight at home, but also in holding up to the conscience of the world the wrongs done to Poland.

Among the exiles were the poets Mickiewicz, Słowacki, and Krasiński, and the pianist-composer Fréderic Chopin. Through their poems and plays, mazurkas and polonaises, the image was created of a noble, romanticized Poland, called upon to suffer defeat and partition at the hands of neighbouring powers, but destined to be born again in glory and majesty. This messianic vision inspired the best of Polish literature and gave a sense of mission to those Poles, both inside their country and without, who were planning and plotting to give it independence once again.

The intensity of the patriotic outpouring of these years is probably unequalled in literature. The fact that it was created by exiles who had hope but little prospect of ever returning to their homes, gives it a poignancy and a sense of nostalgia which little else in literature can show. It is, in a sense, an unreal Poland which shines through these writings. The landscapes of Mickiewicz have the radiance of a summer morning; society is represented as noble and gentle; the presence of evil, in the shape of the occupying powers, is recognized as inevitable, but the ultimate triumph of good appears in the apocalyptic vision of the exiles. The plays of Słowacki and his unfinished epic, *Król Duch*, are concerned above all with the fate of nations and the survival of nationalism. In some respects Słowacki followed the model of his great contemporary Mickiewicz.

Most of the writings of the latter express the same ideas and ideals, though often in mystical and allegorical forms. Most familiar of his works is the epic poem *Pan Tadeusz*, set in Lithuania during the Napoleonic Wars. It is a romantic idyll of country life and family feuds, all happily healed at the end, among the 'middle' gentry of this region. Not a suspicion of the burning social issues comes through to the reader, only the simple pleasures of *szlachta* and peasant and the warm beauty of the countryside which the poet has lost :

> Litwo ! Ojczyzno moja ! ty jesteś jak zdrowie;
> Ile cię trzeba cenić, ten tylko się dowie,
> Kto cię stracił. Dziś piękność twą w całej ozdobie
> Widzę i opisuję, bo tęsknię po tobie.[10]

The rising of 1830 marked the end of the Congress Kingdom; its

---

[10] 'Lithuania, my country, thou art like health; how much thou shouldst be prized only he can learn who has lost thee. Today thy beauty in all its splendour I see and describe, for I yearn for thee.' G. R. Noyes (tr.), in the Everyman edition.

government was suppressed and it was incorporated into the Tsarist Empire, and no one in Europe, except the Poles, protested against this violation of the terms of the Treaty of Vienna. The revolutionary movement next broke out in 1846–48. In Prussian-held Poland it was quickly suppressed; in Galicia, the peasants were turned against the Polish landlords by the Austrian authorities, and a bloody *jacquerie* followed; in Kraków there was a rising against outside control of the city's government; it was suppressed, the independent status of Kraków was abrogated, and the city was absorbed into Austrian Galicia.

Hatred of Prussia and Austria led the Poles in western Poland to be more sympathetic than the facts warranted to Russian rule. Tsar Nicholas was described as 'the most generous of our enemies'. German liberals, on the other hand, favoured the aspirations of the Poles, but on this, the Prussian government blew hot and cold. At one time, fear of Russia and the conviction that invasion from this quarter was imminent led to concessions and attempts to enlist the Poles on the German side against the Russians. As the danger from Russia passed, so the good intentions of the Prussian government evaporated.

In 1848, the 'Year of Revolutions', outbreaks again occurred in Prussian Poland, and Poles were prominent in the widespread risings in the Habsburg Empire. But in Russian Poland all was quiet. The rule of Nicholas I was too firm, and recollections of the suppression of the 1830 rising too vivid for another to be undertaken lightly. Nicholas I died in 1855, and was succeeded by his son, the more liberal and attractive Alexander II. The Russians now attempted in a somewhat restrained fashion to conciliate the Poles. They discovered their Slavic kinship with them; amnesties were scattered broadcast; and a more sympathetic governor was established in Warsaw. But most Poles were as immune to the blandishments of the Russians as they had been to those of the Germans. The intense feelings of the exiles of 1830 now began to be reflected in the mood of the Poles at home. Despite the censorship, the writings of Mickiewicz, Krasiński, and others were read and imitated.

A revolutionary movement was again slowly building up in Russian-held Poland. Carried away by the highly charged emotional climate of the times, national Polish groups rejected reasonable compromises and even their own more moderate and clear-sighted leaders. It seemed as if they had understood all too literally the messianic outpourings of the Polish visionaries : only by suffering could Poland be redeemed. The rising of January 1863 was as badly planned as that of 1830 had been. It spread to Lithuania, but attempts to rouse the peasants of Ruthenia failed : the barrier of language and religion which separated them from the Poles was too great to be bridged merely by revolutionary enthusiasm. The Russian policy of no concessions and ruthless suppression succeeded in 1863 as it had done in 1830. The last Polish revolutionary rising was over until the period of the First World War. It had failed disastrously, and its achievement was to add one more page to the body of Poland's heroic story, and to bring it home to the Poles that they must look for other methods.

The failure and suppression of the rising of 1863 hung like a cloud over Poland for the next half-century. It defined the limits of possible political action. It changed nothing, yet it separates two sharply differing periods. Before it, Poland, with her *szlachta* and her serfs, was still basically feudal; after it, Poland became modern almost overnight. The rising itself demonstrated the futility of romanticism. It also took place at a time of rapid economic and social change.

The most significant change of these years was the ending of serfdom in Russian Poland. This action of the Russians sprang more from a desire to weaken the social structure of Poland and to diminish the power of the *szlachta* than from any liberal or humanitarian feelings. The serfs had been freed on the lands of Prussia in the course of the social reforms carried through at the beginning of the century. In Austrian-held Poland they were liberated by 1811. Their liberation in Russian territory was carried out by imperial decree in 1864. The allocation of land to the peasants was fairly generous, but only because it was made at the expense of the *szlachta*. In this way, the Russians hoped, the antipathy between classes would be intensified, and the peasant would learn to look on the Tsar as his 'little father' and protector against the Polish gentry. The downtrodden peasantry had shown little enthusiasm for the rising; very few of them had ever willingly followed the banner of their lord. But now the peasant had a stake in the land, something which he might lose, and thus something to fight for. Very slowly the Polish peasant was moulded into a Polish patriot.

The middle years of the nineteenth century witnessed also a more rapid development of manufacturing than had taken place hitherto. The cotton-mills of Łódź, Zyrardów, and Białystok, the iron- and steel-works of Sosnowiec and Dąbrowa, and many small factories for woollen goods, linen, footwear, paper, and other consumer goods began to spring up as a market slowly opened up for their products. Labour became more mobile as it became more free. It moved to the cities, such as Warsaw, Łódź, and the towns of Upper Silesia, where an old and feudally operated iron manufacture was gradually being transformed, under the influence of German capital and Western technology, into a Western-style industry. The railway net was spreading more widely and more thickly. Galicia was linked with

Bohemia and Austria; Silesia and western Poland with Berlin. In Russian-held Poland, suspicion of the West and the desire to be separate had led to the adoption of the five-feet gauge. There were no through trains from Berlin to Warsaw, but the line from Vienna, through Moravia and Upper Silesia, to Warsaw, was built with Austrian capital, and at Austria's insistence conformed to the Western railway gauge. Along this line there grew up a succession of small industrial towns for some 50 miles to the south-west of Warsaw.

The spirit within Poland was changing in these years. The Poles had finished with risings. Romanticism and revolution had given way to a pragmatic approach to political and economic questions. Improvement of education, the preservation of language and culture through the simple expedient of using them, the slow building-up of industries, and the improvement of living standards were more likely, it came to be held, to benefit the Polish people in the long run than revolutionary activity. Świętochowski wrote in 1883 that 'destiny has opened before us wide fields for conquests in business and industry. We have never mastered these sufficiently before, and now we can win here more certain victories than were those in which we have put our trust until now.' This was the new, realistic approach.

The quality of government varied greatly between the three states among which Poland was divided. Austrian rule, at one time the most heavy-handed, had now become the most easy-going. Prussia, which had at one time verged on liberalism, now became the most reactionary, and did the most to uproot Polish culture and destroy the use of the Polish language. While the Prussian state did all in its power to restrict the use of the Polish language and the practice of Polish culture, German societies sprang up to 'protect' German *Kultur* in Germany's eastern lands. The German policies, it must be admitted, achieved a measure of success. The campaign against the use of Polish led in some areas to its abandonment. On the other hand, the crudity of German methods provoked an inevitable reaction. The division between politics and religion had never been particularly clear in Poland, and during the nineteenth century the Pole in the western lands used religious channels for the expression of his political views and the institutions of the Church to protect his culture. The parish priest again assumed the role of rallying-point for Polish nationalism. The struggle between German and Pole came in part to be one between Protestantism – specifically Lutheranism – and Catholicism. The former contest the Germans might have won; the latter, they could not. Bismarck's *Kulturkampf* was ultimately a failure, and he probably succeeded only in strengthening Polish nationalism in the western lands by the virulence of his attacks on all its manifestations.

Russian policy was similar in its ends, but differed primarily in the methods by which it was pursued. A brutal policy of Russification was adopted. The name of Poland disappeared from Russian maps. Government officials were Russian, and the system which they administered was an extension of that of Russia. A vigorous censorship was enforced until only a short time before the First World War. The Polish language was treated as if it were only a dialect of Russian, which became for all official uses the preferred language. The University of Warsaw was closed, and the Uniate Church was reabsorbed into the Orthodox. The Russian autocracy was made tolerable only by its hopeless inefficiency.

PART TWO

Land and Resources

Chapter 3

The Territorial Basis of the Polish State

Jeżeli kiedy we tej mojej krainie,
Gdzie po dolinach moja Ikwa płynie,
Gdzie góry moje błękitnieją mrokiem,
A miasto dzwoni nad szmernym potokiem,
Gdzie konwalija woniące lewady
Biegną na skały, pod chaty i sady. . . .

J. Słowacki[1]

THE GEOGRAPHICAL FRAMEWORK within which these changes in the Polish state took place was the great plain of northern Europe. This tract of lowland, so simple and uniform on the small-scale map, so intricate and fragmented in reality, extends from western Germany eastwards until it merges into the vaster plains of Russia and Central Asia. Throughout this extent the land surface rises only locally to a height of more than about 500 feet above sea-level, and its greatest heights do not exceed 1,200 feet. Relief is everywhere gentle; the valleys are broad and open; and the rivers meandering and slow-flowing. Within 'peninsular' Europe the plain is bounded on the north by the Baltic and North Seas; on the south by hills which culminate in the mountain ring of Bohemia and in the Carpathian system. Farther to the east, within the limits of Lithuania, Belorussia, and the Ukraine, these boundaries cease to set limits to the plain, and it extends northwards, through the Baltic provinces, towards the Finnish Arctic, and southwards to the Black Sea, to Moldavia, and the Danube.

The plain is substantially a region of young and relatively soft rocks, which had been reduced to an undulating lowland long before the appearance of the Quaternary ice-sheets. The plain is underlain by rocks of greater age and hardness. In a few localities within the plain these older rocks can be seen, as if through a window cut by erosion through the cover of later deposits. Where this has happened,

---

[1] 'If ever in that my country, where my Ikwa flows in its valleys, where my mountains grow blue in the twilight and the town rings above the chattering stream, where the tree clad banks a-scent with lily-of-the-valley run up the cliffs, cottages and orchards.' M. A. Michael (tr.), in *A Polish Anthology,* ed. T. M. Filip and M. A. Michael (London, 1944).

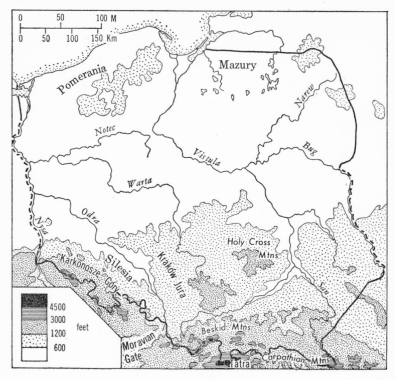

6. Poland: relief and drainage

as in the Świętokrzyskie Góry, or Holy Cross mountains, of south-central Poland, the relief is stronger; the soils are thinner and poorer, but the mineral endowment greater. The older rocks which thus appear as islands in the plain, come to the surface more regularly along its southern margin, where they give rise to the mountains which constitute its southern boundary.

At all stages in her history Poland has consisted essentially of a segment of this plain, though for much of this time she has extended into the mountains and hills to the south. These are complex in both their relief and their geological origins, but only rarely do they constitute a significant barrier to human movement. For much of the last thousand years these mountains constituted a thinly peopled region with scanty resources, through which ran an ill-defined boundary. Beyond it lay the Czech state of Bohemia and the Magyar state of Hungary, and between Poland and them it was both convenient and politically expedient to have such a buffer.

The Polish Plain

There is a fundamental difference in relief, soil, and landscape between the northern part of the plain and the more southerly, and these contrasts have not been without their influence on the course of Polish history. Though the whole plain was exposed during the Quaternary geological period to the ice-sheets which spread southwards from Scandinavia, their imprint has been worn away from its more southerly parts, and today only the north bears the indelible marks of the glaciation.

Four times during the glacial, or Quaternary, period, ice-sheets spread south from the Baltic region, carrying with them a vast burden of gravel, sand, and clay, and at the end of each a change in climate led to a melting of the ice and the deposition over the surface of the plain of the materials which it carried. But before the ice had vanished, it had laid down a vast bank of coarse material along the line of its maximum advance. This was its terminal moraine, fragments of which still give rise to some of the strongest relief in the plain. The melting of each glaciation was accompanied by the discharge of large quantities of water. Huge rivers flowed from the retreating margin of the ice-sheets towards either the Black Sea or the Baltic, cutting wide valleys, and laying down thick deposits of alluvium.

Its first advance took the ice-sheet southward across the European Plain to the foothills of the mountains along its southern margin. The evidence for this glaciation has been almost entirely obliterated by the forces of erosion or covered up by the evidence of the later extensions of the ice. The second advance also took the ice far to the south, but here, too, the long periods of geological time that have since elapsed have seen the disappearance of most of its deposits. The third, called the Central Polish Glaciation, fell short of the limits reached by the first and second. It covered Silesia and reached the foothills of the Bohemian mountains, but eastward across Poland and into Russia, its limit was marked by the higher ground of Małopolska and Podolia. The limit of this glaciation extends eastwards, passing near Orel and Kursk, to the Volga and the Ural mountains. The Ukraine lay to the south of it; Belorussia and Lithuania, as well as Wielkopolska, to the north.

Time has removed the terminal moraines which must at one time have bounded the glaciated area, but it is still possible to trace the courses of the great rivers which flowed from the melting ice-sheets. In part they are still occupied by small streams; in part they survive as depressions in the surface of the plain. As the ice melted away, and the ice-front retreated towards the north, its movement was halted for varying periods of time. At each of these still-stands, morainic material accumulated along the margin of the ice and was left, with the further retreat of the ice, as isolated ridges. Today these constitute the strongest features of the central parts of the Polish plain.

The fourth and last advance of the ice reached a line which runs obliquely across the map from near Zielona Góra in the west to the Vistula near Wrocławek. Thence it continues northward and eastward to the north-eastern extremity of the country. The belt of terminal moraines is then continued by way of Wilno to the Valdai Hills in European Russia. The maximum advance of the fourth glaciation occurred only about 10,000 years ago. The moraines which marked the limit of its advance are still fresh, and to the south and east of Poznań, and from the Vistula north-eastwards across East Prussia, they form the most conspicuous features of the landscape.

The ice retreated from this line in a series of stages, each of which led to the accumulation of looping belts of terminal moraine. Along their outer, or southerly, face, is an apron of sand and gravel outwash, which yields an unfertile soil and usually remains under forest. Within the line of moraine lies an uneven surface, left by the irregular deposition of morainic material. Lakes formed in the depressions in its surface, and in the course of time were interconnected by small rivers. The lakes themselves have tended to fill with alluvium and the peat which forms in their still waters. They are thus not long-lived phenomena of the land surface. Most have disappeared from the plains of Central Poland, and they are numerous now only in those areas which were mostly recently covered by the ice. These are Pomerania and Mazuria, and the continuation of this region north-eastwards into Lithuania and the Baltic region. This is an area of extraordinary beauty. The lakes, almost countless in their number, range from small ponds covering only a fraction of an acre to large water-bodies such as Mamry and Śniardwy, which attain areas of over 40 square miles. The surrounding soil is of no high agricultural value, and much has been left under forest. The dark green of the conifers blends with the pale shades of the broad-leaved trees, the silver of the birches, and the bright green of cultivated clearings and meadows. Small villages cluster near the water's edge and are reflected in its calm surface. It was this environment which Mickiewicz chose as the setting of his rural epic, *Pan Tadeusz*. It was here, too, that Poles and Germans fought their long, sanguinary wars both with the Prussians and between themselves.

The straight coastline which characterizes much of northern Poland has been formed by the waves of the Baltic as they beat against the soft and unconsolidated material of the glacial drift, cutting it into low cliffs and transporting the sand and clay particles along the coast. This movement of the beach material has been in an easterly direction. Its effect has been to smooth the coast, to close the mouths of the small rivers which flow down to the Baltic Sea from the morainic regions of Pomerania and Mazuria, and to form long, narrow sand-spits, which partially close the larger bays.

A result of these changes is that the Baltic coast of Poland and Lithuania is almost devoid of natural harbours. The chief ports of the region lay on the lower courses of the larger rivers, a few miles from the sea. Such is the position of Szczecin on the lower Odra; of Gdańsk, on an arm of the Vistula; and of Königsberg, now the Russian city of Kaliningrad, on the Pregoła (German : Pregel). None of these harbours is good or easily accessible, and when in the 1920s Poland built the new port of Gdynia, it had to be located on an open coast, and protected by man-made harbour-works.

By contrast with these more northerly and more recently glaciated areas of the Polish plain, the regions of central and southern Poland bear only lightly the marks of the glaciation. Over central Poland, the heart of historical Poland, terminal moraines are less conspicuous than in northern. Most of the lakes have filled in and disappeared, and the 'solid' geology, locally at least, shows through the remaining cover of drift. The most evident signs of the extreme changes of the Ice Age are the great valleys, called in Polish *pradoliny*, left by the rivers which carried the melt-water to the sea. Their courses can be traced across the map, from Russia to East Germany. None is today followed by any single river; all are occupied by different rivers in different segments of their course. The valley of the middle Vistula is continued to the west of Toruń and Bydgoszcz by the Noteć valley, and this by the lower Warta as far as its junction with the Odra. To the west of the latter the depression is continued to the north of Berlin until it merges with the valley of the lower Elbe and discharges into the sea below Hamburg. Another such depression lies some 50 miles to the south, and today its course is traced by the Vistula above Warsaw, the Bzura, the upper courses of the Warta and Obra, and by the Odra. Other such depressions can be traced farther to the south, but, being of greater geological age, they are less well preserved in the landscape, and their courses are less clearly distinguished by the segments of river which in turn occupy them.

The historic role of these valleys has been to create obstacles to human movement, and to provide, as it were, a defensive moat for the core-area – Wielkopolska – of early Poland. They did not provide complete isolation; they could be crossed at many points, and the early Polish kings established fortified cities to guard some of them[2].

2 See above, p. 25.

They permitted trade and cultural influences to move across them without great difficulty, but they formed a serious obstacle, as several medieval chroniclers testify, to invading armies.

In southern Poland, the historic provinces of Silesia, Małopolska, and Galicia, the glacial deposits have for practical purposes been removed. The land is made up of rocks, as a general rule hard and soft in turn, which lie roughly from north-west to south-east across the region, giving rise to alternating hilly ridges and valleys, not unlike the sequence of limestone or chalk upland and clay vale in southern England. In a small area of Upper Silesia and adjoining parts of Małopolska these rocks are underlain by coal, which has led to the development of one of the major industrial concentrations of Europe. Farther to the east, in south-central Poland, rocks of yet greater age and hardness break the surface of the land and rise to the high ridges of the Świętokrzyskie Góry or Holy Cross mountains. Though analogous in geological age and composition to the mountains of Wales, this region is one of rounded hills which rise at their highest point, the Łysa Góra, to very little more than 2,000 feet. The poverty of its soil has discouraged the farmer, while the many small deposits of iron-ore and the abundance of charcoal from the forests have made it for over two thousand years a focus of smelting and iron-working.

To the east of the Holy Cross mountains lies the valley of the Vistula, here narrowed between the latter and the limestone plateau, known as the Lublin Uplands – Wyżyna Lubelska, which extends eastwards into Podolia and the Ukraine. South of this varied belt of upland, and lying between it and the mountainous southern border of the state, are the plains of Silesia and south-eastern Poland. These are drained by the upper courses of the Odra, the Vistula, and the many tributaries which descend from the mountains to join them. Although these rivers have brought much coarse detritus down from the mountains, they have also created large areas of soft, rich alluvium which have helped to make this one of the most fertile and intensively cultivated regions of Poland.

The agricultural value of much of southern Poland was greatly enhanced by a widespread deposit of loess. The glacial deposits had consisted of unconsolidated material, much of which was very fine-grained. During the cold and dry conditions which intervened between the advances of the ice and followed its final withdrawal, these deposits dried out and were easily redistributed by water and above all by wind. The loess consists essentially of the fine particles from the boulder-clay redistributed by wind. The lack of vegetation facilitated the process; blowing dust was trapped in sheltered areas, where it sometimes formed deposits of great depth. Elsewhere it constituted merely a thin veneer which has since become mixed with and has in turn enriched the underlying soil materials. On the other hand, loess accumulated to great depths on the Lublin Uplands, on the flanks of the Holy Cross mountains, and in the upper valleys of the Vistula and Odra.

The loess tends to produce a dry soil of great fertility. It is porous, so that its surface dries out readily after rain. It is light and easy to plough, and in the early phases of human history, it was characterized by light woodland easy to clear. The historical significance of the loesslands is that, in contrast with the forested areas of boulderclay, they were relatively open and easy to traverse; that they could be easily cultivated with the simple tools of early man, and in turn rewarded him with a generous return for his labours. The loess regions of southern Poland, in terms of their intrinsic wealth, exceed the clay plains of Wielkopolska; they were densely peopled and possessed an urban development at a relatively early date, and it is an historical accident that it was the Gniezno-Poznań region rather than Silesia or Galicia which became the core-area of the Polish state.

The Mountain Border

The southern border of contemporary Poland is made up of mountains which have always in some degree constituted a barrier to human settlement and have generally been regarded as a 'natural' frontier between Poland and her neighbours. Yet it was not until the present century that a continuous international boundary was established in this mountain region. Before this time, the supposedly natural frontier had not been thought of as a significant barrier to transport or as an obstacle to the extension of national sovereignty. The Bohemian kingdom had, at least since the mid-fourteenth century, extended across the Sudeten mountains to embrace the plain of Silesia. Contrariwise, the Poland of Bolesław Chrobry had extended across the Carpathian mountains to the Hungarian plain, and as late as the second half of the eighteenth century Poland continued to embrace areas lying to the south of the main Carpathian divide. Thereafter, Austria occupied Małopolska and Galicia, until, in 1918–19, the present boundary was established.

The Sudety, or Sudeten mountains, which separate the lowlands of Silesia from those of Bohemia, consist in reality of a series of short ranges, laid out, as it were, en echelon. These are individually not more than about 40 miles in length, and it is possible to pass around their extremities without difficulty. The highest and longest is the granitic range of the Karkonosze Góry, which reaches an altitude of 5,260 feet. But elsewhere the mountains are lower, and their rounded and often forested summits only occasionally exceed 3,500 feet.

The Sudety are separated from the Carpathian mountains by the Moravskábrána, or Moravian Gate. This is in reality a mountain pass on an immense scale. Although its summit lies at only 990 feet, it nevertheless forms part of the divide between the Odra and the Danubian drainage. At its narrowest, the 'Gate' is about 5 miles wide. It contains few physical obstacles to movement, and has since prehistoric times provided one of the most important routeways in the European continent. Its influence has been profound on the historical development not only of the Polish and Czech peoples, but also of the broader Baltic and Danubian regions. Through both the prehistory and history of Europe the movement of cultures and commerce has been canalized by the 'Gate', as they moved between the northern plain and the Danubian basin.

The Moravian Gate and its bordering mountains lie well within the boundaries of Czechoslovakia. The Carpathian mountains which extend eastwards through Slovakia and into Romania, constitute a more formidable barrier than the Sudety. Like the latter, they are made up of a series of parallel ranges, but these are in general higher, more continuous, and less interrupted by gaps and passes. But the Carpathians also rise to rounded and forested summits, and only in the small and compact massif of the Tatra (Slovak : Tatry) does the landscape become really rugged and 'alpine' and only here can permanent snowfields be found. For this short distance of no more than about 40 miles there is no regularly used route across the central Carpathians. But to west and east, in the rolling country of Orava (Polish : Orawa) and Spiš (Polish : Spisz) movement has been easier, and these small regions have long been a disputed frontier between Polish and Slovak cultures.[3]

East of the Tatry the Carpathian range narrows, becomes lower, and is crossed by numerous routes between the Galician and the Hungarian plains. But near the Soviet border, the range becomes broader and higher, and continues into Romania as a formidable obstacle to human movement. The boundary between Poland and Czechoslovakia tends within the Carpathian mountains to follow one mountain ridge after another. It lies toward the north of the broad mountain belt, dipping towards the south only to include within Poland the northern flanks of the Tatra, with the mountain resort of Zakopane. The more northerly ranges of the Carpathian system, known as the Beskidy, lie within Poland. They consist in general of short segments of mountain, truncated abruptly by the deep, narrow, and often gorge-like valleys of the rivers which, rising within the inner fastnesses of the Carpathians, cross them to join the Vistula.

[3] See below, p. 179.

The mountainous barrier which thus encloses Poland on the south, is, like many such barriers, riddled with routeways between the lowlands on each side. Its effect has been, not so much to restrict movement and association – economic, cultural, and political – as to concentrate them at certain points where they can be carried on with a minimum of difficulty and effort. Three such points have been of particular importance in the relations between Poland and the Polish people with their southern neighbours: the Moravian Gate; the routes which encircle the Tatra and traverse the Orawa and Spisz regions; and those which cross the low or eastern Beskidy between Podolia and the north-eastern part of the Hungarian Plain.

Poland derives a certain unity from the river system which drains it. No less than 90 per cent of its area lies within the basins of the Odra and Vistula, and these two rivers derive almost the whole of their drainage from Polish soil. Such a coincidence of hydrographic and political boundaries is rare. It gives Poland undivided control of most of her system of waterways. The Odra, commercially the more important of the two major rivers, rises within Czechoslovakia, on the western margin of the Moravian Gate. It becomes navigable approximately where it enters Poland, and from this point to its mouth in the Baltic Sea, carries much of the bulk commerce of Poland's principal industrial region. Though fed by numerous tributaries from the Sudety, the Odra receives none of significance from East Germany, only a minute area of its drainage basin being actually in East Germany.

The Odra basin is linked with that of the Vistula by several of the valley-like depressions, or *pradoliny,* which were carved by the post-glacial rivers. There is today no natural connection by water between the two basins, but the marshy depressions which have remained from the glacial era lend themselves to the construction of canals. In this way the Vistula is connected by the Bydgoszcz canal with the Noteć and thus with the Odra.

The source of the Vistula is only about 40 miles to the east of that of the Odra. Its course, however, takes it towards the east, where it gathers the drainage of the Carpathians, as the Odra does that of the Sudety. In its upper course the Vistula flows across the broad plain of Galicia. Near Sandomierz it is joined by the San, the most important tributary of its upper course. The Vistula then crosses the uplands of southern Poland, to emerge upon the great plain to the south of Warsaw. From here it takes an irregular course towards the Baltic, in turn following the great glacial valleys and cutting across the belts of terminal moraine, until it enters its delta and divides into several branches which make their separate ways to the sea.

The longest and most important of the tributaries of the Vistula arise close to or even within the borders of the Soviet Union, and the Bug, the longest of them, forms the Polish-Soviet boundary for about 175 miles. These rivers are less useful than the Odra; shifting sandbanks and shallows make navigation difficult; and little has yet been done to deepen and improve them for barge traffic. It is planned to make the Bug navigable and to use it for heavy freight, such as iron-ore, between the Soviet Union and the industrial centres of southern Poland. Very little progress has yet been made in this very ambitious project.

Climate

Conditions on the Polish rivers are directly related to the climate. Poland lies in the same latitude as southern Britain, but it is not, like the latter, exposed to the moderating influence of the sea. Its climate may fairly be described as continental, with severe winters and warm, if not hot, summers. There are nevertheless considerable variations within Poland, and it is possible to recognize no less than four significant variants of the general continental climatic type.

A belt of territory bordering the Baltic coast, and extending inland as far as the great morainic ridges, is distinguished by cooler summers than the rest of Poland, by a shorter period of severe cold in winter, but also by the later arrival of spring, and the earlier coming of autumn and fall of the leaves. Humidity is high at all seasons in this region, and the cloud cover is more persistent and the hours of sunshine fewer than in other parts of Poland.

The moderating effect of the Baltic Sea, which is the cause of these deviations from the average of Poland, ceases to be felt in the moraine country, and the plains of central Poland experience a climate which differs in minor respects from that of northern. Summers are appreciably warmer; humidity and cloudiness are less marked at all seasons; and winters are somewhat colder than near the coast. Within central Poland there is a steady change in the character of the winter from west to east. To the west of Poznań the average temperature in January is about $-1°$ C ($30°$ F). At Brześć on the Soviet border, the January average is fully $4·5°$ ($8°$ F) lower. Spring, in its slow progress from south-west to north-east Poland, comes earlier here than in the coastal region, and summer yields to autumn more slowly. Spring ploughing may begin as much as two weeks before it is possible to begin work in Pomerania or Mazuria. Winters are hard and snow lies long on the fields, but this is in fact the driest season of the year. The heaviest rains come in late spring and summer, when thunderstorms sometimes occur with almost tropical violence.

The hills of southern Poland rise a few hundred feet above the level of central Poland, sufficient to have a measurable effect on climate. Temperatures are at all seasons a degree or two lower, and total precipitation a few inches higher. But the atmosphere is drier and the duration of sunshine greater. Within the climatic region of southern Poland lie two small areas distinguished by the relative mildness of their winters and the greater heat of summers, by the shorter snow-cover of winter, the earlier spring, and the greater length of the growing season. These are the Odra valley in Silesia and the triangular area of lowland between the upper Vistula and the San in Galicia. These areas of more favourable climate are also characterized by their greater extent of loess soil. Both factors combine to make them the most fertile and the most intensively cultivated areas of Poland.

The mountains of southern Poland constitute the fourth climatic region. It is impossible to characterize them in simple terms, for climatic conditions always vary sharply within mountainous areas. Mountains may be said to make their own climate. Temperatures tend to be lower than in the lowlands at all seasons, but under still winter conditions the cold mountain air may slide into the valleys, which fill with cold, raw air, leaving warmer air to bathe the mountain tops. This phenomenon of frost-drainage is not uncommon in all the mountain valleys of the Sudety and Carpathians. Rainfall is very much greater in the mountains than over the plains. In the latter it rarely exceeds an average 25 inches in the year; in the Beskidy it rises to 40 inches, and in the Tatry to over 50 inches. For more than half the year the mountains lie under snow, and in the Tatry snow-patches may linger through the summer.

These climatic variations within Poland, small as they are, nevertheless influence to a considerable degree the use that man has made of the land. There is a difference, on average, of forty days in the length of the growing season between the plains of Silesia and the lake region of Mazuria, and this is sufficient to bring about a considerable variation both in natural vegetation and in cultivated crops.

Vegetation

Poland is by nature a wooded country, and even today no less than a fifth of her surface is under forest. At the beginning of human history tall forest grew everywhere. To the east, in Podolia and the Ukraine, where the rainfall dropped to less than 20 inches in the year, there was natural steppeland, with trees growing only in damp hollows and along the water-courses, but within the limits of modern

Poland it is very doubtful whether there was any wide area of grass-land. Woodland was light, open, and easily cleared by man on the loess soils, but over the clays grew a denser forest of oak, hornbeam, and maple, while alder and willow grew in the marshy valleys, and coniferous trees over the poor sandy soils.

One would nevertheless have found a marked change in the vegetation if one could have made a traverse from south-western to north-eastern Poland. Although the oak would have been found in all parts, the beech, sycamore, and lime were common only towards the south-west. Northward and eastward, with the longer and more severe winters, they thinned away, and the pine and fir became increasingly dominant. In terms of her natural vegetation Poland is clearly transitional between the broad-leaved forest of Atlantic Europe and the coniferous forest of the Baltic.

The changes in vegetation across Poland reflect the variations in climate; they are also adaptations to changes in soil. A plant association dominated by the oak is commonest on the heavy glacial clays; the birch and coniferous trees tend to be most common over the dry sandy outwash and on the patches of blown sand of the moraines.

The natural vegetation cover has been drastically changed by man as he cleared land for occupation and cultivation. But his forest-clearing has been selective. He has cut the trees from the better soils, and has even extended the forest cover over the poorer. The broad-leaved trees, which grew more regularly on the better soils, have greatly diminished relative to the coniferous which are more characteristic of the poorer. Modern reafforestation has been limited to the poorer soils and has generally been restricted to conifers, not only because these are better suited to them but also because they mature more quickly than other trees.

At the time when the Polish state was founded forest clearings were few and scattered, and medieval writers referred not infrequently to the heavily wooded nature of the land. During the eleventh and following centuries forest clearing was pursued on an intensive scale as the steadily growing population created a larger demand for food crops. In this process both monastic foundations and German settlers from the west played an important role. But medieval population growth reached its peak in the fourteenth century, and thereafter tended to decline. Forest clearance ceased over much of Poland, and as in western Europe at this time, there was even some abandonment of land that had been reclaimed in earlier centuries.

It was not until the sixteenth and seventeenth centuries that population began again to grow and to demand more land for cultivation. At the same time iron-working became more widespread and important, and large areas of forest, especially in the hills of south-central Poland, were destroyed to provide the industry with charcoal. The wars of the latter half of the seventeenth century, together with migration to the eastern lands of the Polish state, again restricted population growth in Poland proper. It was thus not until the nineteenth century that forest clearance, in step with population growth, again became significant. During this period the extent of the forest within the limits of historic Poland was reduced from almost a half the total area to appreciably less than a quarter.

Today forest covers about 22 per cent of the land surface of Poland. Large areas were cut over by the Germans during the Second World War, but these have very largely been replanted. Most of the existing forest can be found in three distinctive settings : the damp valley floors and the marshy depressions of the moraine, which are characterized by broad-leaved trees of relatively low commercial value; the areas of sand-dunes and of sandy outwash, which have little or no agricultural value, and are in general planted with conifers; and the mountainous regions, whose steep slopes are covered with mixed or coniferous forest.

Very little of this forest can be regarded as original. The primeval forest has been cut over. Much of what we see today is natural re-growth, but very large areas have been planted by man, and everywhere man has exercised a selective influence on the variety of trees, encouraging or planting those which have a commercial value, and rigorously destroying those which were of no service to him. Today the only area which can claim with any plausibility to be natural forest, unmodified to any significant degree by man, is the Białowieża forest, which now covers an area of about 480 square miles on the border of Poland and the Soviet Union, to the south-east of Białystok. The leached and sandy soils of this region have never been attractive to the peasant, and the forest-based industries, which elsewhere did so much to destroy the forest cover, were never really established in this area.

The nature of soil is a response both to climatic influences and to the nature of the rock on which it is developed. Cultivation, fertilization, and drainage furthermore introduce important conditions, so that in the last resort soil is a 'response to management'. The parent material from which soils are derived over most of Poland is glacial deposits. These range from a heavy, intractable, and almost impervious clay at one extreme to light sands, which are blown by the wind and may even give rise to moving dunes, at the other. The former are difficult to plough and often require draining and liming, but are not in themselves infertile. The latter are retentive of neither soil water nor of soluble soil minerals, and are of very little agricultural value.

The arrangement of minerals within the soil is, by and large, a response to the climatic conditions under which the soil has formed. The two essential and contrary processes are rainfall and its downward percolation through the soil, and, secondly, evaporation from the surface. The essential qualities of the soil depend to an important degree on the relative importance of these two processes. Over most of Poland, the former process is dominant. Whatever the parent material from which the soil is derived, it tends to become leached as rain- and melt-water dissolve and remove soil-forming minerals from the surface layers of the soil. These may be redeposited at a greater depth, but commonly beyond the reach of the roots of field crops. Such is the nature of *podsol,* usually a pale-coloured soil which supports deep-rooting trees, but does not readily support such demanding crops as wheat and sugar-beet. *Podsol,* in varying degrees of development, is found in most parts of Poland.

In the south and south-east, however, the opposite process of evaporation tends to predominate. Under such conditions the moisture which comes from rain or from melting snow mostly evaporates back into the atmosphere. Soil minerals, far from being removed, tend to become concentrated near the surface of the soil and give it the dark colouration from which it derives its usual name of *chernozem,* or 'black earth'. True black earth occurs over only very small areas of Poland, in the drier parts of Galicia and Silesia, where rainfall is low, summers hot, and sunshine prolonged. Elsewhere the climate is too damp and evaporation is on too small a scale for *chernozem* to form.

These two soil types – *podsol* and *chernozem* – mark the extremes, the former one of the least productive, the latter one of the richest, in the world. Over most of Poland soils are intermediate between them. They have been enriched for centuries by the autumn leaf-fall and the accumulated humus has not been wholly dispersed by percolating soil moisture. True *podsols* are extensive only in northern Poland and in the mountains, where the climate is cooler and more humid and coniferous trees, which make only a very small contribution to the soil, tend to predominate.

Poland is not among the better endowed of European countries. Only in parts of southern Poland are soils naturally of a high quality. Elsewhere, in Wielkopolska for example, are soils of intermediate quality but over large areas, especially within the area of the latest glaciation, soils are strongly leached and very poor. Over much of Poland land has been brought under cultivation and is maintained in production only by intensive labour. Large areas are in need of draining and most would greatly benefit from heavy applications of lime and fertilizer. It is against these physical conditions that one must set the present agricultural development of Poland and the current investment in the manufacture of fertilizer.

Polish agriculture has long been dominated by rye and potatoes, which in 1964 occupied respectively 28 and 18 per cent of the cropland. Rye has been since the Middle Ages the staple bread-crop. It will grow, if not flourish, in the poorest soils, and is tolerant of the cool, rainy summers which at times make the cultivation of other crops hazardous. Wheat today occupies less than a fifth of the area that is sown with rye, and this lies almost wholly in those parts of southern Poland which enjoy warmer and brighter summers and possess a superior soil. Oats are grown, primarily to feed the horses, but the area planted has tended to contract in recent years, as tractors come gradually to replace draught animals on the farms.

Potatoes furnish the second staple food of the Polish diet. Like rye, they tend to be tolerant of poor soils and unfavourable weather, and are grown as field crops and in small garden plots in all parts of the country. The summer is too short and generally too cool for maize which comes into its own only to the south of the Carpathians; in Poland it is of negligible importance. Sugar-beet is important on some of the loess areas of the south, and flax, hemp, and tobacco are grown on a small scale in most parts of Poland.

Animal rearing is carried on in all parts. Pigs are the most numerous farm animals, since they can be fattened on agricultural waste. Cattle are also numerous, and the size of the dairy herd has increased sharply in recent years, an indication both of the restoration of farm stock after the destruction of the war years and of improving living standards. Sheep, by contrast, are relatively few, a consequence in large part of the scarcity of relatively dry grazing land, on which they thrive best. Horses still serve as the principal draught animals. They pull the plough on most farms, though tractors are becoming more numerous, and they draw the cart to the small market-towns. Large flocks and herds are rare. Each peasant family usually has a cow or two, a horse, and perhaps a few pigs, and one of the most familiar sights not only in Poland but throughout the peasant countries of eastern Europe, is to see the family cow, or even pig, grazing by the roadside under the watchful eyes of a junior or an aged member of the family.

Mineral Resources

By contrast with the agricultural wealth of Poland, the fuel resources are amongst the largest of any European country and by far the most extensive in East-Central and eastern Europe. A belt of coalfields extends from west to east across Europe near the junction of the northern plain with the hills and mountains of Central Europe.

Amongst the largest of the coal-basins within this belt of territory are those of northern France and central Belgium, of the Ruhr and Upper Silesia. In addition there are several smaller coal-basins, including that of Lower Silesia. All the more important of the world's deposits of bituminous coal were formed during the Carboniferous period of geological time. The coal measures have mostly been removed by subsequent erosion, leaving only the few 'basins' or pockets which are the coalfields of today. At a very much later period of geological time, the Tertiary, physical conditions again suited the accumulation of vast quantities of organic material. Sufficient time has since elapsed for this to be compacted to form only brown coal and lignite, a fuel with a higher ash and water content and a lower calorific value than bituminous coal. Poland has also extensive reserves of this lower-grade fuel, but these have begun to be exploited only comparatively recently. It is the bituminous coal of Silesia which has always formed the principal fuel base of Poland's industries, and formerly one of the country's major exports.

The Upper Silesian coalfield is a basin, roughly triangular in shape and covering an area of over 2,000 square miles. It lies close to the southern border of Poland, and its south-western extremity extends across the boundary with Czechoslovakia. Structurally it consists of a depression, in the midst of which the coal measures lie at a depth of many thousands of feet. They rise towards the margin of the basin, however, and come close to the surface of the ground where they have been exploited since the Middle Ages. Within the basin itself the coal beds are arched upwards in several places, so that in these restricted areas also they come within reach of modern mining techniques. It is in the vicinity of two of these 'islands' within the coal basin that most mining has taken place, and the Upper Silesian industrial region has grown up on the largest of them.

A wide range of types of coal is to be found in the Upper Silesian basin, from anthracitic to the softest of bituminous coals, but among them the qualities which yield the best metallurgical coke for iron-smelting are not the most abundant. In spite of being one of the leading coal exporters[4] today, Poland is nevertheless obliged to import coal of this particular quality. The Lower Silesian coalfield is a small but complex basin enclosed by the ranges of the Sudety. Its volume of output, insignificant beside that of Upper Silesia, does, however, include coal of coking quality, and this gives the Lower Silesian field a greater significance than its size alone would warrant.

Brown-coal and lignite deposits are found in central Poland, where they occur in thick beds at a shallow depth beneath the glacial deposits. Their exploitation on a large scale dates only from the

4 See below, pp. 141–2.

period of planned development. The reserves are known to be immense; extraction of the coal is relatively simple, and though its fuel value is low it is economic to use it in thermal-electric generators built near the pits.

The petroleum resources of Poland were never large, and have now been almost exhausted. They occurred in the folded geological structures which border the Beskidy, where a few pumps are still to be seen. But the volume of production has now sunk to only about 350,000 tons a year, a fiftieth of the output from the oil-wells of Romania.

Metalliferous mining has played an important role in the economic development of Poland, and, by a strange coincidence, a large part of the reserves occur very close to the Upper Silesian coalfield. Prominent among them are the ores of lead and zinc. These occur in the limestone beds of the Trias, a series which overlies part of the coal measures. Both ores were worked during the Middle Ages, when the zinc was used, without being smelted, in the manufacture of brass, and the lead was widely employed in building and later in making shot. The importance of both metals grew during the nineteenth century, and the Upper Silesian region continues today to be the most important source of these metals in Europe. Small quantities of copper have long been obtained from Upper Silesia. Reserves have now been discovered in Lower Silesia, and are now being exploited near Legnica. All the evidence points to their being an important if not large reserve of an essential metal.

Iron-ore, the most important of the metallic ores in modern times, is not abundant in Poland, or indeed in any of the countries of eastern Europe. Iron has been smelted here since prehistoric times, but the ore supply came mainly from very small deposits in the older rocks of the Holy Cross mountains. This region is today strewn with the ruins of ancient iron-works, but the amount of ore now being extracted is quite inadequate to supply even one modern iron furnace. Poland, with today a large and steadily growing iron and steel industry, is overwhelmingly dependent on outside sources for the essential raw material.

Population

The population of Poland must be counted among her foremost resources. In December 1966 it was estimated to number 31·8 million. The birth-rate has long been one of the highest in Europe, and, despite the immense losses suffered during the Second World War, the pre-war level has again been attained. The political division of the territory makes it remarkably difficult to estimate the population of Poland during earlier periods. The fragmentary data suggest a

fairly rapid increase of population during the Middle Ages; a
significant loss as a result of the wars of the seventeenth century;
and a renewed and rapid growth in the eighteenth. It has been
estimated that the historic provinces of Wielkopolska, Małopolska,
and Mazowsze had almost 5 million at the time of the Second Partition and possibly twice this figure for the post-1918 territory of the
Polish state.

Growth was even more rapid during the nineteenth century, and
the population reached 24 million in 1895 within the same area.
Despite heavy losses during the First World War, the total was at
least 26 million at the time when the Polish state was re-established.
During the following two decades, birth-rates remained high, though
lower than during the later years of the nineteenth century. At the
same time, death-rates were somewhat reduced, and the population
crept up to about 31·4 million in 1930, and had almost reached
35 million at the time of the German invasion in September 1939.

Poland's losses during the next six years were greater than those of
any other country except the Soviet Union. The war itself accounted
for over 6 million casualties over and above those who might have
been expected to die during this period. Over half of these died in
German extermination camps. Others died in the course of fighting
and during the suppression of risings, such as the 'Ghetto' Rising of
1943 and the Warsaw Rising of 1944. The transfer of territory added
further to the net population loss. The Recovered Territories are
estimated to have had a pre-war population of about 8,900,000. Of
these about 1,260,000 were regarded as ethnic Poles. Most of the
remainder either fled on the approach of the Soviet army or migrated
to Germany after the incorporation of this territory into Poland. The
German population, swollen by refugees from the bombed cities of
Central Europe, rose to over 9 million, almost all of whom had left
for Germany by 1948.

It had been assumed that the Polish population of the eastern
lands, occupied by the Soviet Union, would be repatriated and settled
in the west. This has, however, happened to only a small degree. The
'lost' lands were predominantly Belorussian or Ukrainian, and
their Polish population was relatively small. In the end, only about
2 million were repatriated, and the western lands were in fact re-
peopled largely by migrants from the crowded lands of central
Poland.

In these ways the population of Poland, of about 35 million within
the 1921–39 boundaries, was reduced to less than 24 million. On
1 January 1949, when migrations may for practical purposes be
assumed to have ended, Poland had 24,078,000 inhabitants. The
catastrophe of the Second World War was followed by a period of

high birth-rate, which has gone far towards restoring the earlier population level. Until 1959 it stood at a level of 25 or more per thousand, but in recent years has dropped to less than 20. By 1960 the population had increased to about 30 million, and in early 1967 was approaching 32.

It is predominantly a young population, with no less than 39 per cent of the total aged less than twenty, and 67 per cent less than forty. In all age groups above thirty women greatly outnumber men, a consequence of the losses during the war years. Before the Second World War about 70 per cent of the population lived on farms and in villages. Since 1949 this population has declined steadily. By 1964, only 50·6 per cent were rural, and at the time of writing (1969) urban population slightly outnumbers rural. This results in part from changes in the structure of agriculture, which have had the effect of reducing the need for farm labour, but in the main it is due to the industrial development of the country and to the expansion of its towns.

The geographical distribution of population still reflects the distribution of agricultural and mineral wealth. The greatest density is found in a broad belt extending across southern Poland from Lower Silesia to eastern Galicia. Not only does this region contain the most valuable cropland, but all the reserves of bituminous coal and most of the metalliferous deposits. An area of relatively dense population extends northwards to embrace most of central Poland.

North-western and north-eastern Poland are the least populous and least developed areas. In the last analysis, this lower population density and, in consequence, the lower frequency and smaller size of towns, is a result of agricultural poverty. Exceptions to this generalization are found on the lower Odra, where Szczecin has developed as a port for the whole Odra basin, and along the lower Vistula, where a belt of more productive soil extends from Bydgoszcz to the sea. On the coast, near the Vistula mouth, are the twin ports of Gdańsk and Gdynia, which, with the surrounding small towns, make up an urban concentration of almost 600,000.

The Village

Until very recent years agriculture employed a majority of the population, and it still contributes a quarter of the gross national product. Poland has always been predominantly a peasant country. The great estates, which had formerly characterized much of it, were greatly reduced in number and size in the course of the land reforms effected between the First and Second World Wars, and were finally liquidated after the Second. Most of the land thus acquired by the state was used to create peasant holdings or to supplement those judged to be too small. In the course of the land reform which followed the Second World War a considerable area, amounting to about 12 per cent of the cropland, was retained as state arms or was converted into collectives. Nevertheless, almost 90 per cent of the land has been allowed to remain in the hands of the peasants.[5]

In some parts of Poland, notably Galicia and parts of Wielko-polska, there has long been an acute overcrowding in the villages and on the land. Farm holdings had by process of division and sub-division become uneconomically small. In some areas land reform offered no relief, as no estates remained to be divided. The recovery of the western lands has provided a partial solution to this problem, by providing a new 'frontier' into which surplus rural population has been able to migrate. In the long run, however, industrialization is likely to be the only solution to the old problem of rural over-population.

In 1960 there were about 3·6 million separate farm holdings, with an average size of under 12 acres. Of these almost a half had less than 7·5 acres. Although a very large number of the micro-holdings were in fact situated near industrial cities, and provided a part-time occupation for factory-workers, there was nevertheless a very large number of extremely small family farms, especially in those parts of southern Poland which had formerly been part of the Austrian province of Galicia.

The nature and intensity of agriculture are determined to a con-siderable degree by the soil and climate. The most intensively cul-tivated areas, that is, those within which the highest percentage of the land is under crops, are found in the regions of superior soil, Silesia and Galicia, with Great Poland coming next in importance. The areas of least agricultural value are naturally the sandy moraine and the ill-drained river valleys. In all these, the land remains heavily forested, and the advance of agriculture, despite the pressure of population and the growing demand for food, has made little impres-sion on the extent of the woodland and the waste.

Official statistics give the village population as about half of the total. The village is in most parts of Poland something very different from the clustered and quaint institution of rural England. In general it is a 'street-village', consisting of little more than a single road, bordered irregularly on both sides by farm cottages with their small patches of garden and orchard and their few farm buildings. The fields stretch away behind the houses to the forest margin or the fields of the next village. The village lacks a conspicuous focus, though it usually has a church, a tavern, and, in the larger, a shop.

5 See below, p. 135.

The cottages vary in plan and style of decoration. Usually they are built of wood and roofed with wooden shingles or thatch. In ground plan they conform more or less to a pattern which is as old as human settlement in this area. They have two rooms, one for sleeping, the other for living and eating, with a central fireplace which serves for cooking as well as heating. A porch is added to the end of some, and much use is made of carved decoration and of colour wash on the walls. The traditional cottage has changed little for centuries, but today is being very slowly replaced by a structure that is more functional and comfortable if not also more aesthetically pleasing. Modern transport facilities, particularly the lorry, allow building bricks, roofing tiles, and cement to reach the villages in quantities sufficient to make a very considerable impact on their general appearance.

An unforgettable picture of the Polish village is presented in Władysław Reymont's novel, *Chłopi*, or 'The Peasants'. This novel is set in the village of Lipce, about 50 miles to the south-west of Warsaw at the turn of the present century. The story revolves around the jealousies and feuds of the land-hungry peasantry of the village, and is presented against the background of one of the finest pieces of nature-painting in literature. The physical appearance of Lipce is today much as Reymont saw it. Agricultural practice has been modified in detail; the outer world today makes a greater impact on it than it did at the end of the last century, when Reymont himself lived on the outskirts of the village and worked on the local railway. Some of the traditional practices described in the novel are now abandoned or carried on in a perfunctory manner; the Jewish tavern-keeper and moneylender has gone, and the symbols of the Party rival those of the Church; but basically it is the same village, the same peasantry, conservative, jealous, quarrelsome, acquisitive, that Reymont portrayed.

The Town

Despite the fact that very little more than half the total population lives in towns, Poland is a well-urbanized country. Official statistics recorded the existence of 787 towns (*miasta*) in 1964. These range from Warsaw, with its population of 1,241,000, and a handful of cities each with more than a quarter of a million inhabitants, down to the immense number of small towns with only a thousand or two. There are, for example, 305 towns each with less than 5,000 inhabitants and in all 517 with under 10,000. These are inevitably closely spaced; they are found in every part of the country, and their chief function has always been to serve as market centres for the surrounding villages. Most have failed to attract manufacturing industries beyond a brick-works, saw-mill, or tannery which serves mainly to process local materials and satisfy local needs. Manufacturing has tended to move to the larger cities with better transport and communication facilities. At the same time the range of peasant interests and activities has broadened with greater ease of movement. The nearby small town is proving to be less attractive than the more distant but larger town with its shops and amenities. The small towns are tending to lose their principal function, that of service centres for the surrounding countryside. The number of those with less than 5,000 inhabitants has declined somewhat since the end of the Second World War, as the smallest of them lost status and became villages. At the same time their aggregate population has fallen by about 10 per cent, despite the large overall increase of population during the same period. The problem of the unviable small town has become a serious one, especially in the less industrialized regions of northern and eastern Poland.

Towns of intermediate and larger size have, on the other hand, increased sharply in size in recent years. Two of them, Łódź and Kraków, now exceed half a million inhabitants, and there are in all nine cities each with more than a quarter of a million inhabitants. The largest is Warsaw itself, since 1596 the capital of Poland. It had been only a small walled town during the Middle Ages, located above a low bluff on the west bank of the Vistula. The river-crossing had become important, and routes radiated eastward and northeastward from the town before Zygmunt III moved his capital here from Kraków. This was at a time when Polish control was being extended over much of Belorussia and the Ukraine. The magnates who were creating vast estates in the east also used the wealth from their land to build town-houses in Warsaw. The old city thus came to be almost surrounded by the palaces of the aristocracy and the less flamboyant houses of the burgesses and merchants.

The old city had a Renaissance air; the surrounding area of palaces came to be marked by a palladian elegance, with here and there a dash of more florid baroque. It was from Warsaw that Stanisław Leszczyński took the architectural style which he developed so tastefully when, as duke of Lorraine, he rebuilt his capital city of Nancy. This was the Warsaw which Canaletto (Belotto) painted in his capacity of court-painter to King Stanisław Poniatowski between the years 1770 and 1780. The Partitions, the Napoleonic Wars, and the Russian occupation interrupted this growth, and when it was resumed in the 1820s, it took on an entirely different character. The city was ringed by the fortresses of the Russians, around each of which building was restricted in order to leave an open field of fire

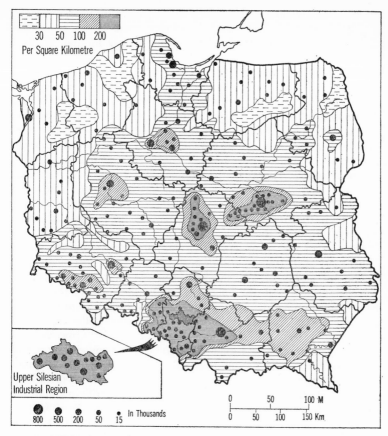

7. Population density and towns. (Data relate to 1965)

for Russian guns. In intervening areas, industrial and working-class suburbs spread west and south-west. The coming of the standard-gauge railway from Vienna to Warsaw in 1845–48 gave a great impetus to factory growth in this direction, so that a ribbon-development of small industrial towns reached many miles from the city. Somewhat more elegant residential areas grew up nearer the river, to the north-west and south-east of the city.

Such were the main lines of Warsaw's development until it again became the capital of an independent Poland. Between 1918 and 1939, the population grew from 760,000 to 1,289,000. The open spaces which had been left by order of the Russians were largely built over. The residential suburbs, like Zoliborz, and industrial suburbs, mainly close to the railway line to the south-west, increased in size. Praga, across the river to the east, became both a residential and a manufacturing quarter, and small towns around Warsaw began to receive its industrial overflow.

This was the city which was more than 80 per cent destroyed during the Second World War. Destruction began when the German forces attacked and captured the city in September 1939. Sporadic destruction followed. In 1943, the Jewish population of Muranów, the so-called ghetto, faced with the prospect of removal to extermination camps, rose against the Germans. The rising was savagely suppressed, and the whole Muranów quarter was reduced to tidy heaps of rubble. It was in the summer and autumn of 1944 that Warsaw suffered most. As the Russian forces advanced across the plains of Mazowsze, and approached the east bank of the Vistula, the Poles in the city rose against the Germans, hoping thus to facilitate its capture by the Soviet army. But the latter waited on the Praga side of the river, while the Germans suppressed the rising, killed most of its leaders, and destroyed the greater part of the city.

The rebuilding of Warsaw has been one of the most striking achievements of post-war Poland. The Old City and its immediate environs, which had been totally destroyed during the fighting, were restored as far as possible to their condition during the eighteenth century, and for part of this the drawings of Canaletto provided the models. This rebuilding is one of the most ambitious and successful attempts ever made at architectural restoration. The only valid criticism that can be levelled against it is that its cost was more than the war-ravaged state could afford, and this is a criticism that one does not often hear in Poland itself. The *Stare Miasto* (Old City) is today a monument to a nation and, as a tablet in the Old Town Square records, to those whose deaths contributed to preserving it.

Most of the eighteenth-century palaces have also been restored, and many now house branches of the government. Elsewhere, however, no attempt was made to preserve the earlier architectural styles. Along the Marszalkowska, formerly the Bond Street of Warsaw, are modern 'blocks'. The Soviet-inspired *Palac Kultury* rises 757 feet from the street and introduces a jarring note with its eclectic Moscow design. Muranów has been rebuilt, with massif blocks of flats replacing the narrow streets of the ghetto, upon the rubble of which in many instances they have been set.

Warsaw has now regained approximately its pre-war size. Its industries have been restored, and to their number have been added many others, including a large steel-works to the north of the city and an automobile factory in Praga. Domestic rebuilding has been slower than industrial, and there has long been acute overcrowding in all the residential areas of the city. At best it consists of large blocks of flats, some of them tastefully designed and set amid parks and open spaces. Warsaw is far from being a city without slums, and some of the latter have been made even worse by wartime damage and inadequate restoration. But these are slowly being replaced by more adequate construction, as the Poles approach the end of their monumental task of rebuilding one of the largest and most attractive cities of Europe.

Łódź, the second largest city of Poland, differs in almost every respect from Warsaw. In contrast with the medieval origins of the latter, it is a product of nineteenth-century industrialization. It is dignified by no ancient monuments, and its wartime damage consisted of little more than the destruction by the Germans of the Jewish quarter. In its face today can be traced the gradual transformation of a few small villages into a sprawling, ugly industrial city, dotted with textile factories of every size and shape.

Łódź owes its growth to the fact that it lay a few miles within Congress Poland, and that at the time when industry was established here, its manufactures could command a market which extended over the whole of the Tsarist Empire. This favourable circumstance did not long continue, but Łódź was able to develop a momentum which carried it forward as the largest and most important centre of textile manufactures in Poland and, indeed, in all eastern Europe.

Kraków has a longer history than Warsaw, which it preceded as capital of Poland, and in the architectural monuments from its past it is even more distinguished. It has been fortunate in having been spared the ravages of war since the Middle Ages, so that it may be said today to epitomize the country's history. The nucleus of the city of Kraków was the fortress, the Wawel, built by the Polish kings in the eleventh century above a steep cliff on the north bank of the Vistula. The city grew up beneath it as a small walled enclosure, with today the fine Romanesque church of St Andrew which survives from this period. During the later Middle Ages, a large extension was made to this urban nucleus, with straight streets intersecting at right angles, a very large market-place, and the Gothic church of St Mary – the *Mariacki* – for which Wit Stwosz in the fifteenth century created his magnificent altarpiece. In the market-place the Renaissance merchants' hall – the *Sukiennice*, or Cloth Hall – was built in the sixteenth century. Around the whole defensive walls were erected, and these in turn have given place to a narrow belt of parks and gardens – the *Planty* – which almost completely encircle the old town.

Within the walls of the Wawel is the cathedral of Kraków, a building of mixed architectural styles which for much of the Middle Ages was the chief burial place of Polish kings. Nearby is their Renaissance palace, built for King Zygmunt I by Italian architects. It now contains a museum and art gallery. Nearby in 1364 Kazimierz the Great founded the University of Kraków. By contrast, nineteenth-century Kraków grew up beyond the green ring of the *Planty*. It was not a heavily industrialized city – indeed, it was not Austrian policy to establish manufactures in Galicia. A number of small factories was established, but Kraków remained until recent years a somewhat conservative, middle-class city and a cultural rather than an industrial centre.

This situation has been changed since the Second World War. A site was chosen about 5 miles to the east of the old city for a new iron and steel works, the *Nowa Huta,* and a 'socialist town' was built for its employees. The suburb of Nowa Huta, with a population of perhaps 100,000, has been incorporated within the administrative boundaries of Kraków. Industrial workers from Nowa Huta rub shoulders in the streets and shops of the city with the older bourgeois element; Kraków is losing its air of old-world detachment and is being absorbed, not altogether willingly, it is said, into the industrial and proletarian society of modern Poland.

Both Poznań and Wrocław share in some degree the character of old Kraków, while participating fully in the developments which are the features of the new. Both are among the oldest cities of Poland, and in their geographical development they have many features in common. In both, the earliest settlement derived from the tenth century or earlier, and was established on an easily defended island in the Warta and Odra respectively. In both instances, the island became the focus of ecclesiastical jurisdiction and is still the site of the cathedral, while later medieval growth took the city in each case to the west bank of the river, where a planned settlement grew up. This latter became the centre of commercial activity; the town hall, or *ratusz*, was built here, and the city's principal churches were built. Both Poznań and Wrocław are today distinguished by their town halls, the former medieval with a Renaissance façade, the latter an exceptionally fine example of late medieval Gothic architecture.

Poznań passed into German hands at the First Partition, and was restored to Poland only in 1918. Wrocław, following the fortunes of Silesia, became part of the Bohemian crown in the fourteenth century and passed to Austria and then to Prussia before its restoration to Poland in 1945. Both became industrial cities during the nineteenth century, with an emphasis on mechanical and metal-using industries. Both suffered during the closing months of the Second World War, and, in the case of Wrocław, the damage was disastrous. In both the wartime destruction has largely been repaired, and they have returned to their former role as large and important manufacturing cities, with a very wide range of industrial production.

Poland's seaborne commerce is handled by the three Baltic ports of Szczecin, Gdańsk, and Gdynia, the last a creation of the 1920s and the others of the earlier Middle Ages. Szczecin, the Stettin of the Germans, lies on the west bank of the Odra, near the point where it begins to broaden into the sheltered Gulf of Szczecin. It is at least as old as the Polish state and in the early Middle Ages was a centre of Viking trade. Its greatest asset was, and still remains, its river, which descends from Silesia and, with its tributaries, drains much of central Poland. River-borne commerce converged on the city, which developed during the Middle Ages as a member of the Hanseatic League. It passed, along with Pomerania, into German hands, and continued until 1945 to be the principal port of eastern Germany. Though lying to the west of the Odra, the city, with its surrounding region, was included within Poland, whose territory might be expected to supply much of the commerce of the port. Both city and docks have now been restored, and receive almost half the number of ships calling at Polish ports, and about a third of the registered tonnage.

Gdańsk, a port of equal antiquity, has played a similar role in the Vistula basin, for whose grain, timber, and other products it long provided the chief commercial outlet. Its history has, however, been more complex than that of Szczecin. During the later Middle Ages it was the principal Hanseatic port of the south-eastern Baltic, and the wealth which accrued from its commerce permitted it to develop as a city of great size and beauty. Though its merchant class was dominated by Germans, it remained a part of the Polish kingdom until the Second Partition, when it was absorbed into Prussia. It remained a part of Germany until in 1919 it, together with its surrounding territory, became the Free City of Danzig, under the sovereignty of the League of Nations, but in customs union with Poland.

Gdańsk was at this time the only port suitably located to satisfy the commercial requirements of Poland, but its citizens who would have the obligation to handle Polish sea-borne trade, showed themselves to be unreliable allies, and the port itself proved to be inadequate for Poland's needs. The Poles found it necessary to establish the third port, Gdynia, to the north-west of Gdańsk, on the short stretch of Baltic coast which they acquired by the terms of the Treaty of Versailles. Gdańsk did not suffer significantly from the establishment of a rival, but it did not grow as it might otherwise have done. It tended to concentrate on the handling of light goods, leaving bulk cargoes for Gdynia, which was equipped to handle them. Nevertheless, German resentment at the status of Gdańsk and at the existence of the so-called 'Corridor' mounted; Gdańsk itself became a centre of Nazi propaganda and intrigue, and its occupation was one of the German aims when, on 1 September 1939, the Germans attacked Poland. When in 1945 Gdańsk was restored to Poland, it was little more than rubble. The Renaissance houses of its citizens and its brick-Gothic churches had mostly been bombed or burned. It had been a city, like the Old City of Warsaw, of very great beauty and charm. The rebuilding has attempted to recapture these qualities, at an immense cost but with considerable success. The Renaissance houses with their stuccoed fronts, their gilding and decoration from the period before the 'Deluge', again border the *Długi Targ* and run down to the Motława, where the Zuraw (Crane-gate) again rises from the waters as if waiting to unload bales from the sailing-ships that once tied up at the city's quays. The docks and shipyards, also restored and rebuilt, lie to the north of the old city, where there is both easier access from the sea and space for the construction of both a modern port and port industries.

Gdynia is a smaller and less attractive city than Gdańsk. There was no estuary to provide a sheltered harbour, and moles have been built to give protection to an otherwise open beach. The docks, in part dug from the coastal alluvium, are equipped primarily for the handling of bulk cargoes, especially coal and iron-ore, for which Gdynia is particularly important. Docks are built on a larger scale than in other ports, and today Gdynia handles a larger aggregate tonnage than either of the other leading ports.

Lack of space prevents a similar examination of other cities. There are no less than fifteen cities, each with a population of over 100,000, eight of them in the Upper Silesian industrial area. Apart from its port cities, which have already been mentioned, northern Poland is not highly urbanized or heavily industrialized. Its largest inland cities, Bydgoszcz and Toruń, lie on the Vistula, and owe much of their importance to their focal position on routes. Bydgoszcz, the German Bromberg, is a large, modern, industrial town; Toruń, one of the largest and most important cities of central and northern Poland during the Middle Ages, and for a time one of the bases of the German knights, has been fortunate to retain many of the monuments of its medieval past, and the old city, still partially surrounded by its medieval walls, has something of the charm of Kraków and Gdańsk.

Central Poland has long had a great number of small towns, a few of which have in the nineteenth and twentieth centuries developed modern industries. Among these were the towns of the Łódź region, which became subsidiary centres of the textile industry. Southern Poland has always been more strongly urbanized. Better soils, greater ease of communication, and denser population have contributed since the earliest years of Polish history to the formation of a closer network of towns. The development of mineral wealth has intensified the process, leading to the emergence not only of the Upper Silesian industrial region, with today thirteen municipalities and a population of about 1½ million, but also the coalmining town of Wałbrzych in Lower Silesia, of Częstochowa, with its iron and steel industry, and the industrial suburb of Kraków. Ancient towns like Opole, Tarnów, Rzeszów, and Lublin have also acquired a variety of light, mechanical, or chemical industries. Lastly, close to the mountains are a number of textile manufacturing centres, most of them of no great size, established here during the nineteenth century or even earlier in order to use the water-power so abundant in this area.

Such in very broad outline is the land which has made up the state of Poland since 1945. About a third of pre-war Poland was occupied by the Soviet Union in September 1939, and with minor boundary changes, has since been retained. A similar proportion of the present area is made up of the Recovered or Western Territories, which had for varying periods of time been in German possession. Legally, Poland is in occupation of these territories pending a peace settlement, but a treaty of peace which has been postponed for more than twenty-five years is not likely to be negotiated. The conditions on which it would have been based have changed drastically. Among the changes has been the Polish occupation and development of the Western Territories, and their integration with the rest of Poland. If some people thought in 1945 that their restoration to Germany was practicable, only the most intransigent could possibly assume so today. Legal niceties to the contrary, Poland no longer 'occupies' the Western Territories; these lands have become in all respects a part of Poland. The historic claim to the boundary of Mieszko's Poland is, in a sense, irrelevant. Poland's claim is predicated on the much more powerful argument of twenty-five years of economic rebuilding, redevelopment, and integration with the rest of the country.

When, at the Teheran Conference (1943), the westward extension of Poland's boundaries was first discussed among the Allies, Churchill observed that Poland would be losing only the forests and marshes of the east and would be acquiring a smaller but richer and better-developed area. This was only partially true. Cropland and agricultural production were seriously reduced by the exchange; the acquisition of Silesia did not make up for the loss of Podolia. On the other hand, the territorial gains rounded out the Polish industrial region in Upper Silesia, ended the technically awkward and politically frustrating division of the industrial area, and gave it an uninterrupted water-route to the port of Szczecin and the Baltic Sea. Poland gained undisputed possession of the two ports of Gdańsk and Szczecin which, together with Gdynia, share the Polish hinterland. What Poland has made of these lands is examined in the next chapter.

Chapter 4

Economic Growth

Jednak wierzę
Ze ludy płyną jak łańcuch żórawi
W postęp.

(J. Slowacki, *Beniowski*)[1]

THE POLAND WHICH disappeared from the political map in 1796 had been a feudal state in which the industrial and middle-class revolution of western Europe had scarcely begun to show itself. The nineteenth century was throughout Europe a period of profound social and economic change. No country was immune to the revolution wrought by the rise of factory industry, the development of railways, the migration of people, the broadening basis of education, and the diffusion of liberal political ideas; but no two countries were influenced by them in the same way. Poland was partitioned between three empires whose attitudes to the revolutionary changes of this century differed radically. The three sectors each blundered into the nineteenth century in its own peculiar fashion. In the Prussian-held areas of western Poland, economic growth and social liberalization were relatively rapid, but at the same time tightly controlled. The Habsburgs, whose inefficiency has sometimes been mistaken for liberalism, restricted industrial growth in Austrian-held Poland, and thus contributed to the grievous rural overpopulation of Galicia. Economic and social changes of the nineteenth century were experienced last in Russian-held Poland. The abolition of serfdom was carried out in a way calculated to cause the maximum embarrassment to the Polish landowners. The attempts at industrialization made in the early nineteenth century[2] had proved to be abortive. They were not renewed on a serious scale, apart from the German-inspired development of the textile industry, until the later years of the century. In the 1880s the government-directed policy of industrial expansion proved to be only a pale and somewhat ineffective imitation of the German.

[1] 'Yet I believe that the peoples, like a chain of cranes, are making their way onwards into progress.'
[2] See above, p. 73.

113

The Polish Republic 1918–39

Such were the three sectors which came together in 1918 to constitute the Republic of Poland : the densely populated and predominantly peasant province of Galicia; the backward and feebly industrialized 'Congress' Poland; and the technically very much more advanced provinces acquired from Prussia, with their developed mining and manufacturing industries and efficient network of transport facilities. It was not until March 1921 that the Treaty of Riga regulated the eastern boundary. Although the western and southern had in general been delimited by the treaties of Versailles and Saint-Germain, it was not until October 1921 that the Geneva Award finally settled the boundary question in Upper Silesia.

The problems of integrating three different economies and three different patterns of autocracy were immense. Even the railway gauge had to be changed in two-thirds of the area of the new state from Russian broad gauge to standard European. A new currency based on the *zloty* finally replaced those of the three former empires. Problems of agriculture and of land-tenure varied between the different parts of the country. The break-up of the thinly peopled estates of Pomerania or East Prussia was no remedy for the acute rural fragmentation of Galicia. In all parts of the country agriculture required a heavy capital investment, not merely to repair the damage and neglect of war, but also to extend crop-farming and create economic farm units. Sufficient capital had not been made available before the economic crisis of the early 1930s put an end to international lending. Nor was it possible to develop a national economy before the political crises of the 1930s gave it a new orientation. The rise of Nazism in Germany led to increased expenditure on defence, and the German invasion of September 1939 terminated all plans for development.

This chapter first reviews briefly the economic problems facing Poland between the two world wars and attempts to evaluate her success in handling them. They are grouped under three heads : money and credit; agricultural reform; and industrial development. The second – and larger – part of the chapter examines the size of physical loss resulting from the Second World War, the socialization of the economy, and the scale and direction of economic growth since the beginning of the economic plans.

Economic Policy

The monetary problem facing the new state seemed the most serious and urgent. It had at first no assets, no national bank, no currency, and very little credit. The first step was to establish the

Polish mark as the new unit of currency. The government inherited no financial reserves, and, except from 1927 to 1930, failed to balance its budget. The demand for goods and services was far greater than their supply and, almost from the start, the government was faced with an inflation which, until 1924, it was quite unable to control. The volume of private saving and investment was negligible during these years; few outsiders had confidence in the stability of the government, and such external investment and credits as the Polish government was able to secure were motivated more by political considerations – the maintenance of the integrity of the Polish state – than by normal investment criteria.

In 1924, the mark was replaced by a new currency, the *zloty,* and the government-owned Bank of Poland was established in order to effect the transfer and to act as a bank of issue for the new currency. A gold standard was adopted, and the *zloty* was pegged at 5·18 to the American dollar. It is generally agreed that the *zloty* was overvalued, and that this was a factor in the economic crisis of the following year.

By 1925 the political and economic situation was improving in Europe. In Poland, however, a tariff war with Germany[3] and bad weather and poor harvests during the previous year combined with the overvalued currency to bring on a renewed financial crisis. Inflation again threatened the economy, and credits to support the *zloty* were for a time unobtainable. It was amid this financial crisis, and in part in consequence of it, that Piłsudski came to power in 1926.

The tide then began to turn. The currency was devalued. The British General Strike provided an unexpected bonus for Poland, whose coal exports for a period dominated the international coal trade. The national budget was drastically trimmed; revenues were increased in particular by the more judicious management of the state monopolies of tobacco, alcohol, salt, and matches; and the budgetary deficit ended in 1926. The prospect of greater political and economic stability furthermore made it easier to obtain loans.

By this date the upward turn in the European and American economy had become marked. The Federal Reserve Bank of the United States and some of the central banks of European countries made loans which supported the *zloty* and at the same time gave the Bank of Poland the reserves necessary for the continuance of its normal functions. The period from the end of 1926 until the onset of the monetary crisis in 1929 was the most stable and prosperous in the history of inter-war Poland. It was, however, a conditional prosperity. The *zloty* had always to be buttressed by import restrictions and by restraints on foreign travel by Poles.

[3] See below, p. 124.

The crisis which began in late 1929 was followed by the withdrawal of short-term loans to Polish banks. Poland began to suffer from the difficulties of all countries which relied heavily on the export of agricultural goods and industrial raw materials. The price for agricultural goods received by the farmer dropped catastrophically, without any commensurate fall in the price of manufactured goods. By 1934 the prices received by the farmer were scarcely more than a third of those of 1928, whereas the price of manufactured goods, which were partly or largely of foreign origin, remained at between a half and two-thirds of the pre-Depression level. Poland's principal non-agricultural export was similarly affected. The price of coal in foreign ports fell disastrously as industrial consumers abroad closed down or reduced their activities and shipping, which had used large quantities of Polish coal for bunker purposes, was laid up.

The early 1930s were a period of acute crisis in Poland, as they were also in much of Europe. By 1934 there were signs of change. Employment conditions began slowly to improve. The state intervened with some success to help the labour market by financing public works. Outside Poland markets very slowly opened up for Poland's exports. By 1936 farm incomes had begun to rise, and there was a real increase in the total value of the national product.

In 1936 also the government at last removed the *złoty* from the gold standard and took steps to control the economy more closely than it had done before. It introduced an ambitious plan of industrial development within the so-called 'industrial triangle' of southern Poland.[4] This necessitated heavier imports of capital goods and gravely endangered the already shaky balance of payments. In order to control this and to prevent a further depreciation of the *złoty* tight curbs were imposed on all foreign trade, and attempts were made to increase the volume of private investment. In the three years that elapsed before the German invasion Poland achieved some success in this sphere of directed economic development. By 1938 the national income had risen to a level about a third higher than before the Depression, and substantial investments had been made in the industrial development of the 'industrial triangle'.

The erratic performance of the economy during the inter-war years and the modest successes of the later 1930s must be viewed against the social background of the country. The divergences in public law and administration, in the development of transport and other services, in the levels of education and in standards of living, between the three sectors that were brought together in 1918 had been considerable, and their reconciliation had presented serious difficulties, not wholly overcome by 1939. The population as a whole

4 See below, pp. 124–5.

remained predominantly rural and agricultural. Almost two-thirds was made up of peasants, and in the eastern provinces of inter-war Poland this proportion rose over large areas to more than 80 per cent. While industrial development, especially in the later years of the republic, absorbed some of this rural population, the population itself rose during the twenty-year period from about 26,282,000 to about 34,850,000, and the birth-rate was highest in those eastern provinces where the proportion of farm population was already greatest and the opportunity for other employment least. There was no time when the economy was not plagued by unemployment or, in rural areas, under-employment, and by the very low purchasing power of the peasantry.

The latter was due above all to the acute rural overpopulation and to the extreme fragmentation of farm holdings. Conditions were most extreme, as has been noted earlier, in the southern provinces which had been under Austrian rule. There much of the agricultural land was already divided into small peasant holdings, almost half of which early in the century were found to be of less than 5 acres. Areas formerly ruled by Prussia and, to an even greater degree, those taken from Russia, were characterized by large estates, in which the characteristic evils of absentee landlords, inadequate capital investment, and unwilling peasant labour had been all too conspicuous.

Over a third of the land in the formerly Russian sector was in large estates on the eve of the First World War, and almost a half was divided into peasant farms. The latter had come to be divided and subdivided with the rapid increase in population, so that there were in effect no farms intermediate between the large estates on the one hand and the very small peasant properties on the other. Agricultural practice had scarcely improved at all during the period of Russian rule. This overwhelmingly agricultural region had in fact become an importer of rye, the dominant bread-crop, while remaining a small exporter of wheat.

In the former Prussian lands agricultural practice was on a higher plane, and there was in normal years a food surplus. The Prussian government had been active during the nineteenth century in taking over land from the *szlachta* and in creating estates owned and administered by Germans. Farming was highly protected; generous farm prices did nothing to encourage agricultural improvements; and the rapidly developing industrial centres created a high level of demand. There were relatively few micro-holdings, and a relatively large number of farms of from 12·5 to 50 acres.

The need for land reform was apparent everywhere. Not only were farms too small, especially in the south and east, but they were also excessively fragmented. At the same time the course of fighting during the First World War had done immense damage to the material equipment of agriculture and large areas had suffered severely from neglect. A land-reform measure was adopted in 1919, subsequently modified, and not really put into effect until after 1925. All estates in excess of 180 hectares (450 acres) were to be sold, but in the areas of low agricultural value the limit was later raised as high as 1,000 acres, and many exceptions were made as much, it would appear, for political as for economic reasons. Furthermore, estates 'which were devoted to highly specialized or unusually productive agricultural enterprises of national importance', a definition so vague as to be susceptible of almost any interpretation, were exempted from the application of the law.[5]

A revised law, however, called for the distribution of half a million acres annually over a period of ten years. About one million acres were divided by 1926. The more favourable economic conditions after 1926 and the relative ease with which peasants could obtain credits encouraged the owners of estates to sell their lands to peasants, and, in fact, the break-up of the former proceeded at a faster rate than had been provided by law. Parcellation was slowed down during the Depression years, but revived in the more favourable economic climate which followed. By 1938, about 6·6 million acres had passed into the hands of the peasants, either to create new farms or to enlarge the size of those which were uneconomically small.

In some parts of Poland, especially in the eastern provinces, the peasants still retained from their feudal past rights of grazing and woodcutting on the wasteland and in the forests. As in western Europe a century or two earlier these rights were sometimes abused, and in any event prevented a more rational and economic use of the land. The land-reform law provided for the division of these lands between the peasant families which had possessed the legal right to use them. The result was analogous to that of the enclosure of the common-lands in England : injustice to many, grave hardship for a few, but an overall increase in agricultural production.

Fragmentation of peasant farms, as distinct from their small size, was particularly acute in the east, since the Austrian and Prussian governments had previously taken steps to reduce the evil. It is said that in 1919 over a third of the total cropland was in holdings that were individually divided into parcels that were absurdly small and widely scattered. The land reform provided for the resurvey of a village and the consolidation of its fragmented parcels of land at the request of only a small minority of its peasants. By 1938, about 6·27 million acres of cropland, about 15 per cent of the cultivated area of

5 Dimitri T. Pronin, 'Land Reform in Poland : 1920–1945', *Land Economics*, vol. 15 (1949), pp. 133–45.

Poland, had been affected in some way by the government's efforts to reduce the waste of fragmentation.

The undercapitalization of Polish agriculture was no less difficult to remedy. Little use was made of fertilizer, and in eastern Poland almost none. Large areas of clay soil needed drainage, and the formation of hard-pan obstructed the flow of ground water and could be removed only by deep ploughing. The cultivation of cash and industrial crops was hindered by poor transport facilities, and the provision of processing plants – flour-mills, sugar-beet factories, oil-seed factories – was inadequate. Above all, the technical competence of the peasant was limited; he was not always receptive to new ideas, and in some parts of eastern Poland a three-field system of agriculture with fallow continued to be practised in open fields. Some of these problems lay beyond the competence of the Polish government to remedy, and could only be solved by capital investment on a scale that was beyond its means. On the other hand, the government provided technical aid as far as it was able, together with model plans for simple agricultural improvements. In this way drainage ditches were cut, tile laid beneath the fields, and farm roads improved. By 1939 about 1·5 million acres are said to have been drained, reclaimed, or improved. The most ambitious and the least successful of the reclamation projects was the attempt to drain the Prypeć or Polesie marshes. This task was technically too difficult, and was abandoned, and the area in question is now part of the Soviet Union, which has also made little impression on its watery wastes.

The Polish land reform has often been criticized as inadequate in both concept and execution. It is true that it fell short of the reforms that were being carried out at the same time in Czechoslovakia and Romania. It was not altogether the fault of the regime that investment in agriculture was not larger, and it is doubtful whether the further division of estates would have contributed greatly to solving the problem of rural overpopulation. The latter was in fact least acute in western Poland, where the German landowners had succeeded in holding on to a relatively large part of their possessions. In the acutely overcrowded south there was very little cropland left to be divided.

The land reform, it has been said, 'failed even to keep up with the increase of peasant population, and the average size of the peasant holdings declined'. The remedy lay not so much in land improvement and land reform as in the development of alternative forms of employment. It is difficult to calculate the size of the rural population that may be regarded as in excess at this time. On the eve of the Second World War, rural population in Poland was one of the densest in Europe, certainly denser than in any area with comparable physical conditions of climate and soil. Wilbert Moore has calculated that in a population dependent upon agriculture of about 19,347,000 in about 1930, no less than 9,922,000 could be regarded as redundant.[6] In other words, the agricultural system could market the same volume of production with an input of about half the actual labour force. Some would regard this figure as too high, but it cannot be doubted that the excessive size of the rural population made reform of the agricultural structure extremely difficult. Given the high birthrate of the rural areas, this condition might be expected to deteriorate.

Despite the problems facing agriculture there was a small increase in the total area under cultivation during the inter-war years. If allowances are made for seasonal variations, the increase in volume of production of the principal food crops was more than commensurate with population growth. A very slow improvement in crop yields was the result of the small technical improvements and investments in agriculture. The fact, however, that yields per unit area of the bread-crops, potatoes, and sugar-beet were up to and occasionally more than 50 per cent better in western than in eastern and even southern Poland is a measure of the improvement that could still be achieved without excessively large investments.

Industry and Industrial Growth

The levels of industrial development in the three segments of Poland which were brought together in 1918 were even more diverse than the conditions of agriculture. By a strange coincidence the meeting-point of the three empires – *Dreikaisereck,* as it was called – was at the confluence of the 'Black' and the 'White' Przemsza, which joined the Vistula above Kraków. This point now lies towards the east of the Upper Silesian industrial region, and, though the rivers ceased to be political boundaries in 1918, the different levels and kinds of industrial growth which the three territories had experienced continued to be reflected in the visible landscape.

The Germans regarded their sector of Poland as primarily agricultural, and, in general, did little to develop manufactures that were unrelated to agricultural production. Their biggest enterprise by far was the mining and heavy industrial undertaking of Upper Silesia. This rested on the foundation provided by the very extensive reserves of coal and the very much less extensive resources in lead, zinc, and iron-ore. Though there had been a little smelting of bog-iron ore with charcoal in the forests of this region before the Partitions, and some

6 Wilbert E. Moore, *Economic Demography of Eastern and Southern Europe,* League of Nations (Geneva, 1945), p. 64. For a discussion of other – and lower – estimates of the surplus, see Nicolas Spulber, *The Economics of Communist Eastern Europe* (New York, 1957), pp. 275–6.

coal had actually been mined as early as the Middle Ages, little real progress was made until the end of the eighteenth century, when most of the coal basin had fallen into Prussian hands.

Large-scale industry owed its inception to the initiative of the Prussian government, which established the earliest modern works at Königshütte, now part of Chorzów. The local landowners and gentry followed the example of the government, so that by 1914 there was within Prussian Upper Silesia, and extending up to the boundary with Russia and Austria, the largest concentration of mining, smelting, and metal-working industries to be found east of the Ruhr. Coal production had been increasing steadily for the previous half-century, and was then at the rate of about 40 million tons a year. It was furthermore priced a little below comparable varieties from the Ruhr, and commanded a market as far west as Berlin, Saxony, and even Bavaria. The local supply of iron-ore had long been inadequate for the local smelting industry, and most of the pig-iron smelted came from Austrian, Swedish, or other imported ores. Coal on the other hand was abundant, though the supply of coking coal was very limited. Nevertheless, pig-iron production on the eve of the First World War reached one million tons, and steel manufacture rose to about 1·5 million. Lead and zinc ores of Upper Silesia occurred mostly within the Prussian sector. They were smelted in a very large number of furnaces scattered through the exposed area of the coalfield. The area constituted at this time by far the most important source of lead and zinc in Europe, and was one of the more important in the world.

Economic development of the formerly Russian sector of the Upper Silesian region was very much less advanced. Indeed, there was no effective industrial growth before about 1880, though there had been a number of abortive attempts. When at last an iron and steel industry was established across the 'Black' Przemsza from Prussian Silesia, it was only after the Russian government had raised a high tariff wall to protect it from German competition. The industrial undertakings of Russian Silesia – Dąbrowa, as it was called – remained small and their range of production limited. It is unlikely that total production at the outbreak of the war was more than 150,000 tons of pig-iron and a rather larger quantity of steel.

The Austrian sector of the Upper Silesian region was the least industrialized. It had been Habsburg policy to establish manufacturing industries in the Czech lands, rather than in the Polish, whose role in the empire was primarily to provide foodstuffs. Though this sector had a few coal-mines and a small production of lead and zinc, no modern iron industry was developed, and the area remained predominantly rural.

When in 1919 new boundaries were drawn in Upper Silesia, the only question was how much of the German sector should be included in Poland. The line drawn, in October 1921, by the Council of Ambassadors[7] disrupted the economy of the region without satisfying the ethnic aspirations of the Poles. Factories were cut off from their fuel supply and their raw materials; cities from their sources of water and of gas. It is not easy to make comparisons between the two sectors into which the former German Upper Silesia was divided. Very roughly, Poland acquired about three-quarters of the coal production and about half the iron and steel capacity, but a very much smaller proportion of the iron and steel fabricating works. After the partition it continued to be necessary for Polish Upper Silesia to supply Germany with crude iron and steel. The assets of individual companies came to be divided between the two countries, and a number of devices were adopted in order to maintain some kind of unity and continuity in their operation. Only the establishment of a limited international regime under the auspices of the League of Nations prevented the formation of two hostile and autarkic industrial complexes within Upper Silesia, with consequences that would probably have been disastrous for both.

Outside Upper Silesia, the former German sector of inter-war Poland contained a few industrial cities, notably Poznań, Bydgoszcz, Inowrocław. Light engineering had been developed in Poznań, and the manufacture of chemicals, especially of fertilizers, in Bydgoszcz and Inowrocław, but most of the manufacturing in former German Poland was closely related to the local agriculture. Distilling, the preparation of tobacco, sugar refining, and leather tanning were the most important.

Apart from a rather feebly developed extractive industry, Galicia had little to show. Some progress had been made in developing the coal, lead, and zinc deposits which bordered on those of German Upper Silesia; the salt deposits of Wieliczka and Bochnia, both near Kraków, had long been worked, and petroleum was obtained from eastern Galicia. But manufacturing industries were, as in much of the German sector, restricted to the processing of agricultural products.

German Poland was the underdeveloped and agricultural fringe of a developed state; the Russian sector was one of the most developed parts of a predominantly underdeveloped country. Its industrialization was in many ways more broadly based than that of western Poland, but at the same time more primitive. Many of its industries had been established here not because of the advantages inherent in the region itself, but rather because it lay relatively close to the West

[7] See below, p. 124.

European sources of industrial technology and entrepreneurial skill, and, at the same time, within the high Russian customs wall and able to command the large and expanding Russian market. This was particularly true of the textile industries which had been established during the nineteenth century at Łódź and its surrounding villages and also at Białystok. At the outbreak of the First World War there were over 600 textile-mills in Russian Poland. Most were very small, employed only a handful of workers, and made little use of mechanical power; but among them were the companies controlled by Poznański and K. Scheibler, which each employed some 8,000 workers and had a share capital of about 5 million American dollars. Most of these large factories were in Łódź, but they were also to be found in Pabianice, Częstochowa, and suburban Warsaw, where Żyrardów had one of the largest factories in the Tsarist Empire.

Second in importance to the textile came the metallurgical and mechanical industries. Their scale was very much smaller, and the chief centres, apart from Dąbrowa, were Częstochowa and Warsaw itself. The manufacture of chemicals was relatively undeveloped and was restricted to the basic acids and alkalis and the preparation of dyestuffs for the textile industry. Factories which processed agricultural products were numerous, but in general very small. They tended to serve the needs of their own restricted localities, and contributed little to the needs of Russia as a whole. The Tsarist government had shown a peculiar ambivalence in its policy towards industrial growth in Poland. On the one hand, it was fully aware of its own shortcomings and desired for strategic as well as economic reasons to build up manufacturing. On the other hand it showed considerable reluctance to allow this growth to take place in the Congress Kingdom, which was in some respects one of the most suitable areas. Freight rates on Russian railways were biased against Polish industries, and the import of raw materials on which this industry was based, such as raw cotton, iron-ore, pig-iron, and coking coal, was burdened by heavy import duties.

Such was the diverse industrial legacy which the Polish republic inherited in 1918–19 : three differing industrial structures, each integrated with a different national economy, all highly protected hitherto, and two of them notably undercapitalized and technically backward. The two most serious problems facing inter-war Poland were the demographic and the industrial, and any easing of the former was predicated on the solution of the latter. In the absence of migration, only the further development of mining and manufacturing could absorb the growing surplus of rural labour. Yet industrial growth was severely handicapped by the cutting-off of the former markets for, among many other goods, the Łódź textiles and

Upper Silesian coal; by the lack of capital for modernization of plant and equipment and for the physical integration of the industries within a single economy; and by the very low purchasing power of the mass of the population. Poland was faced with a far from easy task in finding markets for the fuel and industrial products which had formerly gone to Germany and Russia. In formulating the Geneva Award, the Council of Ambassadors had required Poland to make a certain quantity of coal available to Germany for a period of fifteen years, and had actually required Germany to accept it for a period of three. As soon as this latter period had terminated Germany ceased the duty-free import of Polish coal, and raised a tariff barrier that would exclude it for the future. The German import of Polish coal ceased in 1925, and for her foreign sales Poland was left with a somewhat uncertain market in the Danubian countries. From this dangerous predicament Poland was rescued by the British General Strike, and the cessation of exports of British coal to the Scandinavian countries. This coincided with the completion of at least the earlier work on the new docks at Gdynia and on the new railway linking them with the Upper Silesian region. Poland was able to fill the void created by the British crisis, and continued to strengthen her position in the Scandinavian market until the outbreak of the Second World War.

In most other respects, however, trade failed to revive on a scale that could greatly affect industrial expansion. There was an adverse trade balance through most of the 1920s, and if from 1930 until 1936 the balance was positive, this was only because the government maintained a tight control on imports and foreign spending. Industrial production rose during the years of relative prosperity in the late 1920s, and then declined catastrophically in 1931–32. The potential of the iron, steel, and textile industries was never at any time realized. The peak of industrial production was achieved in 1929 and this level of production was not again reached until 1937. The last complete pre-war year showed an increase in total industrial production over the pre-Depression level of only 19·3 per cent, and much of this was represented by the recent investment in the 'industrial triangle'.

In 1936 the government, which had long taken a prominent role in the ownership and control of industry, began work on a planned industrial development in the so-called Central Industrial Region, a triangular area of southern Poland which covered the upper plain of the Vistula and of its tributary, the San. In the course of 1937 about a billion *zloty* were spent on developing transport and communication facilities in this area and on laying the foundations of new industries. A similar investment was made during the following year; a small plant was established for the manufacture of quality steel; a few other factories were built; and then the Second World War came. The whole undertaking had been motivated as much by strategic as by economic considerations. It was designed to produce armaments and military supplies, and was located as far as practicable from both the German and the Russian boundaries. Its development was cut short by the German invasion, and it was not revived when the war was over.

The Second World War

It is impossible to describe in a few words the effect of the Second World War on the Polish economy. It was first exploited and then destroyed. Any statistical comparison of pre- and post-war Poland is made extremely difficult by the changed boundaries. Some estimate can, however, be made of the physical damage. Warsaw was largely destroyed, and most large cities in the Recovered Territories, such as Gdańsk, Szczecin, and Wrocław, had also suffered immense damage. Factories which had survived the war undamaged had suffered from neglect and lack of maintenance and repair. Some plants in the Western Territories had been stripped by the Soviet authorities as reparation due to them from Germany. Add to this the loss of farm equipment and livestock; the deterioration of the land itself; and the destruction of bridges and transport equipment; and, above all, the loss of some 6 million men and women over and above the number that might have been expected in the course of nature to die within this period.

The Polish government in 1945, when it was again established amid the ruins of Warsaw, faced a far heavier task than that which had confronted its predecessor in 1918. The damage, destruction, and depreciation were incomparably greater than after the previous war, and, though there was for a time some economic aid from the agencies of the United Nations, there were no foreign investments and credits to help rebuild the economy.

The loss of the eastern provinces and the acquisition of the western, called at first the 'Recovered Territories' to emphasize the fact that they had previously formed part of a Polish state, resulted in a net reduction of about 19 per cent of the area of Poland. Churchill's well-known observation that Poland had exchanged poor land for rich is not wholly borne out by the facts. Much of the Western Territories is no more valuable than the Eastern. The extent of cropland was reduced as a result of the boundary changes by more than 11 per cent; that of meadow by 36 per cent; of pasture by 39 per cent; and of orchards and gardens by 37 per cent. The fact that the volume of crops raised on the eve of the war within the newly acquired lands approximately balanced that from the territories lost was a measure of the low level of agricultural practice in the latter.

The gains from the territorial transfer lay in the sphere of mining and manufacturing. The acquisition of the western part of the Upper Silesian industrial region, with the important cities of Bytom (Beuthen), Zabrze (Hindenburg), and Gliwice (Gleiwitz), added materially to industrial production. They also permitted a unified control and direction of the whole industrial region. They gave Poland control of the recently reconstructed and modernized canal, the Gliwicki Canal, which linked it with the navigable Odra, and thus with the port of Szczecin and the Baltic Sea.

At the same time Poland gained possession of the small coalfield of Lower Silesia, of a number of centres of the chemical, textile, and cement industries in Silesia, and of the heavily damaged industrial city of Wrocław (Breslau). The more northerly of the Western Territories were not strongly industrialized, but they included the ports of Szczecin and Gdańsk, and increased Poland's frontage on the Baltic Sea from 40 to about 325 miles.

The territories lost in the east had included two industrial cities of moderate size and importance, Lwów (L'vov) and Wilno (Vilnius), together with most of Poland's small petroleum deposits. The economic value of the manufacturing industries of the Eastern Territories was nevertheless of quite minor importance. The very considerable damage to the cities of the Western Territories makes it difficult to evaluate their industrial significance. On the basis of 1937 or 1938 figures, the area incorporated from Germany increased Poland's bituminous coal production by nearly 8 per cent; that of lead and zinc ores by over 100 per cent; and that of brown coal, which pre-war Poland had used to only a minor extent, by a truly astronomical ratio. If there had been no war damage to industrial installations in the Western Territories, Poland's industrial capacity would have been raised by perhaps as much as 50 per cent. The area acquired was, furthermore, far better equipped with hard-surfaced roads and railways than the territories lost.

Such an analysis of the changes resulting from the transfer of territory omits the significance of the corresponding changes in population. Of the pre-war population of about 8,900,000 in the Western Territories, somewhat more than a million remained after Polish authority had been established. The rest had gone back to Germany, and with them had disappeared a large part of the skilled industrial labour of these provinces. Damage to plant and equipment and shortage of skilled manpower greatly reduced for a number of years the economic value of the Recovered Territories.

What the Polish People's Republic has done with this inheritance is the subject matter of the rest of this chapter. First the mechanism of state control of the economy is discussed; this is followed by an examination of the agricultural and industrial sectors; and the chapter concludes with a review of the growth of the national income during this period and of current economic problems.

Nationalization and the Mechanism of Government Control

Even if the new Polish government had not been ideologically predisposed to a high degree of state control of the economic system, conditions in Poland would have necessitated a radical departure from the system which had existed before the war. At least a third of the capital assets of the country had belonged to Germans who were no longer there. Many of the Polish property-owners could no longer be traced. The Recovered Territories were largely denuded of people, and many industrial and commercial undertakings had been damaged beyond the capacity of their owners to replace or repair them.

The Lublin Committee had assumed control over liberated areas of Poland as soon as the Soviet army had passed through them. It began the reorganization of the social and economic structure of the country long before the fighting had ceased. A land-reform decree, for instance, was published in September 1944, even before the Warsaw Rising had been suppressed by the Germans. The new government thus became possessed of extensive areas of land, part of which it subsequently retained as state farms and state forests. A year later the state assumed the power to direct and control all labour. By an ordinance of October 1945, the obligation of all men up to the age of fifty-five, and of women up to forty-five, to work was decreed. Labour to repair the damage and to restore the economy was declared to be a patriotic duty, and very few were excused from the obligation to register for work and to accept government direction.

Professional persons retained somewhat greater freedom of action, but they too were in time absorbed into some form or other of national organization of the professions. Medical, dental, and nursing personnel were, in October 1948, organized in a national health scheme, and care was taken that even the poorest and least desirable parts of Poland received a fair, if not also an adequate, share of trained medical personnel. Shortly afterwards the pharmacists and veterinarians were similarly incorporated into a state service, and became, like most of the workers, the servants of the state. Professional people, such as lawyers and teachers in private schools and colleges, if they did not become state employees, nevertheless found their scale of payments and the geographical distribution of their services controlled by the appropriate Ministry of the government through the medium of their own professional association.

One of the most serious aspects of the social structure of the new Poland was the small size of the cadres of technically and professionally trained people. This was partially remedied by a closer governmental control of higher education, by the creation of a system of universities and technical colleges, and by requiring all youth to undergo a period of vocational training. Fees were abolished for all higher educational institutions. Admission was to be on the basis of merit, but a relatively high proportion of the total admission was required to be from the families of 'workers'. The exclusion of well-qualified students of middle-class origin became in the 1950s one of the less desirable consequences of the system.

These changes did not come immediately; they were spread over a number of years, and the socialist system of the control of labour and education was not fully established until after 1950. Its creation was accompanied by the nationalization of the means of production. Even before the Second World War the Polish government had participated directly in the national economy through its ownership of a number of industrial undertakings and its monopoly of such goods as matches and salt. This range of activity was of necessity greatly increased after 1945. Its early pronouncements had suggested that the new government would pursue the kind of policy generally associated with European social democracy. It protested its devotion to private enterprise and its desire to establish a balance between the socialized and the private sectors of the economy. Nevertheless, the former grew steadily and it was the latter which withered away.

The nationalization law was not promulgated until January 1946, though the government had in fact already assumed broad powers of control. According to its terms, all assets of Germany and of German nationals were confiscated without compensation. All undertakings included in a prescribed list were nationalized, including all heavy industry, most light industry carried on on a factory basis, and public utilities. In addition, all other enterprises that employed more than fifty persons were also taken over by the state, though provision was made for compensation to all non-German owners. Further, all means of transport and communication, including radio and telecommunications, were nationalized.

The government reserved for itself wide discretionary powers to exclude certain undertakings from the terms of the decree, and also to extend its application to units of production not specified. It also had power to entrust industrial undertakings, whose importance was largely local, to co-operatives run by the workers themselves. Private enterprise fared badly during the following years. Both materials and

skilled labour were scarce, and since the state had assumed the right
to allocate them, it naturally saw to it that the socialized sector was
supplied and staffed, if necessary, at the expense of the private. The
latter declined steadily in importance and in volume of production.
At the end of 1946, rather less than 10 per cent of the gross industrial
output had come from the private sector. By 1950, this had declined
to about 5 per cent, and by 1953 to less than one. At the same time,
wholesale and retail trade gradually passed out of the hands of
private businessmen and shopkeepers, and into the control of the
state, which, in any event, controlled the supply of goods to the shops.

The government had at first looked with favour on the institution
of co-operatives in both agriculture and industry, and had given
them considerable freedom of action. By 1948 this attitude began
to change. The co-operatives were assimilated more and more to the
nationalized undertakings, and came to be regarded as merely an
intermediate stage before the complete socialization of the economy.
By 1948, the Polish leaders no longer professed their desire to maintain a threefold division of the economy : private, co-operative, and
socialized; and declared their objective to be the complete socialization of the economy in the interests of the class-war. In this respect
economic thought followed closely the course of political developments and the growing 'Stalinization' of Poland.

The economy was controlled during this period by the Economic
Committee of the government, or Council of Ministers, and the Committee in turn controlled the Central Planning Board and later the
State Commission on Economic Planning. The Economic Committee
shaped the broad lines of economic policy and was ultimately responsible for the decisions which led to the squeezing-out of the
private and co-operative sectors of the economy. A group of Ministers, whose number tended to increase, was charged each with
segments of the economy : heavy industry, transport, light industry,
internal trade, and many more. They formed a changing pattern as
they divided, subdivided, or merged, according to the needs of those
branches of the economy which they controlled. By 1953, the administration of the national economy was the responsibility of no less than
twenty-six Ministries, each of which had charge of a group of industries and services.

The mechanism of control established by 1950 has, with considerable modification, survived till today. Apart from the not infrequent
changes in the allocation of industrial or commercial activities to this
or that Ministry, there have been changes, particularly during the
Stalinist period, in the direction of streamlining and centralizing the
control of the economy. The tendency was to leave little to the discretion of managers at the local or plant level. A system as rigid

and as hastily constructed as this, functioned imperfectly, and some discretionary power had in fact to be exercised at the local level. More recently the trend has been to exercise less control from the centre, and to leave more to works' managements.

Economic growth has, since the beginning of 1947, proceeded by a series of economic plans formulated by the Central Planning Board and its successor, the State Commission on Economic Planning. The control by the government of industrial production, of transport, of wholesale, and in large measure of retail, trade, as well as of pricing, gives it complete command of the way in which the nation's productive capacity is used. It can to a large degree control demand by manipulating price-levels, and can in the same way draw off purchasing power. It can allocate labour and materials in any given degree to whatever sector of the economy it wishes. If it desires to stimulate capital investment and the expansion of industrial capacity – as, indeed, it has done consistently – it has only to allocate greater inputs to this sector, and, by its manipulation of prices and rationing, to restrict demand for consumer goods. The government, or its Ministries concerned with economic affairs, thus has the power, within the overall dimensions of the national economy, to vary the level of welfare on the one hand and the volume of capital investment on the other.

The first economic plan was drawn up and implemented before government control of the economy had been fully established. It ran from the beginning of 1947 until the end of 1949. This Three-Year Plan aimed at repairing the damage of war and at restoring the economy to at least its pre-war level. In the meanwhile, however, the political climate, and with it that of economic thought, had changed radically. Late in 1947, the political complexion of the government shifted sharply to the left, a process which was completed the following year with the removal of Gomulka from his position as First Secretary of the Party. At the same time the tripartite division of the economy was abandoned as an objective of policy, and the government, now communist in fact if not altogether so in name, set itself to achieve the complete socialization of the economy on the Russian model.

The Six-Year Plan, prepared in late 1948 and in 1949, reflected these changes. It was accepted as part of the law of Poland in July 1950. The detailed plan was never published; instead a summary statement of its objectives was announced. An essential feature was the steady increase of productive capacity during the plan period, by the diversion of current labour and material inputs to capital goods, which would in turn serve to increase total production. In this way the plan called for an increase of over 100 per cent in the gross national product above the 1949 level by the end of 1955. This was to be achieved by a gross investment at two and a half times the level prevailing in 1949. The expected increase in the volume of production of fuel, electrical energy, and crude steel was specified in the plan. A 50 per cent increase by 1955 in the annual volume of agricultural production was called for. This was judged to be necessary to satisfy the food needs of the industrial sector. At the same time no steps were taken to secure a commensurate increase in the production of clothing, boots and shoes, and other consumer goods.

Planning on this scale was new to Poland, and the only available model was that of the Soviet Union, which did not altogether fit Polish conditions. Inevitably, there were mistakes, with capacity less than fully utilized in one place, and inadequate to satisfy urgent demands in another. There were also those who urged the stepping-up of the planned objectives above those specified in the original plan, and those who counselled greater moderation, a slower pace, less overtime, and higher 'real' wages. The atmosphere of the early 1950s was emotionally charged. Party leaders in Poland, under the strong urgings of the Soviet Union, reacted strongly to the political policy of the United States and to economic growth and unification in western Europe. They demanded the shortest and quickest routes to an industrialized and socialized society. This could result only in a higher level of investment from current income, lower *real* wages, and increased labour norms. Plans were thus modified and welfare conditions worsened until they set off the riots of 1956.

Conditions of life were further worsened by a deterioration in the quality of goods produced and very often by a contraction in the range of choice available to the consumer. Each producing unit was assigned a quota. In some instances the figure was unrealistic; in others, raw materials or parts were not available in sufficient quantity; in either event the quality of the product deteriorated. This was equally true of consumer goods and of investment goods, such as the new housing projects. At the same time the choice of varieties to be manufactured was not left to the play of market forces, but was, in many instances, arbitrarily determined by an official of one of the Ministries or by the manager of a factory. The result inevitably was the overproduction of some types of goods and the gross neglect of the needs and desires of whole segments of the community. There is good evidence that decisions in these respects were in favour of the tastes and predilections of the urban dweller and factory-worker, rather than of the peasant.

Over the period of the Six-Year Plan, about 45 per cent of the total investment went into manufacturing and mining. As a result of the expansion of the industrial sector, employment in manufacturing increased from about 1·8 million in 1950 to 2,695,600 in 1955, somewhat less than the planned total of 2·8 million. It was a remarkable achievement, even though it fell short of the sanguine expectations of those who drafted the plan.

The Second Plan ran for the five years 1955–60. It was prepared in the light of changes that had been forced upon the planners in the course of the First Plan. A somewhat higher allocation of credits was made to agriculture and to consumer goods industries, and proportionately less to the heavy and capital goods sector. The events of 1956 were to show how necessary this modification was, and how desirable further relaxations in the austerity of the economic system had become.

The rate of economic growth during the period of the Second Plan and of the Third Plan, which succeeded it from 1960 to 1965, was somewhat lower than during the implementation of the First. Nevertheless, the national income showed an annual average growth of 6·7 per cent during the period of the Second Plan, and this was expected to rise to 7 per cent during the Third. This overall rate of increase compares well with that achieved in western Europe, but was attained at a very much higher cost in reduced consumption and lower standards of living.

Nevertheless, it is possible to see in the small changes in planned objectives and actual achievement some attempt to improve the lot of the people. The Third Plan called for a lower rate of industrial expansion than the earlier plans had done; at the same time, provision was made for a more rapid increase in agricultural production. The result of this is seen in the planned consumption of foodstuffs per head during the period of the Third Five-Year Plan. A somewhat reduced intake of bread-crops is envisaged, but a very much greater consumption of sugar, milk, eggs, meat, and butter. The published figures also indicate an increased domestic consumption (as distinct from production) of cotton and woollen fabrics, of knitwear and of footwear. There has been no revolutionary change in living standards, but the trend through the duration of the last two planning periods has been slowly and consistently upwards.

Agriculture

The agricultural situation in Poland presented problems of exceptional difficulty. These were, in brief, the very high density of farm population and the degree of rural overpopulation, the low level of investment in agriculture, and the generally low productivity of both labour and land. The measures of land reform, carried out during the inter-war years, had proved to be little more than a palliative.

The increase of farm population had by 1939 approximately offset the creation of new farm holdings.

If the reform of the 1920s had been slow and hesitant, that from 1944 onwards was hasty and probably ill-considered. In terms of agricultural land Poland lost by the change of boundaries, and was saved only by the fact that immigration from the Eastern Territories was relatively small. In all, about 9·8 million hectares of agricultural and forest land were expropriated under the land-reform decree of September 1944. Of this, almost 70 per cent lay in the Western Territories. The government subsequently distributed 61 per cent of this land to the peasants, holding the remainder for development as the nucleus of a socialized system of agriculture.

The first post-war Polish government encouraged co-operatives, maintained a small socialized sector, but genuinely desired to perpetuate a system of private farms. The further hand-out of land to less well-to-do peasants may have done something to ensure their loyalty to the regime, but it is very doubtful whether any increase in the number of uneconomically small units was any benefit to the economy. There was a severe shortage of farm animals and equipment, little fertilizer was available, and considerable areas were out of cultivation through flooding or neglect during the war years. At the same time the growing industrial population was creating an increasing demand for farm products.

During the late forties socialized marketing agencies had the responsibility for collecting farm surpluses and retailing them to the urban markets. They failed, however, to attract enough. The government in turn offered higher prices to the peasants, imposed compulsory deliveries upon them, and allowed them to pay their land tax in the form of produce. Overall production was below normal, but the fundamental problem was that the peasant, faced with a marketing system that was unfamiliar and therefore unpopular, and with a pricing system that did not respond to the market conditions, chose to withhold his products. The government's reply was to intensify its system of compulsory deliveries of an ever-widening range of goods, and to adjust its demands to the social and economic standing of the peasant. The contribution of the kulak, or well-to-do peasant, became disproportionately large in comparison with that of the peasant with only a half-dozen acres. In this way the government attempted, for ideological reasons, to eliminate the rich peasant, and thus destroyed the group most likely to cultivate efficiently and produce a marketable surplus.

During these early years the government expressed its belief that collectivization was a desirable objective, but disclaimed all intention of forcing the peasants into collectives. The tolerant attitude disappeared after the political changes of 1947–48. The new Polish leadership was convinced, on both ideological and economic grounds, that the system of private farms had to be replaced by one of collectives. Collective farms were more intensive in the use of labour, at a time when industrialization was making increasing demands for workers; they permitted the use of machines and the employment of more scientific methods than smallholdings, cultivated by a conservative peasantry; they were labour-intensive, rather than land-intensive, and provided an increased output per unit of labour. This was what the circumstances demanded. There were, furthermore, ideological reasons : the need to follow the Soviet model of economic growth; the conviction that the humblest peasant was at heart a capitalist, and that the only person more dangerous to the regime than the poor peasant was the rich one; and the consequent policy of assimilating the farm-worker to the industrial worker.

The nucleus of a system of collectives had been created by the decree of September 1944. It was a considerable time before most of the land retained by the government was in fact organized into collectives. In the late forties, attempts were made to persuade peasants to form collective farms voluntarily. Dissension was encouraged between the peasants with small to medium income and the rich, in the hope that the former would choose collectivization if only out of spite towards the latter. Those who favoured the process were rewarded; those who resisted were discriminated against in the assessment of grain levies, land taxes, and the allocation of fertilizer and supplies.

In spite of these attempts to persuade and compel, collectivization aroused no enthusiasm. In most parts of 'old' Poland it was resisted, and the movement achieved its greatest success in the Western Territories, where the peasants were themselves mostly recent immigrants to the area, and to that degree insecure and more dependent than most on the whim of government officials. Progress was slow until the Six-Year Plan began to be implemented. This embodied collectivization of agriculture as one of its primary objectives. By the end of 1953 government measures were beginning to achieve some small success. There were at this time about 8,000 socialized farms of one kind or another, with more than 1·5 million hectares of cropland. This represented, nevertheless, only about 7 per cent of the total cropland of Poland. By 1955, the number of collectives of all kinds had risen to about 10,000. It had about 200,000 members, but embraced still no more than a tenth of the agricultural land.

The collectives conformed to a variety of models. In the least socialized, the peasants retained possession of their land, and joined together only for ploughing, sowing, and harvesting. The more sophisticated collectives required progressively greater contributions from the peasants. In some the peasants retained only their buildings, farm animals, tools, and equipment. In the extreme form, ownership of all means of production – land, animals, tools, and buildings – became vested in the collective, and the peasants retained only a small garden plot for their private use. Most Polish collectives – from two-thirds to three-quarters of the total – belonged to the latter type. These farms were to make extensive use of mechanical equipment, which was to be supplied, again following the Soviet model, from State Machine Centres, and of fertilizers, to be supplied from the new chemical factories.

The policy of the government appeared to be justified by the higher crop yields in relation both to land and labour, recorded in the socialized sector. This cannot be wholly explained in terms of the system. A high proportion of the collectives was on the superior soils, where agricultural practice had long been on a higher plane than in other parts of Poland. It is not surprising that the Second Plan (1956–60) called for the extension of collectivization to an area of about 5 million hectares, representing from 25 to 30 per cent of the agricultural land.

The rising of the autumn of 1956, however, cut short the process of further collectivization. Many collectives were broken up, and their land redistributed to the peasants, and the creation of new collectives was halted. For the past ten years the government has paid lip-service to collectivization as the ideal system of land tenure in a communist society, but has taken no steps to convert its ideal into reality.

In the earlier plans it was assumed that an increased agricultural output could be achieved in the main by changes in the structure of agriculture, without any large capital investment. The last two plans, however, have allocated a larger share of the total income to agricultural development, and it has been demonstrated that more can be achieved by agricultural research, by greater use of fertilizer, more extensive drainage, and by education than was possible by re-shaping farming on the Soviet model. The gradual change in diet has already been mentioned; it was predicated upon a corresponding change in agriculture – a small decrease in the area under grain crops, a considerable increase in sugar-beet, in fodder crops, and in the number of farm animals. The 1960–65 Plan called for an increase of over 21 per cent in the head of cattle and of 19 per cent in the number of pigs. Crop yields, always liable to fluctuate with the vagaries of the North European weather, have nevertheless shown a steady upward tendency. The following table showing the yield per hectare of certain crops and the volume of production is evidence of at least a moderate degree of success in the agricultural programme in recent years :

	Wheat		Rye		Potatoes		Sugar Beet	
	Yield in 100 kgs. per hectare	Production in thousands of metric tons	Yield	Production	Yield	Production	Yield	Production
1946	8·8	618	9·0	2,763	112	18,710	176	2,983
1950	12·8	1,888	12·8	6,488	138	36,130	222	6,377
1955	14·9	2,134	14·1	7,003	100	27,021	186	7,286
1956	14·5	2,121	13·2	6,558	140	38,052	177	6,428
1957	16·1	2,319	14·7	7,437	127	35,104	225	7,621
1958	15·7	2,321	14·1	7,329	126	34,800	235	8,427
1959	17·3	2,484	15·6	8,113	128	35,698	159	5,975
1960	16·9	2,303	15·4	7,878	132	37,855	256	10,262
1961	19·9	2,792	17·1	8,356	160	45,203	275	11,555
1962	19·4	2,700	14·2	6,685	130	37,817	234	10,075
1963	19·9	3,067	16·3	7,124	158	44,868	287	10,661
1964	18·7	3,042	15·8	6,982	169	48,860	283	12,574
1965	20·6	3,422	18·4	8,289	154	43,263	259	12,314
1966	21·5	3,603	17·8	7,700	169	46,144	313	13,620
1967	22·4	3,934	17·9	7,694	176	48,620	358	15,521
1968	—	4,670	—	8,520	—	50,817	—	14,800

Source: *Rocznik statystyczny, 1968; Production Yearbook, FAO, UN, 1968*

The number of sheep showed little increase, and the number of horses has actually declined since 1950, with wider use of farm tractors. The number of cattle and pigs has, however, increased sharply, with a proportionate expansion in the volume of milk and meat production.

This not inconsiderable increase in agricultural production has been accompanied by a small drop in farm employment and a considerable reduction of the contribution of the agricultural sector to the gross national product. If one may criticize the Polish achievement, it may perhaps be said that the agricultural population has not fallen enough and that the standing of agriculture relative to manufacturing has declined too much. Poland has not yet overcome her problem of rural overpopulation and backward and inefficient agricultural practice. Land is still far too fragmented, with almost 60 per cent of the farms and 28 per cent of the land in holdings of less than 5 hectares (about 12·5 acres). Agriculture remains inadequately capitalized; it still employs too many workers; and crop yields are still by western European standards too low.

	Total Cattle (thousands)	Of which dairy cows (thousands)	Pigs (thousands)
1946	3,910·5	2,748·1	2,674·1
1950	7,200·0	4,850·0	9,350·0
1955	7,912·2	5,454·7	10,888·3
1956	8.353·2	5.599·6	11,560·6
1957	8,264·8	5,766·6	12,325·4
1958	8,209·7	5,931·4	11,958·9
1959	8,352·8	6,024·9	11,209·1
1960	8,695·1	5,884·7	12,615·3
1961	9,168·1	5,915·4	13,434·1
1962	9,589·5	6,022·4	13,616·7
1963	9,841·4	6,070·3	11,653·2
1964	9,939·7	6,013·1	12,918·3
1965	9,947·2	5,920·3	13,779·1
1966	10,390·8	6,013·6	14,251·1
1967	10,767·5	6,142·5	14,232·6
1968	10,530·1	6,056·8	14,676·7

Source: *Rocznik statystyczny, 1968*

	Gross agricultural production; 1950–52 = 100	Agricultural production as percentage of national income	Employment in Agriculture	Agricultural Employment as percentage of the labour force
1949	97·2	42	11,597·5	47·1
1954	104·6	40		
1955	109·9	28		
1957	122·9	26		
1958	126·5	26		
1959	125·4	24		
1960	132·1	23	11,281·1	38·4
1961	145·8	24		
1962	133·7	20		
1963	139·1	21		
1964	140·8	20		
1965	151·7	19		
1966	160·0	19		
1967	164·0	17		
1968	171·0	17		

Calculated from data in *Rocznik statystyczny, 1969*. Note that official statistics give employment only for the socialized industries, and thus exclude most of the farming population.

Manufacturing

The expansion of the manufacturing industries has been the primary objective of all the economic plans of Poland, and has consistently absorbed the greater part of the investment capital. Such an emphasis was inevitable in view of the destruction which the country had suffered and the low level of economic development of much of it. Socialist ideology furthermore considered the expansion of manufacturing industries to be the necessary foundation of every other form of economic growth as well as of higher standards of living. Within the manufacturing sector it emphasized the heavy and investment goods industries almost to the exclusion of consumer goods, at least until the former had achieved their desired degree of growth.

The nationalization of all except the smaller industrial undertakings and of all mineral resources and means of transport clearly facilitated the planning process. It was possible to design an economic plan for the country as a whole and, subject to the availability of materials and labour, to implement it. Socialist planning in Poland was predicated on the assumption that every region should be developed as fully as was consistent with its resource base. This clearly necessitated the development of resources and the foundation in some regions of industries which in a capitalist system would not have been judged to be economic. In the opinion of the planners, the net social advantages more than offset the net economic loss resulting from longer transport hauls and the working of low-grade resources. In practice, however, the planners adopted a less extreme position. Poland was in no position to bear the net cost of the uneconomic location of new industrial plants. There was some degree of dispersion of industry, but many areas remain unindustrialized.

The first plan aimed to restore production to its pre-war level. In certain key products, such as coal, electric power, pig-iron, and steel, production in 1949 equalled or even exceeded that of the last pre-war years. But this was because the change of boundaries brought western Upper Silesia, with its mines and metallurgical works, within Poland. Production within the boundaries of 1945, however, fell considerably short of production within the *same* area in 1938–39. It was to be several years before the war-damaged industries of Wrocław and Szczecin were to be restored.

The Six-Year Plan was intended to create the 'basis of socialism', or, in more familiar terms, to build a large capital goods industry. It was drawn on the model of the Soviet First Five-Year Plan and with Soviet help, and required an increase of 364 per cent in the capacity of machine-building industries by the end of 1955. This presupposed a vast expansion of the metallurgical and related fuel industries, and with the latter was associated a considerable expansion of chemical production. By the end of the planning period total industrial production was to be four times that from the same area in 1938–39, and, since the population had been considerably reduced in the

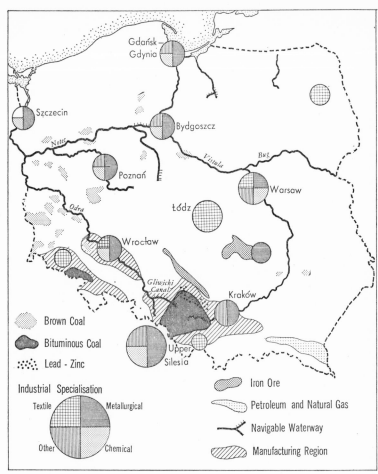

8. The industrial regions of modern Poland

meanwhile, this represented an even larger increase per head. Almost two-thirds of this greatly increased production was to be made up of capital goods.

The plan was not, however, allowed to run its course unaltered. The deteriorating political situation led to the imposition on the already over-burdened economy of the obligation to manufacture increased amounts of military supplies. Expansion in certain fields – in general those oriented towards consumer goods – was curtailed and the planned rates of growth were revised downward. The official claim that by 1955 the industrial plan had been over-fulfilled was based on faulty and inadequate statistics, and was received with some degree of scepticism.

The 1955–60 Plan had been drawn up and its implementation begun before the events of 1956 gave a new twist to public policy. The method of preparing the plan was modified, and local estimates of capacity and potential, made at the plant level, were used. Nevertheless, its initial objectives were generous, and it appears that party stalwarts in the factories and mines were even more sanguine and less realistic in estimating their own potential than the party bureaucrats would have been. Investment in heavy industry continued to take precedence over that in light and consumer goods industries; even greater emphasis was placed on the fuel and power industries. An effort was to be made to increase domestic production of industrial raw materials, in order to cut down on the volume of imports, and the cadre of technically trained persons was to be greatly increased.

The rising of 1956 and the relaxation in the political field which followed it led inevitably to modifications in the planned objectives of the economy; to a reduction in the level of investment in capital goods; and to an increase of that in consumer goods and in non-productive investments such as housing. At the same time, as has been noted, a larger appropriation was made to the agricultural sector.

The industrial expansion of Poland during the period 1950 to 1965 was, in statistical terms, a remarkable phenomenon, even when allowance is made for the fact that in some branches it started from a low level. The official statistics give the following indices of growth :

	1950	1955	1960	1964	1967	1968
Total manufacturing industries	100	212	338	466	587	642
Fuel industries	100	150	175	211	246	267
Ferrous metallurgy	100	181	274	368	443	468
Non-ferrous metallurgy	100	209	273	341	422	450
Machine construction	100	491	805	1,398	1,899	2,200
Electro-technical industries	100	297	832	1,559	2,251	2,500
Transport equipment	100	306	715	1,231	1,713	2,000
Chemical industry	100	228	494	842	1,249	1,400
Building materials industry	100	224	373	490	613	673
Textile industries	100	191	282	338	400	434
Leather goods industries	100	188	291	338	396	426
Food industries	100	156	227	264	299	307
Total capital goods industries	100	230	385	559	722	—
Total consumer goods industries	100	192	291	370	447	—

Source: *Rocznik statystyczny, 1968, 1969*

The average annual rate of growth of industrial production as a whole has been between 7 and 8 per cent. This table shows clearly the disharmony between the rates of growth of the capital goods, or investment, industries, and consumer goods production. A tabulation of the total value of investment during this period, and its breakdown between the sectors and the divisions of each, demonstrates how the investment industries benefited at the expense of all others.

| | Total | In socialized undertakings | In Industry | | In building construction | In transport & communication | In agriculture |
			Total	Of which capital goods			
1946	15,510	55·4%					
1948	23,930	65·6%					
1950	38,625	90·4%					
1952	51,389	96·3%					
1954	63,238	95·9%					
1956	68,580	90·6%	29,191	24,393 83%	1,788	6,165	9,168
1957	73,522	86·2%	29,522	23,836	2,226	6,736	9,544
1958	80,734	85·8%	32,350	24,979	2,052	7,256	9,930
1959	94,355	86·7%	38,026	28,387	2,507	9,093	10,599
1960	99,992	87·6%	39,149	28,900	3,143	10,215	11,955
1961	107,376	88·1%	43,195	34,043	2,942	11,633	13,272
1962	119,082	90·4%	50,044	39,774	4,455	13,089	14,428
1963	122,654	90·4%	52,215	41,908	4,712	13,307	15,828
1964	127,861	90·3%	53,586	43,422 81%	4,531	13,511	18,710
1965	140,767	90·4%	57,549		5,499	15,715	21,870
1966	152,858	90·3%	61,043		6,376	18,263	23,937
1967	170,260	90·2%	67,813		7,742	20,592	26,319
1968	185,102	90·5%	74,395		8,527	21,601	28,633

An Industrial State

On the following pages progress and prospects are examined in the basic sectors of manufacturing. Basic to Poland's industrial development has been the fuel industry. Most of the petroleum resources have been lost as a result of boundary changes, so that resources consist essentially of bituminous and brown coal. The nature and extent of these reserves have already been examined. In terms of potential, there was in fact no limit to the gross tonnage that Poland could produce. The problems during the early years of planned growth lay rather in the varieties of coal available, the poor condition of the mines themselves, and the generally slow rate at which new mines could be opened up and production increased.

As the iron-smelting industry was expanded, the shortage of coking coal became acute. The domestic supply was mainly from the small Lower Silesian coalfield and from a highly restricted area, between Gliwice and Chorzów, of the Upper Silesian. The local supply has had, in fact, to be supplemented by imports from both Czechoslovakia and the Soviet Union. Other shortcomings of the industry could in time be remedied : notably the neglect of the mines during the war years, the shortage of skilled miners, the lack of tools and equipment, and the need to open new, large, and highly mechanized mines. But this took a considerable time, so that coal production failed consistently to achieve its planned objectives and the shortage of fuel held back other branches of industry. By the later 1950s, however, new mines in the central, or Rybnik, section of the Upper Silesian coalfield were coming into production; the construction of relatively pleasant miners' colonies combined with higher wages to attract more labour, and mining equipment was becoming available in increasing quantities.

Coal production thus rose sharply in the 1950s and annual output continues to increase.

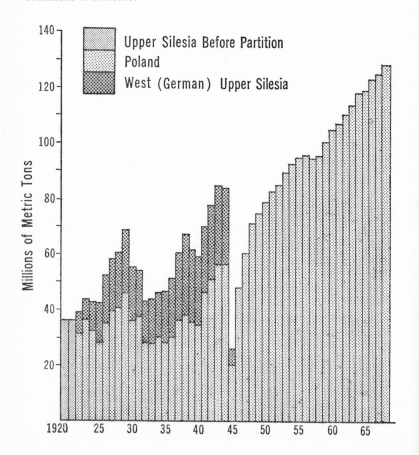

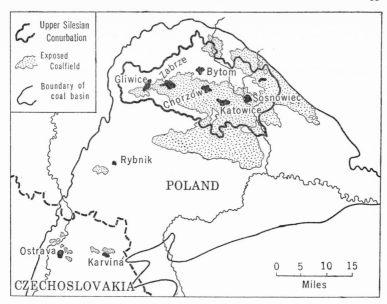

9. The Upper Silesian coalfield and industrial region

Brown coal and lignite were abundant, but little used, in pre-war Poland. The Western Territories contained a few small workings together with very large reserves. In contrast with the bituminous coal, which is found close to the mountains in southern Poland, the brown coal and related fuels are found mostly in central Poland. They occur close to the surface, and lend themselves to extraction with large-scale excavating machinery. Since the fuel has a high water and ash content, and therefore a low calorific value, it is not economic to transport it more than a short distance. Much of it is burned close to the pits from which it is extracted to generate thermal-electric power. Expansion of brown-coal production has been very much more rapid than that of bituminous coal and its growth has been a major factor in the industrial development of central Poland.

A considerable number of hydro-electric installations has been built within the mountains of southern Poland in recent years, but most are relatively small, and their total contribution to the production of electric power does not exceed 2 per cent. The physical conditions of Poland, with the rivers flowing slowly across an almost level plain, do not favour large-scale hydro-electric power production.

The metallurgical and mechanical construction industries have received the lion's share of the industrial investment. Even in 1964, when the light and consumer goods industries were being expanded, they still received 28 per cent of the total industrial investment. This group of industries was given the foremost position in the plans of the socialist countries of eastern Europe, and was considered to be the necessary basis of socialism in all of them. Whether local resources were adequate was never really discussed. Not until ten years after the initiation of the economic plans did Khrushchev raise the question of international specialization within the countries of the Soviet Bloc, the socialist division of labour, as it was termed. By this time it was too late; every country of eastern Europe, with the exception only of Albania, had established its iron, steel, and mechanical construction industries, whether or not these were warranted by their local resources and other circumstances.

Poland was no worse off than her neighbours. Fuel reserves were abundant, though, as has been noted, the shortage of coking coal was a continuing problem. On the other hand, iron-ore reserves were scanty, and intensive prospecting has failed to add appreciably to their volume. The crude production of ore has mounted slowly, but the labour inputs per ton have risen sharply, indicative of the increasingly difficult conditions under which the ore is being mined. The following table shows the volume of ore, the metal content of the ore, and the approximate extent to which domestic needs are covered by domestic production :

	Ore[8]	Fe. content[9]	as percentage of domestic needs[10]
1949	604	233	17
1955	1,699	631	20
1960	2,182	624	13
1961	2,386	672	14
1962	2,436	682	13
1963	2,609	720	13
1964	2,680	740	13
1965	2,861	788	13
1966	3,053	831	13
1967	3,077	838	12
1968	3,050	—	—

It is recognized that Poland must become increasingly dependent on foreign sources of ore, and until recently it was assumed that these would be Soviet. It was, for example, planned to increase Soviet

[8] *Rocznik statystyczny*, 1968.
[9] *Statistical Yearbook*, U.N.
[10] Author's calculation, based on the apparent consumption of blast-furnaces.

deliveries so that by 1965 they would cover 75 per cent of Polish needs. This level has not been reached, and Poland has been obliged to turn elsewhere. There is no overall world shortage of iron-ore, but purchases from sources outside the Soviet Bloc raise payment difficulties.[11]

Before the initiation of the plans, the metallurgical industries were largely concentrated in Upper Silesia, and the centres lying outside this area, as at Szczecin and Częstochowa, were small and old. The plans called not only for a large investment in the older centres and the integration and modernization of their plant, but also for the creation of two entirely new metallurgical combines. These were located, one at Częstochowa, the Bierut Works, only about 40 miles from the Upper Silesian coalfield and very much closer to the only significant Polish reserves of iron-ore, the other near Kraków. This latter, known as the Lenin Works, became the pride and joy of the Polish planners. It was located near the north bank of the Vistula, about 5 miles to the east of Kraków. It was designed to produce up to 2·5 million tons of steel annually, and at the works gates was built the 'socialist' town of Nowa Huta, with a population of about 100,000.[12] In addition a plant was built for quality steel in the northern suburbs of Warsaw.

The mechanical engineering and construction industries have been strongly developed on the basis of the increased metal production. Relatively little expansion has, however, taken place in Upper Silesia. Here conditions were crowded, and much of the area was honeycombed with coal-workings, and incapable of supporting industrial buildings. On the other hand, there have been major developments in Warsaw, where, in particular, an automobile factory has been established; in Poznań, Wrocław, Kraków, and in the Staropolska region to the east of Kielce. Shipbuilding has been expanded at Gdańsk and Szczecin, and both ships and machinery now figure prominently among Polish exports.

The chemical industries constituted one of the least developed branches of manufacturing at the inception of the period of planned development. Their expansion, however, was vital to the success of the plans. Without supplies of fertilizer, agricultural targets could not be met, and agriculture in the Western Territories required large quantities of fertilizer which, before the Second World War, had been obtained from the factories of Saxony. Raw materials for the basic chemicals exist in the salt deposits of southern Poland, in the by-products of the smelting of sulphide ores in Upper and Lower

[11] See below, p. 147.
[12] Nowa Huta is administratively a part of Kraków, from which it is difficult to distinguish it statistically.

Silesia, and in the newly discovered beds of sulphur near Tarnobrzeg in the Vistula valley. Expansion has been rapid during the past twelve years. New works have been built and others greatly extended at Kędzierzyn, Chorzów, Tarnów, and Puławy, and others are either projected or being built.

The expansion of the consumer goods industries has been a great deal less rapid. Though relatively little investment capital has been available for these industries, they have nevertheless undergone some considerable structural reorganization. In Łódź, for example, there had been an immense number of small textile-mills. The smallest amongst them have been closed, and many of the others combined to produce units of more economic size. Nevertheless, even the largest of them continue to operate with a great deal of obsolete plant and equipment.

National Income

As calculated in the socialist countries, the national income is a measure of the value of material production, and excludes that of services and cultural activities not directly related to manufacturing. Calculated on this basis, the national income of Poland increased from a base of 100 in 1950 to 151 in 1955; 208 in 1960; and 262 in 1964. The share of manufacturing has increased steadily throughout the period, and that of agriculture has diminished. Furthermore, though growth has been continuous, the *rate* of growth has tended in recent years to slacken, and is today running at between 7 and 8 per cent per year. At the same time the population was increasing rapidly, so that the *per capita* increase in national income was less marked. The work-force has begun within the last five or six years to receive a large addition from the high birth-rate of the years immediately following the war. It is estimated that between 1966 and 1970 no less than 3·2 million young people will have come on to the labour market.[13] The net increase in the work-force will clearly be a great deal less than this, but it is suggested that 1·5 million, and perhaps a good deal more, jobs will be required outside agriculture. Viewed against the rising population, the economic achievement appears a great deal more modest. Indeed the threat of severe unemployment is now a fact of Polish economic life.

Foreign Trade

It is natural to assume that foreign markets could be developed to absorb the agricultural and industrial surpluses, to maintain full employment, and to provide exchange for the import of raw mater-

13 *Trybuna Ludu* (17 March 1964), quoted J. F. Brown, *The New Eastern Europe* (New York, 1966), p. 109.

ials and capital goods. The situation, however, is far from simple, and prospects for Poland are not bright. The total volume of trade has, it is true, increased at a somewhat faster rate than the national income itself, but in certain key commodities, such as coal, the increase has been negligible. Trade remains overwhelmingly with members of the socialist bloc, at a time when the economy calls more and more for a widely diversified trade. The expansion of trade has been hindered by its bilateral character and by the narrow range of Polish exports. Some of the latter are in diminishing demand, and the quality of others is said to be poor. There has, lastly, been great difficulty in obtaining and granting long-term credits.

Commercial agreements in all the countries of the socialist bloc are negotiated by their governments on a bilateral basis and involve as a general rule a simple exchange of commodities and services. Credits are rarely granted and payments are not made through any form of international clearing account. Trade is, in effect, a form of barter in which the equivalence of commodities is expressed in monetary terms. There is thus a balance in the trading accounts of Poland with most of her commercial partners. The effect of this is to make the economy extremely inelastic, and to prevent the country from benefiting from openings that might develop. Since, furthermore, commerce is conducted in most of the non-socialist world by private commercial institutions, there has been a certain reluctance on the part of non-bloc countries to conduct any large-scale trade with members of the bloc. There is also in certain capitalist countries an irrational objection to doing business with those that bear a 'communist' label.

These conditions make for inflexibility in Poland's trade relations, and inevitably slow down to some extent the rate of commercial growth. It is in part a reflection of these conditions that the percentage of Poland's total trade that is carried on with fellow members of the bloc has in fact been increasing in recent years.

Changes in the general pattern of world trade have tended to affect Poland adversely. Through most of the inter-war years coal had been a major export commodity. Demand remained high during the earlier post-war years, when the Polish coalmining industry had still not fully recovered from the damage and neglect of the period of wartime. Now that this recovery has been made, the foreign market has declined sharply. Poland continues to supply coal on an important scale to other countries of eastern Europe, which, with the exception of Czechoslovakia, have little of their own. East Germany, whose domestic production of bituminous coal is negligible, relies heavily on Polish coal, but it is not difficult to envisage conditions under which Poland would be faced with stiff West German competition in the East German area. The bottom has long since dropped from the Scandinavian market, where the development of hydro-electric power has almost eliminated the consumption of coal.

The East European and Soviet Bloc had been conceived by those who created it and guided its destinies, as an almost self-sufficient economic unit. In 1949 this ideal of near self-sufficiency was brought a stage nearer by the creation of the Council of Mutual Economic Assistance, variously known as CEMA and COMECON. Its membership consisted, in addition to the Soviet Union, of all the East European countries except Yugoslavia. Its object was to assign priorities in industrial production between its member states, to arrange for the exchange of goods, blueprints, and technical knowledge and skill, and to provide mutual help and encouragement. In the course of time a number of commissions – there are at present nineteen – were created, each charged with the supervision of developments in a particular range of industrial production. Overall directions were handed down from the Council which met, infrequently as it proved, in Moscow, to the commissions whose headquarters were each located at some appropriate site within the territory of the member nations.

For the first ten years of its existence, the achievement of CEMA had been of very little importance. The basic reason for this was the fundamental conflict within socialist thought on industrial development. On the one hand, there was the Stalinist ideal of developing parallel ranges of industry within each country of the bloc, so that each could build its own socialism on the approved foundation in heavy industry. On the other, the commonsense opinion held that, in view both of regional variations in resources and of the limited scale of the potential market, specialization as between one country and another was desirable. The former received strong support from nationalistically oriented opinion in each country; the latter was the declared policy of CEMA, and in general the former tended to nullify the latter.

About 1960 Khrushchev revived the somewhat moribund programme of CEMA, and attempted to achieve the ideal of a 'socialist division of labour' within the countries of the bloc. The Balkan members, led by Romania, objected, while the northern tier, consisting of East Germany, Poland, and Czechoslovakia, were prepared to accept some such programme. The Balkan states feared that, with a programme of international specialization, the industrial plums would go to those countries already more highly industrialized, namely the northern tier. They had ambitions to achieve a better balance themselves between industry and agriculture, and saw in Khrushchev's policy only an obstacle to the realization of their ideals.

Romania, which has adopted this policy the most conspicuously, has turned to the West and is building up a broad-based industrial structure with the help of long-term credits from Western countries.

The effect of this failure to broaden the basis of industrial specialization within eastern Europe has, on balance, been detrimental to Poland, which is faced with the loss of markets in the more southerly parts of the East European area. Poland's problem is that she is caught up in an economic system which makes the expansion of trade with non-socialist countries difficult, while the failure of the system itself to function smoothly and efficiently restricts Poland's market within the bloc.

The failure of Poland's export trade to expand with the growth of the economy and to afford the potential conditions of full employment cannot be wholly laid against the imperfect working of the system. To some extent the fault lies within Poland. Quality products might be expected to find their own markets, but there is growing evidence that consumers within the bloc, when given the choice, have preferred Western to Polish products. For the same reason, it is very difficult for Poland to expand her small market in Western countries. There has been in recent years a sharp increase in the value of exports to the new countries. Exports to those of Africa in 1955 amounted to 19 million *zloty*; by 1964, this had risen to 1,191 million. Even after allowance is made for the depreciation of the *zloty* during this period, growth of this order holds out some hope for the country's economic wellbeing. Considerable, if less spectacular, increases have been registered in exports to Asiatic and Latin American countries.

Among the trading partners of Poland the Soviet Union is dominant, with almost a third of the total trade of Poland. Next in importance come East Germany and Czechoslovakia. Great Britain is by far the most important non-socialist country in Poland's foreign trade. The following table illustrates the current direction of Polish trade; the figures are for 1964 :

	Imports from	Exports to
USSR	36·5	32·2
Eastern Europe	27·7	34·3
Industrial West (inc. USA)	24·5	20·5
Other	11·3	13·0
	100·0	100·0

Source: *Foreign Trade of the European Satellites in 1965*, CIA, Washington, 1966

The following table gives a breakdown of Polish trade in 1968 by
the broad categories usually adopted in statistics of foreign trade.

	General Imports		General Exports	
	Millions of *zloty*	Per cent	Millions of *zloty*	Per cent
Live animals	1·6		61·2	
Foodstuffs	421·5		1,263·4	
Raw materials for the food industry	733·6		244·8	
Other raw materials of vegetable and animal origin	1,320·8		449·1	
Fuels, minerals, metals	2,665·4		2,390·9	
Chemicals, fertilizers, rubber	855·4		393·6	
Building materials	73·5		120·0	
Machinery and equipment	3,910·9		3,645·3	
Consumer goods of industrial origin	596.4		1,555·9	
	10,579·1	100	10,106·2	100

Source: *Yearbook of International Trade Statistics, 1969*, United Nations

The most valuable single export is coal, as indeed it has been throughout the post-war period. In 1964 it amounted to 11·5 per cent by
value of the total exports; in 1960 it made up 16·2 per cent of an
appreciably smaller volume; and in 1955, 40·7 per cent. To the coal
export should be added a smaller, but nevertheless important, export
of coke, which in 1964 amounted to 2·8 per cent of the total export.
Second to coal and coal products are agricultural exports, including
fruit and vegetables, refined sugar, and preserved meat. The volume
of these exports has been increasing very slowly, but its market in
Central and western Europe is gravely threatened by the progress
being made in the agricultural sector of the European Common
Market. Manufactured goods, especially the products of the mechanical engineering factories and textiles, make up about a third of
the total exports, and it is in this sector rather than in any other that
Poland looks for any significant growth.

The import trade is dominated by industrial raw materials, among
which raw cotton, raw wool, iron-ore, and petroleum are the most
important. There is a small import of coking coal, which has in recent
years grown with the expansion of the metallurgical branch of industry, of non-ferrous ores and concentrates, and of fertilizers. Pol-
and has now become a net importer of grain; the volume tends to
vary with the weather and consequent yield within Poland, but is
showing an overall increase. This is likely to continue as the population grows, as more land is planted with crops which contribute to
the export trade, and as popular taste demands more wheat and less
rye bread.

PART THREE

The Polish Republic

Chapter 5

The Political Background of Modern Poland

'O wojnę powszechną za wolność ludów prosimy Cię, Panie.'
(Adam Mickiewicz, 1832)[1]

The Heritage of the Past

THE INSURRECTION OF JANUARY 1863 in Congress Poland represented an important landmark in the political history of the Polish nation. While it was fought only against the Tsarist regime and on territories under Russian control, it demonstrated the internal solidarity of Poles in all three of the empires between which Poland had been divided. Profiting from the neutrality of Austria, the Galician Poles publicly manifested in favour of the revolutionaries, helped in the formation of military contingents, organized the import of arms, and welcomed those who were forced to flee Congress Poland after defeat. There is, in fact, good reason to believe that the insurrection would have been suppressed much earlier, had it not been for the aid of the Galician Poles. Even in the area of Poznań, which provided the rising with one of its leaders, Marian Langiewicz, people disregarded the draconian regulations of the Prussian police and gave help to their compatriots.

The uprising was dominated by the same spirit of self-sacrifice and the same almost mystical will to martyrdom as that of 1831. The political aftermath of its defeat, however, displayed entirely different characteristics from those which marked the period of the 'Great Emigration'. There was no mass exodus, and those who did go into exile could no longer rely on the enthusiastic spiritual kinship of members of the Young Europe movement. Some of its most outstanding representatives, such as Garibaldi and Mazzini, were busy in the attempt to realize their dreams; others, such as Kossuth and those who had participated in the German risings of 1848, were slowly recognizing their failure. Indeed, the Polish disaster was the most

---

[1] 'For a world war for the freedom of the peoples, we pray thee, O, Lord' in *Litanja pielgrzymska* (Litany of the Polish Pilgrims) in *Ksiegi narodu i pielgrzymstwa polskiego* (Rome, Instytut Literacki, 1946), p. 98.

eloquent evidence that this heroic chapter of the romantic mid-century struggle for freedom had ended.

The new exiles fundamentally differed from those who escaped to western Europe after 1831. They adhered to the revolutionary ideology of the past, but they failed to adapt it to the new realities of both Poland and Europe. None of their many political groups and programmes presented an effective plan for political action based on the realities of contemporary Poland. They failed to create a new focus of political activity, and their projects, which at best could be considered 'a mixture of acceptable and unrealistic thoughts',[2] were not calculated to win the support of the Poles who remained in their homeland.

For a few years after 1866, the defeat of Austria and her apparent *rapprochement* with France seemed to provide new opportunity for Polish diplomatic manoeuvres. After 1870, however, Bismarck saw to it that Poland ceased to be an international issue. At the same time Polish participation in the Paris Commune did nothing to encourage support from the French government. Moreover, the ever-increasing signs of Franco-Russian *rapprochement* – which placed the ancient friend of Poland on the side of her traditional enemy – tended to reduce the effectiveness of diplomacy as an instrument of Polish liberation.

In consequence, the status and influence of the émigrés was undermined. The moral capital accumulated in the Polish nation by the revolutionary events of the thirties was exhausted (at least for the present). At the same time, Polish society,[3] which until the January uprising had regarded the émigré groups as a common focus of its spiritual and political endeavours, began to develop along different lines in each of the Russian-, Prussian-, and Austrian-held regions of Poland.

In the Russian sector defeat brought about persecution and humiliation. The former Polish kingdom, which was now given the name of the 'Vistula Land', was separated from the predominantly Belorussian, Ukrainian, and Lithuanian provinces, which were renamed the 'Western Territory of the Russian Empire'. In this latter area, which included the Polish cultural centre of Wilno and large Polish minorities, radical measures were taken with the purpose of imposing Russian culture in a minimum of time. Restrictions on the use

---

[2] Henryk Wereszycki, *Historia polityczna Polski w dobie popowstaniowej 1864–1918* (Warsaw, 1948), p. 11.

[3] Despite its division among the three autocratic powers of the European East, the Polish nation managed to maintain a high degree of spiritual and intellectual unity, the aim of which was to replace the lack of a state organization. This community was referred to as *społeczeństwo polskie* (Polish Community) and acquired a special connotation.

of the Polish language in public and the intimidation of those who used it in private were accompanied by confiscation of property of those who had participated in the uprising. Poles were also denied the right to acquire landed property in this area, and, in consequence, the influence of the Polish nobility, gentry, and the city-dwellers was seriously impaired. But the social and political system of Russia was such that those who were prepared to co-operate with the Tsarist authorities were allowed to retain in large measure their traditional privileges.

While it is impossible to determine the actual number of Poles settled in the nine western provinces (*gubernia*) of Tsarist Russia, all available statistics suggest that it was about 2·5 million. In the area of Wilno the majority was Polish. In all western provinces Poles owned around 50 per cent of the estates and controlled the greater part of the agriculture and banking.[4]

More important in the minds of the Poles was the fact that in these eastern borderlands many of the outstanding representatives of Poland's political, artistic, and scientific life were born. Adam Mickiewicz, Tadeusz Kościuszko, Stanisław Moniuszko, Eliza Orzeszkowa, and Jarosław Dąbrowski were born in the Lithuanian-Belorussian provinces, whereas Juliusz Słowacki and Ignacy Paderewski came from the Ukraine. The fact that two of the pupils of the same *gymnasium* in Wilno were Feliks Dzierżyński and Józef Piłsudski is symbolic of the role of the Poles from the eastern borderland in Polish society.[5]

The situation in the Polish borderlands was tragic and demoralizing, but it was more than equalled by that in the Polish kingdom. There, too, more intensive efforts were made to assimilate the region to Russia. The Polish language was gradually eliminated from most of the school system, and was barely tolerated at the elementary level. Russian was introduced as the official language even in local administration. To maintain this policy, which lasted almost without relaxation until the outbreak of the First World War, the ten provinces of Congress Poland were subjected to a mixed civil and military rule, and the system of civil administration was assimilated to that used for military purposes. While Russian hostility was primarily directed against the landed gentry and the hierarchy of the Roman Catholic Church, the entire Polish nation was continually reminded that it was nothing but second-class citizens in their own country. The attempt of the Tsarist regime to gain the support of the

---

[4] For a discussion of the ethnographic and economic situation of the Poles in the *Kresy* see Józef Lewandowski, *Federalizm, Litwa i Białoruś w polityce obozu belwederskiego* (Warsaw, 1962), pp. 15–31.

[5] Ibid., p. 17.

peasantry by agrarian reforms proved to be a failure. Indeed, unwill-ingness of the government to keep its promises in this respect only strengthened the sentiment of nationalism which by then penetrated into the lower classes of Polish society.

This policy of oppression was not pursued entirely without inter-ruptions. During the short-lived period of constitutionalism, after the 1905 Revolution, there even seemed to be hope for a Russian-Polish understanding. But the reassertion of Tsarist autocracy frustrated all attempts at conciliation. The Tsarist policies certainly weakened the powers of resistance of some elements of the population, but failed to shake the nationalism of the masses and of most of their leaders.

Polish nationalism was strengthened by the continuing process of industrialization which, having started as early as the 1820s, reached its peak in the first decade of the twentieth century. Central and western parts of Russian Poland, especially the districts of Dąbrowa and Łódź, gradually changed into the most industrialized and there-fore the most prosperous parts of the Tsarist realm. No doubt indus-trial growth and prosperity benefited primarily the predominantly German and Jewish capitalists. It was accompanied by a higher birth- or at least survival-rate. Changes in the economy greatly in-fluenced the social structure of the Polish nation. The politically powerless upper classes – many of them the sons of impoverished and dispossessed members of the *szlachta* – together with the more enter-prising of the urban population, laid the foundation of a middle class. At the other end of the social spectrum, the peasants, after the abolition of serfdom, flocked to the cities and became part of the industrial proletariat.

The situation of the much smaller body of Poles living in the Prussian provinces of Poznań and Pomerania was incomparably worse than that of the Polish subjects of Russia and Austria. Although they belonged before 1866 to the weakest of the three partitioning powers, their association with Prussia was recognized internationally, and was not a matter for diplomatic bargaining.

Ironically, however, what had seemed to be an obvious handicap, was changed into an element of strength. The relatively prosperous peasants of Prussian Poland, who had acquired ownership of their land as early as the first quarter of the nineteenth century, came to realize that they had to rely only on themselves in their struggle against Prussianism. They were able to use those modest civil rights, which they enjoyed within the framework of the Prussian *Rechtsstaat*, as a defence against a policy of ruthless Prussianization. Yet in their struggle for survival the Poles were faced with formidable odds. Not only the government but also a considerable part of the German nation seemed to agree with the Iron Chancellor's opinion of Prussian Poles that 'if we want to continue to exist, we can do nothing else but eradicate them'.[6] Bismarck proceeded, especially after the creation of the German Empire in 1871, to a systematic Germanization of the entire administrative, judicial, and school systems. The Germanization of the Roman Catholic Church reached its height in the period of the so-called *Kulturkampf*, and the attack on the Church was intended also to weaken the Polish culture which it supported.

In keeping with the general view, which identified the Polish nation with the nobility, the gentry, and the church hierarchy, Bismarck directed his attack against these groups of Polish society. Having already scored considerable successes in dispossessing the Polish gentry, he did not expect much opposition from other social groups, particularly the peasant-farmers and the still quite insignificant urban proletariat. This assumption, however, proved to be wrong. In fact, it was the peasants' sentiment of national solidarity and attachment to their native soil, strengthened by their economic power and organizational skill, that enabled the Prussian Poles successfully to resist the policy of Germanization. Beginning in 1886 the Berlin government passed a number of laws aimed at the expropriation of the Polish farms. By 1914 the sum allotted for this task to the Colonization Commission rose to the enormous figure of over one billion marks. But the German efforts remained largely ineffective. Using their closely-knit financial organizations – co-operatives, loan associations, and banks – the Polish landowners and farmers strenuously resisted this policy. They were helped, not only by their greater numbers, but also by the systematic movement of the German population to the industrialized provinces of west Germany. Thus in the years preceding the outbreak of the First World War the Polish element in the Eastern Marches of the German Empire was stronger than at any time before.

The situation of the Upper Silesian Poles was much worse than that of their compatriots in the provinces of Poznań and Pomerania. Despite the almost miraculous survival of their culture after more than five hundred years of separation from Poland, the Polish inhabitants of this province were severely handicapped in their struggle for national survival against the policies of Bismarck. They belonged to the lowest levels of the Upper Silesian social structure – the industrial proletariat and the agricultural workers. The nobility and the middle classes, who in other parts of partitioned Poland sustained the sentiment of national consciousness, here were German. Poles

[6] Bismarck's letter to his sister of 1861 in Otto von Bismarck, *Die gesammelten Werke* (Berlin, 1924–32, 15 vols.), vol. 14/1, p. 568.

found it difficult to resist the ever increasing pressure of the more powerful and wealthy Germans, backed by the state apparatus of Prussia.

The condition of the Polish population of the Austrian sector was very much better than that of their compatriots in either Russia or Prussia. In Austrian Galicia there were practically no attempts at Germanization after 1867, since in this entirely Polish province there was little opportunity for 'ethnic collision' between the Poles and the Austrians.[7] Another factor favouring the Poles was the preservation of the elements of feudalism in the structure of the Habsburg realm almost until the beginning of the twentieth century. It was in this atmosphere that the members of the numerous Polish nobility and gentry managed to assume prominent positions in the Austrian state even before the introduction in 1860 of constitutional government.

In the years preceding the Austro-Hungarian Compromise (1867) the predominantly aristocratic representatives of Galicia pursued a policy alternating between the promotion of federalism and acquiescence, always of course at a price, with the policies of the Viennese government. Unlike the Czechs, who stood for a radical federalization of Austria and after the *Ausgleich* refused to enter the *Reichsrat,* the Poles participated in parliamentary affairs, though they opposed the policy of centralization. In doing so they tried to realize the demands of the Galician Resolution which had been adopted by the Lwów Diet in 1868. It called for an independent status for Galicia within the Austrian part of the dual monarchy. This was a compromise between the views of the federalists and those which demanded autonomy. It was nonetheless unacceptable to the Vienna parliament, in which the feeling for centralization was dominant.

That the Galician Poles nevertheless managed to put into effect many of their national demands was due to the influence of the Polish aristocracy who remained faithful to the Habsburgs. Their ties to the emperor stemmed from a mixture of political realism and dreams of a reborn Poland under the sceptre of the dynasty. Two other factors tended to mitigate the Galician opposition to the empire. Together with the Viennese government, the Poles had a genuine dislike of the Pan-Slavic tendencies in other Slav lands. The pro-Russian inclination of the Czechs was particularly disliked. The Galician gentry, furthermore, feared that the Viennese government would use the discontent of the peasants, both Polish and Ukrainian, as a weapon against them. Whatever its motivation, Polish policy proved in the end to be successful, and gradually changed Galicia into a centre of Polish national life. It played an important role in

[7] Henryk Wereszycki, 'The Poles as Integrating and Disintegrating Factor,' *Austrian History Yearbook,* vol. II, Pt. 2 (1967), p. 292.

the 1863 insurrection and later came to be regarded as the 'all-Polish Piedmont'. After 1873 Poles participated in almost every Austrian government and even occupied key positions, such as that of Prime Minister. They secured for themselves a high degree of self-government, exceeded only by that of the Magyars; they removed all German officials, and had great success in promoting Polish culture.

However impressive the gains of the Galician Poles, they suffered from two fundamental defects : while they helped the Polish national cause, they were even more favourable to the aristocratic minority which until late in the nineteenth century continued to exercise a monopoly of power. The landed aristocracy made no attempt to introduce economic reforms such as those which characterized developments in Prussian and even in Russian Poland. Equally unsuccessful was the half-hearted attempt to find an equitable solution to the Polish-Ruthenian conflict which assumed dangerous proportions in the half-century preceding the outbreak of the First World War. As Alison Phillips has remarked, 'the Poles used the liberties won for themselves to attempt to impose their culture on the Ruthenes. . . .'[8]

The period between 1863 and the outbreak of the First World War is often regarded as entirely different from that of the uprisings which preceded it. 'The year 1863', wrote A. P. Coleman, 'had freed Poland from its old Emigration and from the temptation to create another.'[9] Indeed, it seemed that the pendulum of Polish history, alternating between periods of nationalist activism and of political realism, had swung in the latter direction. What happened immediately after 1863 in Congress Poland and a few years later in Galicia seemed to involve a fundamental change in the mentality of the great majority of the Polish people and of their political leadership. While the nineteenth-century revolutionaries tried desperately to provoke by their own action a military conflict which would lead to the resurrection of their state, the generation after 1863 was preparing for the advent of a European war which some of them regarded as inevitable. Conspiracy and violent methods were almost entirely abandoned, and were replaced by a policy of so-called 'organic work'. Poles in Russian Poland followed the tactics used by the Poles in Prussia, and emphasized the economic and social development of the entire Polish nation. The economic success of the individual came to be regarded as the most acceptable measure of patriotism and as an indication of the growing welfare of the nation.

[8] Alison Phillips, *Poland* (New York, 1915), p. 216.
[9] A. P. Coleman, 'Poland Under Alexander II : The Insurrection of 1863' in *The Cambridge History of Poland* (Cambridge, 1951), vol. 2, p. 386.

Poles refused to accept the spiritual values of the partitioning powers, and rejected assimilation; yet their apparent acquiescence with the fact of foreign rule resulted in acceptance of the external forms of life in the three empires. This was the concept referred to as that of triple loyalty. It found its philosophical justification in the positivism of Auguste Comte, whose rejection of metaphysics and glorification of the human progress to be achieved through science fired the imagination of the Poles. Loyalty to the existing government was both preached and practised by the school of Warsaw positivists, the Kraków historical school, and by the group known as the *Stańczyks*,[10] whose pro-Habsburg policies repudiated the revolutionary past of the Polish nation and urged 'down to earth' practical work for the welfare of both their own class and the nation as a whole.

No doubt certain adherents of the triple-loyalty policy went far in identifying themselves with the governments under which they lived. They thus blurred the idea of ultimate independence and seemed to relegate it to a very distant future. Yet only a minority of Polish leaders, mostly rightist and conservative, could be considered unyielding protagonists of the idea of compromise (*ugoda*), which came to be regarded as agreement at all costs with the imperial powers. Developments in the middle eighties showed that the antithesis between the heroism of the past and the spirit of conformity and practical accommodation of the present was more imaginary than real. The activities of the Warsaw 'collaborators' and of some of the Galician nobility were more than offset by the nationalist trends of the eighties. At this time the Polish League and the first of the socialist organizations both returned to the idea of militant resistance to the partitioning powers. That this change of mind did not express itself in a reversion to the policy of active uprisings was due to a number of factors. Perhaps the most important were the change in the international atmosphere, which became unfavourable to the Polish national aspirations, and the developments in military science rendering any attempt at armed insurrection hopeless.

At the same time important social developments were taking place. The Poles were gradually changing into a modern nation, characterized by a complex social stratification and permeated even to its lowest levels by the idea of national consciousness. Polish nationalism, however, was not the same in the three different parts of Poland. In those provinces which were under the control of Prussia, nationalism was accepted by a relatively large middle class and by a class

---

[10] The group, which formed the basis of the Polish conservative party, was named after a pamphlet entitled *Teka Stańczyka* – the Portfolio of Stańczyk. Stańczyk was the famous jester at the court of Zygmunt the Old (1506–48).

of educated farmers. On the other hand, in Galicia and in that part of Poland which had become an integral part of the Russian Empire, as well as in Congress Poland, the spirit of nationalism had until recently been limited to the nobility. Here Polish national consciousness continued to be influenced by its aristocratic origins and differed in many ways from the nationalism experienced in the West.

The growing political awareness of the Polish people, which coincided with economic growth and social differentiation, was fundamentally affected by the loss of a political focus after 1863. However remarkable their activities, the representatives of the Polish League in Switzerland were nothing more than a pale reflection of the Polish Democratic Society, the communities of the Polish People, and other radical democratic organizations of the period of the Great Emigration. Nor did they achieve the diplomatic splendour of Prince Czartoryski's Hôtel Lambert in Paris. For over a century the Poles, torn apart and divided between three empires, struggled desperately to maintain their spiritual unity. So long as it was nourished by the common spirit of revolt, the Polish nation, despite internal conflicts, seemed to remain intact. When, however, the idea of violent resistance was abandoned and the Polish people replaced their swords with political arguments, elements of disunity, deriving from long years of separation, began to assert themselves. Moreover, considerations of political tactics forced the Poles to pursue different policies in each of the three empires : 'as irredentists or opportunists, in Poznań, Warsaw, and Kraków, they had to use their own methods of resistance or conciliation, when faced with specific dangers or when taking account of specific advantages'.[11]

The first modern political party appeared in Galicia, where it had developed from the conservative group of the *Stańczyks*. The political growth of the Polish nation was, however, marked by the emergence of many parties, divided in their tactics and to a certain degree even in their ultimate aims. Two of these political parties, operating in all the territories inhabited by Poles, became the most important and eventually came to represent the two main political alternatives in the years immediately before and after the First World War. The first embraced the workers' and the socialist parties, which originated in the late sixties. They were first small, conspiratorial groups – small because of lack of economic development, and revolutionary because of the necessity to operate underground. The increased tempo of industrial growth in the eighties, as well as the renewed trend towards political resistance among the Poles, provided a more favourable ground for the growth of the socialist movement. The first two

[11] Henri Grappin, *Les organisations politiques polonaises,* reprint from *Le Monde Slave,* vol. I, No. 6 (1917), pp. 2–3.

socialist organizations to emerge marked also the beginnings of a significant split within the socialist ranks. *Lud Polski* (The Polish People), an organization founded by Bolesław Limanowski in 1880, adopted a variety of socialism which associated practical action by the workers and peasants with the idea of Polish patriotism and revived the traditions of the national uprisings. The second organization, the Socialist Revolutionary Party, referred to as the 'first' *Proletariat*, was founded in 1882 by Ludwik Waryński and accepted a programme of class struggle, emphasizing the principle of solidarity with the workers of other nations and with the Russian revolutionaries. It was this group which, following the example of the Russian 'People's Will', committed acts of violence and terrorism which led ultimately to its forceful suppression.

The general progress of European socialism, as well as the increased class-consciousness of the Polish workers, led in the last decade of the nineteenth century to the emergence of mass socialist parties. Of these by far the most important was the *Polska Partia Socjalistyczna* (Polish Socialist Party) referred to henceforward as the PPS. It owed its origin to a meeting of eighteen socialist leaders in Paris in 1892, for the purpose of creating an all-Polish socialist party. Its programme, worked out by the Union of Polish Socialists Abroad, combined the idea of Polish nationalism and independence with that of socialism which, it was held, could be achieved gradually and even by legal means. Despite its obvious dependence on the 1891 Erfurt Programme of the German Social Democrats, this association of Marxism with the traditional demands of the Polish people and its indirect repudiation of the concept of the dictatorship of the proletariat, gained for the PPS an almost immediate success among the workers. In one respect, however, the PPS programme remained unfulfilled : the socialist leaders were forced to give up the idea of a single united party in favour of three formally independent political organizations. While in Russian Poland the party was restricted to illegal activities, it managed to elect an underground Central Workers' Committee in which Józef Piłsudski, the successful organizer of the Wilno district, early assumed a leading role. In Austrian Poland the Social Democratic Party of Galicia and Silesia operated openly and legally from 1893, and greatly profited from the able leadership of Ignacy Daszyński. In the same year a Polish Socialist Party was founded in Prussian Silesia and the province of Poznań, and worked until 1913 in close co-operation with the German Social Democrats. The existence of separate parties, however, did not deprive Polish socialism, as represented by the PPS ideology, of a high degree of internal solidarity.

While the PPS derived its spiritual parentage from the 'Polish

People', the second important movement in Polish socialism owed its ideals to the *Proletariat*, and rejected outright all traces of nationalism and patriotism. As early as 1893 a group of internationally-minded socialists seceded from the PPS, under the leadership of Julian Marchlewski and the still very young Rosa Luxemburg. Fascinated by the idea of the proletariat 'without country or nationality' and rejecting the demand for Polish independence, these 'true' followers of Karl Marx founded in 1896 the Social Democratic Party which in 1899 – after being joined by the 'Lithuanian', Feliks Dzierżyński – assumed the name of *Socjaldemokracja Królestwa Polskiego i Litwy* (Social Democracy of the Kingdom of Poland and of Lithuania), here referred to as SDKPiL. Despite the theoretical brilliance of its leadership – and perhaps because of it – the SDKPiL could not compete with the PPS, which 'managed to capture the imagination and attract the support of a considerable section of youth who were eager for action'.[12]

The roots of the second and equally important political movement go back to the Polish League, a secret organization founded in Switzerland in 1887. This body returned to the radically democratic ideology of the Polish Democratic Society founded in Paris after 1830. The composition of the League was sufficiently broad to combine the veterans of 1863 with men who, following the example of the Russian Populists, sought to renew national self-confidence by relying on the peasants. Its programme was broad, embracing both revolutionary ideas and diplomatic action and educational work among the people.

In 1894 the organization changed its name to the National League and extended its activities to all three sectors of Poland. Its original leadership was replaced by members of the younger generation amongst whom Roman Dmowski, the future adversary of Józef Piłsudski and the outstanding representative of Polish nationalism, was the most important. The League organized a series of revolutionary acts, the purpose of which was to force the Russian government to make significant concessions to the Poles, and incurred the hostility of the Russian authorities. There were mass arrests, but Dmowski and a few other members of the League managed to escape to the Galician city of Lwów where in 1897 they founded the *Stronnictwo Narodowo-Demokratyczne* (the National Democratic Party). The League and the new party at first subscribed to the revolutionary idea, but by 1902 they had begun to change their policies, abandoning active resistance against Russian domination in favour of Polish-Russian understanding, going so far as to accept Polish independence

[12] M. K. Dziewanowski, *The Communist Party of Poland* (Cambridge, Mass., 1959), p. 26.

within the framework of the Russian Empire. For Dmowski regarded Germany and not Russia as the principal and hereditary enemy of the Poles. He held that all Slavs should unite against the Germanic *Drang nach Osten*, which would inevitably result in a clash between the Tsarist government and that of Imperial Germany backed by her Austrian satellite. After the Russian victory, which Dmowski foresaw, all Poles would be united in one state under the sceptre of the Romanoffs, and by reason of their cultural superiority they would be able to become fully self-governing and eventually independent. This programme of the new 'realism', with its curious mixture of liberal democracy and nationalism, its readiness to use force, and even to countenance a strong undercurrent of anti-semitism, gained support in all parts of Poland, and gave the National Democratic Party a truly national character. It gained the support of the middle class and the intelligentsia, of the rich peasants, the clergy, the middle nobility, and later even of the workers.

The end of the century saw the emergence of other political parties, especially in Galicia which profited in this way from the relatively liberal conditions of Austria. Here the monopoly, although not the influence, of the *Stańczyks* was broken by the emergence of the Democratic Party and, above all, the *Polskie Stronnictwo Ludowe* (Polish People's Party)[13] which represented the peasants and found an able leader in Wincenty Witos. Even the Ukrainian population of eastern Galicia, despite its under-representation in both the Austrian *Reichsrat* and the local Lwów Diet, created a number of political parties. Of these the strongly anti-Polish Ukrainian National Democrats and the Radicals were the most important. In Prussian Poland the desperate resistance to Germanization reduced the tendency to political fragmentation amongst the Poles. An exception was the Christian Democratic Party, founded in Galicia by Wojciech Korfanty, and later established in the other two sections of Poland.

The Russo-Japanese War of 1904–05 and the subsequent revolution within Russia emphasized the fundamental differences between the conflicting political orientations of Dmowski's National Democrats and of Piłsudski's PPS. Nothing expressed the basic divergence of view of these two men better than their simultaneous visit to Tokyo in mid-1904. Piłsudski offered to the Japanese the services of the Polish revolutionaries; Dmowski warned against such action, arguing that it would only harm the interests of the Japanese and be of no use to the Poles. By the end of 1904 Piłsudski had come to regard

---

[13] In 1913 the Polish People's Party split into two groups: the majority one headed by Witos adopted the symbolic title of *Piast*, thus associating itself with the first peasant ruler of the Polish state; the other much smaller group chose the name of Polish People's Party – Left.

Russian defeat as a signal for revolutionary action. He founded within the PPS a special 'Military Organization', charged with the carrying-on of terroristic and belligerent activities against the Russian authorities. The socialist leader did not change his tactics even after having been repudiated by the majority of the PPS leaders. Dmowski followed the opposite course. He warned against acts of violence, and pursued a policy of moderation and political realism. Diplomatic and organizational work, he believed, were the best methods for the gradual achievement of Polish statehood.

Until almost the end of 1905 the militant elements, which could be found both in the ranks of the PPS and the SDKPiL, appeared to enjoy the support of perhaps the majority of the population of the Russian part of Poland. They organized strikes and demonstrations, and clashed not only with the Russian gendarmes and army, but also with the newly-created National Union of Workers organized by the National Democrats to combat the socialists. Towards the end of 1905, however, the situation began to change. The policy of Russification was eased, the Poles were promised representation in the *Duma*, and some of their political parties, including the National Democrats, were granted legal recognition. These measures and even more the October Manifesto, which promised constitutional government, greatly enhanced the position of Roman Dmowski, whose previous analysis of the political situation thus seemed to be confirmed by the course of the Russian revolution. In the elections to the first and second *Duma*, which were boycotted by the socialists, the National Democrats scored a great victory and, for a time at least, it appeared as if the hopes of the Poles would be fulfilled. As chairman of the Polish delegation in the *Duma*, Dmowski later submitted a serious proposal that Congress Poland be given an autonomous position within the Tsarist realm. The acts of the St Petersburg government flagrantly contradicted Polish expectations and failed even to respect the promises of the October Manifesto. The general atmosphere, however, was marked by religious tolerance and a considerable degree of freedom of speech, press, and assembly, and helped to support the hopes of the Polish people and to enhance the prestige of Dmowski and his party.

On the other hand, developments since the end of 1905 damaged the prestige of the PPS and weakened its influence. Party dissension broke out when the Russian Social Democrats, regarded by Piłsudski and his associates as incapable of revolutionary action, suddenly revealed their potentialities. The strikes and demonstrations organized by the socialist militants were mercilessly crushed by the Russian authorities who used the terroristic acts of Piłsudski's Military Organization as a convenient pretext for further reprisals against the people. There was despondency and demoralization in the PPS, which split into two factions. The majority group gave support to the SKDPiL, which publicly rejected the idea of a popular insurrection in favour of an independent Poland, and declared support for a federal and democratic Russia. Finally, at the congress of the PPS held in November 1906 in Vienna, after a protracted struggle, the majority, composed of the younger party leaders, assumed the name of the PPS – Left, clearly indicating its determination to co-operate with the SKDPiL. Piłsudski's group then constituted itself as the PPS – Revolutionary Fraction. Thus the fratricidal conflict between the two socialist groups served to gain further support for Dmowski's policy.

The change which set in after the dissolution of the second *Duma* – while not strengthening the socialists – gave a fatal blow to Dmowski's entire political concept. The reduction of Polish representation in the greatly weakened *Duma* was associated with a gradual return to the oppressive practices and Russification of the Tsarist bureaucracy. Almost immediately Dmowski began to lose the support of those who regarded his political tactics only as the first step towards full independence, and many returned again to a policy of armed resistance. Dmowski's attempts to organize the neo-Slav movement in 1908, in conjunction with the Czech political leader, Karel Kramář, demonstrated the consistency of his political convictions, but was nevertheless a failure. Whatever its intentions with regard to the solution of the Polish question within the framework of liberal Russia might have been, Russian liberalism was not given a chance. It is not surprising that Dmowski, whose policy was dependent on the victory of liberal constitutionalism in Russia, lost control of his own party. In 1909 he resigned from the *Duma*.

Meanwhile Józef Piłsudski, undaunted by the failure of his revolutionary movement in Congress Poland, transferred his activities to Galicia, since 1863 regarded as a centre of Polish national life. There he took over the command of the illegal organization, the 'League of Active Struggle', and encouraged the growth of a number of other para-military organizations. Of these the most important were the Associations of Riflemen (*Strzelcy*) which after 1910 were allowed to operate openly with the blessing of and some help from the Austrian government. The political counterpart of the military organizations was the so-called Council of the Confederated Parties of Independence, to which members of the Polish People's Party, the Galician Social Democrats, and the PPS, as well as adherents of other splinter groups of the National Democrats, belonged. The aim of this not inconsiderable grouping was to support Piłsudski's endeavour to create a Polish army. Like Dmowski, Józef Piłsudski also foresaw the outbreak of a European war. Unlike his rival, however, he saw the place of Poland on the side of Austria and therefore also of Germany. But his overriding objective was Polish independence. To promote its cause, he was convinced, the Poles must have an army of their own so that in the chaotic situation that was likely to follow the end of the war, they could rely on their own strength. He firmly believed that only thus would it be possible to create by a series of daring *faits accomplis* a strong and unified Poland.

The political defeat in the period of the 1905 revolution did not diminish the stature of Roman Dmowski, nor the validity of his concept of Polish-Russian co-operation – a vision to which such men as Prince Adam Czartoryski and Marquess Alexander Wielopolski had dedicated their efforts.

The First World War and its Aftermath

Thus on the eve of the outbreak of the First World War Piłsudski and Dmowski assumed leading positions in the Polish nation, 'each becoming a symbolic representative of two ways of political thinking and two fundamentally different approaches towards policy problems'.[14]

While the war, which broke out in August 1914, soon became universal, it was not easy for the Poles to recognize it – in the sense of Mickiewicz's vision – as 'a universal war for the liberation of peoples'. The two traditional foes of Polish freedom, the Russians and the Germans, faced each other as enemies, so that a real danger existed that the victory of either might result in the subjugation of all Polish lands under one foreign rule. Moreover, the Poles, whose territories were to suffer that brunt of this first total war, were forced to fight each other as soldiers in the armed forces of the three empires. Their political leadership was faced with an awesome choice. Indeed, the problem of political orientation – with Russia and the Central Powers being the main alternatives – became the basic issue of Polish national existence.

The first and immediate decision was made by Józef Piłsudski, former leader of the PPS and commander of the Associations of Riflemen. Moved by his bitter resentment of Russia[15] and without

---

14 Wereszycki, op. cit., p. 250.
15 Piłsudski's hatred of Russia was influenced not only by his family traditions, but also by his five-year banishment to Siberia. Referring to this tragic experience, he wrote: 'Above all, I have been fundamentally cured of all remnants of past Russian influence. In Siberia I began to hate even more this Asiatic monster covered by a European veneer.'

See 'Jak stałem sie socialistą' (How I Became a Socialist) in *Promień, Pismo póswięcone sprawom młodzeży szkolnej* (Lwów, 1903), No. 8–9, as quoted in Wilhelm Feldman, *Dzieje polskiej myśli politicznej 1864–1914* (Warsaw, 1933), p. 260.

waiting for the news from the war fronts, he threw his minuscule free corps against the Tsarist army. In order to increase the authority of this adventurous undertaking, he declared that he was acting on behalf of a fictitious National Government which, he claimed, had illegally sprung up in Warsaw. This government, he held, appointed him commander-in-chief of the Polish armed forces. If Piłsudski had expected a general uprising in Congress Poland, developments proved him utterly wrong. On the contrary, the declaration of August 1914 by the Grand Duke Nicholas, commander-in-chief of the Russian army, promised unity and self-government for all Poles under the rule of the Tsar. It aroused great enthusiasm among a large part of the population whose rightist representatives declared their loyalty to Russia.

However much applauded by the members of the younger generation, especially in eastern Galicia (and indirectly obstructed by the conservative pro-Austrian elements who feared its revolutionary implications), the partisan-type insurrection urged by Piłsudski in Congress Poland would have endangered not only the cause of the Western Allies but also that of Poland. There seems to be little doubt that a fully-fledged uprising in the western territories of the Tsarist Empire would have seriously affected the Russian mobilization. Consequently, it would have rendered difficult, if not impossible, the diversion improvised by the Russian army at the time of the battle of the Marne, which forced the German command to transfer troops from the West to the East so that the 'two corps that came too late for Tannenberg were to be absent from the Marne'.[16] Almost instinctively, the Polish people in Russian Poland refused to obey Piłsudski's summons. They thus helped to decide 'one of the decisive battles of the world', and in consequence enabled the Western Allies to continue the war and assure both their own and also Poland's ultimate victory.

Although of almost no military significance, this first Polish participation in the First World War helped greatly to build up the personality of Piłsudski. More important was the replacement of the Council of Confederated Parties of Independence by the Supreme National Committee (NKN). The latter united most of the Galician political parties and was entrusted with the organization of Polish Legions, of which the members of the Piłsudski corps were to become the cadres. The committee was dominated by the pro-Habsburg elements, who thought, along with Viennese court circles, in terms of the annexation of Congress Poland and the granting to the Poles of a position similar to that enjoyed by the Hungarians within a reorganized triple empire. This concept was soon proved to be impracticable, in the main be-

[16] Barbara W. Tuchman, *The Guns of August* (New York, 1962), p. 309.

cause of Hungarian and German opposition, but it lingered on in one form or another almost until the end of the war, and greatly influenced the policies of the Galician Poles.

Piłsudski realized the urgent need to secure support from the Austro-Hungarian military command. Accordingly, he did not directly oppose this development, even though it deprived him of the supreme command of the Polish forces, which was entrusted to a Galician Pole serving as an officer in the Austrian army. Nor did he reject the oath of allegiance to Emperor Francis Joseph required of the legionnaires. Yet, in order to maintain a minimum degree of independence, Piłsudski insisted, at least for a time, on the subordination of all Polish organizations, including the Legions, to the fictitious, illegal government created by him in Warsaw. At the same time, he tried to establish direct contacts with the Germans, apparently in order to achieve more independence from Austrian control. That there was constant tension between the Galician political leadership and Piłsudski is evident from the personal feud which developed between him and Władysław Sikorski, the head of the military department of the Supreme National Committee, a conflict which was to have far-reaching political repercussions in the post-1918 Polish republic.

Despite the many obstacles standing in his way, Brigadier Piłsudski, who became commander of the famous First Brigade, succeeded very early in gaining great popularity among the Poles. In fact, his military reputation was much greater than the feats of his still rather small contingent warranted. For Piłsudski's main strength consisted in his political ability. This strength lay in his refusal to accept clear-cut commitments and his conspiratorial talent. Particularly effective was his shrewd mixture of legal and illegal activities, the latter being constantly used as a means to secure for his Polish forces as much legal freedom of action as possible.

Such was the initial purpose of the underground 'Polish Military Organization' which in theory existed after October-November 1914 as an organization parallel to the 'official' Legions. Despite its highly fictitious nature, even at this early stage it provided the means for political and diplomatic manoeuvres and enabled Piłsudski to oversell the value of the Polish contribution to the war. But as time passed the Legions increased in size. They were divided into three brigades,[17] and participated more prominently in the war against Russia.

In mid-1915 the German and Austro-Hungarian forces occupied Congress Poland. This event seemed to offer new opportunities for

---

[17] In addition to the famous First Brigade of Piłsudski, there was the Second Brigade commanded by Colonel Józef Haller, and the less prominent Third, under the command of Bolesław Roja and Mieczysław Norwid-Neugebauer.

unification and for at least a modest degree of self-government, and was regarded by Piłsudski and his associates as inaugurating a new chapter in the Polish struggle for emancipation. They soon realized, however, that the Central Powers had no intention of promoting the cause of Polish independence. It was for this reason that after the fall of Warsaw to the Germans Piłsudski urged former Russian subjects, who volunteered to fight against the Tsarist armies, to join the ranks not of the Legions but of the Polish Military Organization which was under his personal control. Russian Poland was divided into two zones of occupation by the Central Powers, who thereupon introduced a regime which did not inspire the Poles with any degree of confidence. The Germans in particular ruthlessly exploited their sector by using its natural resources and recruiting its workers for the purposes of their own war effort. These losses were not altogether balanced by a more tolerant cultural policy which enabled the Poles to reopen the University of Warsaw.

For many months the Polish issue remained at a standstill. The new occupying powers were unable to come to a decision regarding the future of the country. Oppression and inactivity brought about disillusionment and even discord within both the Legions and the Polish political organizations, which the military administration allowed to continue. Among them, the Inter-Party Political Circle, inspired by the National Democrats, played a significant role. Its policy was one of non-involvement with the occupying authorities, and was referred to as 'Passivist'. It was, however, motivated not only by the secret contacts which its leaders maintained with Dmowski, but also by the unwillingness of many of its members to take any unnecessary risks.

When, towards the end of 1915, the Germans made a few half-hearted concessions to Polish demands, an opportunity was provided for the radically anti-Russian independence parties. They seized it and formed, on Piłsudski's advice, the so-called Central National Committee. Known as the 'Activist' group, the Committee declared itself in favour of a fully independent state to be protected by its own armed forces. Yet appeals of the independence parties to Vienna and Berlin had little effect, causing an ever-increasing frustration over the policies of the Central Powers in Poland. By September 1916 even Piłsudski, profoundly disturbed by the results of his tactics, openly voiced his disagreement and determined to resign the command of the Legions. At this juncture they were changed into a 'Polish Auxiliary Corps', attached to the Austro-Hungarian army.

Ironically enough, it was the German need for manpower, caused by the tremendous losses at Verdun, rather than the endeavours of the 'Activists', which forced the Central Powers to inaugurate a policy of more significant concessions. On 5 November 1916 they announced the creation of a hereditary and constitutional Kingdom of Poland which was to include only unspecified former Russian provinces and be closely associated with the two allied powers. Germany was to control the army, which was to be organized in order to fight the Russians, and also the foreign policy of this new 'independent' state. Despite the subsequent creation of a twenty-two-member Council of State, in which Piłsudski became responsible for military affairs, the position of the 'Activists' remained extremely difficult. The proposed army was to be nothing more than an adjunct of the *Reichswehr*, and the competence of the Council of State was narrowly defined and only of an advisory character. The attempts to create a truly Polish army by changing the Polish Military Organization into a legal body were countered by the German assumption of full control over the Legions, which were to become the core of the future 'Polish Armed Forces' (*Polnische Wehrmacht*).

The tragic dilemma of Piłsudski, who at first accepted the humiliating position within the Council of State, was resolved by developments in Russia. The Russian Revolution of February 1917 changed radically the entire situation of the Polish nation. The programme of federalization announced by the provisional Russian government exceeded anything offered by the Germans. This 'unexpected growth of Polish possibilities and hopes'[18] fundamentally changed the political outlook even of those who until recently had advocated co-operation with the Germans and Austrians. At the beginning of May Piłsudski and his followers refused to support the concept of a German-directed army and opposed the German plans in the Council of State. In July they tendered their resignations from that body. The conflict with the Germans reached its height when the majority of the legionnaires, following Piłsudski's instructions, refused to take the oath of allegiance to the German emperor. Not long after that Piłsudski found himself a prisoner of the Germans in the Magdeburg fortress. Whatever his previous policies might have been, his captivity at the hands of the Germans, who had singled him out as a man dedicated solely to the cause of Polish independence, greatly increased his political prestige and popularity among the people.

Realizing that at last the question of Polish independence had become an international one, the Council of State pressed for further concessions and demanded the reunion and independence of all Polish lands. As a result, in the second half of 1917, the Central Powers appointed a Regency Council to act as a provisional head of

[18] Hans Roos, *A History of Modern Poland* (New York and London, 1966), p. 25.

the Polish state. They permitted the formation of a Council of Ministers, and entrusted the Poles with limited legislative and administrative rights. Indeed, the Bolshevik Revolution and its threat of agrarian reform tended to revive the idea of German-Polish co-operation. This tendency was reflected in the behaviour of the Polish First Army Corps, headed by General J. Dowbór-Muśnicki, which was established in Russia in the summer of 1917, following the March Revolution. The general operated in the Belorussian and east Lithuanian area, which he claimed for the Polish state, and recognized the authority of the Regency Council. By the end of January 1918 his troops had clashed with the Bolsheviks. The struggle against Bolshevism was motivated by a combination of social and national considerations. The communist agrarian reforms were a menace to much of the traditional Polish Eastern Marches. Here the landowners and wealthier classes constituted the essentially Polish part of the population. There was yet another reason which seemed to justify the continuation of good German-Polish relations. No doubt, even the members of the Regency Council and of the governments appointed by it realized that the focus of the Polish struggle for liberation had shifted to the west. They did not want, however, to miss any chance of increasing their power and authority which, they believed, would enable them to serve as a stabilizing element in the anarchical conditions following the final collapse of the Central Powers.

Whatever shreds of belief in German goodwill the organs of this 'Polish state' might have possessed, all were destroyed by the Treaty of Brest-Litovsk (Brześć), signed on 9 February 1918, by which Germany and Austria abandoned their Polish 'ally' and granted to the new Ukrainian state the purely Polish district of Chełm and promised the Ruthenian parts of Galicia and Bukowina the status of an autonomous Austro-Hungarian Crown Land. This development brought about the final breach between the Polish armies operating in the Eastern Marches and the Germans. The First Army Corps, unable to fight both the Germans and the Bolsheviks at the same time, was forced to demobilize. The Second Corps, on the other hand, was strengthened by General Haller's Second Brigade, which broke through the Austrian lines after the Treaty of Brest-Litovsk and refused to capitulate. It laid down its arms only after three days of desperate fighting in the battle of Kanióv, in the Ukraine.

The continued participation of the Regency Council in the ludicrous search for the 'future Polish King' was little more than a sham. Its main purpose was to use the confusion and uncertainty in the east to urge the return of some at least of the border provinces to Poland. This, the Council emphasized, would be 'the best protection for Central Europe against the East'. Almost until the final collapse of the German government the Regency Council was still able to assert its authority. It appointed governments, carried out elections for the Council of State, and even raised a special Polish Defence Force. But the military and political developments, particularly the disintegration of Austria-Hungary, undermined the very foundations of the political system which the Regency Council created. Even its members realized that in the revolutionary atmosphere of post-war Europe they had become an anachronism, and could not long remain. After the separation of Galicia from Austria, on 31 October 1918, the government in Warsaw was overwhelmed. It could take no action against the short-lived Polish republic, established by Ignacy Daszyński in Lublin on 7 November. The Regency Council realized the great popularity of Józef Piłsudski, 'whose personality for many people then served as a political programme',[19] and decided to give him full support in the belief that he alone could stand at the helm of a reborn Poland. On 11 November 1918, one day after Piłsudski's release from prison, the Council appointed him supreme commander of the Polish armed forces. Three days later, it withdrew entirely from the political scene, delivering its power into the hands of Piłsudski who was given the title of Chief of State. This development enabled him to devote all his energy to the establishment of order in the country and the building of a new government.

It might be assumed that Polish independence stemmed predominantly from the efforts, both political and military, of the parties and groups within Poland. In reality, however, the decisive factor in Poland's resurrection was the final victory of the Western Powers and the activities on the side of the Allies of the Polish liberation movement.

Obviously, the original promises of the Russians, who permitted Roman Dmowski and Count Zygmunt Wielopolski to organize a National Committee, would have been of little consequence, had the Tsarist autocracy remained in power. The latter was, at most, prepared to make concessions at the expense of the Central Powers. It was the first Russian Revolution that, aiming at an independent Polish state and army, started a train of events which enabled the Western Allies openly to take up the problem of Polish freedom. Whatever its ultimate aim, the principle of self-determination proclaimed by Lenin served only to emphasize the international significance of the Polish issue.

However, the Polish pro-Allied liberation movement goes back to a much earlier date. It was given a great impetus after Roman Dmowski had departed from Moscow to London in 1915, where he

[19] Andrzej Ajnenkiel, *Od 'Rządów ludowych' do przewrotu majowego* (Warsaw, 1964), p. 21.

directed a propaganda campaign in all the Allied countries. The United States was not bound by any of the obligations which until 1917 tied the hands of the Western Powers. Even before her entry into the war she provided an ideal base for a movement which would necessarily have to be overwhelmingly in favour of the Allies. The organizations of Americans of Polish extraction found an eloquent spokesman in the great pianist Ignacy Paderewski, who spoke up for the Poles first to Colonel House and through him to President Woodrow Wilson. As early as January 1917, Wilson referred to Polish freedom as one of the conditions of peace. In August 1917, Roman Dmowski assumed the presidency of a widespread organization, the Polish National Committee, which established its headquarters in Paris and had representatives in the capitals of the major Allied Powers. Of these by far the most influential was Paderewski himself, who used his moral authority to urge Polish immigrants in America to join the Polish army organized in France by General Józef Haller, who had managed to escape to the West. Before the year was over, the Committee was recognized by all the Allied governments. Its position was greatly strengthened by Wilson's Fourteen Points, which clearly distinguished the genuinely pro-Polish attitude of the United States from that of the Germans and Austrians, then engaged in the negotiations with the Russians at Brześć.

These events were followed by further agreements between the Polish National Committee and the West European Allies. In June 1918, the latter declared themselves in favour of Polish independence, which they termed 'one of the most important guarantees of peace in Europe'. The existence of the Warsaw Regency Council, however, prevented the Allied governments from going further and recognizing the Committee, which they already regarded as the sole representative of Poland, as the government of that country. Paderewski's efforts to bring about an agreement which would enable at least some representatives of the Polish leftist independence parties to join the National Committee foundered on Dmowski's determined resistance. He reproached Piłsudski – and even more the entire Regency Council in Warsaw – for having pursued a pro-German policy.

Thus, when the war ended, the age-old, dual orientation of Polish political life towards West and East, represented by the names of Piłsudski and Dmowski, appeared clearer than ever before. In certain respects there seemed to be agreement between the two antagonists. Both favoured a strong and militarily defensible Poland. Both were ardent patriots and pursued a policy of Polish national interest as they saw it. Yet their political outlook and ultimate aims, as well as the methods they used in promoting Poland's cause, were as different as their personalities. Piłsudski was first and foremost a soldier who believed in the necessity of military discipline and scorned elaborate political programmes and speeches. His few statements embodying a political programme, apart from their emphasis on the army, remained terse and vague. He spoke of 'honour and justice' as those symbols of life which alone could provide a synthesis between individual freedom and man's obligations to society and nation. The 'new Polish man', whose creation Piłsudski declared to be his main political aim, was predicated on the need to induce a military, even a martial, psychology to the whole society. Socialism, to which he originally subscribed, attracted him not by its ideology, but by its revolutionary spirit which, Piłsudski held, coincided with the ideology and tactics of the Polish uprisings. His motto, 'romanticism in aims and realism in methods', revealed him as a leader who, in accordance with the precepts of military strategy and tactics, was capable of using any variety of means, including conspiracy and deception, to achieve his ends.

Dmowski's thinking was both more profound and more complex. He brought a more rational approach to political matters, and tried with an almost doctrinaire obstinacy to adopt a world outlook. His political profile was that of a typical intellectual with conservative leanings. His programme of nationalism – unlike that of his rival – was carefully elaborated; it included not only the creation of a strong centralized state, but also the adoption of the principle of social harmony, and a systematic furthering of commercial and industrial development. A theoretician rather than a man of action, Dmowski used more conventional tactics, determined to a great extent by his political aims.

Neither Piłsudski nor Dmowski could be regarded as adherents of Western-type democracy. Piłsudski's belief in the supremacy of the military and his choice of methods could not be reconciled with the slow and unwieldy processes of the parliamentary system. While more favourable to parliamentary processes, Dmowski and his party had serious prejudices, such as anti-semitism and a determination to assimilate non-Polish nationalities.

One of the first post-war issues on which Dmowski and Piłsudski crossed swords was the question of Poland's future borders. Piłsudski was fascinated by the grandeur of the Jagiellonian tradition and looked forward to the expansion of Polish influence and power by associating in a federal union the nationalities on the western fringes of Russia. Dmowski, on the other hand, was prepared to give up a large part of the pre-1772 eastern possessions of Poland, but exceeded that limit in the west by demanding a longer sea coast and parts of Upper Silesia. He rejected Piłsudski's federalization plans as dangerous and impractical. Instead, he favoured the building-up of an

ethnically homogeneous state, including only those non-Polish territories which had for centuries been within the Polish cultural sphere
and contained important Polish minorities.

Whatever the merits of the two points of view might have been,
the Chief of State and generalissimo was in a position of absolute
ascendancy not only in Warsaw but also in Kraków. He was widely
acclaimed as the saviour 'of the Polish soul' from its frequent tendency towards 'anarchy, disobedience, and weakness'. His exploits as
commander of the Legions and as a fearless opponent of all three
partitioning powers stood him in good stead in the eyes of the masses.
The socialists, disregarding Piłsudski's rather surprising deal[20] with
the Regency Council, hailed him as the builder of future socialist
Poland.

After the failure of the short-lived and radical socialist cabinet of
Daszyński, who willingly liquidated his Lublin People's Republic,
Piłsudski appointed the relatively moderate socialist government of
Moraczewski, who was supported by the PPS and the left-wing
People's Party. Soon, however, the Chief of State realized that only
through co-operation with Dmowski's Polish National Committee
could he and his government receive recognition and sorely needed
help from the Entente. After prolonged negotiations Ignacy Paderewski, a non-party man acting as the representative of the Committee, came first to the National Democratic stronghold of Poznań,
which was still in German hands, and then in the first days of January 1919 to Warsaw. Soon after his arrival an abortive attempt to
seize power was made by rightist elements, including the National
Democrats. Despite rumours that Paderewski had given support to
the conspirators, or perhaps because of them, Piłsudski rather wisely
agreed to an understanding between the Paris National Committee
and his own government. On 16 January 1919 Paderewski became
premier and Foreign Minister of independent Poland. It was in this
capacity that he and Dmowski assumed the responsibility of leading
the Polish delegation to the Paris Peace Conference.

The Polish Phoenix

The defeat of the Central Powers, the unification of Polish political
leadership, and its recognition by the Allied Powers were only the
first steps towards rebuilding the state. Poland was recognized as a
state, but it included only the former Russian sector of Poland and
over half of Galicia. Large territories, claimed by the Poles both in
the west and the east, remained beyond its control. The struggle to

[20] By this step, the purpose of which was to gain an independent non-party
position, Piłsudski indicated that he no longer regarded himself as the leader
of the Polish working class. See Wereszycki, op. cit., p. 352.

secure its boundaries took place at two levels – at the conference table and on the battlefield. Piłsudski had achieved a dominant position in Warsaw. Though at heart he had never accepted Dmowski's formula, he nevertheless allowed him to present his own version of the Polish territorial demands to the Paris Peace Conference.

Early in December 1918, long before the start of the conference, a Supreme People's Council representing all Poles in the German Empire rose in Poznań and took control of the province. It recognized the orders of the Dmowski National Committee, but soon came under the *de facto* control of the Warsaw government. Leadership was assumed by members of the pro-Piłsudski Polish Military Organization, which used the German-Polish clashes occasioned by Paderewski's visit to Poznań to begin a general anti-German uprising.

The issue of the Polish western borders became an important cause of friction between the French and the British. In Clemenceau, the indomitable fighter of French politics, the Poles gained an ardent supporter, who regarded their country as a guarantee against the spread of Bolshevism and a potential ally against the resurgence of German aggressiveness. The British Prime Minister, David Lloyd George, suspicious of French designs to gain hegemony in Europe, opposed Polish claims, covering up his action by extending the principle of self-determination also to defeated Germany.

Despite the relatively favourable reports of the committees of experts and the efforts of Dmowski and Paderewski, the Polish demand for the incorporation of the Poznań province, Pomerania, the south-eastern part of East Prussia, and Upper Silesia, as well as the area and city of Danzig, ran into serious opposition in the Allied Supreme Council. French support for the Poles was wisely linked up with the overall problem of European security. But the French argument, associated as it was with an urgent request for the return to the 1814 Franco-German borders, served more to weaken than to uphold the position of Poland. Lloyd George regarded it as another manoeuvre of the French aimed at establishing their supremacy on the European continent. It was then that he suggested the replacement of proposed strategic boundaries, which he considered a 'typical military view',[21] by a diplomatic solution – extending to France a joint military guarantee by Great Britain and the United States, which would protect her against any future German attack. Clemenceau's reluctant acceptance of this plan, which contained the elements of the future Locarno Agreement, further weakened Poland's diplomatic position.

After protracted and at times very heated negotiations the verdict

[21] David Lloyd George, *The Truth About the Peace Treaties* (London, 1938), vol. I, p. 392.

of the Treaty of Versailles, which dealt only with the Polish-German boundaries, gave Poland considerably less than she had possessed in 1772. Danzig was set up as a 'free city' under the sovereignty of the League of Nations, but was later associated with Poland in a customs union. The actual boundary of Poznań and Pomerania ran to the east of the line demanded by the Poles, and dangerously narrowed the Polish access to the sea, which indeed assumed the nature of a 'Corridor'. As the results of the plebiscite of July 1920 showed, the decision of the Versailles Treaty clauses relating to the disputed areas of Allenstein (Olsztyn) and Marienwerder (Kwidzyń) amounted to a decision favouring the German point of view.[22]

Even greater difficulties were encountered with regard to Upper Silesia, which was not part of pre-1772 Poland[23]. Having abandoned its original plan to transfer a major part of this area directly to Poland, the treaty entrusted the final decision to a plebiscite to be held under the supervision of an Allied Commission. This provision, however, became a source of constant friction between the two countries, which resulted in three insurrections of the Polish workers led by the nationalist Wojciech Korfanty. The last insurrection, which was effectively checked by bands of German nationalists, the *Selbstschutz* and *Freikorps*, took place when the plebiscite had been completed. The Germans received 59·6 per cent of all votes. Encouraged by the British, who feared the consequences of any substantial economic weakening of the Reich, the Germans claimed the entire province, insisting that it must be considered as a whole. On 20 October 1921 the final decision of the Conference of Ambassadors was made known. Poland received 76 per cent of the coal-mines, 90 per cent of the coal reserves, 97 per cent of the admittedly small iron-ore deposits, and a major part of the industrial enterprises.[24]

Lastly, the determination of the western border led, as early as December 1918, to an unfortunate dispute and clash over the territory of Teschen between Poland and Czechoslovakia, both creations of the Paris peace settlement, whose origin and national interest would have seemed to dictate close co-operation.[25] For almost 600 years the duchy of Teschen had formed an integral part first of

[22] The Polish government was highly suspicious of the July 1920 plebiscites in which only a very small percentage of Mazurians and Warmians voted in favour of Poland.

[23] See above, p. 34.

[24] See R. L. Buell, *Poland: Key to Europe* (New York and London, 1939), p. 72.

[25] Tomáš Masaryk, the first President of Czechoslovakia, pointed to the necessity of collaboration in a study entitled *New Europe,* published for private circulation in 1918 in London, writing that 'without a free Poland there will be no free Bohemia, and if Bohemia is not free Poland cannot be free either'.

Bohemia and then of the Habsburg possessions. The historical and economic arguments of the Czechoslovaks were countered by Polish emphasis on ethnic considerations. The Polish claim was overwhelming in the area east of the Olza (Olše) river and in the southern part of the duchy. It was very much weaker when applied to the central part of the province, inhabited largely by the so-called *Ślązaks* who spoke a dialect transitional between Polish and Czech and had a cultural background different from that of the Galician Poles. Many of them claimed a separate identity and in the post-war territorial conflict they sided with Czechoslovakia. The Czechoslovak economic claims were also well founded. The loss of the entire province would have deprived the country not only of the valuable iron- and steelworks at Třinec, but also of coal and coke from the Karviná basin, the chief source of fuel for the Czech industrial cities of Moravská Ostrava and Vítkovice.

Many solutions were proposed, including a plebiscite. The Conference of Ambassadors, acting on the basis of the directives of the Allied Conference at Spa, then announced on 27 July 1920 a partition of the former duchy of Teschen. Both Třinec and the Karviná basin were left in Czechoslovakia, and the rest was adjudged to Poland. At the same time the small districts of Spiš and Orava in Slovakia were also divided, and small areas awarded to Poland.

This decision, reached when the Russian offensive against Poland was at its height, had disastrous consequences on the relations between the two nations. It underscored their political and psychological divergences. It contributed to a political psychosis which, in September 1938, led to the forceful annexation of the Czechoslovak part of the province of Teschen by Poland whose Foreign Minister, Józef Beck, could not forego the 'opportunity' to profit from the dictate of Munich.

While the western border of Poland was determined mainly by peaceful and diplomatic means, the decision in the east was, in the last analysis, left to the force of arms. However deplorable this development might have been, a number of factors made it inevitable. In the first place, chaos and anarchy in the former border areas of Russia, which resulted from the loosening of the hidden forces of nationalism and social discontent, precluded a solution by rational means. Secondly, the policies of the Western Powers were inconclusive and even contradictory; they were unable to decide one way or the other about the Bolshevik Revolution; they did not want to get involved in the problems of Poland's eastern borders. Even more decisive, perhaps, was the audacious policy of Piłsudski, who had never abandoned his federalist schemes and thought the situation favourable for a strong East European federal state under Poland's leadership. He also believed that, once and for all, it might be possible to cripple the power of 'Muscovy'. To achieve this aim, while not entirely rejecting the idea of negotiation, he relied on the prowess and dedication of the constantly growing Polish armed forces.

That romanticism prevailed over his usually realistic assessment of the political and military potentialities of his country is clear from the speech he gave in January 1920 at Lublin. Analysing what he regarded as Poland's great dilemma, he stated :

> Is she to be a state on the level of equality with the Great Powers of the world, or a small state under the protection of the mighty? We have to make a great effort . . . if we want to turn the wheel of history so that Poland can become the greatest military and cultural power in the entire East [of Europe].[26]

Not surprisingly, the Lithuanians, Belorussians, and Ukrainians, themselves imbued with the same strong spirit of nationalism as that which motivated the Poles, resented his grandiose plans to reduce them to mere instruments in the policy of others. Sentiment in the West, with the exception of the French military headed by Marshal Foch, even remained sceptical of Piłsudski's policies. This cautious attitude was best expressed by the Allied treatment of the Polish-Ukrainian conflict in eastern Galicia, which broke out immediately after the collapse of Austria. At first, the Western Powers questioned the wisdom of retaining eastern Galicia within the Polish state, and thus indirectly gave support to Piłsudski's belief in a policy of *faits accomplis*. Nevertheless, his policy proved effective. More than anything else, brilliant manoeuvres by the Polish army, which routed the Ukrainian troops, moved the Allied Supreme Council to acquiesce, at the end of June 1919, in the Polish occupation of the whole of eastern Galicia.

By contrast, the provisions of the Treaty of Saint-Germain, which subsequently transferred sovereignty over this formerly Austrian territory to the Western Allies, were of little consequence. In particular, the decision of the Peace Conference, declaring eastern Galicia to be a League of Nations mandate whose status would be reconsidered by the League's Council within the period of twenty-five years, seemed especially ludicrous.

The events in Galicia, however, were only a prelude to the developing conflict between Poland and the Bolshevik government in Moscow. As early as December 1918 the Red Army started its drive westward, replacing the independent governments of Belorussia, Lithuania, and the Ukraine by radically socialist republics. Thus, by the

---

[26] Józef Piłsudski, *Pisma zbiorowe* (10 vols., Warsaw, 1937–38), vol. V, p. 138.

beginning of the following February, the cities of Minsk, Wilno, and finally Kiev fell into Bolshevik hands.

Such developments were a serious threat to Piłsudski's federal plans. His pride and patriotism were particularly hurt by the capture of the capital (Wilno) and a large part of his native Lithuania, whose union with Poland was the cornerstone of his ambitious federal system. That others thought in similar terms was proved by Paderewski who, in April 1919, submitted in Paris a plan to create a 'united States of Eastern Europe'. Soon afterwards the Poles began their offensive. The capture of Wilno, a personal triumph for Piłsudski, was accompanied by the creation of a special office of Civil Administration for Eastern Territories, directly subordinated to himself. On 22 April Piłsudski issued his manifesto in which he promised Lithuania full autonomy in the solution of its 'internal national and religious affairs'. Less encouraging, however, were the actions of the Lithuanians in Kovno (Kaunas), where an independent republic was proclaimed. Instead of joining Piłsudski's federation, they insisted on the return of Wilno as capital of a Lithuanian state. Undaunted by this momentary failure, the Polish armies continued their drive to the north-east, occupying a large part of what had formerly been the duchy of Lithuania.

Polish success was due largely to the civil war in Russia itself. This struggle fascinated Piłsudski, but he maintained an attitude of neutrality. Indeed, he believed that anarchy and chaos in the border areas of former Tsarist Russia would encourage the emergence of other independent states, especially in the Caucasus, which would become natural allies of a Polish-led federation.

The Polish attitude was thus a significant factor in the final defeat of the counter-revolutionary armies in Russia. 'Piłsudski neither had faith in the ultimate triumph of the Whites in Russia nor did he desire it, knowing full well their poltical outlook'[27] which they expressed in their principle of 'Russia one and indivisible'. Hence he refused the French demand that Poland come to the aid of Denikin. He was unwilling to assume the role of 'the gendarme of Europe' without adequate compensation. Nor did he see any threat in the military conflict between Denikin and the armies of the eastern Ukraine, which accelerated the collapse of the counter-revolutionary effort in the south-eastern part of the Tsarist Empire. On the contrary, the short-lived emergence of independent western Ukraine seemed to play into his hands. Red Army pressure forced his former enemy, Hetman Symon Petliura, to seek his friendship and to agree

[27] Piotr S. Wandycz, *France and Her Eastern Allies 1919–1925* (Minneapolis, 1962), p. 128.

to the cession of eastern Galicia and western Wołyń to Poland. At the same time Piłsudski was able to regroup and strengthen his armies, and gradually to penetrate deeper into the Ukraine.

In December 1919 the Supreme Council, still divided on the policy to be adopted towards Russia, made a public statement on the Polish eastern boundary. Its attempt to fix, even on a tentative basis, the maximum eastern limits of the territories considered 'incontestably Polish' served no useful purpose. Militarily, it was in strange contradiction with the actual situation, since the Polish armies, with full knowledge and even tacit approval of the Western Allies, were already established on average about 180 miles to the east of the proposed 'tentative' line. The Supreme Council's decision, ostensibly based on ethnic considerations, would have deprived Poland of the cities of Wilno and Lwów, which in addition to being predominantly Polish, were closely associated both historically and culturally with the rest of the country.

This boundary proposal, in spite of the statement that reserved to the Poles 'any rights which they might have asserted east of that line', greatly diminished the chances for a peaceful settlement of the Russian-Polish struggle. Indirectly it accepted the claims of the Moscow government and confirmed Piłsudski's conviction that his federal plan could be achieved only through the use of arms. Despite the two attempts of the Moscow government to arrive at an amicable settlement, neither side trusted the other. Both spoke of peace but in reality prepared for war. Moreover, Piłsudski, whose object it was to restrict the Soviets to the territory of Russia proper, believed that a sound peace could be achieved only after a military defeat of the Bolsheviks.

Despite the warnings of the Western Powers and the failure of Poland to gain allies among the Baltic states, Piłsudski, now given the title of Marshal, began on 25 April 1920 an all-out offensive, with the support only of a small Ukrainian contingent. The direction of the Polish advance towards Kiev was to a large degree determined by the attempt to strengthen the position of Poland's ally, Petliura. After an initial success, which led to the capture of Kiev, the fortunes of war began to change. The Bolshevik government, in a sudden surge of energy, rose to the defence of the Ukraine. It combined appeals to the Russian people to resist 'the traditional Polish invader' with statements declaring Soviet victory to be the prelude to world revolution. On 2 July the commander-in-chief of the Russian army issued an Order of the Day which ended with the following words :

The fate of the world revolution is being decided in the west; the way leads over the corpse of Poland to a universal conflagration. On to Vilna, Minsk and Warsaw![28]

By a bold sweep from the north and the south the Russian armies moved towards the centre of Poland. Piłsudski's plans for a federation lay in ruins, and Poland faced the danger of becoming a Soviet republic in association with Russia. After a cabinet crisis in Warsaw, Władysław Grabski became premier. Two weeks later he joined Stanisław Patek, the head of the Polish delegation at the Allied Conference at Spa, and submitted a request for help from the Great Powers. The Western Allies slowly realized the gravity of the Bolshevik threat, but they made Poland first accept a number of conditions, in particular a promise to withdraw to the December 1919 'tentative' line of demarcation; to submit the questions of Lithuania, Teschen, eastern Galicia, and Danzig to Allied decision; and to participate in a peace conference to meet in London. The diplomatic note, which included the armistice conditions, was dispatched to Moscow by a cable signed by the British Foreign Secretary, Lord Curzon. The line of demarcation between the Russian and Polish armies, suggested in the British communication, came to be known as the Curzon Line and played an important role in Poland's subsequent history.

Elated by the success of their armies and treating the British note as a sign of weakness, the Bolshevik leadership decided on further advance into ethnically Polish territory. Fear of being accused of pursuing an imperialist policy led the Soviet Commissar of Foreign Affairs, Georgy Chicherin, to express his desire to end the hostilities by direct negotiations between the Polish and Soviet governments. That this was nothing but a diplomatic cover-up for continued military operations was demonstrated by the dilatory manner in which the Polish reply, expressing agreement with Chicherin's condition, was handled.

Thus by the middle of August Poland's situation seemed hopeless. Lord d'Abernon and General Weygand, it is true, had arrived in Warsaw where they joined the large French military mission, but help for Poland in the shape of munitions and other military supplies was not forthcoming. Germany, Czechoslovakia, and Britain, largely because of the influence of the communist or communist-inspired actions among the workers, prevented larger quantities of arms from reaching Poland. Even more vexing was the attitude of the Danzig workers, who refused to unload British and French ships bringing consignments of military supplies for the Polish army.

It was in this darkest hour of the war that the Poles, under the

28 Roos, op. cit., p. 78.

leadership of Marshal Piłsudski, concentrated all their energy on the defence of their land. Towards the end of July a government of 'national unity' headed by Wincenty Witos took over, and tens of thousands of men enlisted in the newly mobilized armies. By the middle of August the stage was set for the last attempt to 'snatch victory from the jaws of defeat'. On 16 August the Polish armies turned the flank of the over-extended Russian military units which had managed to reach the very gates of Warsaw. Almost immediately, the Soviet troops, threatened by total disintegration, started a retreat which was as hasty as that of Piłsudski, little over two months earlier, had been from Kiev. The victory on the Vistula was followed by two other Polish victories, on the Niemen and the Szczara, so that by the middle of October, when a truce was signed, the Polish armies stood around one hundred miles east of the Curzon Line.

The Russian defeat, which has been described as the 'Miracle of the Vistula', resulted from the close co-operation of the Polish generals under Piłsudski's supreme command. Whatever the merits of the subsequent bitter discussion of the decisive factor in the Polish victory – Piłsudski alone; Piłsudski and his generals; or, as was held by some of Piłsudski's National Democratic opponents, General Weygand – the fact remains that without the dedicated, selfless, and heroic resistance of the Polish soldier and civilian – who repudiated the promises of the Soviets – the results of the struggle would have been different. It was, furthermore, their efforts which saved the European continent, still engulfed in the post-war political and social chaos, from the imminent danger of communism.

In his letter to Clara Zetkin, a leading German communist, Lenin admitted that the real cause of Soviet miscalculation and defeat was the inability of the Bolshevik policy-makers to view the struggle from any viewpoint but that of strict Marxist ideology. With some bitterness he wrote : 'The peasants and workers defended their class enemies permitting our brave Red Army soldiers to die of starvation and ambushed and killed them.'[29]

Another act of the Soviet leadership provided even clearer evidence of its inability to understand the psychology of the Polish nation. This was the creation, on 31 July, in the city of Białystok of a Soviet-sponsored Provisional Revolutionary Committee. Its proclamation, which anticipated the creation of a 'Soviet Socialist Republic of Poland', was felt to be an affront by the great majority of Poles. However significant they might have been in the history of world communism, the names of the Polish communist leaders, such as Feliks Dzierżyński, Julian Marchlewski, or Feliks Kon, were

---

[29] V. I. Lenin, *Sochineniia* (35 vols., Moscow, 1941), vol. 32, p. 149.

unknown to the Polish public. This fact more than anything else betrayed the clumsy purpose for which they were used.

Even before the Soviet-Polish peace treaty was signed, the district of Wilno was again contested. After its capture by the Red Army, it was ceded on the basis of a Soviet-Lithuanian peace treaty to Lithuania. The Warsaw government disputed the validity of this transfer and claimed Wilno not merely by reason of its history and ethnic composition but also because of its long cultural association with Poland. The Poles accused the Lithuanians of un-neutral conduct in allowing Soviet troops to operate on Lithuanian territory. Hostilities followed. At the beginning of September 1919 the Poles appealed to the League of Nations Council, asking it to restrain the Lithuanians and prevent bloodshed. A resolution was passed which drew a provisional line of demarcation between the two antagonists, and a Military Commission was dispatched to the area to enforce the resolution. The commission brought about the Suwałki armistice, which postponed a formal decision of the boundary question. Poland without Wilno was unthinkable to Piłsudski. He secretly ordered General Lucjan Zeligowski to act ostensibly without orders from the Warsaw government and to seize Wilno. This *fait accompli*, one of the first acts in violation of the authority of the League of Nations, aroused widespread hostility to Poland. The Western Powers did not press the issue, largely because they realized that any change would weaken Poland's position in the face of the Bolshevik danger. After attempting to impose a plebiscite, the League Council resorted to mediation but again without success. Towards the end of this period of quasi-independence in 'Central Lithuania' an election for the Wilno Diet was held and resulted in a clear Polish majority. Soon after it had assembled the Diet voted, in February 1922, for incorporation into Poland.

The peace Treaty of Riga was signed on 18 March 1921 and formally ended the Polish-Russian War. It represented a compromise between the maximum Polish demands and the Curzon Line, and followed approximately the border established after the Second Partition of 1793. It ran from the river Dvina on the Latvian border to the west of Minsk, through the Prypeć marshes, and along the river Zbrucz to its confluence with the Dnestr.[30] Poland gained 110,000 square kilometres of Belorussian and Ukrainian territory beyond the December 1919 line, an area in which the Poles were outnumbered by the Belorussians and Ukrainians together. Poland abandoned her Ukrainian and Belorussian allies, while for her part the Soviet Union left the solution of the Wilno question to Poland and Lithuania alone. Each party pledged non-interference in the

[30] See above, p. 244.

internal affairs of the other. The Soviet representative, Adolf Joffe, put up little resistance to the Polish demands—for a number of reasons. Of these the most significant were probably the exhaustion of the Soviet armies and the need to concentrate on the defeat of the White armies in the Crimea and the suppression of the independent regime in Georgia. But ideological considerations were also important. While severely shaken by the Polish experience, Russia appeared outwardly indifferent to territorial losses, since her leaders still maintained their belief in the imminence of world revolution. In a Europe composed of Soviet states, boundaries would be of little consequence.

In the course of the peace negotiations serious differences developed between the 'federalists' and the 'centralists' within the Polish delegation. The victory of the latter, who asked for less territory but favoured its direct annexation and ultimate assimilation, gave the final blow to Piłsudski's schemes. On the other hand, had the Polish eastern borders been decided by the statesmen in Paris, Poland would have gained a great deal less than she won through the dramatic and victorious struggle waged by Piłsudski. The Treaty of Riga inaugurated a period of peace, though the new eastern borders of the republic were formally recognized by the Western Powers only on 15 March 1923.

This belated recognition was due in large measure to hope for the restoration of a non-Bolshevik government in Russia and to the tendency in certain quarters to accuse Poland of 'unrestrained imperialism'. It is clear that this accusation must be viewed in the general context of the European situation and of Polish history and national character. The policy of the Western Powers, alternating between friendship to 'democratic' and enmity to Bolshevik Russia, was bound to irritate the Poles and increase their ambitions. Even more significant was the historical factor. For more than a hundred years the Polish nation had cherished the memory of its past splendour, immortalized in the writings of Adam Mickiewicz and Henryk Sienkiewicz. Poles were still fascinated by the period of their greatest glory, when Poland was one of the largest states of Europe, and, through the ingenious method of federalism, assumed a leading position in the East.

When the world war liberated them from foreign subjection, almost automatically most Polish leaders returned to the dreams of the period of their captivity. The re-establishment of the pre-1772 *Rzeczpospolita* (Republic) became the nation's ambition. Was it not true that for centuries the Poles had acted as bearers of Western culture and civilization in their borderlands, defending them and the rest of Europe from the onslaught of the East? Was it not a fact that many of the most outstanding representatives of Polish spiritual and political life, including Kościuszko, Mickiewicz, and Piłsudski, were born in Lithuania? Thus outdated historical considerations prevailed over practical considerations of political realism. An intense belief in a national mission led the Poles to regard independence, prestige, and honour as the chief political virtues of their nation. The idea of compromise, generally recognized as essential for European peace and stability, was basically alien to Polish political thinking.

Such a political ideology, while understandable in terms of Polish historical experience, failed to realize that the atmosphere of the twentieth century differed profoundly from that of the eighteenth century. The idea of nationalism, which had spread over all the European continent, influenced also the nationalities of the Polish borderlands. These could never regard the Poles, who constituted the aristocratic and propertied classes, as their saviours. This sentiment towards the Poles in the eastern provinces never changed, even though many of the non-Polish population in these lands feared Bolshevism more than Polish rule. Another factor which damaged Poland's reputation was the policy of *faits accomplis*. It irritated the Western public and seemed to lend substance to their accusation of 'imperialism'.

In other ways, however, Poland showed her willingness and ability to co-operate constructively with her neighbours. This was so particularly in the complex system of economic and political collaboration with Germany which the League of Nations had established in Upper Silesia. The international regime created here was 'one of the most curious and at the same time successful international operations of the years between the two World Wars'.[31] In the first years of her existence Poland also subscribed wholeheartedly to the system of international co-operation represented by the concept of collective security, and supported France in the attempt to further international security through the strengthening of the League.

With her 388,000 square kilometres and over 27 million inhabitants the new Poland became one of the largest states of Europe. Like most of the new countries, it was a multinational state, including, in addition to almost 19 million Poles (69·2 per cent), over 8 million non-Poles, mainly Ukrainians, Belorussians, Germans, and Jews who, for the greater part, remained outside the Polish national community. This large number of minorities was a source of weakness, but it was by no means a decisive factor in the ultimate break-up of the state. Poland typified the post-1918 situation of all the new states between Germany and the Soviet Union. Her emergence was made possible by the post-war change in the existing balance of power, which

[31] Norman J. G. Pounds, *Poland Between East and West* (New York, 1964), p. 71.

destroyed one and substantially weakened the other dominant power in East-Central Europe. When the Polish republic came into being, hardly anyone would have believed that within less than two decades another cataclysmic change in the European power-political equilibrium, combined as it was with the revival of old hatreds, would jeopardize the very existence of independent Poland.

Chapter 6

The Polish Political System 1918–39

'W Polsce . . . instynkt wolności w warstwach ludowych jest niemal
równoznaczny z uczuciem niechęci do tych, którzy je dawniej uciskali.
Będzie rzeczą ze wszechmiar pożyteczną, jeżeli . . . niechęć ta znajdzie
swój wyraz w utrwaleniu republiki szczerce demokratycznej.'

(Stanisław Thugutt, 1929)[1]

DESPITE THE DUALITY of Polish national leadership – represented by
Piłsudski in Warsaw and Dmowski in Paris – the first few weeks of
Polish independence were permeated by sentiments of joy and optimism. The romantic dreams and prophecies of the intellectual and
spiritual élite of the period of the Great Emigration were suddenly
fulfilled. Poland assumed a worthy position among the free nations
of the world. For a time, the vision of a glorious future, based on the
idea of freedom and tolerance, seemed to fill the minds both of the
political leaders and the people.

This sudden outburst of enthusiasm, so characteristic of the Polish
national character, paid little attention to the immense problems facing the new state. Even under normal conditions the political, economic, and administrative amalgamation of territories which for over
a century had been under the control of different states would have
presented an enormously difficult task. However, the circumstances
of post-1918 Poland, still in her formative period, were far from
normal. The most important part of the country had been first a
battlefield and then an area of foreign occupation. The destruction
of war was matched by the ravages caused by the ruthless exploitation by the Germans, whose need for metals led to a wholesale removal of industrial machinery to the Reich. While perhaps less
devastating, the Russian evacuation of Poland in 1915 also caused
great damage to her economy. Thus industries were in a condition

---

[1] 'In Poland the instinct of liberty among people is equal to the feeling of
aversion against those who in the past have suppressed it. It would be useful
if this animosity found its expression in the establishment of a truly democratic republic,' Stanisław Thugutt, 'Dlaczego jestem ludowcem i demokratą'
(Why I am a Member of the Peasant Party and a Democrat) in Manfred
Kridl et al., *Polska myśl demokratyczna w ciągu wieków* (Polish Democratic
Thought in the Course of Centuries), Polish Labor Group, New York, p. 303.

of sad disrepair, bordering in certain areas, such as Łódź and Dąbrowa, on total destruction. Similar losses were sustained in the agricultural sector, millions of acres of arable soil not cultivated, the number of livestock sadly depleted, and vast areas of forest destroyed. Particularly serious was the disruption caused by the destruction of the transport system, brought about by the blowing-up of several thousand bridges, demolition of railway stations, and plundering of the railway stock. Last but not least, dwellings in thousands of cities, towns, and villages lay in ruins.

The peasants, many of them displaced from their homes, were on the brink of starvation which only the monumental aid of the American Relief Administration headed by Herbert Hoover helped to alleviate. From the very beginning the country was plagued with almost insoluble financial difficulties – the existence of different currencies, different systems of tax collection, and the inability of governments, overburdened by military expenditure, to balance budgets. As a result, severe inflation set in, which tended to undermine confidence in the Warsaw government.

But the most difficult task, which during the next two decades was never accomplished, was the removal of the fundamental differences between the country's different regions and different social strata. Polish society was marked by a number of glaring contrasts which impeded the process of consolidation. The literate and highly prosperous farmers of the region of Poznań, for instance, were far removed from the downtrodden and partly illiterate peasants of the east and south-east. Workers from the formerly German provinces were accustomed to a higher standard of living than those from Congress Poland and Galicia. On the one hand, there was the sophistication of high society, both social and intellectual, and on the other, the simplicity of the poor and backward countryfolk. After 1918 the influence of the landowners continued to decline, but the rising middle class, especially in the eastern part of the country, retained to a great extent the mentality of the aristocracy. While post-war Poland could hardly be regarded as a 'closed society', very few among the lower classes of society, including the peasantry, managed to rise above their original conditions of life. Within the cities the conflict between the Jews, who had little tendency to assimilate, and the commercial classes continued and was expressed by occasional outbursts of anti-semitism.

The Psychology of Polish Political Parties

The tremendous social and intellectual contrasts only underlined the political split which had characterized the life of the 'Polish community' in the period of captivity. Even in those areas of past

conflict between the Left and the Right, which had been resolved
by the course of history, there remained an after-taste of ill-will and
suspicion, not to be easily overcome. The achievement of national
independence could not eliminate the antagonism between those who
came from the west and those who, in one form or another, participated in the activities of the government set up in Warsaw under
the auspices of the Central Powers. New problems were added to the
old and the tenacity that marked the imminent conflict could be
explained also in terms of a clash of three world outlooks. There
were the adherents, both public and secret, of conservatism, who
tended to insist on old privileges and on the supremacy of the Polish
element over the national minorities. Ranged against this conservative political philosophy, there were the representatives of the new
and lower classes whom the turmoil of war and community of struggle
for independence had brought to the fore. A considerable number of
Poles sincerely believed in the necessity to limit the power of the
government. At the other end of the political scale were those who
believed that the internal unification of Poland – a task of immense
difficulty – could be achieved only by creating a strong authoritarian
government in which power would preferably be vested in one individual alone.

The fact that those who held these opinions were motivated by a
deep desire to preserve Poland and strengthen her national independence was hardly conducive to a compromise. Equally frustrating
was their ability to find precedents for their views in Polish history,
when their methods were applied to the problems of the old *Rzeczpospolita*. No doubt the split between the Right and the Left, accompanied by a weakening of the Centre, was nothing peculiar to Poland,
being characteristic of a number of post-1918 European political
systems. But the relationship of the two factions in Poland was
unusual and bizarre. As subsequent developments proved, authoritarian goals and tactics, which in other European countries were
pursued by the Right, in Poland were embraced and eventually put
into effect by the Left. But this collapse of Polish democracy took
place only after almost eight years of unsuccessful attempts at a
workable parliamentary system of government. There were many
reasons for this failure. Of these at least three deserve discussion –
the multiplicity of political parties; the character of the Polish constitution; and, above all, the psychological aspects of party politics in
Poland. The emergence of political parties was influenced by the
foremost ideologies of contemporary Europe – nationalism, socialism,
democracy, and those derived from the application of the principles
of Christianity to public life. As has been pointed out, 'none of these
dynamic forces were monopolized by any one faction, the peculiar

combinations which emerged from these four constituent philosophies were predestined to make Poland's political life a constantly changing, kaleidoscopic picture'.[2]

While the power-political structure of the Polish republic developed from that of the pre-war period, the formation of political parties and factions was influenced by new and unprecedented problems. Liberation and the adoption of universal suffrage throughout the country brought into political life millions of people who until recently had taken no part in public life or approached it from the narrow confines of their provinces. The task of creating *national* parties, which were to become one of the most influential forces of internal unification, ran an erratic course, impeded by a lack of political experience and tradition, remnants of provincialism, and conflicts of personality. As a result, the consolidation of political loyalties, even among party leaders, was an unwieldy and protracted process. The multiplicity of political groups, partly inherited from the pre-war period, was to be overcome by the organization of blocs composed of kindred parties co-operating on all major issues. Unfortunately, the different blocs more often than not succumbed to fragmentation and even disintegration, giving Polish political life its tendency towards constant combinations and permutations.

Thus the Polish parliamentary system – in order to achieve some degree of stability and cohesion – required two types of coalition. First, a compromise between the individual blocs, with none strong enough to govern alone, was necessary. Secondly – and perhaps more important – there had to be solid agreement within the different factions which made up the individual blocs. The achievement of this dual task proved extremely difficult and its repeated failure was the main stumbling-block in the path of Polish parliamentary democracy. The parties of the Right – dominated by National Democracy – managed to preserve a high degree of cohesion, but the other parties, especially those representing the agrarian and peasant groups, suffered from lack of co-operation, successive splits, and ideological vagueness. It would be tedious to attempt to analyse the complex changes and splits which characterized the political life of Poland before 1926. Yet at least some knowledge of the main forces represented in the *Sejm* is necessary to understand the tragic development of Polish democracy. Of the existing parties the two pre-war antagonists – the National Democrats and the Polish socialists – represented the most important factors within the country.

The National Democrats, having combined with a number of other parties, assumed the name of National People's Union (*Zwią-*

[2] Malbone W. Graham, 'Polish Political Parties' in Bernadotte Schmitt, ed., *Poland* (Berkeley, Calif., 1945), p. 110.

zek Ludowo-Narodowy, known by its initials as ZLN) and emerged as the largest group within the Polish constitutional *Sejm*. The pre-war programme of integral nationalism was made more concrete by the formulation of more definite aims and demands, such as close association between Church and state; insistence on the creation of a strong and highly centralized government; promotion of private enterprise; and the furthering of 'the myth of a solidly national state'. The Union's motto, 'Poland for the Poles', proved attractive for the masses, whereas the adherence of a large number of outstanding personalities gained it the support of the intellectual classes. Its leaders – in addition to Roman Dmowski and Ignacy Paderewski – included such men as university professors Stanisław Głąbiński and Stanisław Grabski, and the former National Democratic leaders of Poznania, Wojciech Trąmpczyński and Marian Seyda, as well as other leading members of Polish society. For the 1922 election the National Democrats organized an even broader bloc of rightist political parties, the Christian League of National Union (*Chrześcijański Związek Jedności Narodowej*), combining the National People's Union with the Christian Democratic and National Christian parties. The League received almost 30 per cent of all votes, securing 163 seats out of 444 in the *Sejm*.

Although much smaller than the combined parties of the Right and even than the agrarian parties, the Polish Socialist Party (PPS) maintained its important position, for two main reasons : first, at Piłsudski's behest, it was the first political party to take over government; secondly, though reduced to relative unimportance after Moraczewski's fall from power, it was to play a prominent role in Piłsudski's seizure of power in 1926. Like the majority of East-Central European Social Democratic parties, it paid lip-service to the programme of orthodox Marxism, emphasizing the necessity of the socialization of major industries and of all communications, as well as the separation of Church and state, and going so far as to recommend the abolition of a standing army and the liquidation of the Senate. In reality, however, considerations of nationalism, as well as loyalty to its ex-member, Józef Piłsudski, caused the PPS to pursue a policy of social moderation. Although Piłsudski had severed his ties with the party in November 1918, the PPS had a number of popular and extremely capable political leaders. Of these the founder of the short-lived Lublin Republic, Ignacy Daszyński; his colleague in the Viennese *Reichsrat*, Herman Lieberman; the member of the executive of the Socialist International Mieczysław Niedziałkowski; and the talented publicist Feliks Perl, were the most important. Despite its relative influence, the party's potential was limited by a number of significant factors. One was its long and fatal association with

Piłsudski; another its strictly urban character; and, last but not least, its fundamentally anti-Catholic orientation in a country where Catholicism and patriotism were traditionally regarded as one.

The third influential factor of Polish politics was a whole cluster of agrarian parties, representing the Polish version of inter-war agrarianism. The original Polish Peasant Party (PSL), whose main representative was its *Piast* branch headed by Wincenty Witos, at first accepted a programme of far-reaching agrarian reforms but, as time passed, progressively shed much of its radicalism, gradually becoming a party of the Centre. It acquiesced in the less than adequate land reform of 1920 and pursued a policy which brought it into close co-operation with the political parties of the Right.[3] It played an important role in most of the pre-1926 coalitions, but its leadership, perhaps because of its involvement in power politics, proved unable substantially to improve the lot of the peasant. The other branch of Polish agrarianism was the more radical Polish Peasant Party which accepted the title of *Wyzwolenie* (Liberation). It stood close to the socialists, deriving its support largely from among the agricultural proletariat. After a short-lived collaboration and even fusion with the *Piast* group, the two parties followed different policies, the discrepancies between them underscored by personal antagonism between Witos and Stanisław Thugutt, an excellent orator and writer, who opposed the rightist orientation of the *Piast* faction. This basic division was accompanied by the emergence of other splinter groups, such as that led by Jan Dębski, which emphasized the absence of disciplined party organizations and common programme characteristic of Polish agrarianism.

The absence of internal cohesion and discipline was even more conspicuous in the case of the ephemeral post-1918 'Centre' parties which, more often than not, were amorphous political formations springing up around individual politicians. Consequently, they had no definite programme, were subject to constant changes, and prepared to participate in different coalitions.

While practically excluded, because of the unsettled condition in the border areas, from the Constituent Diet, the political parties of the minorities (Ukrainians, Belorussians, Jews, and Germans) became an important political factor after the 1922 election, in which they received almost 80 seats in the *Sejm*. Their success, so disappointing from the Polish nationalist point of view, was largely due to an organizational feat, brought about under German leadership, which gathered the majority of the different minority parties into one electoral group. Despite its rather doubtful loyalty to the Polish state, the

---

[3] Another outstanding member of the *Piast* was Maciej Rataj who for a number of years held the position of Marshal (speaker) of the *Sejm*.

Minorities Bloc played a role of utmost importance, as an influential lever between the more or less equally balanced forces of the Polish Right and Left. Indeed, many of the governments bought the support of the minorities by granting them certain concessions, for instance, the Declaration of Warsaw of 4 July 1925, issued on the basis of an agreement between the Jewish Club and the government of Władysław Grabski.

Last but not least, there was the miniscule Polish Communist Party (*Komunistyczna Partia Polski*) which emerged as early as 16 December 1918 from the fusion of the SDKPiL and the left wing of the PPS. From the very beginning the communists set themselves outside the Polish national community. Their programme was based on 'Luxemburgist' internationalism and orthodoxy which went so far as to repudiate the idea of Polish independence and insist on the immediate collectivization of land. No wonder that the overwhelming majority of the Poles regarded the Communist Party as an agent in the service of a foreign power. This assessment was fully confirmed during the Soviet-Polish War when the decision to organize a Provisional Revolutionary Committee in Białystok destroyed the last chances which the communists might have possessed. As if anticipating this result, as early as 1919 they voluntarily accepted the status of illegality, preferring this to any action which might imply the recognition of the Polish state. Later, the communists, appearing under different fronts, scored some minor successes, especially in the eastern provinces.

The atomization of Polish political life – one of its most glaring weaknesses – was largely the result of the system of proportional representation, which favoured the emergence of small political parties. However, as the case of Czechoslovakia proved, multiplicity of political parties did not necessarily lead to the destruction of parliamentary democracy. But the Polish situation was made much more difficult by the mercurial fickleness of party loyalties and by the provisions of the constitution.

The Constitution of the Polish Republic, promulgated on 17 March 1921, was greatly influenced by the developments during the interim period between November 1919 and March 1921 in which Poland was more or less dominated by the powerful personality of Józef Piłsudski, the hero of Poland's liberation. For over three months he alone wielded supreme power within the Polish state. The so-called 'Little Constitution' of 20 February 1919, adopted by the Constituent Assembly as a provisional basic law, vested sovereignty and supreme legislative authority in the unicameral Diet and required ministerial counter-signature for every political act of the Chief

of State, thus at least theoretically curbing his power and subordinating him to the legislature. In practice, however, Piłsudski exercised
great, if not decisive, influence in the formation of almost all cabinets,
reserving for himself the choice particularly of the Ministers of
National Defence and of Foreign Affairs.[4]

An analysis of the final constitutional document reveals that some
of its most important provisions stemmed directly from the past
political conflicts, the two and a half years' political experience of
the Polish state, and the peculiar psychology of post-war public life.
The authors of the new constitution were inspired by the parliamentary system of the French Third Republic. They did nothing,
however, to eliminate its main weakness, namely, the lack of proper
balance between the legislative and executive branches of government. On the contrary, the Polish basic law further intensified this
disequilibrium to the detriment of the executive. The powers of the
lower chamber, the *Sejm*, were very broadly determined. The principles of legal and political, as well as collective and individual,
responsibility of the government to the legislature were especially
elaborated. The upper chamber, the Senate, while playing a secondary role in the legislative process, was used for an additional and
far-reaching limitation of the power of the chief executive. The
President, who lacked the power of veto and of legislative initiative,
had no right to dissolve the Diet, except with the approval of three-
fifths of the Senate. Another significant limitation of the Presidential
power – the importance of which was peculiar to Polish conditions –
concerned the question of the command of the armed forces. This
was vested in the President, but only in time of peace; in time of
war a special commander-in-chief was to be appointed.

By and large, the constitution differed little from those adopted
in Europe in the post-1918 period. It had some of their assets, such
as an all-inclusive bill of rights, and some of their shortcomings, such
as inadequate provisions for local self-government, or those preventing the judiciary from becoming a balancing factor in the lopsided
distribution of power. But none of these deficiencies were of such
importance as those bearing on the powers of the *Sejm* and the
President.

It was with regard to these provisions that the personality of
Piłsudski played a decisive role. The psychology of the parties of the
Right was marked by a deeply engrained fear of the Chief of State.
Many regarded him as a demagogue who, having gone wrong in

[4] In the constitutional crisis of June 1922 the Diet answered the question
somewhat equivocally, stating 'that the initiative in choosing the Prime Minister belongs regularly to the Chief of State'. The actual conflict, however,
ended in favour of Piłsudski who appointed his own candidates. Robert
Machray, *The Poland of Piłsudski* (London, 1936), pp. 157–9.

his wartime political calculation, cleverly built his popularity on the successful endeavours of others, and suspected him of trying to abolish the democratic system of government and replace it by his personal rule. To forestall any such attempt, the Marshal's National Democratic enemies weakened the office of the chief executive so that it might not become a stepping-stone towards autocratic rule – should Piłsudski be elected President of the Republic. Parliamentary omnipotence, which was to serve as another guarantee against the possible pretensions of one man, delivered the country into the shaky hands of unstable and constantly changing coalitions.

Equally distressing was the fact that the constitutional charter never won the respect and support of the Polish people, who refused to regard it as a symbol of the internal unity of the new state. The parties of the Right opposed it because of its allegedly progressive tendencies, those of the Left rejected it because of its failure to comply with some of their fundamental demands. Moreover, the 'assembly-type' government, in which the cabinet in many respects acted as a mere committee of the *Sejm,* exposed all difficulties of parliamentary democracy to public view.

The conditions of political psychosis under which the constitution was adopted were best expressed by the bizarre situation in which both Left and Right – motivated by their unbridgeable discord and their idiosyncracies – defended views and policies which were the exact opposite of their political beliefs. The Right, which originally favoured a strong executive, some of its members flirting with the idea of monarchy, violated its political outlook and tailored the constitution *ad personam,* crippling the power of the President and endowing the *Sejm* – and through it the political parties – with almost unlimited powers. On the other hand, the parties of the Left, which were expected to defend the principle of parliamentary supremacy, declared themselves at first indirectly and then directly in favour of a strong authority which they saw in the personality of their former leader, Piłsudski.

To understand the psychological background of Polish politics it is necessary to realize and appreciate the key role played by the Marshal in post-war Poland. His personality and views became both the negative and the positive symbols of Polish political life. His opponents endeavoured to curb the ambition of a man whose reliability as a democrat they regarded as doubtful and whose tendency towards autocracy they took for granted. This accusation, at least in the first years of the republic, was hardly justified. Again and again, he spoke of a government to be based on the precepts of true democracy and referred to 'our tradition of freedom and tolerance'.[5] He

5 Václav Fiala, *Soudobé Polsko* (Prague, 1936), p. 78.

hastened the election of the first *Sejm,* to which he handed over his
dictatorial powers, and was unanimously re-elected.

However sincere these statements might have been, they did not
and perhaps could not allay the fears of Piłsudski's opponents. For
them he was the natural candidate for the role of dictator. In the
first place, his understanding of government was greatly influenced
by his martial background. While without formal military education,
he had spent a large part of his life in uniform and regarded military
discipline and order as the highest civic virtues. Approaching politics
from the point of view of military tactics and strategy, Piłsudski
proved himself unable to discriminate between the different methods
to be used in the realization of a given aim and to accept the protracted method of making decisions on the basis of negotiation and
mutual concessions. This alone explains why his relationship to an
elected assembly was never devoid of tension.

This tension became especially pronounced with regard to control
over the Polish armed forces. Ever since the foundation of the Associations of Riflemen *(Strzelcy)* and the organization of the famous
Legions, the Polish army had been Piłsudski's main concern. Not
without justification he saw himself as 'the father of the Polish army
and the nation's first soldier'.[6] After November 1918 he combined
the functions of Head of State, Commander-in-Chief, and for some
time also Chief of the General Staff, doing his best entirely to divorce
the military from 'all political influences', particularly those of parliament. His decree of January 1921 on the organization of the high
command of the armed forces vested supreme control over tactical
and strategic war plans in a small body, the 'Inner War Council', to
be presided over by the man designated as Commander-in-Chief in
case of war – Piłsudski himself. The powers of the Minister of War,
who alone was responsible to the *Sejm,* were limited basically to the
technical aspects of the organization of the army. Piłsudski thus
hoped to withdraw all significant military decisions and ultimate
control – which in all democracies in one way or another are under
the jurisdiction of parliament – from the competence of the Diet.
To keep his position of control over the military Piłsudski scornfully
refused the invitation to run for President whom, under the new
constitution, he regarded as a mere figurehead. The ultimate resignation of the embittered Marshal from the last of his military functions
and, indeed, his retirement from public life, in July 1923, bore witness to his intrinsic incompatibility with parliamentary institutions,
especially in their Polish version.

There were other factors which predestined Józef Piłsudski to a
dictatorial position in the Polish state. He enjoyed great popularity

[6] Joseph Rothschild, *Piłsudski's Coup d'Etat* (New York, 1966), p. 25.

and prestige not only among the officers who had fought under him in the Legions and the reconstituted Polish army or among the ranks of his former socialist comrades of the PPS, but also among the masses. His simplicity, martial appearance, terse speech, and ability to combine down to earth political realism with absolute dedication to a great romantically conceived cause – all these qualities of mind and character endeared him greatly to his people. In fact Piłsudski, for many the embodiment of traditional Polish virtues, exuded a curious charm to which few Poles, including many of the Marshal's enemies, could remain entirely immune. No doubt he was fully aware of his popular appeal and of his 'rare ability to elicit the ardent loyalty and the passionate belief in his genius of otherwise sober and critical persons'.[7] This awareness, coupled with a strong sense of mission and innate activism, made it impossible for him to stand aside when the fortunes of the Polish state and nation were, as he sincerely believed, dissipated by the inept, egotistical, and irresponsible policies of the political parties.

One cannot speculate what would have been the fate of Poland, had it not been for Piłsudski's *coup d'état* in May 1926, but there seems to be no doubt that the eight-odd years of Polish democracy, though not entirely without accomplishment, cannot be regarded as successful. The ministry of Paderewski, which replaced the unrepresentative regime of Moraczewski, proceeded as early as the end of January 1919 to at least partial elections for the Constituent Assembly. The representatives of certain provinces still under foreign control had to be appointed. The Diet, where party divisions were subject to constant change, in its final form displayed a clear rightist majority which gradually embarked on a policy the aim of which was to curb Piłsudski's powers.

Besides the drafting of the new constitution, the main problems facing the Diet were agrarian reform and the general reconstruction of a country devastated by war. By the middle of 1919 the combined peasant groups, supported by the parties of the Left, managed – against the rightist opposition – to push through the *Sejm* a resolution calling for a somewhat radical distribution of land among the peasants. Legislative action on this promise was taken only a year later, in the midst of the Soviet-Polish War, when the loyalty of the peasants proved decisive for Polish victory. Much less successful were the efforts to improve the catastrophic economic situation. Indeed, no real action could be taken on any of the economic, financial, political, and legal-administrative issues because of the demands of the struggle for the borders. The needs of the war, in which with one

7 Ibid., p. 368.

single exception[8] the Chief of State played a decisive role, tended to bridge the fundamental differences between the individual parties. National unity was demonstrated by the formation, at the time of the Soviet offensive, of the cabinet of national defence headed by Wincenty Witos.

Only after the termination of the war was it possible to return to normal governmental work. Unfortunately, it was then that the split between Right and Left, and the former's chronic fear and hatred of Piłsudski, appeared as ominous signs of Polish political instability. Internal quarrels over financial and agrarian policies led to the fall of the Witos government and its replacement by a succession of short-lived extra-parliamentary cabinets. In June 1922 the first violent conflict between the *Sejm* and the Chief of State over the latter's power to appoint governments took place.

The internal political discords were compounded by the results of the November 1922 election which confirmed the political atomization of the *Sejm*. Against the greatly strengthened rightist nationalist bloc (Christian League of National Union), which gained 163 seats, there was the loose combination of the Left (185 seats) and, surprisingly, a large bloc representing national minorities with 79 seats. Very significant was the rout of the old discredited Centre parties and the substantial weakening of the PPS. Not counting the composite parts of the rightist and minorities blocs, there were altogether seventeen political parties in the *Sejm*.[9] That this proliferation was not conducive to political stability was proved by the tragic events accompanying the subsequent Presidential election. With the help of the minorities, the candidate of the radical peasants, Gabriel Narutowicz, the Minister for Foreign Affairs, was elected. Two days after the solemn ceremony in which Piłsudski transferred his powers of Chief of State to the new chief executive, Narutowicz was assassinated. The assassin, a rightist fanatic, explained his motive – indignation because the Head of the Polish State was elected by non-Polish votes.

The subsequent orderly election of the pre-war socialist and friend of Piłsudski, Stanisław Wojciechowski, and the appointment of a non-party cabinet under General Władysław Sikorski could not heal the malaise of Polish political life. The conflict between the parties of the Right and Piłsudski became for all practical purposes unbridgeable. Sikorski restored order, but the efficiency of his government was

[8] For Piłsudski's offer of resignation see Wincenty Witos, *Moje wspomnienia* (Paris, 3 vols., 1964), vol. II, pp. 290–91.

[9] The number of parties continued to increase, so that by May 1926 the total number amounted to 59, of which 31 were represented either in the *Sejm* or the Senate. Twenty-six were Polish and 33 represented the interests of the ethnic groups. See Rothschild, op. cit., p. 9.

Results of National Elections of 1922 in Poland

Parties	Vote for *Sejm*	Seats in *Sejm*	Seats in Senate
Right			
Christian League of National Union	2,551,000 (29·1%)	163	49
Centre			
Polish Centre	260,000 (3·0%)	6	—
Bourgeois Party	30,000 (0·3%)	—	—
National Union of the State	38,000 (0·4%)	—	—
Left			
Polish Peasant Party *Piast*	1,150,000 (13·1%)	70	17
Radical Peasant Party, *Wyzwolenie* (Liberation)	963,000 (11·0%)	49	8
Radical Peasant Party	116,000 (1·3%)	4	—
National Workers' Union	474,000 (5·4%)	18	2
Left Polish Populist Party	59,000 (0·7%)	1	—
Polish Socialist Party (PPS)	906,000 (10·3%)	41	7
Polish Communist Party	121,000 (1·4%)	2	—
Minorities			
Bloc of National Minorities	1,401,000 (16·0%)	65	26
Galician Zionists	177,000 (2·0%)	5	—
Jewish Populists	50,000 (0·6%)	1	—
Zionists (Western Galicia)	81,000 (0·9%)	2	—
Ukrainian Peasants		5	—
Border Union	48,000 (0·6%)	1	—
Scattering	206,000 (2·3%)	—	2

Figures compiled from *Bulletin Periodique de la Presse Polonaise*, No. 125 (12 December 1922), pp. 1–2, as indicated in Malbone Graham, *New Governments of Eastern Europe* (New York, 1927), p. 499.

greatly affected by the erratic and irresponsible behaviour of the political parties. The press, which at least in part was inclined to sensationalism, did not inspire confidence in the new government and parliament. No wonder that in this atmosphere of mistrust and demagoguery the economic situation took a sharp turn downward. No one was willing to make the extraordinary sacrifices which alone would have brought economic improvement. Most disturbing was the continued depreciation of the Polish mark, which frustrated all attempts to balance the budget. The threat of bankruptcy and the sudden *renversement des alliances* of the *Piast* group of the Peasant Party, which assumed the position of the new Centre, pulled down Sikorski's ministry. In May 1923 it was replaced by a political cabinet based on a Right-Centre coalition headed by Wincenty Witos.

The seven months of this second Witos ministry proved fatal for the future of Polish democracy. A number of factors forced the government to take measures which made it, and to a certain extent the entire parliamentary system, universally unpopular. The economic ills which had plagued the previous regime remained unsolved, while the situation continued to deteriorate because of the constant rise in the cost of living, which in turn brought about serious labour unrest. Despite the imposition of a capital levy, the workers' dissatisfaction mounted, reaching its zenith in a series of strikes which, in the month of November, resulted in violent riots in Kraków, suppressed with bloodshed by the troops. Last but not least, the greatly watered-down version of the Land Reform Act of 1920, forced upon Witos by his rightist allies, caused disaffection in the ranks of his own party and precipitated his fall in December 1923. Thus the question of the sorely needed land reform remained on paper for another two years.

There were other, in the long run more significant, conflicts which characterized Witos' second premiership, especially the head-on clash between him and Piłsudski, who was greatly annoyed by the cabinet's attempt to take over the direction of military matters and who began to regard the parliamentary system as the real cause of maladministration and political chaos. During June and July 1923 Piłsudski dissociated himself entirely from the regime, parting with his cherished military posts of Chief of the General Staff, Chairman of the Inner War Council, and designate Commander-in-Chief of the Polish Army in time of war. Voluntarily accepting legal, though not political, retirement, the Marshal observed the political scene with the utmost apprehension. This feeling changed to alarm when the new government started to reorganize the supreme command of the armed forces, as established by himself, and systematically to appoint his adversaries to positions of control.

Piłsudski did not change his negative attitude towards Witos' successor, Władysław Grabski, despite the attempts of the Defence Minister, Sikorski, to entice the Marshal back into military command. Sikorski's plan for the reorganization of the supreme command, which would leave ultimate control in the hands of the War Minister and not of the Inspector-General of the Armed Forces – a position which was being prepared for Piłsudski – only annoyed the irascible Marshal. In fact, Sikorski's behaviour tended to rekindle their mutual rivalry.

Having obtained full powers from the *Sejm*, Grabski, in his additional capacity as Minister of Finance, was at long last able to introduce his programme of increased taxation, reduced expenditure, and the divorcing of financial affairs from political control. The re-establishment of a balanced budget, the introduction of a new currency, the *złoty*, as well as the creation of the *Bank Polski*, endowed with the exclusive right to issue banknotes, brought an almost immediate, but short-lived, improvement in the financial situation. In the second half of July 1925, however, a number of factors – bad harvest, failure to obtain adequate American loans, and the outbreak of the German-Polish tariff war – combined to threaten all Grabski's achievements. As was to be expected, the renewed atmosphere of economic crisis, expressed by the fall of the *złoty*, increased the number of unemployed, and the organization of further strikes plunged the country into a new political crisis.

Grabski's ministry found itself under fire from Right and Left, both accusing him of extreme radical measures. The passing of the second Land Reform Act failed to win over the peasants, who suffered a terrible blow in the fall of world grain prices, and their confidence in Grabski waned. His difficulties proved insurmountable. The opposition of the minorities and the ever-growing pressure of the military group 'invisibly' organized by Piłsudski caused the most successful of parliamentary premiers to resign in November 1925.

Grabski's successor, Alexander Skrzyński, made one last attempt to overcome the economic difficulties and the chronic 'crisis of confidence' by parliamentary methods, and managed to create an all-national cabinet in which the PPS was also represented. Another important gesture of conciliation was the removal of Sikorski and his replacement by Piłsudski's trusted henchman, General Lucjan Zeligowski. But none of these measures proved sufficient to restore the shattered morale of Polish parliamentarians. The attempt of the rightist Finance Minister, Jerzy Zdziechowski, to solve the economic crisis by a draconic deflation policy, while bringing about a definite economic improvement, again resulted in political discord. Claiming that the 'man in the street' was to bear the burden of economic recovery, the socialists resigned from the coalition, precipitating the fall of Skrzyński on 5 May 1926. The sudden and unexpected demise of the Polish parliamentary system followed.

No doubt there were many reasons why Piłsudski, the First Marshal of Poland, staged his *coup d'état* on 12–15 May 1926. The internal and external conditions of Poland had reached a stage of utmost emergency with which, it seemed, purely parliamentary methods could not cope. Post-war Poland's contrasts and antagonisms had caused what the Marshal and his adherents – and, rather reluctantly also, some of his opponents – regarded as political paralysis. Yet the main and immediate motive of Piłsudski's action was the continuing degradation of the army, a development which he could not tolerate.

Backed by those high officers of the army – mainly former members of the Legion – whose units Żeligowski had transferred to the vicinity of Warsaw during his tenure as War Minister, Piłsudski decided to strike just as Witos, at the head of a new Right-Centre coalition, managed to form a new government. Piłsudski had at first hoped that no officer would have the temerity to oppose by force of arms the First Marshal of Poland. But after a dramatic interview with President Wojciechowski on the Poniatowski Bridge across the Vistula, he found himself in the unenviable position of a rebel. He led an armed insurrection against a regime which may no longer have been fully representative of the political opinion of the nation, but nevertheless was still the legal government. What was supposed to be an 'armed demonstration',[10] destined to bring about a 'voluntary' resignation of the Witos government, suddenly changed into a regular military encounter. Whatever may have been his personal opinion, Wojciechowski upheld the authority of the government and was determined not to betray his constitutional oath. He led his cabinet and those troops which remained loyal to them in the not entirely hopeless resistance against the insurrectionists.

There followed three days of heavy fighting between the two armies. The railway strike organized by the PPS and the railway unions decided the outcome. This action virtually strangled the governmental forces within Warsaw, cutting them off from reinforcements approaching the city from the west. On the night of 14 May the Witos government and the President (whose dignified behaviour had made him at least the moral victor in the conflict) resigned and cleared the field for Piłsudski and his adherents.

Piłsudski stated that 'only after a difficult internal struggle did he decide to proceed to a test of strength with all its consequences'.[11] For the next nine years he and his nation were to suffer from these 'consequences', which eventually changed Poland into an authoritarian state and her main representative into a fully-fledged dictator. The PPS leaders and membership, without whose aid Piłsudski might have lost his bid for power, were soon to regret their loyalty to their erstwhile leader.

Piłsudski's 'Guided' Democracy

The May victory emphasized the importance of a special group found within both the civilian and military organizations of the Polish state. These were the so-called 'Piłsudskists' – the steadfast adherents of the Marshal, who unconditionally and without any afterthought recognized his moral authority and wisdom. Almost

---

[10] The determination to avoid an armed conflict flows clearly from the pledge 'given on my honour' by Piłsudski to President Wojciechowski on 9 May that he would never raise his 'hand against the right of the legal government in Poland'. See Władysław Grabski, 'Ostatnie Rozmowy Piłsudskiego z Wojciechowskim', *Kierunki*, No. 14 (15 May 1960).

[11] *Kurier Poranny* (13 May 1926), as quoted in Józef Piłsudski, *Pisma zbiorowe*, vol. IX, p. 9.

automatically, and indeed logically, they tended to assume leading positions in the Polish political and governmental systems. Despite his sincere efforts to forget the fratricidal conflict and to create an atmosphere of conciliation, the new master of Poland could not avoid giving precedence to this group and promoting its members to positions of power and honour. Such action was dictated not only by practical considerations – it stemmed also from the entire personality of Józef Piłsudski. One simply could not expect a man who regarded honour and loyalty as the greatest virtues to pass over those who in a 'soldierly' manner had responded to his call and 'order'.

Had its individual members possessed the energy and determination of their leader and the moral and intellectual qualities equal to their new tasks, the gradual emergence of a new governmental élite might have resulted in a great strengthening of the state. Alas, these representatives suffered from a number of shortcomings which only gradually appeared on the surface and exercised a harmful influence on Polish life. They lacked administrative competence and their attitude to those they had defeated left much to be desired.

Significantly, Piłsudski's advent to power was not the result of mass political backing. The group closest to him, *Klub Praca* (the Labour Club), was composed of technologically inclined intellectuals and – apart from providing the first post-*coup* premier, Professor Kazimierz Bartel – was numerically unimportant and politically colourless. The so-called *Naprawa* (Reform Group), which was destined to gain the support of young intellectuals for Piłsudski's cause, emerged only after the *coup* and remained relatively uninfluential. Thus one can say that Piłsudski came to power because of his immense popular appeal, helped at the same time by the dissatisfaction and political frustration prevalent among nearly all strata of Polish society. This meant in fact that members of almost all political parties, acting as individuals, gave support to the new regime. Indeed, many of Piłsudski's former enemies wished him well or at least believed that he should be given a chance.

That the Marshal consciously steered away from any definite political affiliation was proved not only by his continued enmity towards the Right-Centre parties, but also by his cool and increasingly unfriendly attitude towards the parties of the Left, particularly the PPS, which played a decisive role in his final victory. In trying to dissociate himself from political partisanship, he went so far as to express doubts as to the continued validity of such recognized distinctions as 'Left' and 'Right'.

Such an agglomeration of supporters created an impression of national unity which was the Marshal's ultimate aim. Yet his 'camp' suffered from two serious defects. First, it had no programme.

Although not regarded as a shortcoming, such a fault showed up the inability of its component parts to agree on basic political issues and Piłsudski's lack of a definite plan for leadership. Instead of a programme he gave his supporters a watchword for action – *sanacja* – which translated into English meant 'moral sanitation'. As interpreted by the Marshal, *sanacja* was a systematic elimination of corruption, incompetence, administrative disorder, and partisan greed, accompanied by the somewhat hazy aim of 'moral regeneration' for the entire Polish nation. The lack of content, characteristic of the concept of *sanacja*, was at first quite successfully replaced by Piłsudski's personal charisma. It was believed that he alone could save Poland from disintegration and lead her towards political maturity. In the thirties, however, the lack of a programme became a serious liability, lending to the Marshal's repressive action against the recalcitrant politicians all the characteristics of personal vindictiveness. Even more tragic was the situation after his death, when his successors, unable to perpetuate his mystical influence, fell back on even more autocratic practices, thus building a wall between them and the masses.

The absence of a programme underlined the second defect of the Piłsudski 'camp'. It continued to be divided into a number of groups and categories, each of varying importance, the main criterion being its relationship to the Marshal. Piłsudski himself, still encountering resistance against his policies, ended by recognizing only one measure of loyalty. Forgetting his pre-war ties with the socialists, he relied on those who had served with him in the Legions, had acted under his command in the underground Polish Military Organization, or had taken an unequivocal stand on his behalf during the May *coup*. Thus a 'praetorian' guard came into being which gradually rose to prominence and eventually pushed other adherents into less significant positions. While some members of this new élite were still imbued with the conspirator-like mentality of their past underground activities, all were military men accustomed to approach problems from a military point of view and having nothing but scorn for the ways of the civilian. Commands and orders tended to replace reason and discussion in their councils. As members of this class progressively occupied the most important posts of command, the Polish state and society became excessively militarized. This process was accelerated during the late thirties and reached its zenith at the time of Piłsudski's death and after, when the Polish government was frequently referred to as that of the 'colonels'.

The fact that the core of Piłsudski's adherents were military men was not sufficient to repel the Polish public, which entertained considerable respect for the soldier. The character of these 'soldiers', however, soon became a matter of serious concern. The more idealistic among them failed to understand party life once the object of their dreams – independent Poland – had been created. Like their commander they had little understanding of the socio-economic problems of society and state. As one observer put it,

> the different leading positions were occupied by 'smooth operators', who only associated themselves with the Polish Legions and *ex post facto* managed to acquire some military certificate, rather than genuine legionnaires, many of whom did not compete for leading positions.[12]

No wonder that, as a group, they could not match the moral standards of the man whose ideas and heritage they tried to represent. However patriotic and dedicated to the cause of Poland they might have been, their crude and unsophisticated craving for power tended to become a divisive element in the Polish body politic.

Profoundly shaken by the unexpected armed conflict, after May 1926 Piłsudski adopted an attitude of moderation and conciliation. His moving tribute to the dead on both sides who, he declared, had given their lives for Poland but whose blood would produce a 'new crop of brotherliness', was undoubtedly sincere. So was his apparent humility when he admitted his own share of guilt. His words imploring 'God, the All-Merciful ... to turn aside His avenging hand from us'[13] were an echo of his awareness of human frailty and of the soft and melancholy atmosphere of his Lithuanian motherland. No doubt the demands of politics prevented him from maintaining his original stance of forgiveness and restraint. The May *coup* plunged him into a maelstrom. His ruthlessness four years later, even if accompanied by familiar doubts and misgivings, was a logical conclusion of the turbulence he had engendered.

Piłsudski's supporters, both civilian and military, did not possess that degree of human understanding and statesmanship. The originally mild purge of the civil service by the first Bartel administration increased its momentum after the renewal of the conflict with the opposition. The organs of local administration especially usurped powers greatly exceeding those they had possessed before the May *coup*. Even the goodwill of the central authorities in Warsaw, which tried to remedy many of the injustices, could not curb the autocratic tendencies of the lower organs of government.

While perhaps more understandable, the behaviour of the

---

[12] Václav Fiala, op. cit., p. 20. The author added that approximately 15,000 legionnaires (surviving from the original 30,000) by the mid-thirties had grown into the 240,000-strong Union of Legionnaires.
[13] Piłsudski's order to the armed forces of 22 May 1926, reprinted in Piłsudski, op. cit., vol. IX, p. 11.

Marshal's military adherents remained remote from his ostensible intentions. The three commanding officers of the troops who had remained loyal to the government were kept in prison without trial for over a year, one of them (General W. Zagórski) disappearing under conditions giving rise to suspicions of political murder. Others, including Piłsudski's old rival Władysław Sikorski, were forced to resign. Had it not been for the Marshal's protection, many other members of the army high command would have suffered. On the other hand, a large number of low-ranking officers did not escape the consequences of their decision to back the constitutionally elected government. The vindictiveness of the May victors, which stemmed from their privileged position in the army, dealt a serious blow to the internal unity of the armed forces.

The energetic and disciplined hand of the Marshal and his supporters eliminated much of the chaos and anarchy characteristic of the previous regime. The *coup* also brought about a closer integration of the individual Polish provinces. The constitutional amendment of 2 August 1926 increased the power of the President, enabling him to dissolve the *Sejm* and the Senate and issue decrees with the force of law subject to subsequent ratification by parliament. As a result legislative action could be taken with greater ease and executive decisions put into effect more speedily. The government was authorized to spend money up to the amount of the preceding year's budget, if the *Sejm* failed to approve a new budget by a certain date. Steps were taken to ensure that no one political party or group could paralyse the legislative and executive branches of government and bring the administrative system to a halt. While constitutionally on doubtful grounds, the regime's initial practice of appointing members of the cabinet on the basis of their expert knowledge tended to increase the quality of the governmental apparatus.

On the other hand, Piłsudski's immediate entourage began to show its lack of experience for running the complex mechanism of a modern state. The initial economy measures were soon abandoned and the number of civil servants, who were expected to obey unquestioningly the orders of the government, exceeded in the middle thirties the total of the pre-May 1926 period. The military members of the Piłsudskist 'establishment', who gradually penetrated into the civilian administrative system, took over offices for which they lacked the necessary qualifications. But political promotions in the army were just as detrimental as military influence in government. The fact that in many cases important commands were entrusted to Legion veterans and those of the Polish Military Organization (POW), while professionals trained in modern military strategy and tactics were passed over, could hardly contribute to the overall mor-

1 Eighteenth-century Warsaw. Krakowskie Przedmieście, seen from Castle Square. Painting by Canaletto (Bellotto)

2 Władysław Aleksander Łubieński, Primate of Poland, with his retinue at the election of King Stanisław II Augustus Poniatowski. Detail of a painting by Canaletto (Bellotto)

3 Castle Square, Warsaw, today. Completely destroyed in World War II; rebuilt in original style. The column is a monument to Zygmunt III. The tall building in the distance is the rebuilt cathedral

4 Village in Małopolska, near Ojców. Note the traditional building style, with wooden thatched cottages

5 Town square and town hall (*ratusz*), Tarnów, southern Poland. The Renaissance style of the latter derives from the sixteenth and seventeenth centuries, a period of prosperity in this region

6 Peasant market in a small town in the Warsaw region. Note the traditional design of the carts, almost always horse-drawn. The only innovation is the use of old car tyres on their wheels

7 The Old Town Square (Stary Rynek), Warsaw, rebuilt in original seventeenth- and eighteenth-century style

8 The late medieval town hall at Wrocław, one of the finest examples of municipal architecture in Central Europe

9 The rebuilding of the centre of Warsaw

13 Tadeusz Kościuszko (1746–1817), patriot. In the American War of Independence he became adjutant to General George Washington and later leader of the Polish uprising against the partitioning powers

10 Pyrzyce (Pyritz) in western Pomerania, fifteen years after its destruction during the Red Army's advance. The buildings, largely wood, were completely destroyed. Only the church and the medieval town walls and gates survived

11 Łódź, the late nineteenth-century textile-mill, erected by Poznański, and, to the right, the 'palace' which he built for himself. The factory still operates; but the palace is now the seat of the urban government of Łódź.

12 'We were, we are, and we shall remain on the Baltic, the Odra, and the Nysa'. A public display of political intentions on a building in Szczecin

14 Józef Piłsudski (1867–1935)

15 Gdańsk, September 1939. The German attack on the Westerplatte

16 Warsaw, September 1939. German bombing in progress; an oil depot in flames

17 Warsaw, September 1939. The results of German bombing

19 Clearing the rubble. The start of the rebuilding of Warsaw in 1945

20 Stanisław Mikołajczyk (*2nd from left*), former Prime Minister in exile and leader of the Peasant Party, in New York in 1950, with, on his left, Vladko Macek, former vice-premier of Yugoslavia, and Ferenc Nagy, former premier of Hungary

22 Adam Rapacki, Polish Foreign Minister 1956–68

21 [*opp.*] Władysław Gomułka, re-established as First Secretary, addresses a
mass rally in Warsaw on 24 October 1956

23 General de Gaulle in Zabrze, summer 1967

24 Mieczysław Moczar, President of the Union of Fighters for Freedom and Democracy

25 Józef Cyrankiewicz, Polish Prime Minister, toasts Alexei Kosygin of the USSR and Willi Stoph of East Germany at the end of a *Comecon* session in Warsaw in May 1970

26 Cardinal Stefan Wyszyński, Primate of Poland, with his chaplain at Częstochowa during the celebrations to mark the millennium of the Polish State in 1966

ale and quality of the armed forces. No wonder that after the 1939 catastrophe indignant voices claimed that obsolete military doctrine was partly responsible for the military defeat.

When he came to power, Piłsudski endeavoured to reap the rewards of his illegal action without having to bear the burden of its revolutionary character. He upheld the powers of the acting President, the speaker of the *Sejm*, Maciej Rataj; formally respected the competence of parliament; and went so far as to tolerate the existence of an opposition. Yet his insistence on legality was largely a well-conceived stratagem, for he allowed his name to go forward as a candidate for the Presidency. When elected, he refused to serve – to the utter consternation of his leftist supporters, stating rather cynically that he had run only in order 'to legalize his activities'.[14] Instead he suggested the election of the colourless and pliable Ignacy Mościcki. In both elections the opposition put up a counter-candidate and this caused the Marshal great chagrin and dissatisfaction. The only constitutional basis of Piłsudski's power was his absolute control over the military establishment as Minister of War and Inspector-General of the Army. In the latter function he took over the supreme command of the armed forces, in keeping with the reinstated decree of 1921. These two offices he held until the end of his life.

While behaving in a conciliatory manner, Piłsudski was in no way prepared to give up any of the *de facto* powers which he had gained by the *coup*, believing over-optimistically that the parties of the *Sejm*, having recognized their defeat, would be willing voluntarily to do his bidding. It was this lack of psychological insight which tended to aggravate the continued struggle between him and his associates on the one hand, and the parliamentary opposition on the other.

No doubt Piłsudski's initial measures and policies encountered no ostensible resistance. This was true, for instance, of the appointment of the Bartel government of experts, welcomed by many because of its composition and as an indication of goodwill on the part of the Marshal. The same can be said of the amendment to the constitution which was adopted in August 1926. It greatly increased the authority of the executive, giving the President an almost unlimited right to dissolve the National Assembly and to rule 'in case of urgent necessity' by means of decree-laws in the intervals between the sessions of the *Sejm*. In addition, the chief executive was authorized to issue decrees having the force of law on the basis of broad enabling acts passed by parliament. The continued validity of such decrees was made dependent on the subsequent approval of the *Sejm*, to which

---

[14] *Kurier Poranny* of 1 June 1926, reprinted in Piłsudski, op. cit., vol. IX, p. 33.

they were to be submitted within two weeks after the beginning of a session. In view of the latent difficulties of past legislatures, the government's new budgetary powers, referred to above, were a significant step in the consolidation of its authority. In other ways, too, the power of the executive was increased and stability and continuity – the two qualities which previous regimes had lacked – became distinct possibilities.

The reaction of the parties to the amendment signalled a momentous change in their political behaviour. When faced with a basic constitutional issue, for the first time they pursued policies corresponding to their true political principles. The rightists supported the bill, expressing a desire that the reform be accompanied by others eliminating proportional representation, raising the voting age, and changing the electoral districts to the detriment of the minorities. On the other hand, the socialists, disturbed by the provisions relating to decree-laws, voted against the amendment. Their opposition, however, was lukewarm as they did not visualize the manner in which the right of dissolution especially would be used.

But soon all the opposition parties found themselves engulfed in a bitter conflict with the regime. Parliamentary defeats and votes of no-confidence in the individual members of the government were countered by a refined, highly 'legalistic' use of the right of dissolution. Before 1926 was out Piłsudski had himself taken over the premiership. Abandoning entirely the traditional coalition concept, he formed a cabinet which included former or apparent leftists and conservatives, and the energetic General Felicjan Sławoj-Składkowski as his Minister of the Interior. At the same time he gave other military collaborators important positions within individual Ministries, thus allowing the future rulers of Poland, the 'colonels', to penetrate the administrative apparatus.

Not surprisingly, while trying to combine the new 'tougher'[15] line with the semi-constitutional use of the *Sejm*, Piłsudski was faced with a more hostile and more outspoken opposition than before. To strengthen his position he gained the support of the traditional landed aristocracy, as well as that of the industrial spokesmen. His meeting with the industrialists, however, was of much deeper significance. The negotiations which took place at the castle of Prince Janusz Radziwiłł, in Nieśwież, gave a psychological boost to the regime, still uncertain of its position in the country. The Marshal himself, a member of an impoverished gentry family, was attracted to the old-time aristocrats, sharing some of their inclinations and

---

[15] Three critics of the regime, including the former National Democratic Minister of Finance, Jerzy Zdziechowski, were brutally beaten up by assailants in army officers' uniforms, whose identity 'could not be established'.

believing that close contact with these representatives of past Polish grandeur would lend him further prestige. Politically the agreement accomplished two things. First, by splitting the rightist bloc it dealt a heavy blow to Piłsudski's National Democratic opponents. Secondly, it provided the regime with an excellent opportunity to inaugurate, in accordance with its appeals for national unity, its new policy of 'social equilibrium'. In practice, this orientation meant a *status quo* for agrarian policy and a rejection of all 'social experimentation'. Surprisingly, even then the PPS, which must by then have realized the direction of its former hero's policies, did not oppose him, but only the 'monarchists and reactionaries in his cabinet'. Moreover, Ignacy Daszyński continued his secret conversations with Piłsudski, his 'old friend' and comrade.

Another significant gain of the *sanacja* regime was the establishment of a *modus vivendi* with the Roman Catholic Church. Largely through the influence of the hierarchy and that of the Vatican the Piłsudski government managed to bring about, if not an understanding, then at least an accommodation, with this powerful factor in Polish national life, whose opposition would have represented a formidable obstacle.

The immediate reaction of the National Democrats was entirely different from that of the parties of the Left. As early as December 1926, Dmowski had founded the Camp of Great Poland (*Obóz Wielkiej Polski*), which aimed at unifying all nationalist elements for the purpose of combating the *sanacja*. In keeping with the general trend in East-Central Europe, it regarded itself as a *movement*, not as a *party*, and its organization and aims were strictly autocratic, imbued with the spirit of militant nationalism, while its anti-semitism was even more pronounced than before. With its definite ideology, the Camp of Great Poland found a ready response among the student youth, which was greatly attracted by its radicalism and élitist concepts.

A variety of factors, of which the action of Dmowski and the lack of consistent support in the *Sejm* were perhaps the most important, caused Piłsudski to abandon his policy of relying on the support of his adherents in other political parties. With a view to the approaching election, he decided to give the *sanacja* movement a formal organizational structure. He entrusted this task to his close henchman Walery Sławek who, in December 1926, founded the 'Non-Party Bloc of Co-operation with the Government' (*Bezpartyjny Blok Współpracy z Rządem*; referred to as BBWR in keeping with its Polish initials). Fundamentally opposed to party alignments, this new body could hardly be regarded as a party. Its main goal was to co-ordinate the efforts of those who defected from the existing political parties and to propagate the fundamentally negative and vague concepts of the *sanacja,* combined with an increased emphasis on the interests of the state. BBWR also strove for the adoption of a new constitution. Its leadership consisted of elements which eventually proved to be incompatible – the technocrats of Bartel's Labour Club (*Klub Praca*) and the members of the Association for the Reform of the Republic, referred to as *Naprawa,* on the one hand, and the military hard core of the 'Piłsudskists' on the other. Apart from the traditional conservatives and the landed aristocracy, who had broken with the National Democrats, the *sanacja* movement was joined by individuals from different political groups. Many backed the BBWR for purely opportunistic reasons, desiring to reap the rewards of co-operation with the regime.

Soon the BBWR began to erode the positions of practically all parties, especially the *Piast* peasants, the Christian Democrats, and the parties of the Left. For all its impressiveness, the new bloc suffered from the same defects and indecisiveness which until 1930 characterized Piłsudski's semi-constitutional regime. It lacked a genuine programme and its policies were largely self-defeating. The BBWR endeavoured to destroy the party political system in Poland, but operated as a party itself, representing another attempt on Piłsudski's part to rule with the 'voluntary' agreement of the parties. The result of the 1928 election, in which a large number of parties took part, failed to eliminate political fragmentation. Despite the aid which the BBWR received from the government, both financial and in terms of direct help from the state administrative apparatus, the BBWR received only about a quarter of all votes (120 seats in the *Sejm* and 46 in the Senate), and was closely followed by the parties of the Left which, taken as a whole, increased their representation. Indeed, in the voting for the *Sejm* the three[16] parties of the Left had more popular votes than the government party, being deprived of their primacy only by the operation of electoral arithmetic. (They obtained altogether 119 seats in the *Sejm* and 20 in the Senate.) The magnitude of the defeat of the Right-Centre parties which, of course, bore the brunt of the BBWR attack, seemed to indicate that the public had sanctioned Piłsudski's *coup.*

Yet the new composition of parliament failed to improve the government's position. It did not dissuade Piłsudski from his unrealistic and highly dangerous notion that the *Sejm* – in deference to

16 The parties of the Left – after the departure of the small *Praca* (Labour) group, which joined the BBWR – consisted of the PPS, the *Wyzwolenie,* and the post–1926 Party of the Peasants (*Stronnictwo Chłopskie*). In November 1928 the group took the name of the Co-ordinating Commission for the Defence of the Republic and Democracy.

his moral position in the nation – should support the regime unconditionally. He failed to realize that the new Diet, particularly its leftist parties, the moral victors, would not be prepared to abdicate their constitutional rights. Its first meeting, however, which was devoted to the election of the speaker (Marshal) of the *Sejm*, dealt a heavy blow to Piłsudski's illusions. To his amazement and anger, the *Sejm* defeated his candidate, Kazimierz Bartel, and elected the socialist Ignacy Daszyński. This development signalled the beginning of a conflict between the *sanacja* and the socialists, and foreshadowed the formation of the so-called *Centrolew* – an opposition coalition of the parties of the Left and Centre.

Resigning in favour of Bartel, now premier for the second time, Piłsudski ominously expressed regret at his decision after the Soviet-Polish War 'to do nothing and leave Poland to itself', despite the fact that 'he could have destroyed like vermin the *Sejm* composed of harlots'.[17] This declaration was only the first of many similar statements in which the Marshal used vulgar and abusive language against the opposition, thus further widening the gap between his trend towards absolute dictatorship and the insistence of the *Sejm* majority on the principle of parliamentary sovereignty. The scope of the conflict covered practically all aspects of government – freedom of the press, the issue of the so-called 'discretionary' funds, and the entire problem of parliamentary control over governmental expenditure, which the constitutional amendment left vague and unclear. The dispute over this basic right of all legislatures reached its zenith in March 1929 when the *Sejm*, led by the PPS leader Herman Lieberman, proceeded to the impeachment of the Minister of Finance, Gabriel Czechowicz, for having spent over half a billion *złoty* without parliamentary authorization. Pointing out that this enormous sum was the budgetary surplus for the year 1927–28, the first after many years of deficit economy, Piłsudski, who had authorized the expenditure, maintained that the government had a moral right to use such funds at its discretion and refused to submit the matter to the *Sejm* even for *ex post facto* approval. While the bulk of the money was used for the improvement of the port of Gdynia – the pride of Poland – this fact alone, in the opposition's opinion, could not excuse such unconstitutional behaviour.

Even before the issue was terminated by the somewhat inconclusive judgement of the Tribunal of State, Piłsudski induced Mościcki to dismiss the more conciliatory Bartel and appoint Kazimierz Świtalski Prime Minister with a hard-line cabinet, half of its members either generals or colonels. As a result of this hardening of the

---

[17] Józef Piłsudski's interview with the editor of *Głos Prawdy* of 1 July 1928, reprinted in Piłsudski, op. cit., vol. IX, pp. 113, 118.

Marshal's policies, the opportunistic and somewhat unprincipled contacts between Daszyński and Piłsudski were abruptly discontinued and both sides mustered their forces for a final showdown. On 31 October Piłsudski, acting on Świtalski's behalf, appeared at the opening of the parliamentary session accompanied by about one hundred officers, who assembled in the vestibule of the parliamentary building. Thereupon Daszyński refused to open the session 'under the threat of bayonets'. The *Sejm* did not meet until December 1929. By then the Centre-Left (*Centrolew*) bloc of six parties[18] was firmly constituted and led by Daszyński. Its first act was to overthrow the Świtalski cabinet.

Surprisingly, despite his radical views about the *Sejm*, the Marshal relented. For the third time, Bartel, the opponent of the stridently anti-democratic 'colonels', was appointed premier with a cabinet predominantly composed of moderates. This sudden reversal of the trend towards full dictatorship seemed to provide a ray of hope that the extremes of autocratic rule would after all be avoided.

That this did not happen was because the Centre-Left parties, succumbing to illusions about their strength, refused at ruce which would mean the preservation of the *status quo*, and insisted on the abandonment of the semi-constitutional system and return to full democracy. Under such circumstances the apparently good-will ministry of Bartel did not last long. In March 1930 it was replaced by the cabinet of Walery Sławek, composed almost entirely of Piłsudski's more radical adherents. Sławek's cabinet, in which Sławoj-Składkowski held the portfolio of the Interior, managed to maintain itself only by proroguing the *Sejm*. Its position was made more difficult by the fact that economic prosperity brought about by Piłsudski's political stabilization and the overall world economic situation came to a sudden end. While economic crisis provided arguments for the Centre-Left opposition, it also strengthened the position of those who believed that poverty, price increases, and unemployment could be combated only by authoritarianism.

The latent crisis caused the Centre-Left parties to take the conflict outside the *Sejm*. In June they organized a Congress for the Defence of Law and Freedom in Kraków and adopted a manifesto calling for the abolition of the concealed dictatorship of Piłsudski and promising that any attempt at a new *coup* would be resisted by force. This action, it seems, was the 'last straw' as far as the Marshal was concerned. He ordered Sławoj-Składkowski to collect material against the Centre-Left leaders to be used as evidence of their seditious and subversive activities. On 25 August 1930, Piłsudski took over the

[18] *Centrolew* was composed of the three parties of the Left, the National Labour, *Piast*, and Christian Democratic parties.

reins of government for the second time, his first act being the dissolution of the National Assembly and a call for a new election to be held in November.

At the beginning of September about ninety leaders of the Centre-Left opposition and a number of representatives of the Slavic minorities were arrested and illegally detained in the fortress of Brześć. Among them were Wincenty Witos, leader of the *Piast* peasants; Herman Lieberman of the PPS; the leader of the *Wyzwolenie* (Liberation) Party, Kazimierz Bagiński; and Wojciech Korfanty of the Christian Democrats. Any election carried out after such an action alone would have been regarded as irregular. The subsequent electoral campaign, in which the meetings of the opposition were broken up, anti-government lists of candidates simply cancelled, and the demagogic watchword 'with or against Piłsudski' launched, caused the November voting to lose all the characteristics of a free election.

As expected, the BBWR emerged victorious. Out of a total of 444 seats in the *Sejm* it secured 247, and of the 111 Senate seats it obtained 76. The Left-Centre parties, including the PPS, suffered a serious setback, receiving only 82 and 14 seats respectively. Even more devastating was the defeat of the parties of the national minorities which lost well over 50 per cent of their previous strength. On the other hand, the National Democrats, now known as the National Party, by reason of their tight organization and radically nationalistic programme, increased their representation to 60 seats in the *Sejm* and 12 in the Senate. The government party achieved its aim, but not entirely, for it was denied the two-thirds majority necessary for the adoption of a new constitution.

When faced with the armed might of the *sanacja,* the threats of the opposition proved to be of no avail : the masses did not rise against the regime in the defence of freedom. On the other hand, the acts of violence and, above all, the Brześć action, caused a revulsion in practically all strata of Polish society. Even Piłsudski's supporters, who otherwise favoured the curbing of parliament's power, regarded his behaviour as excessively cruel and unnecessary. The opinion of the intelligentsia – which on this occasion spoke for the entire people – was voiced in the dignified but firm protest of the professors of the Jagiellonian University in Kraków followed by that of all other institutions of higher learning. Though released in December 1930, the main defendants were tried only at the end of 1931 on trumped-up charges of plotting a *coup d'état,* and condemned to up to three years in prison. Some, including Wincenty Witos, managed to escape to Czechoslovakia.

There is reason to believe that Piłsudski himself was overwhelmed by the tragic consequences of his ill-advised and hasty action. Once again, the idealism of his vision of a free, prosperous, and happy Poland clashed with the methods which he chose in order to put his ideal into effect. Viewed in retrospect, the outrages of Brześć were nothing but a logical escalation of the events of May 1926, when the irascible Marshal had first used unconstitutional and forceful means to remedy a situation which he regarded as degrading for Poland. Only thus can one explain why a man who in the pre-war period had set out to liberate his people from the shackles of tyranny could change into a dictator. While difficult to assess, the state of his health, which affected his nervous system, rendering him irritable and inclined to outbursts of anger and spells of depression, certainly influenced his behaviour. As pointed out by one observer, 'ever since the 1926 *coup* Piłsudski was dying, day after day, for nine long years'.[19]

Yet his political acumen and strong sense of mission did not allow him to reconsider and reverse the course of his policies. On the contrary, the tragic logic of events caused the Marshal to become more and more dependent on his immediate entourage, the coterie of 'colonels' whose power after 1930 continued to increase. Embittered by the internal political conditions, Piłsudski entrusted to this group the administration of internal political affairs under his guidance, limiting himself mainly to the formulation of military and foreign policies.

While deprived of all power, the opposition forces continued and even increased their activities. The bitter realization of defeat and the continuing economic crisis, which affected not only the unemployed worker but also the small and especially landless peasants, brought about in March 1931 the amalgamation of the three agrarian parties into a new Peasant Party (*Stronnictwo Ludowe*), which found not only leadership, but also a symbol, in Wincenty Witos and adopted a radical confiscatory land-reform programme. The PPS, which declared itself in favour of far-reaching social reforms, entered into close co-operation with the peasants.

Sławek's successor, Aleksander Prystor, aggravated the worsening economic conditions by his lack of imagination. Draconian economy measures were introduced. These, in turn, tended to strangle the economic life of the country and were countered by the organization by the PPS of mass strikes. Consequently, the BBWR, setting parliament aside, voted a far-reaching Enabling Act, making it possible for the government to rule on the basis of administrative decrees.

After the Brześć affair, the BBWR made an attempt to gain the co-operation of the National Democrats whose policies, for the most

[19] Jules Laroche, *La Pologne de Piłsudski* (Paris, 1953), p. 219.

part, it emulated. Competing for the support of youth, the government party was forced gradually to adopt radically nationalist and quasi-fascist slogans and even policies. This orientation was in direct conflict with the programme and activities of the Youth Legion (*Legion Młodych*), which was originally organized by the BBWR, but fell out with its parent body because of its insistence on radical social reforms. More successful were the two opposition youth organizations – the National Radical Camp (*Obóz Narodowo-Radykalny*) and the agrarian Union of Village Youth (*Związek Młodzieży Wiejskiej*), referred to as the *Wici*. The former was a splinter group of the National Party imbued with an extremely nationalistic and Nazi-type ideology. While very vocal, it had a small following. After less than two months it was banned for its alleged participation in the murder of the Minister of the Interior, Bronisław Pieracki, but continued its activities as an underground organization. While associated with the Peasant Party, the *Wici* organization, which recognized Witos as its ideological leader, propagated ideas even more radical than those of its parent party. The thinking of the youth organizations clearly indicated the widening gap between the founders of the state and the generation which reached maturity in the period of the economic and political crisis.

One of the main preoccupations of the ailing Marshal was the preparation of the new constitution which would express the post-1930 political realities of Polish life. The new document represented a combination of the United States Presidential type of government and contemporary authoritarian tendencies, and the singular concepts of one of its authors, a well-known lawyer Stanisław Car. At the same time, however, it was greatly influenced by the political thought and experience of Piłsudski. It lacked the liberalism of previous Polish constitutions, emphasizing the interests of the state at the expense of those of the individual. Two of its aspects lent it an élitist character. It elevated the office of President to a position of decisive influence. His broad powers to issue decrees under the 1926 amendment were further increased : in important matters of state the Presidential decree-laws did not require the Prime Minister's counter-signature (Article 56). Further, the election of the President was entrusted to an Assembly of Electors, which was limited to citizens of special distinction. The second élitist element of the constitutional charter was the enlargement of the power of the Senate. Now on a par with the *Sejm*, it was to be composed of two-thirds elected and one-third appointed members. One important prerogative of the President proved to be of legal, and also political, significance in the near future. It concerned his right to appoint his own successor 'in time of war' (Article 24).

The new document, its main characteristic a fundamental restriction of parliamentary control, represented a somewhat unusual example of constitutionalism. While rejecting autocracy outright, the constitution was intended to 'guide' the Polish nation to an eventual unrestricted system of democracy. As emphasized by practically all its interpreters, it was tailored to fit the personal characteristics of one man. Unfortunately, this man – Józef Piłsudski – was mortally ill at the time of the adoption of the basic law. He might even have been unaware of the highly irregular manner in which it was adopted – on 26 January 1935. On that day the opposition deputies, because of their small number condemned to the role of passive onlookers, decided to abstain from the *Sejm* proceedings in protest against the scornful behaviour of the majority. The constitutional *rapporteur,* Stanisław Car, immediately tabled the motion that the still rough draft of the new basic law be adopted. Before the alarmed opposition deputies could arrive, the balloting was over and the majority had begun to sing *My pierwsza brygada* ('We, the First Brigade'), the song of Piłsudski's Legions.

But the First Marshal of Poland did not live to assume the leading position of President under the new constitution, which went into effect on 23 April 1935. He died on 12 May.

Piłsudski's Successors

Towards the end of his life Marshal Piłsudski became a dictator who by using harsh and ruthless methods imposed his will on the Polish nation. But in post-war Poland he was the most determined and efficient personality of the contemporary political leaders. His regime brought about a definite improvement in public order over the anarchic conditions of pre-1926 parliamentary democracy. Despite his growing tendency towards authoritarian interference with government, the quality of public administration was greatly enhanced. Unfortunately, in the last years of his life, when he reserved his declining energy for military and foreign policy issues, the group of his *sanacja* subordinates allowed the administrative services of the country to take on an entirely political character.

It may well be that the economic improvement which followed Piłsudski's 1926 *coup* was to a large extent influenced by international factors; but it was to the credit of the government which he had chosen that the opportunities offered to it were used. It balanced the budget and achieved a surplus which enabled Poland to combat the effects of the economic crisis. Only in 1933 was the government forced to proceed to an internal loan; its success was another proof of the soundness of its financial policies. No doubt some of its accomplishments were due to deflationary measures which stood in the way of economic progress, but their immediate effectiveness could not be denied.

Piłsudski's understanding for the 'man in the street' caused him to pay attention to the interests of the economically underprivileged members of Polish society, particularly workers and small farmers. But his exaggerated emphasis on the interests of the Polish 'state' made little allowance for a systematic social policy. One could hardly reproach Piłsudski for his inability to deal with agricultural unemployment – the perennial problem of the Polish economy. Its solution would have required massive industrialization which could have been carried out only with substantial foreign loans and investments. To secure them in the circumstances of the early thirties was far beyond the possibilities of Poland.

Last but not least, Piłsudski sensed almost instinctively that the main problems of the new state were those of political unity, territorial integrity, and independence. These, he believed, could be secured by the *sanacja* regime's 'guided democracy' and the building-up of a strong army – a task for which he appeared to be eminently qualified. He elevated the armed forces to the sublime position of the main rallying-point of the Polish nation. He evoked in the masses a profound sentiment of responsibility for the defence of the state, transcending political or class differences. Surprisingly, this leading military figure of inter-war Poland neglected to provide his army with modern implements of war. Also, his military commanders continued to adhere to obsolete strategic and tactical doctrine.

Unfortunately, Piłsudski's assets were offset by the tragedy of Brześć, the emigration of outstanding national leaders, and the relegation of the opposition to the impotent role of mere bystanders. His determination to infuse military discipline into Polish public life unwittingly destroyed the political acumen of a large part of his compatriots. His premature death caused immense grief to most Poles, irrespective of their social or political standing. The seven-day funeral ceremonies in Warsaw and Kraków seemed to unite the entire nation. In one respect fate proved kind to the Polish leader. It cut the thread of his life at a time when Polish independence seemed to be firmly secured. From another point of view, however, premature death deprived the Marshal of the opportunity to make amends for the acts of violence and ruthlessness which had accompanied his ascent to power.

Many Poles, while grieving over the passing of the great Marshal, expressed genuine concern about the future of a dictatorship without a dictator. Despite his dedicated patriotism and high motivation, Józef Piłsudski ended his life by 'delivering power into the hands of a "clique" of colonels, whom he allowed to rise in the shadow of his personality and who, after his death, would be able to cover up their arbitrary authoritarianism with his name'.[20] The authority of the dead Marshal proved insufficient to curb the ambitions of his successors, whose approach to government caused hardening of autocratic rule, government malpractices, and even corruption.

Piłsudski's death marked a new stage in the history of the *sanacja* regime. The power-political vacuum was filled by a special type of collective leadership. As pointed out by the official mouthpiece of the government, *Gazeta Polska*, rule had been transferred into the hands of Piłsudski's 'oldest and most trusted collaborators'. Of these three represented the 'hard core' of the regime – President Ignacy Mościcki, Prime Minister Walery Sławek, and General Śmigły-Rydz who, allegedly in keeping with the wishes of the late Marshal, was appointed Inspector-General of the Polish Armed Forces. Despite his generally recognized political inexperience, if not *naïveté*, Śmigły-Rydz almost automatically became a member of the ruling triumvirate.[21] In addition to this highest élite, other members of Piłsudski's entourage ranked high as potential participants in the collective leadership. Among them the former premier, Aleksander Prystor; the successful Minister of the Interior of the Brześć period, General Felicjan Sławoj-Składkowski; and the Foreign Minister, Józef Beck, were the most prominent.

Piłsudski did not leave a political testament which would provide clear guidance for his successors. In their quest for the correct interpretation of the true meaning of the teaching of their late master, the new leaders of Poland were greatly handicapped by the fact that the legacy of Piłsudski's rule, while rich in action, was lacking in theory. It provided an inadequate basis for the formulation of fundamental policies. But the authoritarian trend expressed in the new constitution, whose moral and political orientation was ascribed to Piłsudski, seemed to indicate the direction to be followed. Rightly or wrongly, Piłsudski's successors concluded that Poland should continue to develop towards stricter and more rigid autocracy, bordering at times on practices to be found in contemporary totalitarian societies.

This unfortunate trend was expressed by two legislative measures – the law concerning the election of the President, and the new electoral laws – both of 8 July 1935. The former elaborated the constitutional provisions on the Presidential election, the latter provided for a new regulation of the electoral procedure. It was important because in practice it disregarded the principle of free, secret, equal, direct, and proportional suffrage expressly retained in the new constitution.

[20] Laroche, op. cit., p. 225.
[21] See Léon Noel, *L'Agression allemande contre la Pologne* (Paris, 1946), p. 26.

It reduced the size of the *Sejm* (from 444 to 208) and effected its 'depolitization' by denying political parties the right to nominate candidates. By granting this right to district electoral colleges – organized along corporativist lines – the electoral law further underlined the élitist tendencies of the April constitution and delivered the *Sejm* into the hands of the government. Composed as they were of delegates of local and municipal councils and of a number of professional organizations, the colleges could not but follow the wishes of the *sanacja* regime. Even more élitist was the system introduced for the election of the Senate. The two criteria for membership in the Senate electoral colleges – personal merit and confidence of citizens – reduced the number of those entitled to vote to bearers of high orders, officers, people with university education, and officials of territorial administration, etc., the majority of whom were government employees. In addition, the appointment of one-third of the Senate was entrusted to the discretion of the President of the Republic.

Sadly enough, one of the main authors of the new electoral laws, Prime Minister Sławek, honestly considered them to be the fulfilment of Piłsudski's dream of the final destruction of 'Sejmocracy' and the replacement of professional politicians by experts. In reality the new system left no scope for the opposition in the legislative organs, doing away even with the remaining unimportant remnants of parliamentarianism. No wonder that the opposition parties put up a desperate but ineffective resistance against the new electoral system. Realizing the hopelessness of their situation, they decided to express their protest by abstaining from the election. Despite the elaborate nature of the electoral procedure and the government's attempt to present the election as a new type of non-political voting the venture proved to be an absolute failure. Even in keeping with the official figures, which were hotly contested by the opposition, only 46 per cent of persons entitled to vote participated in the *Sejm* election. This fact alone was a serious defeat for the regime. Equally distressing was the failure to secure an 'apolitical' legislature composed predominantly of experts. Instead, regime politicians, especially those belonging to the 'colonels' group, as well as representatives of the eastern conservative estate-holders, were elected. Last but not least, the defeat of the dissenters from the Peasant Party, who allowed their names to be put on the official list, clearly demonstrated the unbreakable unity of the peasant opposition. The regime gained great majorities in the eastern, predominantly non-Polish, provinces, whereas in larger cities and western provinces as little as 30 per cent of the electors took part in the balloting. Altogether 184 Poles, 19 Ukrainians, 4 Jewish representatives, and one Russian were elected. The representation of the minorities, while somewhat higher than in 1930, resulted from a 'deal' between the regime and certain minority groups whose candidates were included on the lists. Not surprisingly 133 deputies were members of the BBWR.

Of the 96 members of the Senate, 64 were *elected* and 32 *appointed*. Among those elected the majority were high state dignitaries and military men, 45 belonging to the government bloc and only 4 to the Ukrainian minority. The 32 senators appointed by the President (including 2 German, 2 Jewish, and 2 other Ukrainian representatives) further increased the strength of the regime.

The election – despite the government's attempt to describe it as a consolidation of power by those favouring 'creative state work' – marked the beginning of the internal struggle within the ruling élite. The first conflict developed when President Mościcki refused to follow Marshal Piłsudski's recommendation that he vacate the Presidency in favour of Sławek. Indignant over this refusal, Sławek resigned as Prime Minister. Having subsequently dissolved the BBWR – regarding it rather naïvely as superfluous in the new 'depoliticized' governmental system – this personally honest and perhaps most dedicated adherent of Piłsudski deprived himself of his main source of political power.

His action greatly weakened the strength of the group of 'colonels'. At the same time it narrowed down the number of leading contestants for the late Marshal's position to two : President Mościcki, who displayed unexpected political shrewdness; and Śmigły-Rydz, whose political inexperience was offset by the support which he received from the emerging army *junta*. Gauging the resistance against the totalitarian-type election, the President appointed a civilian, the former *Wyzwolenie* member Marjan Zyndram-Kościałkowski, to the premiership. Both he and his cabinet, which included only two colonels, represented a step towards a more liberal government, one that would be able to deal with the economic crisis which hit Poland with full impact soon after Piłsudski's death.

The new Prime Minister, determined to combat unemployment, reform the tax system, and re-establish a balanced state economy, introduced a number of radical measures intended to revive the economic life of the country. But even under normal conditions his task would have been difficult; in a Poland split by internal discord, with her government denied popular support, it became insuperable. Kościałkowski's difficulties were increased by the opposition of the Śmigły-Rydz group and a refusal to co-operate on the part of the 'militarized' civil service.

Kościałkowski found support in the ranks of the *Naprawa* movement, representing the left wing of the Piłsudski camp. On the other hand, the government was weakened by the conflict with its own youth organization (*Legion Młodych*), the Moraczewski socialists, and the trade unionists, who joined the opposition. The dissolution of the BBWR, too, deprived the Kościałkowski cabinet of much of its support, rendering it more vulnerable to attack by the 'colonels', who were opposed to its liberalizing tendencies. While trying to conciliate the Left, the premier realized that substantial reforms would shatter the very foundation of the post-1926 system to which he also adhered. It was this strange dilemma that tied Kościałkowski's hands and finally brought about his downfall. The appointment in May 1936 of a 'strong' government under Felicjan Sławoj-Składkowski, including two generals and three colonels, marked the victory of the Śmigły-Rydz forces.

President Mościcki thereupon withdrew into the background. The new Prime Minister skilfully manoeuvred Śmigły-Rydz into the political limelight. While the cabinet continued to be divided into the Mościcki and Śmigły-Rydz factions, Składkowski's relationship to the Inspector-General was that of a military subordinate to his commander. In July 1936 he circulated a decree elevating Śmigły-Rydz to a position of precedence next after the President of the Republic, to whom all officials, including the premier, should show 'respect and obedience'. Finally, the appointment of Śmigły-Rydz to the exalted position of Marshal of Poland completed the measures intended to elaborate and give substance to the myth of the new 'leader' of Poland. Despite his outstanding military record, this mild and sensitive man, who combined the study of military science with painting and had only recently begun to take an interest in politics, was hardly suited for the role into which he was pushed.

The decisive positions within the state remained in the hands of the 'colonels' who of necessity shared their power with economic experts. It was in parliament, which had not lost all its importance, that the governmental bloc's lack of unity, both political and ideological, made itself felt. Walery Sławek, aided by the speakers of the Senate, Aleksander Prystor, and of the *Sejm*, Stanisław Car, attempted to follow more independent policies of mild opposition.

To counter their influence, but above all to widen the basis of the regime, Śmigły-Rydz, acting at the suggestion of his military advisers, returned to the idea of a government party. This was organized by Colonel Adam Koc in the first months of 1937 and assumed the name of Camp of National Union (*Obóz Zjednoczenia Narodowego*), generally referred to as *Ozon*. Its aim was to give the new leader a group of followers similar to that possessed by Piłsudski. Unlike its predecessor, the BBWR, *Ozon* followed the pattern of a hierarchically organized totalitarian party. It combined the idea of nationalism with that of Catholicism, making use of vague and demagogic economic slogans. To put it more crudely, *Ozon* appealed to the nationalism of the Right and tried to take the wind out of the sails of the Left by promising certain socio-economic reforms. The expectation that *Ozon*, because of its radicalism and mild anti-semitism, would draw members away from the National Party remained unfulfilled. A mass party only on paper, it drew its strength mainly from among officers, state employees, and government-financed organizations, thus becoming a weak replica of the BBWR.

Tendencies towards totalitarian methods lent the internal political split, which characterized the whole post-1926 political development of Poland, a new dimension. The two large opposition parties – the Peasant Party and the PPS – found an effective rallying-cry in the necessity to organize a common defence of the republic against creeping totalitarianism. The Peasant Party, led by the former Marshal of the *Sejm*, Maciej Rataj, manifested its absolute control over the Polish countryside. It organized immense meetings protesting against the policies of the regime and introduced a novel weapon, the peasant strike, which called forth a violent reaction on the part of the authorities. Ideologically important were the activities of the so-called *Front Morges*,[22] organized by Ignacy Paderewski, Wincenty Witos, and General Haller. Its manifestos directed to the Polish people appealed to the intelligentsia by their call for the creation of a 'government of national confidence'. The PPS also increased its activities, becoming the vanguard of anti-government resistance in urban centres. In 1937 the opposition was strengthened by the emergence of the Labour Party (*Stronnictwo Pracy*) which resulted from the unification of the Christian Democrats with the National Workers' Party. Its leaders, such as Józef Haller and Wojciech Korfanty, commanded great prestige among Poles. In 1938, the opposition parties were joined by the small Democratic Party (*Stronnictwo Demokratyczne*), which actively opposed the policies of *sanacja*, nationalism, and anti-semitism.

The communists, associating themselves with the unimportant, more extremist, groups within the PPS and the Peasant Party, managed for the first time during their twenty-year existence to score some gains too. But the official leadership of the two parties rejected the Popular Front concept as incompatible with their policies. The period of communist opportunities, however limited they might have been, was only of short duration. Having succumbed to the most

---

[22] *Front Morges* was a name used to indicate close co-operation of leading Polish patriots who met on Swiss soil in the home of Ignacy Paderewski, Morges.

dangerous deviationism of 'Trotskyism' and 'bourgeois nationalism',[23] the Polish Communist Party incurred the wrath of Stalin. In the course of 1937 many of its leaders, having been enticed into the Soviet Union, were summarily dealt with by the NKVD and the party itself dissolved because of its contamination by 'agents of Polish fascism'.[24]

Following the example of other European autocratic movements, the *Ozon* leaders made an attempt to outpace the fascist successors of the dissolved National Radical camp – the 'ABC' group and the *Falanga* led by Bolesław Piasecki. The governmental bloc used the services of Piasecki's associate, J. Rutkowski, to organize the Union of Polish Youth, which was to be based on totalitarian concepts. This idea of Colonel Koc misfired. The Union remained only a small group, being unable to compete even with the semi-legal fascist elements in the cities and among the students whom it was supposed to replace. With the exception of Warsaw the fascist extremists had a very small following, the great majority of young people giving support to the opposition parties.

The political plans of Colonel Koc were successfully opposed by the Sławek–Prystor group, which suddenly realized the discrepancy between their former socialist ideals and the reactionary tendencies of the regime. Equally important was the anti-totalitarian stand taken by the intellectually-oriented *Naprawa* group. It replaced its advocacy of enlightened despotism, to which it had adhered during Piłsudski's lifetime, by a liberal stand opposing a purely one-party form of government. At the end of 1937 Colonel Koc resigned as head of *Ozon*; he was replaced by General Stanisław Skwarczyński, a more liberal adherent of Piłsudski. Following closely on the abortive attempt of Mościcki to gain the PPS for closer co-operation with the government, the change in the *Ozon* leadership clearly indicated the abandonment of its totalitarian tendencies. It was reduced to the status of a regular political party, giving up its hierarchical structure and going so far as to organize a parliamentary club. Of course, this development did not mean return to parliamentarianism, but *Ozon* lost all political significance.

In mid-1938 the internal struggle within the 'Piłsudski camp' again flared up when Walery Sławek was elected to the office of Marshal of the *Sejm*. This highly emotional man declared his intention to restore the non-party bloc which he himself had dissolved. His aim, he emphasized, was to re-establish 'the political and moral values of the late Marshal'. The subsequent deadlock between the cabinet

[23] Dziewanowski, op. cit., p. 154.
[24] 'The Eighteenth Congress of the Communist Party of the Soviet Union', *World News and Views* (6 April 1939), p. 382.

15

and parliament was resolved by dissolution of the latter in September 1938. In taking this action, President Mościcki indicated somewhat vaguely that the new parliament would take up the urgent problem of revising the electoral laws.

The new elections, however, were still conducted on the basis of the élitist and highly undemocratic procedure of 1935, forcing the opposition parties to abstain. *Ozon*, which again assumed the role of the governmental bloc, scored an even greater victory than before. Of the 208 *Sejm* members 161 were aligned with the regime. The Senate was solidly composed of pro-government senators. Despite all indications to the contrary, the development towards totalitarian monolithism gained an almost inexorable momentum. Characteristic of the political situation were the subsequent municipal elections which took place at the turn of 1938 and 1939. Being conducted on a democratic basis, in the great urban centres and in the countryside they resulted in victories for the opposition parties, especially the PPS. Together, they won over 60 per cent of all votes.[25]

Despite these appearances Poland did not become a totalitarian state along the lines of Nazi Germany and Fascist Italy. Although totalitarian tendencies existed, they were ultimately repudiated not only because of the influence of the opposition, whose opinion was not silenced and which carried on limited political activities, but occasionally also by the representatives of the regime. No doubt there were considerable restrictions on the freedom of the press; the police and even the civil service were frequently used for illegal purposes; and the judicial system lost much of its independence. Most shameful was the existence of the notorious concentration camp at Bereza Kartuska, which had been founded as early as 1934, but acquired its bad reputation only during the rule of Piłsudski's successors. However deplorable, it was in no way comparable to Nazi concentration camps.

The fact that Poland had not become a totalitarian state has also been explained by the opposition's attitude to defence. Ever since 1926 the Polish opposition parties had voted almost unanimously for the military budget and, when issues of national defence were at stake, tended to forget their opposition. This attitude became conspicuous in 1939 when Poland was suddenly faced with the menace of Nazi totalitarianism. It was then that the 'Brześć exiles' were allowed to return to their homes, so that when the fatal blow came, in September 1939, the Polish nation faced it with unity and determination.

From the political point of view the 'reconciliation' – caused as it was by the impending catastrophe – could not conceal the bank-

25 Buell, op. cit., pp. 116–17.

ruptcy of the Polish experiment in autocratic government. It would be ludicrous to argue that the inexperienced, undisciplined, and irresponsible pre-1926 regime represented more than a mere semi-democracy. But Piłsudski's 'guided democracy' and, to a much greater extent, the authoritarianism of his successors proved to be no more capable of solving Poland's main problems. In fact, the four years or so of the rule of the 'colonels', who spoke glibly about the military preparedness of their country, did nothing to modernize its armed forces.[26] After 1934 Poland, unable to cope with the ravages of the economic crisis, could no longer compete with the systematic rearmament drive of her two powerful neighbours, falling behind in terms of quality and quantity and losing much of her significance.

The most tragic aspect of the last five years of the pre-war Polish national existence was the progressive emasculation of politics. It started under Marshal Piłsudski and reached its peak under the rule of his successors. The adoption of an anti-liberal view of politics, the erosion of the true meaning of parliament, the erection of unconstitutional institutions, and the elimination of the opposition – all this tended to undermine the belief of the Polish nation in the effectiveness of democratic methods.

Poland's Foreign Policy

The introduction of total warfare in the First World War did not destroy the utility and significance of traditional diplomacy. For a number of reasons even the smaller states of post-war Europe were enabled to play at least a limited role in the international political arena.

Apart from the pluralistic character of the League of Nations, the main cause of this phenomenon was the substantial weakening of Germany and Russia – the two colossi of Europe which for over ten years were prevented from asserting themselves in the European power-political struggle. Of similar importance was the character of French superiority over the European continent. France was never free from British interference and her policies, fundamentally of a defensive nature, did not prevent the members of the so-called 'French System' from pursuing their own foreign policies.

Under these circumstances Poland, the largest and militarily by far the most important state of the 'new' Europe, soon assumed a relatively important position in international councils. She enjoyed, more than any other of the new states, a broad scope of independence in the regulation of her external affairs.

[26] Typical of the regime mentality was the slogan *silni, zwarci, gotowi* ('strong, united, ready') which created an artificial sentiment of military strength.

What were the foundations of Poland's foreign policy? Of the many factors which determined its formulation, historical traditions, geography, and internal political developments were of decisive significance. A society which regarded its regained statehood in terms of the historical injustices inflicted upon it, was greatly influenced by the experiences of its past.

Past Polish grandeur was a constant challenge which encouraged the Great Power (*mocarstwo*) complex, especially of the nation's political leadership. This complex was reflected in Piłsudski's and all other subsequent federalist plans, in the belief in Poland's mission to protect Europe from Bolshevik danger and, last but not least, in the fateful decision 'to go it alone' in her complex relations with Nazi Germany. The initial close association of Poland with France, as well as sympathy with Hungary, also stemmed at least in part from the experience of history. While of little consequence from the point of view of military defence, geographical considerations providing for the foundation of Polish national existence were of immense importance for the contacts of the renewed state with the outside world. Thus the solution of the problem of the city of Gdańsk (Danzig) and that of Polish access to the sea, regarded as unsatisfactory both by Poles and by Germans, almost immediately gave rise to friction between the two states. In fact, Poland's location between Germany and Russia represented the fundamental problem and eventually the insoluble dilemma of her foreign policy. It determined Poland's relationship not only to these basically inimical powers, but also to France and her system of alliances and, indeed, influenced her overall position in Europe. Lastly, Poland's external policies were influenced by her internal political system. There seems to be no doubt that the hardening of Polish authoritarianism enhanced the chances of a limited understanding between Piłsudski and his Foreign Minister, Józef Beck, and the militaristic regime of Adolf Hitler.

It is extremely difficult to trace a meaningful division of the twenty years of the inter-war foreign policy of Poland. Such an attempt would imply, at least indirectly, a judgement far exceeding the limits of a critical analysis. The sole purpose of any division of Poland's international relations should be a better understanding of their aims, the methods used for their realization, and of their actual consequences.[27] From this point of view, the German-Polish Agree-

[27] Thus the following division of inter-war Polish foreign policy has been suggested: I. The initial pro-French era (1919–26); II. Period of stabilization and weakening of French ties (1926–32); III. Attempt at independent foreign policy (1933–38); IV. Third Europe policy (1938–39).
The second stage is associated with Foreign Minister August Zaleski, whereas the latter two stages are usually referred to as Józef Beck's era.

ment of January 1934, which represented an attempt to deal with the basic problem of Polish national existence, can be regarded as a dividing line between two different policies. In a general way, policy preceding that date was based on co-operation with France, acceptance of the French system of alliances, and reliance on the League of Nations multilateral concept of international security. After that date Poland, which in 1932 signed a treaty of non-aggression with the Soviet Union, made an attempt at establishing an equilibrium between her two powerful neighbours. While maintaining her alliance with France, the new relationship to Germany, which many Poles regarded as evidence of Great Power status, inaugurated a number of policies whose contrast with those of the pre-1934 period was unmistakable.

The cooling of relations with the French was accompanied by outright enmity against France's ally, Czechoslovakia, aggressiveness against Lithuania, and a belief that the time had come for Poland to assume the leadership of what Beck regarded as the 'non-committed third' of Europe. Symptomatic of this new approach to international relations was the acceptance of the German concept of 'bilateralism' and the rejection of the League of Nations idea that peace and security should be based on multilateral undertakings. As stated by Beck, 'Poland was no longer prepared to ally itself with doctrinaire blocs or to allow our country to become the instrument of policy which it has not itself fixed'.[28] While convincing arguments were put forward to justify the new policy, its net result was clearly negative. The events preceding the outbreak of the Second World War demonstrated its unfeasibility. Yet the return to a more concrete and on the surface more far-reaching guarantee – readily given not only by France but also by Britain – did not save Poland from a crushing defeat.

As one student of the pre-1933 situation pointed out, 'although their motives were mutually exclusive, Germany and Russia shared at least one common interest : to destroy Poland's independence, or at least to reduce her to political impotence'.[29] As a result, it was not surprising that the 1922 Rapallo Agreements and the subsequent co-operation of the general staffs of Germany and Russia were recognized by the Poles as a deadly menace to their national existence. While perhaps less effective than it has been generally assumed, up to 1926 German-Soviet co-operation successfully checked any military action which the Warsaw government might have contemplated in support of the French-Belgian occupation of the Ruhr. Indeed,

---

[28] Quoted Buell, op. cit., p. 333.
[29] Josef Korbel, *Poland Between East and West* (Princeton, 1963), p. 5.

commonly shared hatred of Poland became one of the most solid ties uniting the two outcasts of Europe.

The immediate post-war history of Polish-German relations was nothing but a series of incidents keeping animosity between the two countries at its highest pitch. Again and again, Germany declared her unwillingness to recognize the loss of her eastern provinces, being determined not to miss any opportunity to harass and weaken her eastern neighbour. Both the conservative military and the progressive civilian leaders of the post-1918 Reich pursued a cold war against Warsaw and did their best to influence world public opinion so that it would recognize the Berlin point of view that Poland was nothing but a *Saisonstaat* – one of the most monstrous results of the unjust Versailles settlement. Significantly, the gradual re-admission of Germany into the European community, expressed in the Locarno Agreements, was preceded by the outbreak of a tariff war between the two states, which proved highly injurious to Poland's economic interests and was relentlessly pursued until the German-Polish Agreement of 1934.

In a similar fashion the Soviet Union – obsessed as she was by the danger of a new Western intervention – regarded Poland as the main exponent of capitalist imperialism. The Polish-Soviet relationship was compounded by a number of difficult and almost insoluble problems. For Poland feared communism as much as the re-admission of Russia into the fold of European nations; she believed in the danger of a new communist-sponsored Pan-Slavism; and, not surprisingly, viewed her relationship to her eastern neighbours in the terms of the 1919–20 war which had enabled her to push her borders beyond the ethnically Polish area. Despite occasional attempts at *rapprochement,* such as the 1922 Moscow conference on the reduction of armaments or the July 1924 consular convention, the relations between the two states remained strained, each accusing the other of having constantly violated the provisions of the Treaty of Riga. Complaining about Poland's maltreatment of her Belorussian and Ukrainian minorities, the Moscow government organized occasional raids on the Polish border areas, forcing Warsaw to proceed to the organization of a special corps of frontier guards. At the same time the Soviet government made full use of its subsidiary weapon, the Comintern, which regarded Poland as one of its main targets.

To counter this dual danger to Poland's territorial integrity and even national independence Marshal Piłsudski – having proved the military strength of his country by defeating the Soviet armies before Warsaw – turned to France, Poland's traditional friend. Diplomatically forgetting some of his misgivings about post-1918 French policies, especially the critical attitude of Paris towards his eastern policy, the

Marshal displayed a high degree of political acumen. He travelled to the French capital and personally negotiated a treaty with the then most powerful state on the European continent. In the Treaty of Alliance, signed on 19 February 1921, the signatories pledged themselves to 'concert on questions of international policy', to enter into economic collaboration, and 'to concert action in case of unprovoked aggression against the territory of the two parties'. They undertook also 'to consult each other before conclusion of agreements relating to Eastern Europe'. Of equal significance was the secret military convention, insisted upon by Piłsudski, which provided for mutual aid in case of German aggression and a somewhat circumscribed obligation of France to aid Poland in case of Soviet aggression. France, however, was expressly absolved from the duty to send troops to fight on Polish territory.

Thus started an alliance which for a number of years came to be regarded as the axiom of Polish foreign policy and the mainstay of the so-called French system of alliances. Unfortunately, Poland's relationship with Czechoslovakia, the second potentially most important member of the French alliance, was far from satisfactory. The wound caused by the division of the former duchy of Teschen, which the Poles refused to recognize as permanent, was exacerbated by a number of other factors. Thus the first political treaty between the two states, which was signed in 1921, remained unratified and only gradually did the two nations begin to realize the community of their interests. On different occasions, such as the 1922 Genoa Conference, or during the common endeavour to secure the signing of the 1924 Geneva Protocol, Poland and Czechoslovakia pursued identical policies. This development reached its zenith in 1925, when a comprehensive commercial and, in part also, political treaty was signed. Even then, however, differences of a political and also psychological character failed to bring about a more far-reaching and permanent *rapprochement* between the two countries.

The short-lived period of Polish-Czechoslovak co-operation was influenced at least to a certain degree by the friendly relations between Poland and Romania, Czechoslovakia's partner in the Little Entente. As early as March 1921 these two western neighbours of Soviet Russia, both fearful of Soviet territorial revindications, signed a defensive alliance directed against 'an unprovoked attack against their eastern borders'. But the attempt to work out a definitive organizational framework for close Polish collaboration with the Little Entente remained unsuccessful.

The bitter feud between Poland and Lithuania, caused by the Polish seizure of Wilno, was not terminated by the Western acceptance of the *fait accompli* brought about by Polish arms. Lithuania refused to recognize the decision of the Conference of Ambassadors, closed her borders, and interrupted diplomatic and all commercial relations with Poland and, indeed, regarded herself as being in a state of war with that country. The 1925 Polish Concordat with the Vatican – generally regarded as an approval of the Warsaw point of view – further aggravated the tense relations between the two states. Despite repeated attempts to end this highly irregular situation, Lithuania, which enjoyed the support of the Soviet Union, maintained her uncompromising stand until 1938.

While not the beginning of a new stage, the Locarno treaties of 16 October 1925 prepared the ground for a gradual development which ultimately brought about a fundamental reorientation of Polish foreign policy. Stemming from a number of considerations – of which France's continued search for security and the new 'fulfilment' policy inaugurated by the German Foreign Minister, Gustav Stresemann, had been the most important – Locarno was accepted by the majority of the French public with approval and even enthusiasm. This complex of treaties sealed, by means of a mutual guarantee agreement, the *status quo* on the western borders of Germany, at the same time providing through arbitration treaties for a peaceful settlement of disputes between Germany and France and Germany and Belgium. No such security, however, was granted to Germany's eastern neighbours, Poland and Czechoslovakia. They had to console themselves with mere arbitration treaties with the Reich. In order to provide her eastern allies with the guarantees which Germany, Great Britain, and Italy refused to give, France entered into separate treaties of alliance with them. While more precise than the previous treaty with Poland of 1921, which remained valid, the new agreement was more limited because of its dependence on the operation of the Covenant of the League of Nations.

Whatever the expectations of the authors of the Locarno Pact might have been, subsequent developments proved that both its provisions and its ideology, rather optimistically referred to as the 'spirit of Locarno', did not substantially increase European security. In France and in Britain it helped, in a similar way to the 1928 Pact of Paris, to create an atmosphere of false security. In Germany it increased the pressure for a future 'peaceful' settlement of the territorial conflict with Poland. It provided fuel for a discussion, albeit unofficial, about the possible settlement of the issue of Polish Pomorze and Gdańsk whose return to Germany, it was held in many quarters, would secure European peace.

The hopes of the Western Powers that the German-French understanding would weaken the ties of the Reich to Moscow also proved unsubstantiated. The 'spirit of Locarno' failed to prevail entirely over that of Rapallo. For Stresemann saw to it that the *rapprochement* with the West and German entry into the League of Nations would be balanced by continued German-Russian collaboration. The so-called 'neutrality' treaty, concluded in the spring of 1926, again hinted at the possibility of concerted action by the two countries against Poland. This menace was underscored by the increase of military co-operation between the *Reichswehr* and the Red Army.

No wonder that – despite all protestations to the contrary – the ties between Poland and France underwent an imperceptible but definite change. 'While there was no unanimity of views in Poland, and grave domestic issues somehow obscured the importance of Locarno, many people sensed danger in the pact.'[30] This perhaps undesired effect of Locarno on France was best expressed by Paul Reynaud who, writing in retrospect, observed that his country 'adopted a policy of an ostrich' or 'perhaps' – and this he regarded as much more serious – 'Locarno already contained the spirit of Munich'.[31] Poland was disillusioned and realized the futility of her belief that common action of the First World War Allies might bring Germany 'to its senses'. At first this undercurrent of deep disappointment was drowned in the customary expression of French-Polish friendship. As time passed, however, the fact that Poland failed to secure a permanent seat in the League of Nations Council coupled with the intense *crescendo* of German revisionist propaganda, to which even some elements of the French public tended to succumb, rubbed in the feeling that Poland had become the subject of the policy of others. Particularly vexing was the support offered by the Berlin government to the ceaseless stream of complaints by members of the German minority who made full use of the system of the international protection of minorities, as well as the more elaborate provisions of the Upper Silesian Statute. This constant harassment of the Polish government, which in the European forum was presented as a constant menace to peace, tended to undermine Polish sympathy for the League of Nations. It was these and other feed-back effects (*Rückwirkungen*) of Locarno which aggravated Polish dissatisfaction.

Yet, when in May 1926 Piłsudski seized power, at least on the surface of things, Poland seemed stronger externally than internally. The republic was still shielded by its alliances with France and Romania; held its own in the League, where it eventually secured a semi-permanent seat in the League of Nations Council; and maintained correct, if not friendly, relations with a number of other governments, such as those of the Baltic states (excepting Lithuania)

[30] Piotr Wandycz, op. cit., p. 365.
[31] Paul Reynaud, *La France a sauvé l'Europe* (Paris, 2 vols., 1947), vol. 1, pp. 47–8.

and the Little Entente. The 1926 *coup*, however, had far-reaching repercussions for Polish foreign policy. Until 1930 Marshal Piłsudski permitted public discussion both in the *Sejm* and in the press of internal political problems, but his idea of 'democracy' did not allow such discussion in relation to the aims and means not only of the military but also of the foreign policies of his regime. Such important matters, Piłsudski held, would have to be decided by him alone. This new approach explains why for a relatively long period of time the fundamental assumptions of Polish foreign policy remained unchanged. During the first five years of his regime Piłsudski devoted his energies to the building-up of the army which he considered to be the main instrument of foreign policy. The protracted struggle with the internal opposition, whose militant resistance was broken only by the 1930 Brześć action, also prevented the Marshal from giving the full imprint of his personality to the conduct of external affairs.

Yet even in this ostensibly inactive period, which was marked by the diplomatically immaculate and politically cautious behaviour of Foreign Minister August Zaleski, at least some elements of the new 'foreign policy style', imposed by Piłsudski, could be clearly discerned. Warsaw's foreign relations lost much of their rigidity and Poland, rather surprisingly, managed to profit from the hated Locarno Agreements and the 'spirit' which they engendered. She cleverly exploited the justified fear of the Russians that Locarno and its aftermath would alienate Germany from her pro-Soviet policies. In turn, by reacting to the overtures of the Kremlin, the Warsaw government aroused the fear of Berlin that its partner might abandon its traditional anti-Polish stand. It was by these methods that Poland gradually acquired more freedom for political manoeuvring. By the end of the twenties both Germany and the Soviet Union pursued their own paths in the regulation of their relations with Poland. The signs of a possible Polish-German *rapprochement* were countered by renewed Soviet efforts to induce Poland to sign a non-aggression treaty. Their result, the so-called Litvinov Protocol of February 1929, represented a regional supplement to the Briand-Kellogg Pact, to which not only Russia and Poland, but also Romania, Estonia, Latvia, and eventually also Lithuania, subscribed. While of doubtful value from the point of view of international security, the Litvinov Protocol represented the first break of the hostile encirclement of Poland.

Relations with Germany remained unchanged, especially when Stresemann's unimaginative successors, unable to keep the equilibrium between East and West, had to compete with the extreme nationalism of the growing Nazi movement. With the appointment of Maxim Litvinov to the office of Commissar of External Affairs, Soviet foreign policy, having deviated somewhat from the diplomatic aspects of Rapallo, became more flexible. In particular, it began to draw closer to France and expressed willingness to adopt a more positive attitude towards Poland. Whatever its motivation might have been – and there is reason to believe that it stemmed from the internal and external weakness of the Soviet Union – the sudden goodwill of Moscow was taken up by Warsaw, which by the end of 1930 was ready to extend its new 'political outlook' to the sphere of Polish external relations.

This 'new look' was closely associated with the personality of Józef Beck, one of the closest collaborators of Marshal Piłsudski, who in 1930 became Under-Secretary for Foreign Affairs. While both Zaleski and Beck depended with regard to major problems entirely on the will of the Marshal, there was an immense difference in their political thinking. A man of scholarly tendencies, Zaleski, during the major part of his tenure, was engaged in delicate dealings with the *Sejm*, and, personally at least, was never prepared to destroy all contacts with the democratic public. Beck, on the other hand, had an entirely different background. Having co-operated, as an army colonel, with Piłsudski in the 1926 *coup*, he had reached political maturity at a time when 'the clatter of officers' sabres could be heard in the corridors of the *Sejm*, when soldiers pledging their allegiance to the teachings of their Marshal prevented the regular opening of the Polish legislature'.[32] As a result, Beck was not burdened with the 'heritage' of parliamentary responsibility and eagerly accepted, in military fashion, all the commands of his chief. This attitude was best expressed at the Wilno meeting in 1934 of the former legionnaires to whom Beck reported on the Polish denunciation of the treaty relating to the international protection of minorities as follows : 'The commander gave the order and we put it into effect.'[33] Whatever criticism can be levelled against Beck's policies, he definitely cannot be reproached for not having conscientiously executed the orders of his chief. Indeed, so long as Piłsudski was capable of conducting the affairs of state, it was his ideas, methods, sympathies, and antipathies which determined Polish foreign policy.

Piłsudski brought to Poland's complex international relations the same conspiratorial, militaristic, and emotional elements which characterized his handling of internal policy matters. In fact, the international scene of inter-war Europe seemed to be perfectly suited to

[32] Václav Fiala, op. cit., p. 142.
[33] In his conversation with Hitler Beck referred to himself 'as the Foreign Minister who had to carry out the great schemes of Marshal Piłsudski'. See Józef Beck, *Final Report* (New York, 1957), p. 95.

his brilliantly original and unorthodox, but politically adventurous, concepts which regarded surprise and diversion as characteristics of a good foreign policy.

It was with this ammunition, both conceptual and tactical, that the Marshal and Beck set out to build Poland into a Great Power. Faced with the mounting attacks of the Germans, Piłsudski, the arch-enemy of the Russians, continued his efforts for a final settlement with the Soviet Union. On 24 July 1932, Russia, having shoved aside the objections of Germany, signed a Treaty of Non-Aggression with Poland, reaffirming the validity of the Riga Treaty (including its border provisions) and imposing on the signatories the duty 'to refrain from taking aggressive action against or invading the territory of the other Party. . . .'

Soon after this success, which greatly enhanced the prestige of Poland, Beck replaced Zaleski as Foreign Minister, thus being given an opportunity further to develop his policy of equilibrium between Germany and the Soviet Union. The treaty with Russia, which seemed to assure Polish security in the east, encouraged the belief that – despite the continued animosity of the Germans – a similar agreement might be arrived at also in the west. This development was accompanied by a number of events which foreshadowed pro-found changes in the European political system, amounting almost to a *renversement des alliances*, which took place after 1934.

Throughout 1933 Poland's foreign orientation alternated between the old policy of alliances and the temptation to establish her as a balancing factor between her two powerful neighbours. That the latter policy prevailed was due to a number of reasons. First, the wavering behaviour of France was causing serious concern in War-saw. Her attitude towards the revision of the Peace Treaties (whose main target at the time appeared to be Polish Pomerania); her lack of resistance to German rearmament; and, above all, her apparent acquiescence in Mussolini's proposal for a Four-Power Pact re-affirmed Piłsudski's fear about the reliability of his ally. Whatever the truth in the story about the Polish leader's plan for a preventive war,[34] there is reason to believe that a determined military stand by

---

[34] The issue of the preventive war allegedly suggested by Piłsudski has be-come a subject of great speculation. While indications of such an intention can be found in the dispatches of a number of diplomats (as well as in memoirs), evidence of definite Polish military preparations and negotiations with France is missing. One can assume that, particularly in April 1933, Piłsudski was not averse to such action.

See Wacław Jedrzejewicz, 'The Polish Plan for a "Preventive War" against Germany', *Polish Review*, vol. XI, No. 1 (1966), pp. 62–91; also Anna Cienciała, 'The Significance of the Declaration of Non-Aggression of 26 February 1934', in Polish German and International Relations: A Reappraisal', *East European Quarterly*, vol. I, No. 1 (1967), pp. 16–18.

France against Germany would have been eagerly supported by Poland. The second reason for Poland's decision was the behaviour of Nazi Germany. After having clashed violently with the Poles, Adolf Hitler suddenly changed his tactics. He abandoned entirely the Rapallo policy and offered friendship to Warsaw, undoubtedly realizing the tremendous assets to be gained from the additional worsening of Franco-Polish relations and the disintegration of the French system of alliances. While perhaps of less significance, the German appreciation of Polish power, so undiplomatically under-estimated by Paris, had a definite value for the prestige-conscious Piłsudski and Beck. Last, but not least, the achievement of an agreement with the rising power of Hitlerite Germany at the time of her isolation and relative weakness was regarded as good diplomacy which was bound to bear fruit in the future.

Such was the background of the Declaration of Non-Aggression and Understanding signed on 26 January 1934. The treaty, which briefly referred to the continuation of the existing obligations of both signatories to other countries, emphasized their determination to act together on all subjects concerning their mutual relations and never to use force in the settlement of their disputes. The Declaration was to be good for ten years.

The Polish policy of 'equilibrium', inaugurated by the German-Polish Declaration, has been subjected to severe criticism. In particular, Poland was accused of having helped Nazi Germany out of her isolation, contributed to the destruction of the system of collective security, and dealt a final blow to the French defensive system, regarded as the last obstacle standing in the way of German imperialism.

Yet, when considered from the strictly Polish point of view, the new policy, which did away with the 'iron ring' of Rapallo and seemingly diverted Nazi expansionism from Poland, did not necessarily appear to be harmful to Polish national interests. That it turned out to be one of the main instruments of Hitler in his drive for European domination was due to two factors – Polish weakness and the subsequent policies of Minister Beck.

The reaction of the anti-Nazi elements in Europe was perhaps best expressed by the distinguished Romanian historian Nicolae Iorga, who wrote :

Poland extended its hand to Germany at a time when everyone in Germany burns with a desire for revenge and endeavours to restore everything that Poland has taken away from it. Poland went to Berlin in order to receive a gracious assurance that everything has been forgiven. It turned its back on France which in all uncertainties is the living symbol of the preservation of treaties.[35]

The maintenance of independence and impartiality between her two basically antagonistic neighbours proved to be a task beyond the strength of the Polish republic. The concept of 'equilibrium' bound the hands of the Polish policy-makers, denying them exactly that freedom of action it was intended to secure. While ostensibly dead, the 'spirit of Rapallo' hung over the heads of the Polish leaders, constantly forcing them to take actions which would prove their strictest neutrality. In view of the ever-growing German aggressiveness and the traditional anti-Russian tendencies of Warsaw the new policy was soon bound to acquire a definitely anti-Soviet bias.

More harmful from the point of view of the Polish national interest were three other by-products of the post-1934 policies. Despite the attempts, especially of the military, to maintain the traditional ties with France, Poland became more and more alienated from her ally. Barthou's plan for an 'Eastern Locarno' was rejected by Poland, and the Franco-Soviet-Czechoslovak alliance of May 1935 was regarded with the utmost suspicion. The militarization of the Rhineland revived French-Polish co-operation, but not for long. The visit of Śmigły-Rydz to Paris, and the loan which Poland received from France, only slightly improved relations between the two states.

Another equally detrimental effect of the 1934 Declaration was the inauguration by Beck of a policy aiming at the creation of an East-Central European bloc stretching from the Baltic to the Aegean. This 'Third Europe' idea, however attractive it might have appeared as an experiment in regional organization, in reality was fraught with great danger. It was unrealistic as it presupposed co-operation between states as disparate as Sweden and Bulgaria, or Lithuania and Greece; it was aggressive, if not imperialistic, being based on the assumption of the destruction of Czechoslovakia and the coercion of Lithuania; most importantly, the 'Third Europe' project could not be realized because of the lack of enthusiasm and even resistance of its potential members and, above all, because of the veto of Hitler whose goals were not local – as Beck erroneously believed – but global, endeavouring to take control of the entire European continent.

Connected with the concept of the *Intermarium*, as the idea of the 'Third Europe' had been at times referred to, was the determination of the Polish government, in which the opinions of Beck prevailed,

---

[35] 'Antipathetic Politics', *Neamul Romanesc* (25 September 1935), quoted Fiala, op. cit., p. 313.

not only to tolerate but directly to support the destruction of Czechoslovakia, Poland's southern neighbour. The fact that Warsaw put forward its territorial demands against Czechoslovakia on the occasion of the September 1938 Munich Agreement, unwittingly becoming a partner of Nazi Germany, could hardly be regarded as serving the true interests of the Polish republic. While securing the annexation to Poland of the industrially rich western part of the province of Teschen, the action of Warsaw helped to destroy the bastion covering her south-western and southern flank. As emphasized by one student of the Czechoslovak and Polish crises,

the existence of Czechoslovakia in its pre-Munich borders greatly hampered the freedom of movement of the German army in both western and eastern directions, and the fact that Czechoslovakia possessed a comparatively strong air force posed a significant danger to the most important industrial centres of Germany. After Munich the military potential of Czechoslovakia was paralysed and the threat to France and, above all, to Poland (as well as the states of the Central and Lower Danubian basin) was tremendously increased.[36]

This judgement has been supported by another analysis of Beck's policies : 'What was to serve as a condition for the development of ambitious plans, in reality opened to Hitler the way to Rumania and to the borders of the Ukraine.'[37]

In fact, after the elimination of Czechoslovakia, the German-Polish pact lost much of its usefulness for Hitler, who by then was prepared to proceed to the next stage of his struggle for Europe. In this Poland. which was expected to make far-reaching concessions, no longer figured as an equal partner but as a mere German satellite to be used in the German crusade against the Soviet Union.

The dismemberment of Czechoslovakia, beginning on 15 March 1939, demonstrated Poland's critical situation. With one stroke Hitler destroyed whatever hopes the Polish Foreign Minister might still have had in the possibility of the emergence of a 'Third Europe'. Instead, with the creation of the German satellite state of Slovakia, Poland found herself almost entirely encircled by either inimical or clearly unfriendly powers. The achievement of a common border with Hungary by the latter's annexation of the former Czechoslovak province of Subcarpathian Ruthenia was of no military significance, being overshadowed by the growth of German military might and economic as well as political penetration into south-eastern Europe.

[36] Henryk Batowski, *Kryzys dyplomatyzny w Europie* (Warsaw, 1962), p. 51.
[37] Hans Roos, *Polen und Europa* (Tübingen, 1957), p. 356.

The Polish leadership's, particularly Beck's, flirtation with Germany turned out an absolute failure. As during the First World War the West 'came to the rescue' of Polish independence. While motivated by their own national interests, the decisions of the British and the French to resist further German aggression coincided with the cause of Poland. Alarmed by the seizure of Prague, Neville Chamberlain gave Poland a unilateral promise of aid, should her independence be threatened. In deference to considerations of Polish prestige this guarantee was changed in the month of April into a provisional and, on 25 August, into a fully-fledged treaty of mutual assistance. In it the British government guaranteed not the borders but the national independence of Poland in case of direct or indirect aggression. The provisional treaty was followed on 28 April by Hitler's denunciation of the 1934 German-Polish Declaration and the unleashing of a violent anti-Polish campaign. France declared her solidarity with Great Britain, although she signed a new military convention with Poland only on 4 September 1939.

While formidable on the surface, the Western guarantees at best could be regarded as promises for the future. The Western Powers were militarily weak and the only effective aid which could be given to Poland – an all-out offensive against the western border of Germany – was both materially and psychologically out of the question. As Winston Churchill pointed out, only the Soviets – had they become part of the Western Alliance – could have given immediate support to their western neighbour. But, quite understandably, the Poles refused to be saved from the clutches of Germany by the tender mercies of the Soviets. It was this refusal, as well as the clear reluctance of France and Britain, to combine with the 'Bolsheviks', that prevented the creation of the 'grand alliance'.

What the Poles and their allies entirely failed to appreciate was the possibility of the revival of the 'Rapallo' policy. Its precondition – the renewal of German-Polish enmity – was strengthened by two other new, but extremely significant, facts. While determined to solve the dispute with Warsaw by military means and, indeed, only too eager to test the re-created Germany army, Adolf Hitler could not disregard the traditional fear of German strategists, namely that of a war on two fronts; the Soviet dictator, Joseph Stalin, having weakened his army and country by bloody purges, was only too eager to postpone the 'final struggle'. Moreover, for Stalin the prospect of a major conflict within the capitalist world offered both ideologically and politically unprecedented opportunities.

Such was the background of the famous German-Soviet Treaty of 23 August which precipitated the Nazi attack against Poland. Of course, when the war started, the Polish government was unaware of the Secret Additional Protocol signed by the Foreign Ministers, Molotov and Ribbentrop, on the delimitation of spheres of influence between the two states – a protocol that envisaged a fourth division of Poland.

Chapter 7

Poland in Exile

'We have got to beat Hitler,' I said, 'and this is no time for quarrels and charges.'

(Winston Churchill, April 1943)[1]

WHATEVER THE SHORTCOMINGS and mistakes of their political leadership, the Poles faced the ordeal of war with a spirit of sacrifice and dedication. The initial encouragement which they might have derived from the alliances with France and Britain, was soon dispelled by the inability of the Western Powers to come to their aid. Thus Poland had to face the terrible onslaught of the most powerful military machine the world had ever seen alone. Irrespective of the actual military significance of the aggressive action of the Soviet Union on 17 September, the sudden attack from the east demonstrated the full extent of the Polish tragedy.

The five years of Polish participation in the Second World War were marked by three characteristics. The Nazi invader, who occupied the major part of ethnically Polish territory, was unable to induce any of the representative figures of the nation – including those who had co-operated with the Germans during the First World War – to play the ignominious role of 'Polish Quislings'. The attitude of the Polish masses was one of determined resistance which even the terror of the SS and the Gestapo failed to break.

Secondly, a relatively large part of the governmental apparatus and a sizeable contingent of the army managed to find their way to the West. There, the armed forces were increased in size by conscripts and volunteers from among Polish nationals living abroad. Of greater significance was the army of General Władysław Anders, which in the middle of 1942 transferred from the Soviet Union to the Middle East and later to Africa. As a result, the Polish government, which was established first in France and then in London, disposed of considerable armed forces which greatly contributed to the combined Allied war effort.

Most important, perhaps, was the ability of the exiled govern-

---

[1] Winston S. Churchill, *The Second World War*, vol. IV: *The Hinge of Fate* (Boston, 1948; London, 1950), p. 761.

ment – which legally, although not politically, was derived from the defeated regime – to maintain a considerable degree of consistency despite the immense pressures to which it was exposed. Equally remarkable was the capability of the Polish exiles to maintain contacts with the representatives of the non-communist underground military organization on Polish soil, which spoke for the overwhelming majority of the nation.

Valour in Defeat

The spirit of national unity permeating the whole of Polish society at the moment of the first clashes tended to engender over-optimism, which was totally oblivious of the military weakness of the country. Apart from the obvious disparity of strength, a number of other factors weakened Polish power of resistance. Following the advice of the Western Powers not to incite Hitler's fury, the Warsaw government delayed its general mobilization so that a large part of the Polish armed forces was unable to participate in the fighting. Another factor was the psychologically understandable, but strategically unsound, decision of Marshal Śmigły-Rydz, who 'within a few days lost control' over the military operations,[2] and the general staff to spread the numerically inadequate Polish divisions along the entire German-Polish border. Thus no central reserve, from which the gaps in the defensive system could be filled, was created. Nor did the Polish High Command fully appreciate the military significance of the new route of attack through the Moravian Gate, provided by the destruction of Czechoslovakia. In fact, the Polish general staff lacked a strategic plan comparable to the minutely prepared German offensive. The Soviet intervention – the effect of which was more psychological than military – cut off important units of the Polish army, which was prevented from escaping to Romania.

Yet all these handicaps – coupled as they were with a catastrophic lack of armour and aircraft which, in most cases, was destroyed on the airfields – did not prevent the lower commanders from displaying remarkable tactical skill. Almost pathetic was the heroism of the Polish soldier, who fought valiantly against insuperable odds, as well as the valour of the Polish civilians, especially those in Warsaw, which defended itself until the last days of September against a merciless bombardment.

The country, which lay prostrate at the mercy of the victors, was divided by the agreement of 28 September into two parts. All territory east of the line running along the rivers Pissa, Narew, Bug,

---

[2] This was the assessment of Smigły-Rydz by Anders in his conversation with Stalin. See Władysław Anders, *Mémoires (1939–1946)* (Paris, 1948), p. 159.

and San was annexed by the Soviet Union. Nazi Germany, on the other hand, divided the newly acquired regions into two different sectors. The so-called 'Incorporated Eastern Territories' (*Eingegliederte Ostgebiete*) were made an integral part of the Reich, which was extended well beyond the pre-1914 boundary between Russia and Germany. The second sector was the purely Polish area which somewhat later was given the name of General Government. In reality, the latter was nothing but a German protectorate.

While the Nazi measures were based on the right of conquest, the Kremlin took a number of actions in order to justify both morally and legally its seizure of territories belonging to the Polish republic. The Soviet action, it was stated, was based on the right of self-determination of the 'West Ukrainians' and the 'West Belorussians', who represented a clear majority of the population of the annexed area.

10. Poland after the Fourth Partition (main changes 1939–45)

Their 'democratically' elected assemblies voted in favour of incorporation into the Ukrainian and Belorussian republics of the Soviet Union. The city and region of Wilno was ceded to Lithuania which in 1940, together with the other Baltic states, Latvia and Estonia, became a part of the Soviet Union as an 'independent' republic. While duly registered by the amendment of the Soviet constitution, these changes could not alleviate the immense suffering of hundreds of thousands of Poles deported to the Soviet Union.

Soon after German victory the 'Incorporated Eastern Territories', despite their overwhelming Polish character, were subjected to a policy of forceful Germanization. It was ordered by Hitler himself and put into effect by Heinrich Himmler, the head of the SS formations and Commissioner for the Strengthening of German Nationality. In keeping with the pseudo-scientific criteria of Nazi racial theories the population was divided into three categories : those whose racial composition seemed to make them more amenable to denationalization; those who were to be expelled to the east; and finally Poles who because of their intellectual background were destined to extermination. By all methods – cultural, social, and economic – a large part of the population of this 'incontestably German soil' were to be forced to become German. Yet the majority resisted the 'generous' offer to be inscribed on the German ethnic list (*Volksliste*), thus choosing the fate of a people with practically no rights. Their conditions of work, their pay, and rations were far inferior to those of the Germans. Their cultural institutions, including universities, secondary schools, and to a certain extent even elementary schools, were closed. Above all, thousands of Polish intellectual leaders were imprisoned in concentration camps.

The fate of the so-called General Government, which was treated as a German colony, was no better. Finding no Pole prepared to take over the reins of government under the occupation authorities, the Nazis appointed a purely German administration which was located in Kraków and headed by Governor-General Hans Frank, a man whose reputation as a leading Nazi lawyer was more than matched by his fanaticism and ruthlessness. Under his rule the General Government of Poland became a 'residue area' into which all Poles who were expelled from the western regions were herded. The cities and countryside were mercilessly plundered, the population was reduced to starvation level, and hundreds of thousands of men and women were deported to the Reich for compulsory labour. Implementing the diabolical plan to deprive the Polish nation of its intellectual leadership, the SS proceeded to outright 'liquidation' of thousands of Polish intellectuals, deporting others – including the whole faculty of the Jagiellonian University in Kraków – to Nazi concentration

camps. After the defeat of France the Nazi administration took certain measures for revitalizing the economy of the area, particularly
its agriculture, and for the improving of its transportation system.
The main purpose of this action, however, was to use the General
Government, cynically referred to as the 'Polish Homeland', as a
base for the coming attack against the Soviet Union.

Most tragic was the dreadful fate of the 3½ million Polish Jews.
Many of them, after having been subjected to humiliation and torture, were killed outright. Others were concentrated in ghettos, such
as that of Warsaw, from where they were gradually deported to the
infamous extermination camps of which the one in Oswięcim became
a lasting memorial of Nazi depravity and sadism.

Speaking of the Jews at a session of his cabinet, Frank stated :

As far as the Jews are concerned, I want to tell you quite frankly
that they must be done away with in one way or another. . . .
Gentlemen, I must ask you to rid yourself of all feeling of pity.
We must annihilate the Jews.[3]

The Nazi atrocities committed in Poland have been best described
by Himmler himself. His statement in summer 1941 demonstrated
that even his distorted mind shrank from the atrocious crimes per-
petrated at his behest by the SS units. This flows from his monstrous
admission that :

It is much easier in many cases to go into combat with a company
than to suppress an obstructive population of low cultural level,
or to carry out executions or to haul away people or to evict crying
and hysterical women.[4]

It was not surprising that soon the chasm separating the Poles
from the Germans became unbridgeable. Of course, the immediate
aftermath of defeat and loss of independence – the suddenness of
which could not be easily understood – was a feeling of apathy and
despondency. But soon it was replaced by severe criticism of the
government whose incompetence, it was held, was largely responsible
for the national catastrophe. Having assessed the tragic situation of
their nation, those Polish leaders who remained in the occupied
country proceeded to a systematic organization of a resistance movement. The commanders of the defeated army, acting in co-operation
with four former opposition parties – the PPS, the Peasant Party, the
Labour Party, and the National Party – gradually built up an under-

[3] United States Chief of Counsel for the Prosecution of Axis Criminality,
Nazi Conspiracy and Aggression (Washington: Government Printing Office,
1946), pp. 891–2.
[4] Ibid., pp. 553–4.

ground movement which was eventually to acquire fame throughout the entire free world. As early as the end of September 1939, when the non-political 'Service for the Victory of Poland' was founded, the first measures for the creation of a clandestine army were taken. By the beginning of 1940, this organization, having changed its name to League for Armed Struggle (*Związek Walki Zbrojnej*), had almost 100,000 members. Even more impressive was the ability of the Poles to build up a system of underground civilian administration. Leaders of both the military and civilian branches of the national resistance movement – General Stefan Rowecki (known under his assumed name as 'Grot'), and the PPS leader, Mieczysław Niedziałkowski, acted as delegates and representatives of the Polish government-in-exile. Despite occasional disagreements, they never lost radio and courier contacts with their legal government abroad. Much less successful were the initial attempts to expand the activities of the underground movement so that they would cover also the areas annexed by Germany and the Soviet Union. In the latter territories attempts at organization – which were regarded as being directed against the Soviet state – were practically impossible because of the deportation of more than a million Poles into the interior of Russia.

After the German invasion of Russia in June 1941, which caused a tremendous extension of German manpower resources, the Polish underground organization stepped up its activities. In February 1942 the military contingents of the different political groups were unified in the so-called Home Army (*Armia Krajowa*), generally referred to as AK, which began to operate in practically all parts of the Polish republic. The ever-increasing terror of the German occupation authorities, expressed by such drastic measures as the eviction of Polish peasants from their native soil, further consolidated the power of the Home Army, which created special commandos and conspirator groups to execute the different tasks of military resistance. Until the August 1944 uprising the Home Army engaged in relatively few large-scale operations. Yet it rendered great services to the Allied cause. Apart from effective acts of sabotage, especially of the railroad system, and 'counter-reprisals' against the most reprehensible representatives of the Nazi occupation authorities, its most productive was the gathering of military intelligence. The Polish underground provided the Allies with information on the development and sites of the V-rockets, thus enabling their air forces to paralyse German production of this terror-weapon. By the second half of 1943 the AK, whose leadership after the arrest of General Rowecki was taken over by General Bór-Komorowski, had well over 300,000 members.

While not directly associated with the AK efforts, the pathetic revolt of the practically unarmed remnants of the Warsaw ghetto in April 1943 provided another aspect of the anti-Nazi resistance in Poland. It represented one of the most tragic and gruesome events of the Second World War.

The growth of the organizational framework for military resistance was accompanied by a constant build-up of what some referred to as the 'secret government'.[5] Being engaged also in acts of resistance, at least for a certain period of time, the civilian branch of the Polish underground competed with the military one. Represented by the co-operation of the four large political parties, which for a relatively long time had claimed almost a monopoly of political power, the civilian organization went through a number of changes, finally emerging in February 1944 as the Council of National Unity (*Rada Jedności Narodowej*). This organ included representatives of the smaller political groups and co-operated with the official delegate of the government-in-exile. After the arrest of Professor Piekałkiewicz, Jan Stanisław Jankowski, the deputy premier in the last wartime cabinet of Tomasz Arciszewski, held this important position.

Like its government-in-exile the underground liberation movement in Poland also faced during the Second World War a number of serious crises. The first arose when the Nazis attacked the Soviet Union, and an enemy of Poland became an ally of the Western Powers. Even more disturbing was the diplomatic split between Moscow and the London government in 1943. The most serious test of endurance and moral fibre for the Polish underground resulted from the August 1944 Warsaw uprising and its tragic consequences.

The sudden outbreak of hostilities between the two traditional enemies of Poland – when almost overnight the Soviet enemy became a much appreciated ally of those powers in which the Poles had placed their trust – reopened the painful issue of Soviet-Polish relations. Following the instructions of their London government, the members of the underground resistance did not change their anti-German orientation. Despite their determined refusal to recognize the Soviet occupation of eastern Poland, they heeded the warning of General Władysław Sikorski that any action against the Russians would be disastrous as it would create the impression that the Poles had sided with Hitler.

The tactics of the Home Army, as formulated by Sikorski and accepted by the leadership of the Polish resistance movement, envisaged the possibility of Soviet-Polish co-operation. It was agreed that a head-on clash with the Nazis should be avoided as long as possible

[5] See Jan Karski (pseud.), *Story of a Secret State* (Boston, 1943).

so that the Poles would remain strong enough to take over power immediately after the expected German collapse. Both Sikorski and his government, while uneasy about Russian behaviour, believed that the strength and prestige of the Western Powers would prevent the Soviets from violating the integrity and independence of the Polish republic.

The split between Moscow and the government-in-exile seemed to confirm the fears of those members of the Polish underground movement who were less optimistic about the possibility of post-war Soviet-Polish co-operation. But – with the exception of a small group of the extreme rightist elements (the so-called 'National Fighting Forces') – the bulk of the AK, following instructions from London, even increased their anti-Nazi activities, bringing considerable aid to the Red Army, now approaching the borders of pre-war Poland. When they were crossed, on 4 January 1944, the Home Army units 'came into the open' and staged a number of uprisings, as envisaged by the strategic plan Burza (Tempest) which called for the co-ordination of activities between the Polish underground movement and the approaching Soviet troops. The Soviets readily used AK aid, but refused to recognize Polish sovereignty over territories east of the Curzon Line. Eventually they proceeded to the disarming of the Polish units and the deportation of many of their leaders to the Soviet Union. Despite this bitter disappointment, the Home Army continued to fight the Germans and to offer its co-operation to the Red Army, believing that this display of inter-Allied unity would strengthen the position of their government-in-exile.

Although the development of the war clearly demonstrated the unwarranted optimism of the exiled government and its representatives in Poland, only a minor part of the resistance forces turned against the Russians. Equally small was that part of the Polish public which changed sides and joined the Soviet-sponsored liberation movement. Yet during 1944 the situation of the Polish national resistance movement continued to deteriorate. The moral firmness of its members and the support of the overwhelming majority of the nation were of little avail in the struggle against the Soviet-supported organs of the Polish communists and their fellow-travellers.

The tragic predicament of the underground movement reached its peak in July 1944, when the Red Army, greatly profiting from AK aid, crossed the river Bug into territories west of the Curzon Line. Soon after that the Soviet government recognized its own creature, the Polish Committee of National Liberation, as the de facto government of Poland. As more territory was being wrested from the Germans, this body, referred to as the Lublin Committee, aided by the

Soviet security apparatus, started a ruthless liquidation of the civil and military organs of the Polish underground movement.

This critical situation for the Polish cause contributed to the decision of Bór-Komorowski to stage a mass uprising in the Polish capital. Anticipating an early attack by the victorious Soviet forces, whose guns could be heard in the Warsaw suburb of Praga, and responding to the appeal of the Soviet-controlled Kościuszko radio station in Moscow, the Home Army, backed by the entire population of the city, rose in revolt against the enemy on 1 August 1944. This uprising, approved by the London government, was to enable the Poles 'to welcome the Red Army to the free capital of an exhausted but undefeated nation'.[6] Undoubtedly this was an action of a body recognizing the authority of the exiled government, but it was by no means intended as an anti-Soviet demonstration. Its aim, apart from the natural tendency to take revenge against the Nazi tormentors, was to prevent Warsaw from becoming a battlefield between Soviet and Nazi armies.

On the other hand, it was clear that a Polish victory in Warsaw would have greatly improved the standing of the London government, which the Soviet leaders regarded as the main obstacle to their political aims in Poland. As stated by Winston Churchill, 'they did not mean to let the spirit of Poland rise again in Warsaw. Their plans were based on the Lublin Committee. That was the only Poland they cared about'.[7] That is why the Soviet offensive came to a sudden end. The Western air forces were prevented from bringing more adequate supplies to the beleaguered city by the Russian refusal to allow the use of their airfields for aerial shuttle operations. Stalin expressed his true opinion in his communication dated 22 August to Churchill and President Roosevelt by referring to the insurrectionists as a 'group of criminals who embarked on the Warsaw adventure in order to seize power'.[8] After sixty-three days of heroic resistance Warsaw was forced to surrender to the Germans.

The defeat of the Warsaw uprising greatly enhanced the position of the Lublin Committee and contributed to the demoralization and progressive disintegration of the AK and what remained of the underground Polish administration. Those same men who had willingly risked their lives and fought alongside the Red Army against the common enemy were branded as traitors and exposed to various forms of terror, directed especially against the commanding officers

6 Edward J. Rozek, *Allied Wartime Diplomacy. A Pattern in Poland* (New York, 1958), p. 236.
7 Winston S. Churchill, *The Second World War*, vol. VI: *Triumph and Tragedy* (Boston, 1953; London, 1954), p. 141.
8 Ibid., p. 136.

of the underground units. By the end of 1944 the *Burza* plan had lost practically all its *raison d'être*. While AK members continued to fight against the Nazis, after the Soviet victory they refused to come out into the open and again disappeared underground. Thus on 19 January the London government found it necessary to dissolve the Home Army. No wonder that a few members of the AK joined the remnants of the 'National Fighting Forces' and put up a desperate guerilla resistance in the Beskidy mountains. Against these 'enemies' of the people' the security organs of the new regime and the NKVD unleashed a merciless campaign. Finally, on 27 March, fifteen leaders of the Polish underground movement accepted the Soviet invitation to consult on the normalization of Polish political life. Despite express guarantees of personal safety all disappeared without trace. Only about forty days later did the Soviet government announce their arrest on charges of anti-Soviet activities. In June 1945 they were condemned – after having made 'a full confession' – to long terms of imprisonment. This tragic epilogue did not end the persecution of the leading members of the Home Army. Indeed, action against them represented the first phase of the Stalin-type liquidation of the antagonistic classes.

The Government-in-Exile

Having crossed the Romanian border on 17 September 1939, the defeated Polish government was interned and prevented from exercising its authority. After some difficulty, the appointment of a new government, which secured the legal continuation of the Polish republic, was made possible by the use of the 1935 constitution.[9] Władysław Raczkiewicz, the former speaker of the Senate and an adherent of Piłsudski, who was eventually appointed President, was not an inspiring leader. The new government found its strong personality in Sikorski, Piłsudski's erstwhile opponent. His power was greatly enhanced by the solemn declaration of Rackiewicz, in his own name and that of his successor, that they would not use the enormous powers conferred on the President by the 1935 constitution, and that they would carry out their duties in close co-operation with the Prime Minister. Sikorski formed a government composed of the leading members of the four large opposition parties and a few non-party men, and established its headquarters in the French city of

[9] The first appointee of President Mościcki was General Bolesław Wieniawa-Długoszowski, the Polish ambassador in Rome, a known favourite of Marshal Piłsudski. His name, however, was rejected by the French government and, at the suggestion of the ambassador in London, Count Edward Raczyński, Raczkiewicz was chosen. See Count Edward Raczyński, *In Allied London* (London, 1962), pp. 40–4.

Angers. There, the Polish governmental organization was regularized by the appointment of a twenty-four-member National Council (*Rada Narodowa*) – a semi-parliamentary body created for the purpose of advising the government and controlling its administrative apparatus. Owing to the fact that its president, the venerable Ignacy Paderewski, was prevented by ill-health from fulfilling his functions, the leading role in the National Council fell to the acting President, Stanisław Mikołajczyk, secretary-general of the Peasant Party and close associate of its leader, Wincenty Witos.

While the great majority of the Polish representative figures were members of the former opposition parties, the supporters of the old regime were not entirely eliminated, holding important positions in the army and the diplomatic service. But the energy and prestige of General Sikorski managed not only to hold the disparate forces together, but also to instil into his co-workers and the entire Polish community abroad a determination to carry on a vigorous struggle against the Nazis. By far the most important asset of the government was its ability to organize, within a surprisingly short period of time, considerable armed forces which were immediately offered to the Western Powers.

The French capitulation caused the Polish army to suffer great losses. In fact, only a minor part of the mobilized manpower, together with the government, managed to reach British shores. There, after an initial internal crisis caused by the attempt of the adherents of the old regime to seize power, the government and the armed forces were reconstituted, strengthening their position by establishing close contacts with the British. The Polish air force especially, organized within the framework of the Royal Air Force, distinguished itself in the Battle of Britain. The position of the London government was further strengthened by the establishment of friendly relations with the United States, whose President promised to supply the Poles with American weapons and permitted the recruitment, of course only on a voluntary basis, of US citizens of Polish origin.

The subsequent history of the exiled government in London was marked by three events, each exposing the Polish leadership to immense pressure and causing a serious internal crisis. Two of them – the Nazi invasion of the Soviet Union and the Katyn affair, which was followed by the Soviet breach of diplomatic relations with the Poles – could be objectively assessed and directly, even though ineffectively, countered by the exiled government. The third event – the preliminary decision on the eastern borders of Poland made by the heads of state of the three leading powers of the United Nations at Teheran – remained secret for a longer period of time and therefore could not be easily opposed. Indeed, Teheran initiated a period during which Polish affairs became one of the major points of concern and friction between the United States and Great Britain, on the one hand, and the Soviet Union, on the other.

The Nazi attack against Russia forced the Polish government to seek reconciliation with the Kremlin. It was not easy for the Poles to accept as an ally a state with which until recently they had considered themselves to be in a state of war. Sikorski, however, approached the problem from a realistic and statesmanlike point of view. Having, as early as June 1940, considered the possibility of a *rapprochement* with the Soviet Union, he believed sincerely, even though somewhat over-optimistically, that Stalin would be prepared not only to change his attitude towards the Polish government, but also to return the territories occupied in 1939.

The Soviet-Polish agreement of 30 July 1941 seemed to indicate the way towards better Soviet-Polish relations. It provided for the re-establishment of diplomatic relations, co-operation in the war against Germany, general amnesty for Polish prisoners in the Soviet Union, and the organization of a Polish army on Russian soil. In one all-important aspect, however, the agreement fell short of Polish expectations. While the 1939 Molotov–Ribbentrop pact on the partition of Poland was declared to be invalid, the actual issue of the future borders remained undecided. Faced with the insistence of the British that nothing should be done which might cause dissension among the Allies at that crucial phase of the war, Sikorski had little choice left but to hope that subsequent developments might favour the Polish claim to the 1921 borders. He might have tended to believe that the 'camaraderie of arms' might diminish Soviet unwillingness to recognize the justice of the Polish point of view, but at the same time he was fully aware of the gravity of the problem. This is clear from his insistence on obtaining from the British and the Americans a written statement declaring as null and void all territorial changes since 1 September 1939. Even these declarations turned out to be disappointing. The Americans limited themselves to a communiqué given to the press by Sumner Welles emphasizing, in connection with the treaty, 'the US policy of non-recognition of territory taken by conquest'. The British complied with the Polish request in a special note addressed to the government-in-exile. But its effect was largely vitiated by the subsequent statement of Anthony Eden in the House of Commons that the declaration was not intended as a guarantee of the Polish borders by the British government.

No wonder that the issue caused internal dissension both in the National Council and in the government. Three Ministers, including the Foreign Minister, August Zaleski, and General Kazimierz Sosnkowski, resigned in protest against what they regarded as a serious

violation of Polish national interests. Despite its lack of constructive-
ness the opinion of the pessimists proved to be correct. The organization of the Polish army in the Soviet Union almost immediately ran
into serious trouble. The release of Polish prisoners-of-war proceeded
at a very slow pace; those who were released complained of being
inadequately supplied with food and other amenities of life; the staff
of General Anders, the designated chief of the Polish army, failed to
establish the whereabouts of several thousand officers. When, at the
end of 1941, Sikorski paid a visit to Moscow, none of the issues
could be satisfactorily dealt with. On the other hand, in his conversation with the Polish leader, Stalin insisted that there will be 'very
slight alterations in the pre-war boundaries of Poland'. The nature
of these alterations was clearly established first by drafting into the
Red Army Polish subjects of Belorussian, Ukrainian, and even Jewish
origin, and later by the Soviet decision to regard Poles from eastern
Poland as Soviet citizens. Two outstanding representatives of Polish
Jewry, Henryk Ehrlich and Wiktor Alter, who made an attempt to
organize a Jewish contingent within the Anders army, were arrested
and – as it was revealed only in 1943 – condemned to death and
executed.

Further disagreements over the equipment, the use, and finally the
food rations, of the Polish army eventually resulted in an arrangement between Anders and Stalin providing for the transfer of over
70,000 men and about 35,000 civilians to Iran. Having been re-
trained in the Middle East, Anders' army played a prominent role
in the Italian campaign, distinguishing itself particularly in the
dramatic capture of Monte Cassino.

By the end of 1942 the tension between the Polish government-in-
exile and the Soviets had greatly increased. No doubt there was much
truth in the Russian criticism of the unofficial Polish campaign of
hatred and scorn against the Soviet Union and her army. The Poles,
however, could point, undoubtedly with full justification, to the in-
human treatment meted out to them when in Russian captivity and
to the unwillingness of the Soviet government to regard them as
soldiers. The activities of the few extreme rightist groups in the
Polish army did not serve the Polish interest, as they were used by
uncritical admirers of the Soviet Union for attacks against the exiled
government, which they branded as reactionary.

The agenda of the Polish embassy in the Soviet Union after the
departure of Anders' contingent gradually dwindled to diplomatic
formalities. Both parties regarded each other with utmost distrust
and intentionally avoided discussing the main issues separating the
two governments. From January 1943 an exchange of diplomatic
notes took place dealing with the future Polish-Soviet borders. The

Soviet demand for the recognition of the Curzon Line was indignantly refused by the Polish government-in-exile. This unfavourable development in relations between the two 'allies' reached crisis-level when, on 5 April 1943, the German command announced the discovery of a mass grave of about 10,000 officers in the forest of Katyn, near Smolensk. It was stated that they had been killed by the Russians in 1940. This was a tragic denouement of the Polish authorities' efforts to secure the release of the missing officers who, according to repeated Russian assurances, were at liberty, 'when they were in truth foully murdered'.[10] While fully understandable, the Polish request for an International Red Cross investigation was considered in Allied circles to be politically unwise as it provided the Kremlin with a pretext for breaking off, on 25 April, diplomatic relations with the Polish government-in-exile. Yet the breach would have come anyway, as by then Stalin had decided to create a pro-Soviet Polish liberation movement, both civilian and military, operating on Polish soil.

The subsequent history of the Polish government-in-exile centred around the unsuccessful attempts of the British and American governments to heal the breach in the Allied ranks. As presented by the Soviets the conflict between the two governments stemmed from two basic issues : the refusal of the Poles to recognize the Curzon Line as the future Soviet-Polish border and the nature of the London government which, the Kremlin held, was dominated by reactionaries and enemies of the Soviet Union. In this uneven struggle a number of decisive factors worked against the exiled government.

In the first place, the Polish position was weakened by the tragic death of General Sikorski in an air accident. The new premier, Stanisław Mikołajczyk, while capable of combining genuine patriotism with statesmanlike moderation, did not enjoy the authority of his predecessor.

Equally detrimental to the Poles was the growing belief in unofficial and even official British and American circles, which approached the war mainly from a military point of view, that Polish intransigence with regard to the border issue weakened Allied unity and, in the last analysis, was harmful to Poland herself. This belief was best expressed by Winston Churchill. His arguments, at least from the British point of view, were not without substance.

The vital interests of the United Nations coalition, he held, required the continued resistance of the Russians, whose contribution to the war effort was of such a magnitude as to override other considerations, including those of the future eastern borders of Poland.

[10] Stanisław Mikołajczyk, *The Pattern of Soviet Domination* (London, 1948), p. 39.

Churchill indicated that whatever the conditions of the final victory might prove to be, 'the Soviet Union would be overwhelmingly strong and Russia would have a great responsibility in any decision she took with regard to Poland'. He also believed that 'one of the main objects of the Allies was to achieve the security of the Soviet western frontiers'.

These arguments – despite their air of power-political cynicism – could be reconciled with the British view of the justice of the Polish government's territorial claims. Speaking in the House of Commons in February 1944, Churchill stated that the British government 'never in the past guaranteed . . . any particular frontier line to Poland'. Nor did it 'approve of the Polish occupation of Vilna in 1920'. Churchill referred to the 1919 British view which was 'expressed in the so-called Curzon Line', clearly implying that this view remained unchanged.[11] Whatever scruples he might have had, they were dissipated when the idea was accepted that Poland's territorial losses in the east would be compensated in the west at the expense of Germany.

It was this British reasoning – supported either directly or tacitly by the Americans – that explained the Western attitude at the first meeting of the three heads of state in November–December 1943, when Stalin's insistence on the Curzon Line was unopposed. Churchill underlined the importance of Poland for Great Britain, but suggested that 'it might move westwards, like soldiers two steps "left close". If Poland trod on some German toes, that could not be helped, there must be a strong Poland.'[12]

Although the details of the first meeting of the 'Big Three' were divulged to the government-in-exile only much later, Teheran marks a decisive event in the history of the Polish government in London. Thereafter it was condemned to a mere rearguard action, its support in the West considerably diminished. As time passed and the Red Army, together with the representatives of the Soviet-sponsored Polish liberation movement, penetrated into Polish territory, the position of Mikołajczyk and his associates continued to weaken. They were exposed to ever-increasing Allied pressure that they accede to the Soviet demands and accept the Lublin Committee as a negotiating partner. It is clear that both Churchill and Roosevelt failed to realize that the Polish problem involved much more than the agreement on the future borders and a compromise over the composition of the future government. Indeed, by the end of 1944 Stalin had reached a point of no return – he was bent on the Soviet-

11 Ibid., p. 39.
12 Winston S. Churchill, *The Second World War*, vol. V: *Closing of the Ring* (Boston, 1951; London, 1952), p. 362.

ization of Poland and for this purpose he needed a pliable Polish government.

This conclusion has been fully confirmed by the failure of Mikołajczyk's mission to Moscow in October 1944. When, on his return to London, his colleagues refused to accept a 'compromise', which he halfheartedly recommended, Mikołjaczyk resigned as Prime Minister, on 24 November. His successor, Tomasz Arciszewski, who had only recently escaped from Poland, was a veteran PPS leader opposed to a policy of compromises. While prepared for a friendly solution of the Polish-Soviet dispute, he insisted on 'a just and equitable settlement with participation of both sides', which would respect 'the sovereignty and freedom of the new Polish state'. He was unwilling, however, to deal with the Lublin Committee.

Whatever the Poles might have done, their action would have had no effect on the behaviour of Stalin. He encouraged the action of the Lublin Committee on 31 December 1944 by which it declared itself to be the provisional government of Poland, granting it within five days the recognition of the Soviet government. The Western leaders refused to recognize the new government but could do nothing to dislodge it from its position or in any meaningful fashion support the demands of the London Poles. As a result, at the conference of the 'Big Three' at Yalta, held at the beginning of February 1945, the problem of the Polish borders and government was again discussed without the participation of Polish representatives. In the final communiqué, which was unanimously adopted and issued on 11 February, the Curzon Line was declared to be the eastern border of Poland. While the conference had discussed at great length the future western border of Poland, the communiqué simply stated that 'Poland must receive substantial accessions of territory in the north and west'. The final statement of the leaders of the three Great Powers represented an almost inexplicable defeat for the Western point of view. The existing provisional government, composed entirely of Soviet-sponsored Poles, was declared to be the basis of the future Provisional Government of National Unity to be formed by the 'inclusion of democratic leaders from Poland itself and from Poles abroad'. Although the reorganization of the present government was made a condition of its recognition by the Western Powers, who also insisted on the speedy 'holding of free and unfettered elections', these two conditions could hardly cover up the magnitude of the British and American defeat.

After Yalta, the Arciszewski government lost all contacts with the Western Powers, the negotiations on the composition of the future National Unity government being carried out only with Mikołajczyk and the representatives of his Peasant Party. Even so they were

17

extremely difficult, dragged on for a number of months, and were concluded only because of Churchill's personal intervention. Only two former members of the Polish government-in-exile accepted invitations to join the 'new' government – Mikołajczyk and Jan Stańczyk, a member of the PPS, who dissociated himself from Arciszewski and the government-in-exile.

The recognition of the Provisional Government of National Unity on 5 July 1945 by Great Britain and the United States entirely eliminated the former Polish government-in-exile from international councils.

PART FOUR

The People's Republic

Chapter 8

Poland a Soviet Satellite

'Nie dziw, że nas tu przeklinają,
Wszak to już mija wiek,
Jak z Moskwy w Polskę nasyłają
Samych łajdaków stek.'

(Adam Mickiewicz, 1823)[1]

THE SOVIETIZATION OF POLAND, which started immediately after the entry of the Soviet army into Polish territory, was marked by four distinctive features. First, the country came entirely under the control of the Soviet Union which unilaterally determined its new geographical shape. Secondly, the new masters used all their power and influence to promote the cause of Polish communism. While there were sporadic instances of active and even armed resistance on the part of the anti-communists, on the whole the process of Sovietization continued unopposed.

The third characteristic of the communist victory, which Poland shared with the rest of East-Central Europe, was the rapidity of cataclysmic changes in society. Unlike Russia, which had become a totalitarian state only gradually, Poland had changed into a Stalin-type dictatorship less than three years after the end of the war. Last but not least, the great majority of the Polish people, despite the hopelessness of active opposition, remained hostile to communism. The Communist Party developed very slowly, but soon changed into a special class divorced from the rest of the nation. Both its lack of success and isolation were due to a variety of causes. Of these resistance of the peasants and influence of the Roman Catholic Church were the most important.

Poland on the Map of Europe

The Second World War radically changed the external conditions of Polish national existence. The Polish People's Republic – as the new Poland is referred to – is smaller by one-fifth than its pre-

---

[1] 'It is no wonder that they curse us. Indeed already ages have passed since only packs of scoundrels are being sent from Moscow to Poland', Adam Mickiewicz, *Utwory dramatyczne, Dziady* (Kraków, 1948), p. 241.

war predecessor. It had lost 46·5 per cent of its former territory to the Soviet Union. In the west it gained the major part of the former German province of East Prussia, the entire area of former eastern Germany up to the rivers Odra and western Nysa, as well as the city and environs of Szczecin on the western bank of the Odra. This new western border resulted from the Potsdam Agreement of July 1945. By it the territories detached from Germany were put 'under the administration of the Polish state', and 'the final delimitation' of the border was reserved to the final peace conference. The fact, however, that the same Potsdam Agreement sanctioned the expulsion of the German population from the territory under Polish control strangely contradicted the 'provisionality' of the border settlement. While not recognized *de jure* by a number of Western powers, including the United States, the Odra–Nysa Line, which is regarded by the Polish and communist bloc governments as final, became a *de facto* international boundary.

Thus the 'new' Poland moved approximately 130 miles westwards. She acquired considerably shorter borders and a much longer seacoast on the Baltic, including three major ports. The so-called Western Territories greatly increased the industrial potential of the country, which became the owner of the major part of the great Silesian coal-basin and other natural resources. In addition, Poland gained a highly developed industrial establishment which provided a solid foundation for a transformation into a modern industrial state. With her 121,130 square miles Poland is the largest and undoubtedly the most important state of East-Central Europe.

This geographical shift was accompanied by important changes in the ethnographic, social, and economic structure of Polish society. For the first time in her modern history Poland became homogeneously Polish and Roman Catholic. In 1968 her population passed the 32-million mark and is constantly growing. In the post-war period the government achieved a sounder balance between industry and agriculture, which enabled it to embark on a process of further industrialization, during which Poland changed from being a backward, predominantly agricultural, community into an industrial society. The percentage of the population depending for its livelihood on agriculture had fallen from 60 per cent in 1931 to 38·7 per cent by 1960; correspondingly the number of those dependent on industry had by 1960 increased to well over 25 per cent of the total population. As a result, there was a sharp decline in the rural population : from 72·6 per cent in 1931 to 51·9 per cent in 1962. The urbanization of Poland is continuing in proportion to her industrial expansion, alleviating, though not entirely removing, the tedious problem of agricultural over-population characteristic of the pre-1939 period.

However significant, none of the many post-war changes was comparable to that of Sovietization. Its importance can be understood only if reflected against the historic relationship of Soviet communism to Poland.

The Soviet Communist Party and the Polish Question

Karl Marx and Friedrich Engels had little appreciation for the Slavs, whom they regarded as the main representatives of European reaction. Lagging both socially and economically behind Western societies, the individual Slav nations were totally unprepared for a liberal democratic, let alone a socialist, revolution. This was true also of the Poles, who were still a typical peasant people without a middle class and a class-conscious proletariat. Yet both founders of modern socialism tended to exclude the Poles from their general condemnation of the Slavs. They attacked Polish nationalism as reactionary, but believed that this shortcoming was more than offset by the Polish tendency towards revolution. However impractical Marx might have been, with him propensity to revolution ranked high among the virtues of men and nations.

Indomitable Polish resistance against what Marx regarded as 'the dark Asiatic spirit' of Tsarism induced him to embrace the cause of Polish independence. It was not surprising that Marx's revolutionary socialism found a number of leaders among the Polish exiles. Some, such as the two generals of the 1863 Warsaw uprising, Jarosław Dąbrowski and Walery Wroblewski, were among the outstanding members of the Parisian Commune. The former was killed fighting on the barricades, while the latter survived to become a close associate of Karl Marx and member of the General Council of the First International. Marx's inability to recognize the significance of the national idea prevented him, however, from grasping the true nature of the Polish revolutionary movement.

Subsequent developments proved that the primary motivation of the Polish revolutionaries was the idea of nationalism and not that of socialism. This fact had an important influence on the character of Polish socialism when it made its appearance in the last two decades of the nineteenth century. The great majority of its followers supported the Polish Socialist Party (PPS), which was permeated with the ideas of traditional Polish patriotism. While it paid tribute to Karl Marx because of his stand in favour of an independent Poland, in most cases it used Marxian theory only in so far as it could be adapted to the actual needs of the country, especially its struggle against Russia. Only a relatively small section of the Polish socialists became associated with the Social Democratic Party of the Kingdom of Poland and Lithuania (SDKPiL), which regarded itself as an uncompromising adherent of orthodox Marxism and rejected all forms of revisionist thought, especially those of the PPS.

The most characteristic feature of the SDKPiL was the nature of its leadership, which 'was perhaps the most remarkable elite of dedicated professional revolutionaries next to that of the Bolsheviks'.[2] The personalities of Feliks Dzierżyński, Julian Marchlewski (Karski), Karl Radek, Adolf Warszawski (Warski), Józef Unszlicht, Leon Tyszka-Jogisches, and, above all, Rosa Luxemburg represented a unique group of cosmopolitan socialists, which provided Polish, German, and also Russian socialism and later communism with great talent, leadership, and inspiration.

Outstanding among the founders of Polish Marxian socialism was Rosa Luxemburg, who definitely ranks among the most important representatives of Marxist theory and practice. She was distinguished for her independence of judgement which caused her at times to consider critically the views of other socialist leaders and theoreticians, including those of Marx and Engels. In contrast with the clear-cut support for Polish independence of the latter, she consistently opposed the idea of nationalism and saw no future for an independent Poland in the coming era of European socialism. Despite her leftist leanings, she came into conflict also with Lenin, the leader of the Left in the international socialist movement. Rosa Luxemburg was highly critical of Lenin's underestimation of the revolutionary role of the workers, contrasting it with the fundamental significance of the spontaneous action stemming from the 'healthy revolutionary instinct of the masses'. Of equal significance was her rejection of Lenin's autocratic and highly centralistic concept of the party in the period of the dictatorship of the proletariat.

In many respects, of course, the difference between the two socialist leaders was one of tactics. Thus Luxemburg insisted on the socialization of agriculture, implying, at least indirectly, the opportunistic nature of Lenin's promises of land distribution. The same was true of Lenin's approach to the right of self-determination for Poland. Theoretically at least, his understanding of the Polish question was identical with that of Rosa Luxemburg. If he nevertheless expressed himself, as early as 1913, in favour of Polish independence, he did so not because of his pro-Polish bias, but solely in order to promote the cause of revolution. Lenin firmly believed that Polish nationalism, as well as that of the other nations of the empire, represented a tremendous force which could be harnessed for the destruction of Tsarism.

Irrespective of the policy of the Bolsheviks, the Polish Social Democrats – even before the October Revolution – declared themselves in

[2] Dziewanowski, op. cit., p. 32.

favour of strict solidarity with the Russian proletariat and rejected as un-Marxian the idea of an independent Polish state. Thus they followed in the footsteps of their erstwhile leader, Rosa Luxemburg, who in the meantime had changed her nationality and become one of the leaders of the left-wing German Social Democrats. 'Luxemburgism', a term which was later used to indicate the unorthodox ideas of Polish communism, continued to plague first the SDKPiL and then the Polish Communist Workers' Party.

Lenin's understanding of the Polish question was best demonstrated at the Seventh All-Russian Conference of the Russian Social Democratic Labour Party in April 1917. The Resolution on the National Question, which was adopted at that meeting, solemnly declared 'the right of all nations forming part of Russia to secede and form independent states'. At the same time, however, the resolution contained an element of ambiguity. The criterion of the right of nations to secede, which alone could guarantee 'complete solidarity among workers of the various nations', was the judgement of the proletariat. Moreover, this right 'must not be confused with the expediency of secession of a given nation at a given moment'. In keeping with their past policies, the members of the SDKPiL led by Feliks Dzierżyński repudiated the idea of self-determination for the Poles and asked for the incorporation of their country into the future Russian state. Replying somewhat later to his Polish comrades, Lenin only underlined the duplicity of his views. He repudiated their opposition to Poland's separation from Russia but, at the same time, stated :

> But these people fail to understand that to enhance internationalism it is not at all necessary to reiterate the same words. In Russia we must stress the right of separation for the subject nations, while in Poland we must stress the right of such nations to unite.[3]

In their uncompromising internationalism the doctrinaire leaders of the Polish Social Democrats paid little attention to the wishes of Lenin and carefully avoided any action which might have even implied the possibility of future Polish independence. Thus they attacked indignantly the policies of those political parties, including the PPS, which took an active part in the building-up of the provisional state structure under the auspices of the Central Powers. After the Bolshevik revolution the members of the SDKPiL, both in Poland and on Russian soil, declared themselves unequivocally in favour of absolute unity with the 'brotherly victorious proletariat of Russia'.

[3] V. I. Lenin, 'The Speech on the National Question' of 12 May 1917 in *Collected Works* (New York and London, International Publishers, 1929), vol. XII, pp. 311–12.

Yet the difference between Lenin's position and that of the Polish Social Democrats was more apparent than real. Indeed, his flexible and highly dialectic formula of self-determination made it possible for his regime to adopt an ambivalent attitude towards Polish independence. As Stalin expressed it, the Bolsheviks could give full support to an independent proletarian Poland; oppose full emancipation of a bourgeois Poland; or, if necessary, give up the idea entirely, sacrificing the independence of the Poles to the interests of the proletarian revolution. It was the latter policy which the Bolsheviks pursued in the months following the October Revolution. They insisted on Polish independence during the Brest-Litovsk negotiations. But, when the very existence of the Russian proletarian state was imperilled, Lenin willingly delivered Poland into the hands of her enemies.

Only the Allied victory redressed the ignominy of Brześć, freeing the hands of the Soviet regime and enabling the Poles to declare national independence. The new state, however, found little sympathy with the Polish Social Democrats and their Russian Bolshevik protectors.

While a number of outstanding Polish Marxists became associated either with the Bolsheviks or with the German *Spartakusbund,* within Poland the SDKPiL and its PPS-Left ally embraced a highly unrealistic policy characterized by progressive alienation from the sentiments of the Polish people. At first it seemed as if the internal situation – marked as it was by economic misery, political chaos, and unemployment – would provide conditions favourable for a radical socialist movement. As in other parts of the European continent, also in Poland a definite radicalization, if not in action, then at least in aims, took hold of the masses. Local councils of workers and peasants almost spontaneously sprang up in different parts of the country. But few of these bodies were dominated by the SDKPiL and even fewer had a truly revolutionary character. Thus even the short-lived 'people's government' of Lublin pledged its support to the PPS leadership and through it to Józef Piłsudski. With the exception of the Dąbrowa industrial basin, the activities of the councils of workers' deputies and their military arm, the 'People's Guard', remained insignificant. The attempted revolts were liquidated with relative ease by the equally weak forces of the Warsaw government. By and large the country turned its back on the prophets of a radical proletarian movement, clearly indicating that nationalism and not socialism was the predominant sentiment in Polish hearts.

Unperturbed by these developments, the leadership of the SDKPiL proceeded, on 16 December 1918, to the merger with the PPS-Left and the creation of the Communist Workers' Party of Poland

(*Komunistyczna Partia Robotnicza Polski*; KPRP). Its founders displayed a singular lack of psychological understanding. The programme which the party adopted was such as to offend the innermost feelings of the great majority of Poles. At a time when they were rejoicing over their newly-won independence, the communists called for a world revolution and the establishment of the dictatorship of the proletariat. The frantic endeavour of Polish patriots to build up the new state administration was countered by a call for the reconstitution of the bankrupt councils of workers' deputies. Above all, in a typical Luxemburgist manner, the communist programme stuck to the idea of a speedy development of collective and communal farming. As if all this were not enough, the new party dismissed the idea of an independent Polish state. It was stated that in a situation characterized by the victory of communism in Russia and the imminent victories of proletarian revolutions in Germany and the rest of Central Europe, the issues of independence, national frontiers, and a national army were of no consequence. Poland, the KPRP believed, was nothing but a *Saisonstaat* which would be swept away, becoming a part of 'the international camp of social revolution'.

In the subsequent months the Polish communist leadership showed no political acumen whatsoever, succumbing to the errors which Lenin described as 'infantile diseases of communism'. Over-optimism, belief in the imminent collapse of capitalism, doctrinaire and uncompromising application of what they regarded as Marxism, and over-confidence characterized the tactics of the communists, especially their leader, Julian Marchlewski. It was this frame of mind which caused the KPRP to boycott the 1919 election for a bourgeois parliament – a 'doomed' institution which the communist leaders regarded with utmost scorn. The same ideological rigidity and barren theorizing prevented the party from exploiting its surprising successes in the elections to the workers' councils, especially in the urban areas. By the second half of 1919 even these potentially revolutionary bodies broke up, partly because of the repressive measures taken by the government.

Preference for 'conspiratorial methods' was best expressed by the Polish Communist Party's decision to refuse to comply with the Warsaw government's order that all associations and organizations should be allowed to exist only after registration with the state authorities. Unwilling to 'soil their hands' with the 'semi-feudal' Polish state, the party leaders willingly accepted the status of illegality.

The Soviets, too, did not view the new Polish government with much favour. Their 'second thoughts' were expressed by a reinterpretation of the right of self-determination, now given a more restrictive meaning. This interesting transformation was entrusted to Lenin's aide, Joseph Stalin, a man whose 'brilliant' career was to be paved by innumerable 're-statements' of what were regarded as fundamental principles of Marxism-Leninism. Acting as Chairman of the Commissariat for Nationalities, Stalin first stated, uncompromisingly, that the right of self-determination belonged to the 'party of the proletariat'. Later he went so far as to declare that 'the so-called independence of a so-called independent . . . Poland . . .' was only 'an illusion',[4] and hinted that such independence concealed dependence on Western imperialism. Thus, in the Soviets' opinion, the new Poland was a state dominated by the gentry and the bourgeoisie – a creature of the imperialist West.

As stated by one student of international communism, 'the *fait accompli* of national independence destroyed the chief stumbling block to co-operation between the Russian Bolsheviks and the SDKPiL'.[5] This was the main reason why the KPRP, disregarding the previous warnings of Rosa Luxemburg, became one of the first parties to join the newly founded Communist International. While constantly 'out of step' with the Comintern directives on many theoretical problems and practical policies, the party began to lean more and more on its Russian comrades. Because of their strongly internationalist and cosmopolitan background the Polish communist leaders were able to rationalize their behaviour which, in the eyes of the average Pole, was equivalent to treason. The intervention of the Red Army, the Polish communist leaders argued, could not be regarded as 'an invasion' or an 'expression of imperialist tendencies', but more appropriately as 'an embodiment of the principle of solidarity of the international proletariat'.[6]

The Polish communists were soon given the opportunity to prove the courage of their convictions. After the failure of the secret negotiations between Lenin's and Piłsudski's representatives, the Polish armies resumed their attack against the Soviets in April 1920. The initial Polish successes were soon reversed and the Red Army started its astounding offensive against the Poles, which changed into a grandiose attempt to spread the gospel of communism in western Europe. To Poland and her Communist Party fell the 'distinguished' role of a bridge between the Russian and the German, and finally also the European, proletarian revolutions.

The communist campaign was conducted on three levels : most important and decisive, of course, was the military and political

[4] Joseph Stalin, *Marxism and the National and Colonial Question* (New York, International Publishers, n.d.), p. 79.
[5] F. Borkenau, *World Communism. A History of the Communist International* (Ann Arbor, 1962), p. 102.
[6] See Dziewanowski, op. cit., p. 82.

operation of the Soviet Union. Much less effective was the endeavour of the Comintern, which mobilized a contingent of professional revolutionaries to aid and advise the Polish communists in their destructive work. On the third level there were the activities of the Polish communists. As the offensive gained momentum, it assumed more and more a class-war character – a war directed against the Polish bourgeoisie and capitalism, whose domination over the peasant masses was to be broken by the application of the 'genuine' right of self-determination. The Bolsheviks declared that they would not negotiate peace with the present Polish regime but only with Soviet Poland.

Lenin and the majority of the Soviet leaders betrayed their true intentions when, acting against the opinion of Trotsky and Kamenev, they decided that the Red Army should cross the Polish-Russian ethnographic line and make a bid for the capture of Warsaw. Considerations of world revolution prevailed over Poland's national interests. Lenin's decision was enthusiastically approved by the second meeting of the Comintern which started on 19 July 1920. The majority of the Polish delegates were swept away by the intoxication of victory and expectation of great events.

The Red Army capture of the city of Białystok on 2 August 1920 enabled the KPRP to establish a Provisional Revolutionary Committee for Poland to act as the core of the future Polish Soviet Republic. Even at this moment the party proved unable and unwilling to abandon some of the basic characteristics of Luxemburgist orthodoxy. The issue of Polish independence was intentionally blurred and the small peasants, while they were to be allowed to keep their farms, were told that large estates and forests would not be distributed among them but nationalized. In its pamphlet propaganda the Białystok group took no account of the obvious sentiments of patriotism and national solidarity so evident among the Poles. If anything, the creation of the Committee was regarded as an insult and it helped to arouse the indignation of the Polish masses whose revulsion against communism came to be identified with the centuries-old hostility between the Russians and the Poles, thus contributing to the final victory of the Warsaw government.

Even after this débâcle, only gradually recognized by the Soviet leaders, the small Polish Communist Party still retained some influence. Its importance, however, was essentially vicarious. Preparing for a future revolution in Germany, both the CPSU and the Comintern continued to cultivate their Polish comrades who, it was still held, commanded the bridge to the West. In Poland itself, however, the party was condemned to a lingering, illegal existence and forced to hold sessions of its representative organs abroad. Above all, it lost the last vestige of respectability, being considered a group of agents in the pay of an enemy power. Thus it had little chance to profit from the general instability of the twenties, even though after the 1919 elections it managed to secure some representation in the *Sejm,* especially from among the Ukrainian and Belorussian Social Democratic groups.

Only at the 1923 congress in Moscow did the KPRP leadership – not without much hesitation – adopt a new programme almost entirely cleansed of the traditional Luxemburgist heresies with regard to the national and agrarian questions. The hitherto despised Polish state was recognized and its independence in the period of transition from capitalism to socialism was upheld. Last but not least, the right-wing leadership of the KPRP offered co-operation to the PPS and its former leader, Piłsudski.

The developments after the Fifth Comintern Congress, which met in 1924, confirmed the final collapse of hopes for a German revolution. Even then the KPRP retained its position as the *enfant terrible* of international communism. In the struggle between Stalin and Trotsky, its leaders publicly sided with Trotsky and supported the defeated German communist leader Heinrich Brandler. As a result, the Polish communists shared the defeat and censure of those who were accused of rightist opportunism. It was then that Stalin for the first time emerged as the decisive factor in the history of Polish communism. As chairman of a special Polish commission, he proceeded to a far-reaching purge of the party, replacing the rightist leadership of Adolf Warski (Warszawski) by a new one composed of left-wingers led by Julian Leński (Leszczyński).

After 1924 the KPRP lost much of its independence, its organs being appointed and its operations financed by the CPSU through the Comintern. Having quite appropriately dropped the adjective 'Workers', the 'new' KPP went through the same process of Bolshevization as the other 'sections' of the International. The Poles, however, could not avoid continued conflicts with the Comintern, thus enabling it to interfere unilaterally with both their personnel and ideological policies. The KPP leadership, hesitating rather desperately between the Left and the Right, pursued a policy calling for worker–peasant co-operation and support for the demands of the minorities. At the same time, it pegged its hopes on the rapidly approaching internal political crisis in Poland. Mistaking Piłsudski for a revolutionary, who would plunge the nation into a bloody civil war, the KPP decided to back him and the PPS in the May 1926 *coup d'état.* Seen in retrospect, its feverish activity, which called on all leftists to create a United Front against Witos, seems more than ridiculous.

Piłsudski paid no attention to these 'would-be supporters', sending some of their leaders to prison for the duration of the crisis. While the KPP policy was supported by the Comintern, it was again Stalin who stated that 'our Polish comrades have, in this case, committed a very grave blunder'.[7] Rather than being caused by foreign influences, the Polish error was due to the highly doctrinaire bent in the KPP leadership which approached political tactics from the point of view of rigid Marxism and failed to consider Piłsudski's personal characteristics.

Moreover, in the years to come the Polish communists failed to take full advantage of the authoritarian trend of the regime and the growing economic crisis. The party was weakened by the aftermath of the fiasco of May 1926, which continued to split its ranks. Much more important, however, was the absolute subordination of the party to the Kremlin-dominated Comintern. Like its Soviet counterpart, the Polish party became almost pathologically 'security conscious', succumbing at times to veritable witch-hunts of saboteurs, spies, police agents, and secret adherents of Trotsky. While some gains were achieved, especially among the non-Polish nationalities, the communists failed to secure that degree of respectability which would enable them to make considerable inroads into the positions of the traditional Polish political parties. Thus all their efforts to bring about a United Front of all anti-fascist progressive forces, which started almost two years earlier than in the international communist movement, were repudiated by the *Centrolew* combination of the PPS and the Peasant Party. The occasional successes, such as the heroic communist-led participation of the Jarosław Dąbrowski brigade in the Spanish Civil War, could not improve the status of the party.

Finally, in the middle thirties the Polish communists lost whatever influence they might have had in the international communist movement. Gradually their leaders found themselves in the unenviable position of outcasts. At home they 'were considered to be slavish followers of a foreign power, while the Soviet government regarded them with suspicion....'[8] Their background of Luxemburgist intellectualism, which brought them dangerously near to the doctrines of Trotsky, as well as their tendency towards factionalism, made them an ideal target for the terroristic purges instigated by Stalin in the middle thirties.

During the Great Purge of 1937–38 almost the entire leadership of the KPP, including members of its right and left wings and the Polish members of the Executive Committee of the Comintern, were

[7] *International Press Correspondence* (24 June 1926), pp. 286–7.
[8] Dziewanowski, op. cit., p. 149.

executed or otherwise liquidated. The NKVD went so far as to 'invite' men from the remote Spanish battlefield to be dealt with summarily or sent to various forced-labour camps. At the beginning of 1938 the party was dissolved by the Comintern without any reasons being given for such drastic action. Only at the Eighteenth Congress of the CPSU did D. Z. Manuilsky, speaking of the factional strife in some communist parties, state that the KPP also harboured 'Fascist and Trotskyite spies' and was contaminated by 'agents of Polish fascism'.[9]

After 1938 the Polish Communist Party disappeared entirely from the list of communist parties. One can only guess at the reasons for Stalin's action. It may well be that in matters of foreign policy it augured the final abandonment of the ideological plateau in favour of one destined to defend the narrow interests of the Soviet state. Some observers associate the liquidation of the Polish communist leaders with the approaching reorientation of Soviet foreign policy. As stated by Boris Souvarine, who was personally acquainted with many of Stalin's victims, 'Stalin loathed them because of their evident intellectual and moral superiority and because he regarded them as an obstacle to a possible agreement with Hitler'.[10]

The behaviour of the Kremlin towards Poland in 1939 all but destroyed the last remnants of communism in that country. Those few communists who continued to regard themselves as party members suffered from lack of leadership and, what was worse, from utter disillusionment in their Marxist-Leninist faith. No wonder that they succumbed to ideological disorientation. They did not participate in the anti-Nazi resistance, leaving the field entirely clear for the activities of the London-directed underground movement. Before June 1941 the situation of the Polish communists, who managed to carry on certain activities in Russian-annexed eastern Poland, was made more difficult by the uncertain and vacillating behaviour of the Kremlin.

After the Nazi attack against Russia Stalin was forced again to recognize the importance, both political and military, of the Polish 'bridge' and its main representative, the Polish government-in-exile. However, his idea of a 'strong and independent' Poland, to be created after the victorious end of the war, did not conform to the views of the London Poles. Having realized that they would not accept his dictates, Stalin returned as early as January 1942 to the ideological approach to the Polish question. This at first imperceptible change was signalled by the revival, in January 1942, of the Communist

9 *World News and Views* (6 April 1939), p. 382.
10 Boris Souvarine, 'Comments on the Massacre' in Milorad M. Drachkovitch and Branko Lazich, *The Comintern* (New York, 1966), p. 176.

Party to operate in the Polish underground. While it was given a new name, Polish Workers' Party (*Polska Partia Robotnicza*; henceforth referred to as the PPR), it could not improve the tarnished record of communism. It was for this reason that the new name omitted the adjective 'communist' and openly rejected the unpatriotic pre-war traditions of the SDKPiL and of Polish communism. Discarding the usual communist clichés, the PPR presented itself as a spokesman for Polish nationalism and a partisan of national unity. Like the communist parties of other Slav nations, the Polish communists paid tribute to the principle of Slav solidarity and relegated the idea of communist internationalism to the background. In its proclamations the PPR declared as its main aims the achievement of national liberation and of social justice. The party also founded its own resistance movement, the People's Guard, which, however, remained insignificant in comparison to the huge Home Army. When, in November 1945, Władysław Gomułka became First Secretary of the party he rejected the idea that the improvement of the lot of the working class 'could be resolved only by revolution along Russian lines'.[11] He went so far as to find kind words for some of the policies pursued by the pre-war PPS.

Simultaneously with the revival of the Polish Communist Party a broader political body was being prepared – to serve as a counterweight to Sikorski's government-in-exile. This was the so-called 'Union of Polish Patriots', whose main aim was to pose as a true representative of Polish national interests. Officially, it appeared only in May 1943; in reality, however, it started its activities as early as 1942. Last but not least, preparations were made for the organization of a Soviet-sponsored army on Russian soil to be composed of Polish deportees to the Soviet Union.

Only after the final change in the fortunes of war and the breaking-off of diplomatic relations with the Polish government in London in April 1943 was it possible to put the three instruments of Soviet policy in Poland into full operation. In the first place, the *Kościuszko* division of General Zygmunt Berling was organized and provided with traditional Polish army uniforms. The name of the same great Polish patriot was given to the radio station broadcasting to Poland under the auspices of the Union of Polish Patriots. To create an impression of strength for the pro-Soviet liberation movement the PPR gave the impetus to the founding of a popular front-type organization – the National Council of Poland (*Krajowa rada narodowa*, KRN), which declared itself to be the supreme legislative body of the country. It came into being at the end of December 1943 and decided

[11] Władysław Gomułka, *W walce o demokrację ludową* (2 vols., Łódź, 1947), vol. II, pp. 126–7.

18

that lower councils should be set up on the different administrative levels of government. Presided over by the 'Muscovite' Bolesław Bierut, it was composed of the representatives of the PPR, of a few members of the splinter group from the extreme left-wing Polish socialists who had separated from the socialist underground organization, and other unimportant radical peasant and democratic bodies.

By the beginning of 1944 everything seemed to suggest that not the London government, but its communist competitor backed by a powerful Soviet protector, would play a leading role in post-war Poland. Yet the response of the Polish people to the 'liberators' from the East remained fundamentally negative. The average Pole retained his loyalty to his exiled government and to the underground Home Army. Only enmity and indifference towards communist-inspired activities can explain why the first internal strife within the PPR – between the subservient Bierut and the more nationalistic and independent-minded Gomułka – passed unnoticed by the Polish public. For communists of all shades and their fellow-travellers were regarded as unacceptable by the great majority of Poles.

The victorious advance of the Red Army caused further defections to the communists and their supporters. When, on 20 July 1944, the Red Army entered what the Kremlin officially regarded as Polish territory, the leaders of the PPR, the Union of Polish Patriots, and other small political groups created a new political body to serve as the supreme executive organ within the country. It was given the name of Polish Committee of National Liberation and subsequently referred to as the 'Lublin Committee' after the first large Polish city in which it was established. While headed by a leftist socialist, Edward Osóbka-Morawski, and including a number of non-communists, its policies were determined by the PPR. The committee's first act was the adoption of a carefully worded and patriotic declaration, the so-called July Manifesto, addressed to the entire Polish nation. In it the idea of democracy (to be derived from the 'broad principles' of the 1921 constitution) was emphasized as the main characteristic of the future governmental system. The manifesto scrupulously avoided anything that might hurt the feelings of the nation; its only 'revolutionary' feature, the promise of a fundamental land reform, was welcomed by the great majority of the people.

Following in the wake of the victorious Red Army, the Lublin Committee and the KRN took control of the territories captured from the Germans. Moving strictly within the limits prescribed by the Soviet authorities, they gradually increased both the scope and intensity of their rule and issued administrative decrees on a whole variety of important political and economic questions. The tragic failure of the August 1944 Warsaw uprising, which clearly demonstrated the impotence of the London government and demoralized the loyalist forces, greatly strengthened the communists in their surge for power. On the last day of 1944 the Lublin Committee organized itself into a provisional government, whose non-communist veneer could not cover up the fact that in reality it was firmly controlled by the PPR.[12] Within less than a week the new government received official recognition by the Kremlin. After the Soviet armies, accompanied by Polish contingents, had captured Warsaw, the provisional government moved into the Polish capital, assuming under the guidance of its powerful protector – 'full sovereignty' over the country.

It was this body which according to the Yalta decision was to become the basis of the future 'democratic' government of Poland.

The Sovietization of Poland

The most characteristic feature of the process of Sovietization in Poland, which started immediately after the Red Army had crossed the Polish border, was its almost total dependence on the active aid of the Soviet Union. Without it and, above all, without the presence of the Soviet armed forces on Polish soil the PPR would have failed to gain the support of some non-communist elements, which alone enabled the 'Lublinites' to pose as an all-national movement. With few exceptions, those who 'went along' were opportunists who, having sensed the general trend of political development in eastern Europe, decided to throw in their lot with the winning side. The inability of the Western Powers to assert themselves in determining Poland's future tended to confirm the 'correctness' of the decision of these pliable politicians and to discourage those who tried to resist the communist tide.

The Yalta decision – far from saving what still could be saved of democracy in Poland – greatly strengthened the power and prestige of the Polish communists. The Lublin government's position of ascendancy was confirmed. The demand that it be reorganized on a more democratic basis was little more than a pious wish which could have no effect on the political situation within the country. Whatever the Big Three might have decided, it could not stop the progressive Sovietization carried out by the Polish communists.

As was to be expected, the creation of a Provisional Government of National Unity – a result of protracted negotiations in Moscow – failed to infuse democratic freedoms into the stifled conditions of Polish political life. The fact that the final phase of these negotiations coincided with the sentencing of the leaders of the Polish underground movement, who about three months previously had been

[12] Churchill, *Triumph and Tragedy*, p. 235.

arrested under mysterious circumstances by the Soviet authorities, did not augur well for the future of political freedom.

While the new twenty-one-member 'coalition' government theoretically contained seven non-members of the Lublin group, its composition was a serious violation of the 20 June agreement in Moscow, which had promised the Peasant Party at least one-third of all important positions in the new government. Furthermore, the 'coalition', in which the PPR, the PPS, the Peasant Party, the Democratic Party, and the Christian Labour Party participated, was largely a fiction. Despite the presence, even in some relatively important posts, of a few pre-war leaders, the socialists fell under the control of a group of left-wingers who, in November 1944, fraudulently adopted the traditional name of PPS. They were headed by the politically insignificant Osóbka-Morawski and opposed by the great majority of the pre-war PPS rank-and-file, headed by Zygmunt Żuławski. Of the minor coalition 'partners' the Democratic Party had practically no influence; the activities of the Labour Party, which found an energetic leader in Karol Popiel, who had returned from exile in London, were soon curbed by governmental interference. Even more important, the Peasant Party was faced by a competitor, which used the same name, and even in the Lublin Committee period tended to serve the communist cause. Two of its leaders were appointed Ministers on the Peasant Party quota.

The only capable personality determined to oppose the creation of an entirely communist system was Stanisław Mikołajczyk, the Second Deputy Premier and Minister of Agriculture in the new government. Despite the enthusiastic support he received from the members of his Peasant Party and from a great number of Poles, he was faced with overwhelming odds which neither he nor anyone else was able to cope with. His decision to join the Provisional Government of National Unity was criticized by many of his compatriots, who decided not to return to Poland and to remain in exile. The head of the Peasant Party, it was argued, provided the new communist leaders with an aura of sorely needed legitimacy and legality. Moreover, Mikołajczyk was accused of having made it possible for the Western Powers to 'wash their hands' over the fate of their former ally and to pretend that the true interests of Poland had been preserved.

Weighty as these arguments might have appeared, one could hardly reproach him for lack of patriotism or even for making a diplomatic blunder; for there were important reasons clearly in favour of his decision. While improbable, the likelihood of Western support, which had been promised him, could not be easily dismissed. More important, however, was the attitude of the Polish public which – without regard to its desperation after the tragic outcome of the struggle for the reconstitution of a free Poland – called for at least some aid from those who had represented it during the arduous years of the war. There was much justification in Mikołajczyk's words : 'I felt it my duty, as one who has sent Polish soldiers into battle, to share the fate of my own people in those most difficult days.'[13]

He was soon to realize, however, the isolation and hopelessness of the cause for which he and the majority of his compatriots had fought. Even before the Potsdam Agreement, designed to bring both internal and external stabilization to Poland, the Peasant Party was exposed to the intolerance of its communist 'coalition partner'. During the hearings at Potsdam, at which Mikołajczyk for the first time was informed of the enormous economic concessions made by the 'Lublinites' to their Soviet ally, a semblance of national unity was maintained. However, the stipulation adopted at Potsdam that the Polish government hold 'free and unfettered elections', in which 'all democratic and anti-Nazi parties' would be allowed to participate, carried as much authority as the preceding decisions made at Yalta.

Almost immediately after the signing of the declaration, all opponents of communist supremacy, above all Mikołajczyk and his party, were exposed to an organized campaign of intimidation. The communist-dominated government gradually set in motion all its formidable means of coercion. The Ministry of Public Security, headed by the Moscow-trained Stanisław Radkiewicz, the voluntary Citizens' Militia, and the Internal Security Corps displayed a high degree of ruthless efficiency so reminiscent of their model, the Soviet security agencies. In fact, the two-odd years during which the Peasant Party tried to enforce at least some of the solemn promises made by the communists at Potsdam, were marked by an uninterrupted series of acts of violence directed not only against the irreconcilable enemies of the new regime operating underground, but also against all potential antagonists of communism. The new army, which included, particularly in the higher ranks, a considerable number of Russian officers, also added to the strength of the pro-communist forces.

Having failed to bring about the fusion of the two peasant parties, Mikołajczyk found it necessary to change the name of his own group to Polish Peasant Party (*Polskie Stronnictwo Ludowe*; PSL) so that it would dissociate itself from the pro-communist policies of the 'Lublin', bogus Peasant Party (SL). Of similar significance was the refusal of the PSL to join the so-called 'democratic bloc' promoted by the PPR to serve as a united front of all permitted political parties. As a result, Mikołajczyk's party was in a peculiar position, being

13 Mikołajczyk, op. cit., p. 134.

both part of the coalition and simultaneously a spokesman for opposition political views. This fact enabled it more successfully to oppose the political machinations of the communists. At the same time, however, it exposed itself to the discriminatory and terroristic practices of the regime, which accused the PSL of sheltering former Piłsudski supporters and the National Party. After protracted negotiations the Polish Peasant Party was allotted only 52 instead of the 145 seats to which it was entitled in the National Council, which became a provisional parliament. Yet the party continued to grow, so that by January 1946 it had around 600,000 members and became a true competitor of the Communist Party.

In order to strengthen its position, the PPR – which managed to unite the socialists, the Democratic Party, and the SL in the 'democratic bloc' – interfered with internal conditions within the PPS. It gave active support to its opportunist leadership, enabling it first to force the rightist Żuławski group to join the party and then to maintain full control over its activities. Realizing its inability to gain a larger popular following, however, the PPR continued to operate under the screen of extreme patriotism, insisting on a special 'Polish way' towards the establishment of socialism, of which the main characteristics, it was argued, were respect for small and medium private property and enterprise and repudiation of the Soviet notions of the dictatorship of the proletariat and the collectivization of agriculture. Peasants were to receive allotments acquired by the confiscation of all estates of over 50 hectares (125 acres) of arable land. The Catholic Church, the formidable spiritual opponent of communism, was not directly attacked. The regime insisted only on curtailing its temporal activities.

Yet the frantic attempts of the communists to gain popular backing proved of little avail. Their main support continued to be the Soviet Union whose army was in firm control of Poland. It was the protection of Moscow that enabled the Warsaw regime to continue the build-up of the security forces and to reserve all important levers of power to the communists, whose influence and authority were greatly enhanced by the creation of the economically significant Ministry of Recovered Territories. This was entrusted to Gomułka, Secretary-General of the party and First Deputy Premier in the government. While their programme spoke of national unity and social justice, the communists did not conceal their final aim – the achievement of an absolute monopoly of power. They were not willing to tolerate any political force which would be genuinely independent of their control. This was particularly true of the Polish Peasant Party, whose progressive elimination in no way differed from similar actions undertaken in other People's Democracies.

Mikołajczyk's party found itself opposed by the entire 'democratic bloc' which used all possible methods to weaken the PSL hold over the majority of the Polish population. Thus the peasant leader's greatest strength, his staunch resistance against foreign intervention, was used with great skill against him and his party. Such intransigence, the communists hinted, might encourage Moscow to 'incorporate Poland outright into the Soviet Union'.[14] As early as July 1945 Gomułka referred to Mikołajczyk as 'a symbol of all anti-democratic elements, of all that is the enemy of democracy and of the Soviet Union'.[15]

In its endeavour further to postpone the long overdue elections and to confuse public opinion, both domestic and foreign, the regime devised a clever subterfuge which was to demonstrate the degree of support which it received from the people. This was the so-called referendum which took place on 30 June 1946. In it the Polish electorate was asked to vote 'yes' or 'no' to the following three questions :

Are you in favour of the abolition of the Senate?
Are you in favour of the economic reforms – nationalization of industry and land reform?
Do you want the new western border with Germany to be permanent?

The nature of the questions put the PSL in an extremely difficult position. Obviously, it could not recommend to its members to vote negatively on the last two questions. However, the negative reply to the first question which the party leadership advised was suppressed by the government so that it seemed as if the provisional government enjoyed majority backing.

The effect of the referendum helped to create the psychological atmosphere of apprehension and fear in which the subsequent elections were held. A new electoral law provided the regime with far-reaching opportunities for illegal manipulation, and the unleashing of a violent campaign against all the political opponents of the new system. The Labour Party of Karol Popiel, which intended to join forces with the peasant opposition, was subjected to a number of repressive measures ending in the removal of its leader and his replacement by a docile follower of the communist lead. Much more severe, however, was the action taken against the leaders and members of the Polish Peasant Party. It fell victim to a systematically

14 'A History of the PPR – Materials and Documents,' Archives of the Polish Underground Study Trust, London, as quoted in Dziewanowski, op. cit., p. 2.
15 *Zarys historii Polskiego ruchu robotniczego 1944–1947* (Warsaw, 1961), p. 155.

organized terror which did not shrink from acts of physical violence, torture, and even assassination. Responsibility for these acts, as well as the subsequent electoral fraud, must be ascribed to the communist leadership, which used the organs of state security for a merciless crushing of all opposition. With almost a million voters disfranchised, the PSL candidates struck from the electoral lists in ten districts, and the electoral committees dominated by the PPR, the result of the elections, which took place on 19 January 1947, was a foregone conclusion.[16]

After the elections Poland was quickly transformed into a one-party totalitarian state. The office of Prime Minister was taken over by a pro-communist member of the PPS, Józef Cyrankiewicz, while Bolesław Bierut was elected President of the Republic. The representatives of the PSL had no place in the new government, which was composed only of the communists and their faithful allies. With its 28 seats in the Constituent Diet of 444, the PSL was no longer able to put up any resistance against the measures taken by the communist-controlled 'democratic bloc' coalition. Eventually, the regime subjected the remnants of the PSL to outright persecution, which forced its leaders – including Mikołajczyk – to escape to the West. In November 1947 the new PSL leadership ceased opposition.

For some time it appeared as if the PPS – because of pressure by its older leaders and rank-and-file – might assume the function of a quasi-opposition element. These hopes, however, were entirely frustrated by the arrests in mid-1947 of a large number of leading socialists and the new leadership expressed itself in favour of the amalgamation of their party with the PPR. In preparation for this step about 150,000 'unreliable' members of the PPS were expelled, its leading position was lost, and the communists became the largest party in Poland. However, the fusion, so carefully prepared by Cyrankiewicz, was delayed because of the outbreak of a serious crisis within the Polish Communist Party.

It had very soon become clear that for a section of the PPR leadership the policy of appealing to Polish patriotic sentiment was much more than mere tactics. Indeed, it soon appeared as a reflection of deep convictions among the native group of communists headed by Gomułka himself. No doubt he went along with a policy which resulted in the destruction of all genuine opposition. His belief in the necessity of an 'independent Polish road to socialism' prevented him from accepting unquestioningly the Stalinist version of proletarian internationalism. He was opposed to hasty and compulsory collectivization, expressed doubts about the utility of the Cominform, and

---

[16] For an eyewitness account of the 19 January 1947 election see Mikołajczyk, op. cit., pp. 201–29.

did not favour harsh action against Tito. Nor did he approve of an all-out campaign against the Church. As pointed out by one observer, Gomułka combined 'combating of active anti-communism' with the 'tactics of the "safety valve" '.[17]

Even more dangerous for Stalin was Gomułka's independence of judgement and action. The speech which he delivered on the occasion of the founding of the Cominform was conspicuous 'because of its lack of bombast and especially excessive praise, thanks, and other expressions of gratitude to the Soviets, which characterized the majority of other statements'.[18] Unlike the other members of the PPR leadership, he and his associates failed to sense, or simply chose to disregard, the new atmosphere of triumphant Stalinism. To his amazement and bitter disappointment he found himself in almost complete isolation.

Gomułka's feud with the Stalinist group headed by Bierut came to a head at the meeting of the Central Committee of the PPR in June 1948, when his analysis of the history of the Polish communist movement was severely criticized. In the following months Gomułka fought desperately with the Politburo members, trying to avoid the humiliation of the ritual of recantation. When he finally gave in at the meeting of the Central Committee in September 1948, the nature and setting of his recantation were entirely different to those of the other purged East European communist leaders. No doubt the accusation levelled against him by Edward Ochab that Gomułka would 'become the symbol for the bourgeoisie, for the rich peasants, for reaction . . .'[19] was severe. It was strangely reminiscent of Gomułka's attack against Mikołajczyk in 1945. Yet the atmosphere of the gathering was one of sorrow and resignation rather than of vindictiveness. The speeches of his opponents were a mixture of appeals and cajolery. Moreover, Gomułka's recantation, however humiliating, was unique in the period of Stalin-type purges. Having accepted his guilt, the fallen leader exclaimed almost defiantly that 'there must be some elements of a Polish road to socialism'.[20]

After September 1948 the PPR embarked on a new course, marked by a sudden emphasis on the fundamental importance of the Soviet model. The compulsory nature of the CPSU example, hitherto carefully concealed, was now openly regarded as the main criterion for the building of Polish socialism.

Gomułka's final liquidation was preceded by the fusion of the Socialist and Polish Workers' parties. In December 1948 the Polish

---

[17] Hansjakob Stehle, *The Independent Satellite* (New York, 1965), p. 29.
[18] Eugenio Reale, *Avec Jacques Duclos. Au Banc des Accusés à la Réunion Constitutive du Kominform à Szklarska Poremba* (Paris, 1958), pp. 27–8.
[19] *Nowe Drogi* (September-October 1948), p. 63.
[20] Ibid., p. 143.

United Workers' Party (PUWP) was founded. Three socialist leaders, including Cyrankiewicz, who became Secretary-General of the new party, were included in the PUWP eleven-member Politburo. But they had no influence on its policies. The new party expressly subscribed to the traditions of the Polish Social Democrats and the prewar Communist Party. The PPS tradition combining socialism with nationalism was repudiated. In its Ideological Declaration the 'special Polish way to socialism' was rejected and the Stalinist interpretation of People's Democracy as a different brand of the dictatorship of the proletariat accepted.

The Period of Stalinism

By the beginning of 1949 the party and the country were engulfed by Stalinist terror which penetrated into all spheres of life. The party changed into a replica of the Soviet Communist Party. Bierut, as party chairman, assumed the position of a Polish dictator. His influence was enhanced by the fact that he had spent several years in the USSR, which connected his political career with the CPSU. This, it was held, enabled him to read Stalin's mind better than any of his colleagues.

Beirut became the object of a personality cult similar to that enjoyed by Stalin. Yet his position was definitely weaker than that of his predecessor and the other leaders of East European communist parties. His power was checked by two other representatives of Polish Stalinism : the deputy premier, Jakob Berman, whose influence in ideological matters earned him the title of 'grey eminence'; and Hilary Minc, a dogmatic economist, who built his position on the emulation of Soviet economic policies. Both were the oldest and most influential members of the Politburo. Despite his services to the communist cause, Cyrankiewicz, who had contributed to the liquidation of his own party, the PPS, never achieved political distinction, being overshadowed by the communist members of the Politburo. Among them Stanisław Radkiewicz, the Moscow-trained Minister of Public Security, soon became one of the most dreaded persons in Poland.

To this communist leadership fell the unpleasant task of finally liquidating Gomułka and his accomplices. Their cases were taken up in November 1949 at the Central Committee plenum, which was imbued with an atmosphere of fear and hysteria. Unlike his associates – Zenon Kliszko and Marian Spychalski – Gomułka refused to yield to concerted attack. He found enough courage to repudiate additional charges levelled against him and to strike back by pointing out that he alone was being made scapegoat for all the shortcomings of the party. As expected, his dignified defence was of no avail. Together with his friends he was deprived of his party and government positions and forbidden to participate in party work. In 1951 he was detained in his home, obviously in preparation for a public trial. That he escaped the tragic fate of Slánsky, Rajk, Kostov, and the other victims of Stalinist terror in eastern Europe can be explained by the fact that his deviationism was originally shared by almost all of those who subsequently acted as his judges.

In the period between September 1948 and November 1949 the party was subjected to three major purges of 'nationalist deviationists', affecting almost a quarter of party membership. Victims of the purges suffered the same indignities as those inflicted upon their non-communist predecessors. In certain cases they were tortured during investigations. Yet it seems that in Poland there were fewer executions than in the rest of the communist world and perhaps also fewer forced-labour camps. Even the most fanatical communists could not fail to realize that in the eyes of the Polish public the purges were nothing but an overlapping of the hated Russian practices into eastern Europe. The new political system was supported by a huge, well organized, and ruthless security police directed by Radkiewicz, supervised by Bierut himself, and closely co-operating with the Soviet NKVD.

The period of Stalinism was a systematic introduction of contemporary Soviet methods into all fields of public life. Some communist leaders went so far as to demonstrate their loyalty to Stalin by 'anticipating his requirements'.[21] As stated by Bierut, the members of the PUWP were to develop 'a consciousness of the leading role of the CPSU'. The *Nowe Drogi* stated in an issue devoted to Stalin's seventieth birthday that 'the name of Stalin was indissolubly linked with the hearts and minds of the Polish working class'.[22]

The PUWP systematically infiltrated into all government organs. The few non-communists still holding important positions were dismissed and replaced by communists. Traditional Polish organizations, such as the peasant and Catholic youth movements and the popular Boy Scout organizations, were either dissolved or put under rigid party control. All non-party associations became tools of the regime.

The Six-Year Plan, elaborated by Minc and inaugurated in 1950, was based on Soviet economic practices. Industrialization, its main characteristic, served the interests of Poland in its general purposes. Unfortunately, in many cases the benefits of industrial planning were vitiated by the fact that the plan paid more attention to the needs of the Soviet Union than those of Poland. Senseless emphasis on the

---

[21] Richard Hiscocks, *Poland. Bridge for the Abyss?* (London, 1963), p. 145.
[22] *Nowe Drogi* (1950 special issue) quoted ibid., p. 146.

production of capital goods and organizational shortcomings pressed down the already low standard of living. Politically, the speedy growth of a class of industrial workers broke the traditional social set-up and provided the regime with new means of control and indoctrination inapplicable to a peasant society. The industrial workers, whose unions were changed into state organs, were put into the straitjacket of Soviet work practices, such as the Stachanovite system and socialist competition. Despite the increasing momentum of the Polish industrial economy, the people derived little profit from their labours.

The era of Stalinism in Poland was marked by a vicious campaign against the two basic forces of Polish national life – the peasantry and the Roman Catholic Church.

While less intensive than in most of the other Soviet East European satellites, the campaign of collectivization was especially insidious, as it was directed against the very backbone of the Polish nation, and encountered bitter opposition. Non-fulfilment of deliveries to the government, wholesale slaughter of cattle, and over-consumption were associated with determined resistance against the PUWP. Party leaders realized the danger of applying agricultural policies which in the Soviet Union required draconic measures to be put into effect. At first they were forced to press rural collectivization along Stalinist lines. When failure became apparent the party had to go slow and make many concessions. But no radical changes were made in the treatment of agriculture, which continued to be the Cinderella of the Polish economy. Emphasis on policies aiming at 'socialization of the countryside' could not cover up the alarming decrease in total agricultural production caused by the inability of the regime to gain at least some degree of support among the peasants. By 1953 the Six-Year Plan had exceeded its goal for industry, but in agricultural production it remained at 12 per cent below its target. Even after the death of Stalin the agricultural programme adopted in March 1954 at the Second Congress of the PUWP remained vague and ambivalent. Both Minc and Berman reaffirmed the Stalinist principle of collectivization. Politically, the degree of resistance in the countryside provided the most accurate measure of the failure of communism in Poland.

The Polish peasants instinctively rejected the complex doctrines of communism. The opposition of the Roman Catholic Church was of a different nature. It was based on solid organization and discipline combined with the political experience and diplomatic adroitness of the Catholic hierarchy. In a Poland which after 1945 had become almost 100 per cent Catholic, the traditional role of the Church to act as the main representative of Polish national traditions became even more important. It commanded the loyalty of the overwhelming majority of the people and derived further strength from its spiritual association with the West. Faced with so powerful an adversary, the communist leaders tried to avoid, or at least postpone, an outright trial of strength. They knew that Soviet backing – which in many cases proved to be their main asset – would be highly detrimental in a clash with the Church. Thus the regime preferred to pursue for as long as possible a policy of 'peaceful co-existence'. To provoke Polish Catholicism by militant atheism along the lines of orthodox Marxism-Leninism would have deprived the communists of the benefits of their initial tactics – to appear as a popular, patriotic, and truly Polish party.

The unilateral denunciation in September 1945 of the 1925 Concordat with the Holy See was more in keeping with future policy towards Catholicism. But this action had been made possible by the policy of the Vatican which continued to recognize the London government and made no definite arrangements with regard to ecclesiastical jurisdiction in the former German territories recovered after the war. The Polish government could make a clear-cut distinction between the Germanophile Vatican and the Polish episcopate with which it desired to live in peace.

At the same time, however, the regime prepared itself for the struggle against its powerful antagonist. As early as November 1945 the organization of the so-called 'progressive Catholics' was founded by Bolesław Piasecki, a man whose fascist past did not recommend him to any position in 'People's Poland'. Yet Piasecki managed to ingratiate himself not only with the Soviet occupation authorities but also with Gomułka. His organization, better known as the 'Pax' movement (after the name of the publishing firm which it owned), achieved even before the advent of Stalinism some influence and considerable freedom of action. In a country in which private enterprise was eliminated it carried on commercial and industrial activities along 'capitalist' lines, enjoying at the same time practically all the privileges of state enterprises. The PPR and later its successor, the PUWP, gave Piasecki's movement full support. 'If he was not their agent, he did his best to act like one.'[23] However objectionable from the point of view of Marxist doctrine, Piasecki's theory on the separation of the 'socio-economic system', which Christians were free to support, from 'the materialistic philosophy of communism', which they had to oppose, was made use of by the regime. Introducing the

---

[23] Adam Bromke, *Poland's Politics: Idealism vs. Realism* (Cambridge, Mass., 1967), p. 83. The author attributes Piasecki's decision to 'side with the Communists against the overwhelming trend of popular sentiments in Poland' to a mixture of 'opportunism and political realism'.

idea of ideological 'multiformity', Piasecki's teaching provided the government with an opportunity to split the ranks of Polish Catholicism, particularly by separating its lay leadership from the ecclesiastical hierarchy.[24] This intention was confirmed by the regime's simultaneous organization of a group of so-called 'priest-patriots', who collaborated with the government and condemned the activities of the Polish episcopate. The lack of success of these dissidents demonstrated the firmness of the clergy.

The defeat of Gomułka and the advent of Stalinism upset the precarious balance of power between regime and Church. By the end of 1948 the Polish communists had inaugurated a campaign of active atheism, directing their first attack against Catholic writers, some of whom were arrested, and the Catholic youth group, which was dissolved. Catholic publishing houses were nationalized. Responding to this challenge, paralleled in other parts of the communist world, Pope Pius XII issued, in July 1949, a decree excommunicating all Catholics who were members of a communist party or its willing tools. Such Catholics were to be denied the sacraments.

The government regarded the papal action as a provocation and retaliated with a number of measures designed to cripple the power of Polish Catholicism. The Pope became the target of violent attacks and a decree on freedom of conscience and religion was passed which introduced harsh penalties for priests refusing to administer sacraments because of political considerations. Measures were taken against various Catholic institutions, particularly schools, which in many cases were put under the control of the anti-religious Society of Children's Friends. Of special importance was the confiscation of the largest church welfare organization, *Caritas,* which was responsible for a whole variety of charitable activities and administered the considerable contributions received from American Catholics of Polish origin. *Caritas* was placed under the control of 'patriotic priests' and members of the organization of 'progressive Catholics'. The most damaging blow, intended to break the political position of the Church, was the abolition of its exemption from land reform. All its estates in excess of 50 hectares (which were reserved to the individual parishes) were confiscated without compensation. While the revenue from this land was to be used for religious and charitable purposes, including the support of aged clergy, it was placed under the administration of a government-controlled Church Fund. This measure provided the regime with another powerful weapon against the independence of the episcopate.

If the unity and determination of the Church remained unimpaired, this was due to a large extent to its leader, Archbishop, and

24 See Stehle, op. cit., p. 109.

since 1953 Cardinal, Stefan Wyszyński, the Primate of Poland. Despite his insistence on the defence of the rights of the Church, Wyszyński realized that further aggravation of the already tense Church–state relations might result in a violent conflict – a head-on collision which neither he nor the regime desired. This was the background of the agreement, at times referred to as *modus vivendi*, signed in April 1950. It was the first genuine accord between a communist government and the Catholic Church. Both parties made considerable concessions. The episcopate scored a definite success by preserving the supreme authority of the Pope in spiritual matters and with regard to church jurisdiction. This victory, however, was bought at the price of important political concessions. The Church pledged support for the regime in all temporal matters, going so far as to promise to instruct the clergy not to resist the expansion of the co-operative movement in the Polish countryside.

The armistice did not last long. To break the continued hold of Roman Catholicism and its representatives over important segments of the nation, the regime could not afford to live up to the terms of the 1950 agreement. The unsettled problem of the ecclesiastical administration in the newly acquired territories of western Poland served as a convenient pretext to break the *modus vivendi*. The Vatican set up only temporary administration in the western provinces by appointing temporary apostolic administrators, pending the final settlement of borders by a peace treaty. The Polish government regarded this action as inimical to its vital interests. It deposed the administrators and replaced them by capitular vicars elected by the local diocesan chapters. At the same time it resumed its anti-religious activities. Religious instruction in schools was restricted to the minimum and in certain areas discontinued; the number of theological faculties was drastically reduced; and the publication of Catholic periodicals stopped. Hundreds of priests, including bishops, were arrested and tried on trumped-up charges of anti-state activities. Many were accused of having violated the constitutional prohibition of misusing Church and religion for political ends. By decree of April 1953 the government reserved for itself control over all church appointments and the right to dismiss members of the clergy whose activities violated law or public order. All church dignitaries were ordered to take an oath of allegiance to the Polish People's Republic. In the autumn of 1953 the show-trial of the bishop of Kraków, Jan Kaczmarek, was followed by the arrest of Cardinal Wyszyński, who was detained in a monastery. Finally, in December 1953, those bishops and vicars capitular who were still free took the prescribed oath of loyalty to the state.

On the surface, the state had won a decisive victory over the

Church, which was condemned to a slow and lingering death. But persecution, as well as the increasing activities of the Pax organization, which in 1955 merged with the 'priest-patriots', failed to break the unity of the Church. More than before Catholics clung to their clergy whose resistance, symbolized by Wyszyński, helped to strengthen the nation's defence against atheism. The Catholic Church gained the support of all those who opposed the government, including even those members of the intelligentsia who in the past had pursued anti-clerical policies. Support for Catholicism became a political demonstration against the regime whose repressive policies against the Church could be continued, but only at a heavy price. Every anti-Church measure was accompanied by a sizeable decrease in the overall economic performance of the country.

Particularly oppressive was the influence of Stalinism in the realm of education, culture, and the arts. As in the Soviet Union, educational syllabuses at all levels were changed so as to serve the needs of the new social and political system. Special emphasis was laid on systematic indoctrination of children, who were to be isolated from the influence of family and Church and brought up in the spirit of militant communism. Admission of students of peasant and worker origin into institutions of higher learning was accompanied by the exclusion of those from 'bourgeois' families. By this method, the regime's educationalists believed, a new intelligentsia more inclined to accept communist values would emerge. The universities were deprived of their traditional academic freedoms and subjected to state and party control. Elaborate educational planning, organized so as to serve the needs of industry, contributed to the decline in educational standards.

Another aspect of post-1948 development was the regimentation of cultural, artistic, and intellectual life. All expressions of art, especially literature, were to be given socialist content and subordinated to the philosophy of 'socialist realism'. The regime managed to gain adherents among the younger generation of writers, but only a few of these were able to grasp 'the Marxist theory of socialist perspective'.[25] The older, more mature, writers remained silent. As subsequent developments proved, the moves of the communist strategists 'on the battle map of the war for men's minds' ended in dismal failure.[26]

By 1953 the Soviet Union appeared to have consolidated its control over the life of the PUWP and the Polish state. All major deci-

[25] Ludwig Krzyzanowski, 'Literature' in Oscar Halecki, ed., Poland (New York, 1957), p. 235.
[26] Czesław Miłosz, The Captive Mind (New York, 1955), p. 212.

sions were made by the Kremlin. Warsaw could decide only on minor issues and enjoyed some leeway in the choice of tactics to be used in policy implementation. By a cruel irony of fate men who had inherited the proud traditions of revolutionary Marxism, such as those expounded by Rosa Luxemburg, became abject servants of Stalin whose totalitarianism was even more oppressive than Tsarist despotism.[27]

Moscow employed a whole variety of methods to control its Polish dependency. Of these the most important was the Soviet hold over the Polish armed forces and particularly over the organs of public security. The former was achieved by the appointment of Konstantin Rokossovsky, a Russianized Pole, to the office of Deputy Prime Minister and Minister of National Defence. His importance was enhanced by his 'co-optation' into the Party Politburo. A number of Soviet officers and specialists were attached to the Polish army, some acting as political agents.

Soviet influence over state security was even more pronounced. Until December 1945 its main organ was the Ministry of Public Security, built up on the Soviet model and including a number of Soviet experts. This department was headed by Radkiewicz, the Moscow-trained representative of Stalinist ruthlessness. In the Polish governmental set-up the public security apparatus played a dominant role, overshadowing that of all other Ministries, including those in charge of the economy. In addition to the Office of Public Security (*Urząd Bezpieczeństwa Publicznego*, popularly referred to as *Bezpieka*), it was composed of a number of other agencies and military units, such as the Citizens' Militia, which performed regular police duties, prison guards, the Internal Security Corps, and the Frontier Guards. Of special importance was the Voluntary Reserve of the Citizens' Militia, used for the purpose 'of combating banditry'. In addition, specialized units were entrusted with police duties, such as the Railroad, Postal, Forest, and Industrial Guards, operating under the supervision of the individual Ministries. By far the most important was the Central Office of Public Security, its individual departments, and its subordinate offices. These organs were there to ensure the political reliability of citizens : they issued personal identity cards and maintained personal records of the population. With a few exceptions, the organization of public security in Poland was a replica of that in the Soviet Union.[28]

Stalin's death did not immediately affect the character of the

---

[27] Bromke, op. cit., pp. 69–70.
[28] For the organization of the Polish National Security forces see Kazimierz Glabisz, 'The Armed Forces and National Security' in Oscar Halecki, ed., *Poland*, pp. 164–75.

Polish system of government. Despite the traditionally anti-Russian mentality of the Poles, Stalinist practices outlasted his death by more than one year. The reason for this strange phenomenon must be sought in the changed character and the increased strength of the Polish United Workers' Party – no longer an unimportant faction but a powerful élite disposing of adequate means to impose its will. Because of its privileged position, the party had all the characteristics of the 'New Class', as described by Milovan Djilas. The luxurious life of the higher echelons, securing for them better salaries, special stores, and even arrangements for special health care, contrasted drastically with the misery of the average Pole.

Yet developments after autumn 1955 proved that as elsewhere in eastern Europe, in Poland the 'monolith' of Stalinism was by no means so solid as was generally assumed. Having been put together in haste and having no other foundation but fear and terror, it could cover up but not eliminate its internal weakness. When, after Stalin's death, one of the pillars of terroristic control was removed, the hidden discontent within the countries of the Soviet Bloc gradually made itself felt.

Chapter 9

The 'Glorious October' and its Aftermath

'W interpretacji rewizjonistów VII Plenum i Październik – to dwa różne pojęcia. Pod obłudnym hasłem obrony Października rewizjoniści łamią i atakują uchwały VII Plenum.'

(Władysław Gomułka, 1957)[1]

As in other states of the communist world a wide gap arose between party and people. In Poland not only the leaders but also the rank-and-file of the PUWP failed to realize their alienation from the overwhelming majority of the nation, evident at the Second PUWP Congress in March 1954. It was attended by 1,128 delegates, of whom 272 were workers and 108 peasants. Well over 600 were party functionaries, state officials, and members of the intelligentsia, all of whom held decisive and best-paid positions in Polish society.

Living in a world of its own, the party bureaucracy failed to read the signals of the times and was unprepared to make more important concessions to the concept of the 'New Course'. A few reforms of an organizational character along the lines of the Soviet example were adopted. The 'cult of the individual' was condemned and the 'principle of collective leadership' introduced. In practice it meant that the First Secretary of the party, Bierut, gave up his post of Prime Minister, being replaced by Cyrankiewicz. The necessity for economic reforms was recognized. Apart from these changes the congress brought nothing new.[2]

The power-political structure within the party remained the same. The communist leaders realized that more important changes might lead to the undermining of their positions. Soon, however, the accumulated injustices of the past were uppermost in people's minds, and the party was pushed into a defensive position. A development started which in two years brought about momentous changes in the PUWP and seemed to augur genuine liberalization and greater independence of the Soviet Union.

[1] 'In the interpretation of the revisionists the VIIIth Plenum and October are two different concepts. Under the hypocritical slogan of October the revisionists destroy and attack the resolutions of the VIIIth Plenum.' Władysław Gomułka, *Przemówienia* (Warsaw, 1959), p. 39.
[2] For the slow advent of changes in Poland see Bromke, op. cit., p. 86.

The Polish 'Thaw'

The initial economic reforms of the 'New Course' were mainly promises to correct the most obvious and glaring shortcomings of Polish economic planning. In October 1953 the party openly confessed that the current Six-Year Plan, through its emphasis on industrialization, left practically no scope for the improvement of the pitiably low standard of living. To improve this shortcoming, the cause of widespread hostility against the government, the party promised increased production of consumer goods, better housing, and higher agricultural investments. As pointed out by one observer, 'the Polish New Course was rather an admission of the inadequacy of the existing plan than a programme which it was seriously intended to fulfil'.[3] Real changes in economic policy started only in 1956 after the Twentieth CPSU Congress.

Much more important was the 'Thaw' in the political and cultural spheres. At the end of 1954 a reorganization of the public security services took place. Its main impetus – apart from events in the Soviet Union – was the revelations of a high official of the Ministry of Public Security (the dreaded *Bezpieka*), Lt-Colonel Józef Światło, who had defected to the West. His broadcasts describing the practices of the Polish police caused consternation among the people and great embarrassment in the party. As a result the Ministry of Public Security was abolished and its chief, Radkiewicz, was relegated to a position of lesser importance. Most of the high officials of the Ministry were dismissed from government service, two were expelled from the party Central Committee, and one was sentenced to five years imprisonment for 'systematic violation of the law'. By the end of 1954 many prominent victims of Stalinist terror, including Gomułka, had been secretly released from prison.

The main advocates of liberalization were writers, university teachers, and students. It became clear that ten years or so of communist rule had failed to change the opinions of the Polish intelligentsia. No doubt the relaxation of the rigid controls on Polish literature was influenced by stirrings among Soviet *literati* after Malenkov's reforms. The Soviet spark, when it touched Polish soil, flared up into a flame which ultimately devoured the artificial structure of communist supervision over Polish cultural life. Faithful to the tradition of nineteenth-century Poland, which regarded the writers as representing the conscience of the people, Polish authors turned against the hypocrisy and inhumanity of the regime. During the course of 1954–55 the great majority of pre-war writers were rehabilitated and readmitted into the Union of Writers. Many young

[3] Hiscocks, op. cit., p. 173.

authors, motivated by 'pangs of conscience' over their past 'sins', indignantly turned against a system which had induced them to forget their mission. Typical of this attitude was the behaviour of Adam Ważyk, a poet who from being an admirer of Stalin changed into a determined opponent of the regime and critic of contemporary social reality.[4]

The writers found enthusiastic supporters among young people, especially students, who took an important part in the liberalization movement. Although they had grown up under German occupation and later communism, they had remained largely unaffected by communist indoctrination. National traditions, family influence, as well as loyalty to the Church, were still at the top of their list of values.

The confrontation of traditional Polish ideals with communist drabness and the mendacity of official slogans called forth sullen opposition against the regime. Far from becoming 'products of social-ist morality' and 'young builders of socialism', young people turned their backs on a system which, apart from the hypocritical teaching of communist puritanism, did nothing to satisfy their spiritual and material needs. After many years of resignation and despair opposi-tion to communism had become their main obsession. They furiously demanded what the communist regime lacked and was incapable of giving to them – bearable living conditions, human happiness, and better prospects for the future.

This ferment, which started soon after Stalin's death, was given a great impetus by the World Youth Festival held in Warsaw in the summer of 1955. Contacts with young Westerners opened the eyes of the Polish youngsters to whom 'it brought the first dizzying re-minder that there could be joy in just being alive'.[5] After this, Polish youth sought self-expression in turning to the West. American jazz, dances, films, and even dress – in fact all that had a Western label – caught their imagination.

That this fervour did not remain limited to externals was due to the activities of students who gave both form and substance to the craving after freedom. Western literature and the renewal of con-tacts with the Western world increased their desire to restore freedom of expression in Poland. Students' theatres and cabarets sprang up in university centres, serving as media for subtle criticism of the regime. At the end of 1955 the students took over the publication of a Warsaw weekly, *Po prostu*, until then one of the colourless

---

[4] Wazyk's *Poem for the Adults*, voicing his bitter disappointment with this social reality, was representative of the change of mind of those who had initially succumbed to the lure of communist propaganda.

[5] Flora Lewis, *A Case History of Hope* (New York, 1958), p. 57.

periodicals of the official youth organization. Almost overnight *Po prostu* changed into a mouthpiece of the Polish reformists. Its analytical approach to the tenets of Marxism-Leninism and its attacks against the incompetence of the party gained it great popularity all over the country.

The PUWP leadership, suffering from an incipient internal split, made practically no sanctions against the rebels. It gave way to the reform movement, believing that it would be able to control its development. The party went so far as to admit publicly its responsibility for the sad state of Polish literature and promised to avoid past mistakes. It was in this atmosphere that a general debate on party cultural policy took place. Outstanding representatives of Polish literary and artistic life attacked the senseless enforcement of 'socialist realism' and the system of rigid control over all artistic production. Later, the discussion was extended to other aspects of Polish life : its dreariness, hypocrisy, and harshness were subjected to scathing criticism. More courageous party members, who had not succumbed to the demoralization of Stalinism, joined the reform movement. As a result, the 'Thaw' penetrated into party publications, such as the semi-official *Nowa kultura* and even the ideological mouthpiece of Polish communism, *Nowe Drogi*. The necessity of re-establishing contacts with the people was recognized as the first aim of the PUWP. In the autumn of 1955 the party leadership cautiously reopened discussion on the possibility of a specific 'Polish way to socialism' – an issue which during Stalin's life had been regarded as anathema. Basing its arguments on the writings of Lenin, *Nowe Drogi* concluded that 'we have paid too little attention to that which is innate in our movement, in our historic road . . .'[6]

The Twentieth CPSU Congress of February 1956 gave a tremendous boost to the endeavours of the Polish reformers. Views which until recently had been put forward with the utmost care and many reservations were suddenly given official sanction. Above all, the approbation which the Congress gave to the concept of 'separate paths to socialism' of the individual communist parties and states gave full justification to the policies promoted by the Polish reformists. The representatives of the Warsaw regime found it necessary to express themselves in favour of a radical reappraisal of the fundamental concepts of socialism. Cyrankiewicz stated that 'a great unceasing revaluation of many things, which is far from complete yet, is taking place at present in the whole country. . . .' He added that it was necessary to reject 'the ballast of dogmas which have fettered

[6] 'For an Increase of Our Creative Effort and Ideological Work,' *Nowe Drogi*, No. 14 (September 1955), as quoted in *News from Behind the Iron Curtain*, vol. 4, No. 12 (December 1955), p. 14.

free thought and have frequently become an obstacle and brake in our march forward. . . .'[7]

Psychologically important was the secret speech of Nikita Khrushchev repudiating the terroristic practices of Stalin. In a country whose history was marked by a century and a half of struggle against Russian oppression, the condemnation of Stalin was more important than elsewhere in eastern Europe. For the overwhelming majority of the Poles 'Stalinism and communism were one and the same thing'.[8] Hence Khrushchev's revelations were almost automatically applied to the whole communist system. The Twentieth CPSU Congress brought about a rewriting of the official post-war history of Poland. The communist leaders and part of the Polish public registered with great satisfaction the declaration that the charges levelled against the KPP, as well as its dissolution and the ruthless liquidation of its leaders in 1938, were 'based on evidence falsified by provocateurs who have since been exposed'.[9] In the eyes of the Polish non-communist public this declaration was viewed as a confession of ideological bankruptcy.

The Polish reformers very cleverly used the lessons of the Twentieth CPSU Congress for purposes of further liberalization. Their efforts were made easier by the unexpected death of Bierut, only a few weeks after the condemnation of his Soviet model. Bierut was succeeded by Edward Ochab, whose orthodox ideological past at first prevented him from realizing the immediate urgency of fundamental reforms in the organization and practices of the Polish state and party. Initially, he attempted to follow a middle of the road policy. He indignantly condemned the 'cult of the individual' and other practices of Stalinism, underlining the importance of the 'Polish road to socialism'. But the basic orientation of the PUWP was to remain unchanged. This attitude of the new First Secretary was expressed in his treatment of Gomułka and his revisionist associates, Spychalski and General Wacław Komar. Responding to popular clamour, he announced their release from prison, adding that Gomułka's arrest in 1951 had been unjustified and without foundation. This concession to public opinion was accompanied by a statement criticizing Gomułka's 'opportunistic and nationalistic deviation' as a clear violation of socialist internationalism.

At the same time liberal elements in the party, backed by the non-communist public, proceeded to the second stage of Polish liberalization. Its aim, openly declared, was a revival of democratic institutions and the elimination of everything standing in the way of

[7] Ibid., vol. 5, No. 5 (May 1956), p. 45.
[8] Dziewanowski, op. cit., p. 258.
[9] *Trybuna Ludu* (19 February 1956).

democratic ideals. Party and government were forced to take a number of measures for the renewal of political life. The *Sejm*, which since the end of 1947 had been nothing but a meaningless rubber-stamp for the executive acts of the regime, was suddenly infused with new vigour. At its April meeting Cyrankiewicz himself declared that in future the *Sejm* would reassume its deliberative, controlling, and legislative functions. He repudiated its recent helplessness and the withholding of information necessary for the fulfilment of its key role in Polish society. For the first time the *Sejm* witnessed more genuine debate and, on the adoption of a new abortion law, it abandoned its practice of unanimous vote. The five Catholic deputies voted against the law, basing their opposition on their Catholic world outlook.

One after another, the main representatives of the Stalinist regime were removed from positions of influence and power. At the beginning of May 1956 Jakob Berman, the chief ideologist and interpreter of Polish Stalinism, resigned as deputy premier and member of the Politburo. He lost all political influence. Soon afterwards the former PPS member Adam Rapacki took over the Ministry of Foreign Affairs. Despite the fact that, together with Cyrankiewicz, he had been among the most enthusiastic advocates of the merger of the PPS with the communists, Rapacki was known for his nationalistic and liberal sympathies.

The most important measure of liberalization was the amnesty granted by the *Sejm* to tens of thousands of political prisoners and the reduction of the sentences of others. Again the burning issue of past police atrocities was reopened and further punitive measures were taken against those regarded as guilty of gross violations against socialist legality. In April the former Minister of Public Security was dismissed from the cabinet. Another result of the reappraisal of the past was the rehabilitation of the wartime Home Army whose members had been for years subjected to vilification and constant harassment. This persecution, it was stated, was unjustified, having been based on Stalin's theory of the intensification of class struggle in the last phases of the building of socialism. Thus Stalin's doctrine had prepared a terrible fate for 'the soldiers of the Home Army – soldiers who believed that they were fighting for a free and democratic Poland and shed blood for this cause'.[10] While it involved only enlisted men and not officers, this gesture of reconciliation was one of the most tangible results of the liberalization and democratization process.

It was the writers, journalists, and the more enthusiastic members of the young intelligentsia who made full use of the opportunities

[10] Radio Warsaw on 27 March 1956, as reported in *News from behind the Iron Curtain*, vol. 5, No. 5 (May 1956), p. 43.

offered by the de-Stalinization campaign. Following the example of *Po prostu*, a large number of other periodicals, occasionally including even the official party organ, *Trybuna Ludu*, engaged in a systematic attack against the different expressions of the 'cult of the individual'. Almost invariably, they based their arguments on the long forgotten tenets of Marx's teaching – his emphasis on search for knowledge, his scepticism, and his refusal to be bound by blind clichés of past or contemporary dogmas. The search for the true meaning of socialism became an obsession and gave rise to a lively intellectual life, especially in the ranks of the younger generation. Under the sponsorship or influence of *Po prostu* numerous discussion groups composed of party and non-party members were founded in the larger Polish cities. Of these the famous 'Crooked Circle Club' in Warsaw was the most radical and influential.

The same quest for truth characterized the meetings of the official Council for Culture and Art. Expressing the thoughts of the majority of Polish *literati*, the leading poet, Antoni Słonimski, rejected the idea that the party should be responsible for literary de-Stalinization. The Writers' Union, too, which Słonimski described as the 'Red Salvation Army', should be limited to its 'appropriate functions'. No organization, but the writers themselves, acting as free individuals, could bring about the improvement of Polish cultural life. Condemning the 'mythology of the era of fear', Słonimski complained about the appearance of new myths :

> Now they say that the responsibility for the past belongs to the cult of the individual. This I found formulated by the chief Marxist theorist, Professor Schaff. Let us follow this formula to the end. First of all, [let us not refer] to the cult of the individual, but to the individual himself. Further, it is not the individual, but the system, which permits the individual to conduct such dangerous activities.[11]

At the same time, however, Słonimski – like many others – did not lose his faith in the socialist cause, regarding the abandonment of the true heritage of Marxism as the main reason for Poland's shortcomings.

In the realm of economic life the promises of two years ago were replaced by concrete planning. Even the former representatives of Stalinist thought recognized the necessity of a thoroughgoing reform. This reform, it was emphasized, was to be based on 'free scientific

[11] Antoni Słonimski, 'For the Restoration of the Citizen's Rights', *Przeglad Kulturalny* (5, 11 April), as quoted in *News from behind the Iron Curtain*, vol. 5, No. 6 (June 1956), p. 9.

discussion', decentralization, and democratization, as well as the introduction of certain elements of market economy considered as the only guarantees for improvements in the standard of living.

Liberalization and efforts to introduce a breath of democracy, had they remained limited only to the members of the educated classes, would have been of little avail. That the reform movement assumed nationwide proportions was due to the strike and subsequent riots of workers in the city of Poznań in June 1956. This spontaneous rebellion, which was followed by similar outbreaks in other industrial centres, proved that the regime had lost whatever sympathy it might have gained even among those traditionally held to be the backbone of communism – workers who contrasted promises of future abundance with day-to-day misery. They protested against low wages, intolerable increases in work norms, shocking housing conditions, and other economic privations. Events in the *Cegielski* works in Poznań were symbolic of their mood. Once their demands, voiced by a delegation sent to the Warsaw Ministry, were rejected, they went on strike, a strike which soon changed into open revolt against the security police and the local party authorities.

The fact that during the demonstrations the workers carried banners calling for 'bread and freedom' underlined the political overtones of the uprising. It was suppressed only after the arrival of military reinforcements from Warsaw, but not before serious losses both in dead and wounded had been sustained. Over 300 workers were arrested. The riots caused the government great embarrassment as they occurred during the Poznań international Fair, which was attended by many foreign visitors. The initial reaction of the regime, as expressed by the radio address of Cyrankiewicz, was by no means unequivocal. While the Prime Minister admitted the validity of the workers' complaints, he attributed the Poznań events to 'agents of imperialism' determined to obstruct the democratization process and government efforts to improve the lot of the workers.

Reference to foreign imperialists carried little persuasion, as all Poles knew that the disturbances were caused by economic disorganization and lack of contacts between the workers and the regime. Even before the issue could be dealt with by the party, the government had restored to the *Cegielski* workers the first instalment of unjustly collected taxes and removed from their positions two Ministers responsible for negotiations with the workers. The Poznań insurrection and its aftermath brought about an acceleration of the internal political crisis within the PUWP. It precipitated the conflict between reformists and Stalinists at the Seventh Plenary Session of the PUWP Central Committee, at the end of July. The 'conservative' Stalinists, led by Zenon Nowak, used the meeting for their counter-attack against the policy of democratization, which they identified with opposition to the Soviet Union. They used the issue of the Poznań uprising as a convenient pretext for demanding a return to ideological orthodoxy and repression against the protagonists of liberalization. Like their Soviet protectors, they saw behind the Poznań riots the machinations of foreign imperialistic agents and their Polish henchmen.

This hack interpretation was almost entirely abandoned by Cyrankiewicz, and especially by Ochab, who now appeared as spokesman for the liberal faction. The riots, Ochab stated, had been caused above all by the excessive bureaucracy and 'soullessness of the authorities'. To avoid such happenings in the future, the party must establish close relations with the workers, promote their freedom to criticize, and help to establish the rule of law and respect for civil rights. The resolution adopted by the Seventh Plenary Session of the party Central Committee included many of the ideas advocated by Ochab. It declared itself in favour of continued democratization, emphasizing not only the ideology of Marxism-Leninism and the usefulness of profiting from the CPSU example, but also the necessity to express 'the national interests' of Poland.

The same session of the Central Committee declared the resolution of 1949 expelling Gomułka, Spychalski, and Zenon Kliszko from the PUWP to be null and void. All three were formally readmitted into the party fold. Kliszko was appointed Deputy Minister of Justice. Three new members and two new alternate members of the Politburo were co-opted, all of them in favour of the policy of democratization. Foremost among them was the Foreign Minister, Rapacki, and Stefan Jędrychowski who replaced the Stalinist Eugeniusz Szyr as head of the State Planning Commission.

Gomułka's star was now in the ascendant. During the seventh plenum he had been frequently referred to. His position was strengthened by the almost universal belief in his patriotism, the determination with which he had resisted Stalinist pressure, and the dignity with which he had borne the humiliation to which he had been subjected. The peasants remembered him because of his opposition to collectivization and even the party rank-and-file hailed him as a sincere and convinced communist. Rightly or wrongly, the personality of Gomułka – the innocent victim of Stalinist terror – became a symbol of a better Poland based on a more liberal and democratic system. Gomułka's gradual readmission into the political arena only intensified the split within the party leadership. It was characteristic of the internal confusion in the PUWP that both factions – the

Stalinist *Natolin* group and the reformist *Puławska* faction – tried to gain Gomułka to their side.[12] Even after he had decided to join forces with the reformers, the contest remained for some time in the balance. But developments favoured the anti-Stalinists, especially when Ochab abandoned his orthodox past and threw his weight behind them. By late summer and early autumn the intoxicating spirit of revolt against a hated tyrannical system was approaching its climax. While drawing their strength from enlightened public opinion and many of their active supporters from among the non-communists, the reformers operated strictly within the framework of the PUWP. It was not surprising that they were unable to keep pace with growing popular demands voiced at different public demonstrations. Of these the celebration of the three hundredth anniversary of the crowning of the Blessed Virgin of Częstochowa as 'Queen of Poland' at the monastery of Jasna Góra was by far the most important. Over a million people took part in this pilgrimage, which turned into a mass protest against the oppressive policies of the Warsaw regime. The empty throne of Cardinal Wyszyński, carried in the centre of the procession, gave clearly political overtones to a religious celebration.

Meanwhile the intellectual revolt spread and the protests of Polish Marxists gave it greater intensity. Leszek Kołakowski, the brilliant philosophy instructor at Warsaw University, accused the Stalinists of 'crushing all capacity for individual and collective activity of a creative nature in economic, political, and cultural life'.[13] Even Adam Schaff, Professor of Philosophy at Warsaw University and the leading party ideologist, openly admitted that among intellectuals Marxian ideology enjoyed little support and authority.

Aroused by the events in Poznań, workers started a movement calling for the liberation of trade unions from their subservience to party and state. This demand was accompanied by agitation for the introduction of workers' councils along the lines of Yugoslav workers' self-government. At the end of August, the Central Committee of the PUWP itself dispatched a delegation to Yugoslavia to study the operation of workers' councils with a view to recommending the extent to which they might be used in Poland. Soon after this – without waiting for the initiative of the party organs – workers in a number of larger industrial enterprises introduced workers' councils,

---

[12] The conservative or Stalinist faction was named after the château of *Natolin* near Warsaw where it usually met; the reformers were sometimes referred to as the *Puławska* group after their meeting place in *Puławska* street in Warsaw.

[13] 'The Intellectuals and the Communist Movement', *Nowe Drogi* (September 1956), quoted Hiscocks, op. cit., p. 206.

acting independently of the official trade unions and participating in the running of the individual plants.

The intellectual debate reached its climax during September and early October. Leading Polish economists, Oskar Lange and Edward Lipiński, openly attacked the centralistic and bureaucratic apparatus as an impediment to economic progress. Lipiński went so far as to insist that collectivization of agriculture, stemming from a soulless application of political dogma, did not suit the conditions of Poland and had brought the country to the brink of agricultural bankruptcy. This criticism, backed by public opinion, forced the party to proceed to immediate economic reforms. Agricultural machine-stations were abolished. Machines would be sold to the peasants. Unsuccessful collective farms were closed down. The Five-Year Plan was changed by increasing investment in agriculture, housing, and social welfare. Greater emphasis was laid on the production of consumer goods.

Indicative of the changed conditions were the judicial proceedings against the Poznań demonstrators, which opened at the end of September – perhaps the first fair trial in 'People's' Poland. The accused were allowed to defend themselves and their counsel spoke with unheard-of freedom in defence of their clients. They pointed out that not the workers but the unbearable conditions of work were the main causes of the riots. Even the prosecution admitted that most of the excesses were due to police brutality. The Stalinist version of the causes of the insurrection, still adhered to in the Soviet Union (which attributed it to the influence of 'imperialist conspirators'), was definitely rejected. As a result, the sentences were relatively mild.

At the beginning of October a tacit co-ordination of the activities of the protagonists of liberalization and democracy took place. The workers stood solidly behind the intelligentsia, which in turn found a number of courageous spokesmen, especially among the youth. *Po prostu* and its editors spoke on behalf of the overwhelming majority of the Poles, infusing radicalism into other organs of the press and providing a focus for the democratization movement. Shoving aside the last vestiges of fear – the main characteristic of Stalinism – the reformers formulated a political, economic, and cultural programme. They demanded freedom of the press, which would permit public discussion of all the pressing problems of Polish society; they insisted that the *Sejm* assume a position of leadership in the state and exercise genuine control over government; they were in favour of economic reforms which would replace the dogmas of the past by a decentralized and imaginative management of industry, and do away with collectivization of agriculture.

Far from trying 'to turn the clock back' the reformists were motivated by realism, accepting the basic political and economic changes in post-war Poland. Instead of clamouring for the return of pre-war conditions, which they rejected, reformists called for 'humanistic socialism', adopting many of the aims and practices of traditional Polish socialism. They rejected the communist-sponsored democratic socialism and advocated 'socialist democracy'. This aim, they realized, could be put into effect only by a radical change in the leadership of the party and state. To be effective, such change would have to be accompanied by a purge of the party apparatus at all levels. It was this aspect of liberalization that called forth stubborn opposition from the 'conservatives', who regarded any change in the existing *status quo* as endangering their positions.

By the beginning of October the stage was set for the final showdown between the two factions. The Stalinist minority, led by Zenon Nowak, relied on its control of the party bureaucracy and, if necessary, on Soviet aid. The advocates of change were greatly strengthened by the control of the Internal Security Corps, headed since the end of August by General Wacław Komar, an old adherent of Gomułka. In addition, the reformists received encouragement from abroad. Recognizing that 'knowledge of the experience of Yugoslavia' was indispensable for the progress of Polish democratization, they established 'brotherly relations' with the Yugoslav government and party. Even more important were the assurances given to Ochab in Peking on the occasion of his visit to the Eighth Congress of the Chinese Communist Party.

The resignation of Hilary Minc foreshadowed the return of Gomułka. After the session of the Politburo of 15 October it was announced that 'Comrade Gomułka took part in the meeting'. However important, the tactics of the reformist faction were not the only reason for its success. Its victory was due to the support which it received from the masses who – perhaps imprudently but none the less sincerely – believed in the possibility of major changes which would secure for Poland internal freedom and external independence.

The October 1956 Revolt and Its Aftermath

The events of the Eighth Plenary Session of the Central Committee of the PUWP, which started on 19 October and lasted for three days, represent a milestone in the modern history of Poland, as well as that of Polish and international communism. The future of Polish liberalization hung in the balance when, on 18 October, Nikita Khrushchev informed the Polish leaders that a Soviet delegation would attend the meeting of the Central Committee of their party. It was obvious that the Soviet comrades' uninvited participation was intended to strengthen the Polish conservatives and prevent radical changes in the leading organs of the PUWP.

Ochab's announcement on the morning of 19 October that the representatives of the political and military leadership of the Soviet Union had arrived in Warsaw to 'consult' with the Polish leaders fell like a bombshell. Recognizing the gravity of the situation, Ochab adjourned the meeting. Meanwhile Gomułka and his three adherents, Spychalski, Kliszko, and Ignacy Loga-Sowiński, had been co-opted on to the Central Committee. Reformist attempts to have them elected members of the new Politburo without discussion were unsuccessful.

Despite Soviet protests the Poles refused to admit the Russian delegation, which – apart from Khrushchev – included such luminaries as Mikoyan, Molotov, Kaganovich, and Marshal Ivan S. Koniev, into the Central Committee session. Instead, the representatives of the two parties met at the Belvedere Palace, the former seat of Polish presidents. Four leaders of the PUWP, among them Gomułka, were appointed delegates for the negotiations. Thus the man whose return to power the Soviet leaders were determined to prevent participated in the Soviet-Polish conversations.

As reported in the October issue of *Nowe Drogi*, the first encounter of the two delegations was far from friendly.[14] Khrushchev denied Gomułka the right to speak on behalf of the PUWP, called Ochab a traitor, and accused the Poles of spreading anti-Soviet propaganda, thus endangering the very existence of the whole socialist camp. Above all, the Soviet leaders were very bitter about the proposed changes in the PUWP representative organs. In the middle of the discussions reports came in that Soviet troops were marching towards Warsaw. The Polish negotiations refused to continue the talks under the threat of 'Soviet military intervention' and implied that, if necessary, they were prepared to meet force by force.[15]

Many factors worked in favour of the 'rebels' and enabled them successfully to resist Soviet pressure. Despite the feverish activity of the Natolinists, who went so far as to contemplate a *coup* with the aid of the Soviet army, the great majority of the Polish leaders put up a united front against the Soviet demands. They refused to be impressed by the fact that the Russian delegation included an unusually large contingent of senior officers and that Khrushchev and his associates repeatedly resorted to threats and attempts at intimidation. This Soviet behaviour was overshadowed by mass demonstrations by thousands of workers and students who pledged their loyalty to the cause of the reformers and put themselves at the disposal of

---

[14] See the report of Aleksander Zavadzki in *Nowe Drogi* (October 1956), p. 16.
[15] A good description of the 19 October crisis can be found in Lewis, op. cit., pp. 210–19.

the Internal Security Corps commanded by General Komar. His troops occupied all important buildings, including the radio station, and took up positions on the approaches to the capital. Equally, if not more, important was the fact that the non-communist majority of the nation made it plain whom it would support in case of a Soviet-Polish conflict. As a result, Gomułka's threat to give a radio broadcast on the facts of the dispute to the entire nation was a powerful weapon which Khrushchev could not afford to disregard.

He and the other members of the Soviet delegation realized that any attempt to suppress the reform movement by violence would lead to a bloody conflict between the two states. Moreover, they knew that disturbances in Poland, the largest of the East European countries, might have served as a spark which would ignite the fires of smouldering rebellion in other parts of the area. Such developments would have frustrated the policy of decompression, to which the Soviets under Khrushchev were committed, and would most certainly have undermined the Russian leader's position in the Soviet state and party. Weighing these risks with the risk of trusting Gomułka and his supporters, Khrushchev – with an extraordinary psychological insight – decided on the latter policy. His decision was made easier as Gomułka and Ochab left no doubts about their determination to continue the Polish-Soviet alliance within the framework of the Warsaw Pact. As subsequent developments were to prove, Khrushchev's analysis of Gomułka as a devoted and sincere communist proved to be correct.

Despite its statement that the discussion had been held 'in an atmosphere of party-like and friendly sincerity', the communiqué issued in the night of 19 October proved that in its main purpose Khrushchev's mission had ended in failure. The agreement that Polish-Soviet discussions should be continued in the near future in Moscow was a tacit recognition of the right of the Polish communists alone to decide on the composition of the leading organs of their party. On the other hand, the Poles expressed their desire to make peace with the Soviet Union. The CPSU delegation left Warsaw in the early hours of 20 October.

In the morning of that day Gomułka delivered a long address to the members of the Central Committee. This first statement after his return to power was characterized by both moderation and firmness. In the best style of a disciplined party member Gomułka displayed little personal resentment at the treatment he had received after his purge in 1948. He reserved his criticism for the past mistakes of the regime. Speaking of the nation's economy, he recognized the increase of the productive capacity of Polish industry. But he pointed out many shortcomings in the industrialization process, especially failure to improve the workers' living conditions. He condemned 'juggling with figures which showed a 27 per cent rise in real wages', but could not cover up widespread discontent. Speaking of Poznań, Gomułka declared that the workers 'gave a painful lesson to the party leadership and the government'. While he welcomed participation of the workers in the management of industrial plants, he warned against hasty measures.

Particularly severe was his criticism of past agricultural policies. Having declared himself against any form of compulsory collectivization, he stated that the yields and harvests per hectare of individual farms were greater than those of state and co-operative farms. The latter, he implied, should be dissolved, if manifestly unproductive. In his general approach to the economic management of the state Gomułka warned against the rigidity of doctrinaire planning which failed to pay attention to Polish realities.

Condemning the atrocities of the period of the 'cult of the individual', Gomułka stated that democratization was 'the only road leading to the construction of the best model of socialism in our conditions'. But, he emphasized, the process of democratization must not be used to undermine socialism. The party must retain its leading role; 'freedom of criticism in all its forms' should be exercised in a manner which is 'creative and just'. Subscribing to the principle of equality, independence, and friendship in Soviet-Polish relations, Gomułka declared 'the abolition of exploitation of man by man' to be an immutable socialist tenet. 'The roads of achieving this goal can be and are different.'[16]

The nine-member Politburo elected on 21 October included in addition to Gomułka four close co-workers – Ochab, Loga-Sowiński, Jerzy Morawski, and Stefan Jędrychowski. The representatives of Stalinist orthodoxy, Marshal Rokossovsky, Zenon Nowak, Franciszek Jóźwiak, and Franciszek Mazur, were excluded. The Secretariat, now headed by Gomułka, remained unchanged.

The results of the Eighth Plenum were regarded as a clear victory not only by the reformist group within the party but also by the non-communist majority. Gomułka's subsequent statements, similar in tone to his first address to the Central Committee, seemed to reflect the mood of the nation. This explains the wave of enthusiasm and emotion which swept over Poland. The non-communists regarded the PUWP's new orientation as a mere beginning of a policy auguring the return to Poland's national traditions. If put fully into effect, Gomułka's programme would punish those responsible for past terror,

16 The full text of Gomułka's address can be found in Paul E. Zinner, ed., *National Communism and Popular Revolt in Eastern Europe* (New York, 1956), pp. 197–238.

eliminate Stalinists from important positions, and fundamentally change the basic assumptions of the Polish state. Communist reformists were convinced that in Gomułka they had found a man who would lead the nation towards truly democratic socialism. His militant and intolerant post-war communism seemed to have been entirely wiped out by his revolt against Stalin in 1948 and his subsequent imprisonment, which had earned him general admiration. His influence and prestige were such that during the Hungarian Revolution he managed to control wholesale anti-Soviet passions. When, in keeping with old Polish traditions, widespread sympathy for Hungary demanded more than mere moral support, the public responded to his request to remain calm, disciplined, and 'realistic', thus avoiding any action which might serve as a pretext for Soviet intervention.

It seemed that Gomułka's triumph had opened a new phase in the history of post-war Poland. Changes in the party were followed by organizational and personnel changes in the government and administrative services. A number of men compromised by their past were removed, together with some whose sole qualification for office was their PUWP membership. The decline in Soviet influence was demonstrated by the replacement of Rokossovsky by Spychalski, and the dismissal of a number of Russian senior officers who had acted as 'advisers' in the Polish army. The fact that almost immediately after his return to Moscow Rokossovsky could assume the position of Soviet Deputy Minister of Defence demonstrated the true nature of his mission in Warsaw. Other important changes included the appointment of Gomułka's supporter Władysław Bieńkowski as Minister of Education; the removal of the conservative Szyr from the department of construction; and the abolition of the Committee of Public Security, whose functions were now divided among different central offices, the Ministry of the Interior in particular.

The reorganization of the Council of Ministers by reducing the number of Deputy Prime Ministers from seven to three (one of whom was to come from the United Peasant Party) greatly strengthened the authority of the individual Ministries. These in turn contributed to greater efficiency in government through further decentralization and greater use of experts irrespective of political affiliation.

The reformist trend made itself felt in practically all aspects of the economy. The chairmanship of the Trade Union Council was taken over by Loga-Sowiński who replaced the Natolinist Wiktor Kłosiewicz. The regime gave tacit support to the Workers' Councils which after October sprang up practically everywhere in Poland. While their competence was left somewhat vague and much more restricted than their Yugoslav counterparts, the decree setting up the councils seemed to imply that they would assume a position of importance.

Their purpose, it was stated, was 'to implement the working-class initiative with regard to its direct participation in the administration of enterprises.'[17] At the same time they were expected to serve the new regime both politically and economically, acting as a tool for the sorely needed boost to workers' morale. The regime, at least for a while, tolerated the time-honoured weapon of the workers – the strike – thus abandoning one of the basic principles of communist orthodoxy.

The reform in planning, whose rigidity and inefficiency was generally recognized, led to the abolition of the State Commission on Economic Planning. In order to prevent the repetition of a situation in which one man – Hilary Minc – had become the economic dictator of the country, planning was entrusted to a Planning Commission of the Council of Ministers. Its competence, which in the past had tended to cover all aspects of the economy, was curtailed so that it could 'concentrate on general, overall, and long-range planning'.[18] In order to secure the advice of experts an Economic Advisory Council was created to act as a sort of brains trust serving the Commission and cabinet. Oskar Lange, the American-trained economist, became the chairman of this body. Realizing the inability of the socialized economic system to cover all the needs of modern society, the government adopted a programme aiming at the encouragement of handicrafts, limited private trade, and even certain services.

One of the most revolutionary changes took place in the realm of agriculture. Gomułka's suggestion that unproductive co-operatives be dissolved gave the signal for a nationwide development which within less than three months brought about a total collapse of collectivization. The number of collectives sank from about 10,600 to around 1,700. The return to private agricultural economy was encouraged by an increase in the price of grain and the abolition of compulsory milk deliveries.

The events of the 'Glorious October' – as the 1956 revolt was generally referred to – greatly enhanced the general trend towards full liberalization in social and intellectual life. As one observer put it,

> the restraint and unanimity of the preceding period gave way to a sudden outburst of intellectual vivacity, to the mushrooming of clubs, newspapers, and discussion circles, to large-scale contacts with the West and relatively unrestrained travel abroad.[19]

Alone in the communist orbit, Poland enjoyed an almost full

---

[17] *Trybuna Ludu* (20 November 1956).
[18] See *East Europe*, vol. 6, No. 2 (February 1957), p. 8.
[19] Zbigniew Brzeziński, *The Soviet Bloc. Unity and Conflict* (New York, 1962), rev. ed., p. 345.

freedom of the press. Except for the partly self-imposed censorship on news from Hungary, the newspapers formerly a 'weapon of the drive leading to October now became self-appointed spokesmen of what October was to mean'.[20] Lack of instructions rendered the functioning of the official censorship impossible, so that liberal and 'revisionist' writers enjoyed unrestrained freedom. The availability of Western newspapers was accompanied by the discontinuation of the jamming of Western broadcasts.

The educational system was freed from the deadening influence of communist doctrine. Teachers were allowed to present a more balanced picture of Polish history, including its most recent phases. At university level the generally hated and highly ineffective compulsory courses in Marxism-Leninism were replaced by courses in modern philosophical trends. Sociology and psychology again became a part of the university curriculum. The intellectual climate of all institutions of higher learning changed profoundly when those scholars who had been dismissed because of their political convictions were allowed to return. The official youth organization disintegrated and young people looked forward to the building of an organization which would endeavour 'to renovate the life of the country and to restore to socialist practice its humanistic essence . . .'

Particularly important – because of their moral and national implications – were two other measures of the Gomułka regime : reconciliation with the Roman Catholic Church and a more favourable settlement of Soviet-Polish relations.

Soon after the termination of the Eighth Plenum Cardinal Wyszyński and other members of the Catholic hierarchy were released from prison or detention. Assuming the duties of Primate once more, Wyszyński negotiated a new *modus vivendi* between Church and state which appeared to be based on a realistic assessment of the power and interests of the two. While the state did not lose its influence over ecclesiastical appointments, its power was limited to making objections to church nominees. The most tangible result of the agreement was the reintroduction of religious instruction into schools. While it was not made a part of the regular school curriculum, priests and other teachers of religion were appointed by the school authorities in agreement with church representatives.

All this seemed to imply that a change of heart on the part of the PUWP leadership had taken place. Because of the Church-state agreement, welcomed by the majority of the nation, the episcopate

[20] Lewis, op. cit., p. 241–2. The Polish press followed with horror the developments of the Hungarian revolution. To restrain the expressions of undisguised anti-Soviet sentiment, which would provoke the Soviet Union, the regime imposed a partial press censorship.

assumed a loyal attitude towards the new regime. In his sermons Cardinal Wyszyński emphasized the necessity of patience and moderation as the main virtues of all Catholics. Hand in hand with the favourable development in the Church's fortunes went the improvement of the position of Catholic intellectuals and writers. The Catholic intellectual monthly *Znak* and the weekly *Tygodnik Powszechny*, suppressed during the Stalinist era, were allowed to reappear as organs of the Catholic Clubs of Progressive Intelligentsia organized in a few large cities. The group responsible for *Tygodnik Powszechny* assumed the name *Znak* (after the monthly) and found an extremely competent leader in Stanisław Stomma. While not allowed to form a political party which – along the lines of the Peasant Party – could join the National Front, five deputies of the *Znak* group were elected from among the non-party candidates.

The second measure which greatly increased the prestige of Gomułka and his regime concerned the new relationship of Poland and the Soviet Union. Despite continued Polish insistence on the recognition of the principles of equality and independence, the discussions in Moscow in November 1956 took place in a friendly atmosphere which prepared the ground for future cordial relations between Khrushchev and Gomułka. The communiqué on military and economic co-operation, issued on 18 November, represented a compromise. It provided the Soviet leaders with assurances that Poland would not dissociate herself from the Warsaw Pact nor take other measures injurious to Moscow. The relations between the two governments seemed to be as firm as ever. The communiqué referred to their 'indestructible union and fraternal friendship' which would benefit 'the peoples of the two countries' and 'further the interests of strengthening peace and security throughout the world'. No doubt the almost grim 'realism' of this pro-Soviet sentiment reflected the fact that the Polish leaders had the fate of Imre Nagy and his friends at the back of their minds.

In return for their promises the Poles gained considerable concessions from their Soviet 'partners'. The new relationship between the Polish People's Republic and the USSR, it was expressly stated, would be based on 'complete equality, respect for territorial integrity, national independence and sovereignty, and on non-interference in internal affairs'. More important than the agreement on the temporary stationing of Soviet forces in Poland, which formally respected the sovereignty of the Warsaw government, were the economic gains which Gomułka secured from his Soviet ally. Debts to the Soviet Union were cancelled, long-term credits were advanced for the purchase of grain and other commodities. Equally important was the decision of the Soviets, then the main importers of Polish coal, to abandon their policy of exploitation and increase the prices paid to Warsaw to a level approximating that of the world market. The fact that only a few months later Poland managed to secure Western, especially American, loans underlined the success of the new regime and the status of independence it had gained since the October revolt.

While Gomułka's promise 'to enable people to elect and not merely to vote' remained largely unfulfilled, the new electoral process gave considerable freedom of choice from among the members of the PUWP, the United Peasant Party, and a host of non-party candidates, all running on the common list of the National Front. The voters were given the right to cross out the names of those candidates for whom they did not want to vote.[21] The electoral law was opposed from two quarters – the Stalinist hard-liners, who dreaded its liberal features, and the non-communist majority which desired a genuine multi-party system.

It was not surprising that the election, in which only the National Front list was submitted to the electorate, confronted Gomułka with his first serious challenge. The unwillingness of the regime to allow political opposition – an action which would have called forth a violent reaction from the Kremlin – gave rise to apprehension that the non-communists, by abstaining from the election, would jeopardize Gomułka's position and strengthen the hand of his conservative opponents. Equally dangerous was the possibility that the voters might delete an excessive number of communist names, including some communist leaders, from the National Front lists, thus damaging, if not undermining, the authority and prestige of Gomułka's regime. To prevent such a development Gomułka himself, on the eve of the election, made a dramatic radio appeal to the Polish nation. Urging his compatriots to participate in the election, he stated :

> The call for the deletion of the communist candidates from the voting lists is synonymous not only with the deletion of socialism in Poland; the deletion of our party's candidates is synonymous with the deletion of Poland from the map of Europe.[22]

Thus the Polish leader changed the election into a popular referendum – a plebiscite in which Polish citizens were asked to accept or reject the changes brought about by the momentous events of 1956.

While greatly aided by the Catholic Church, which urged all Catholics to participate in the elections, Gomułka's triumph was due above all to the symbolic role which he played before, during, and immediately after the October revolt. Soon after the election the fact

21 See below, pp. 358–9.
22 *East Europe*, vol. 6, No. 5 (March 1957), p. 9.

that 'Gomułka was a symbol, but not the architect of the Polish October' caused the unity and co-operation of the majority of Poles to come to an end.[23] Having won the struggle against Soviet imperialism and Stalinism at home, the Polish leader lost his crusader's halo and reverted to what he had been throughout his life – a man dedicated to the cause of communism. Ever since he had left school at the age of fourteen, Gomułka's sole intellectual armour, main political tool, and principal criterion, by which he judged and later also decided all issues of life, had been Marxism-Leninism, which he had studied on his own. He was not doctrinaire by nature, being capable of a realistic and even pragmatic approach to problems. Yet his commitment to communism was such that, in cases of doubt, he almost automatically sought refuge in communist ideology and practice.[24]

Recompression

General enthusiasm for the new regime prevented the public from noticing a few facts, the importance of which was realized only when reflected against Gomułka's subsequent policies. As early as the first days of the Glorious October period, the new leader of Polish communism had insisted on the party's monolithic leadership of the working class and its absolute monopoly of power. Less than one month after his assumption of power he revealed his true convictions by extolling the security organs, not only because of their positive role in the October upheaval, but also as an indispensable institution of socialist Poland, defending her against forces of international reaction, as well as any 'attempts aimed against the political line mapped out by the leadership of the party'.[25] Thus Gomułka clearly indicated that he had never ceased to believe in the necessity for violence as a means of political struggle. Soon after the election he warned against 'hesitant' elements in the ranks of the intelligentsia and began to dissociate himself from the more radical members of the liberal faction. Instead of giving support to this group, which had played a key role in his return to power, Gomułka diplomatically assumed a central position, opposing both the rigid dogmatism of the Natolinists and the extreme tendencies of the reformers.

Thus started the, at first, imperceptible but, as time passed, increasingly radical withdrawal from the policies of liberalization. The threat of the Natolin faction, which retained considerable strength in the Central Committee, forced the new First Secretary to continue

23 Brzeziński, op. cit., p. 331.
24 Ibid., p. 332.
25 Paul E. Zinner, op. cit., p. 303.

to accept the aid of a few reformist liberals, irrespective of his determined opposition to the 'barren intellectualism' and tendency towards useless theorizing characteristic of their group. His main supporters, however, were the party professionals, headed by Ochab and Roman Zambrowski, who also regarded the radical 'liberalizers' with the utmost suspicion. It was the internal party struggle alone which tended to determine Gomułka's policies. He and his faction continued their attacks against the Stalinist dogmatists, but at the same time stepped up their onslaught against the liberal extremists, now generally referred to as 'revisionists' and declared to represent the greatest danger for the party and the socialist system. The emphasis of this rather amorphous group on such values as 'integral democracy, freedom for everybody, and free play for political forces' was condemned as an attack on the very foundations of the party – the dictatorship of the proletariat and the principle of class struggle.[26] Moreover, the Workers' Councils were deprived of all political power and much of their administrative competence. They were expressly denied the right of collective ownership of the individual factories in which they operated. In October 1957 the mainstay of the liberalization and democratization movement, the weekly *Po prostu*, was banned because of its alleged 'nihilistic and deviationist tendencies'. Its suppression, which was accompanied by the expulsion of its editorial board from the party, was followed by two days of violent student riots in Warsaw.

The behaviour of the intellectuals was declared to be one of the main reasons for political regression in Poland after 1956. In the opinion of party leaders the intelligentsia had abandoned the tenets of Marxism-Leninism and succumbed to pseudo-liberalism, thus becoming tools of the bourgeoisie. Suspicion and fear of the intellectuals was greatly strengthened in the spring of 1958 by the defection of Colonel Paweł Monat to the United States. His previous service as military attaché in Peking and in Washington enabled him to divulge confidential military and intelligence information to the Americans, which caused great embarrassment to the Warsaw government. The action of Monat, whom Gomułka regarded as a typical product of the liberal atmosphere of October 1956, caused the Polish leaders to harden their policies.

From 1958 onwards the liberal faction was pushed into a defensive position. The pressure of the government was directed in the first place against writers, journalists, and scientists. While still a far cry from the crude methods of Stalinism, the renewed emphasis on conformity and the introduction of rigid censorship caused bitter dis-

[26] This opinion was expressed by Roman Zambrowski, member of the *Puławska* faction. See *East Europe*, vol. 6, No. 5 (May 1957), p. 31.

appointment in the ranks of the literary élite, many of whom gave up writing and retired from public life. The PUWP again started to interfere with their organizations and urged them to pay more attention to the interests of the communist regime. Gradually the government began to introduce various 'administrative' measures against those who exceeded the limits imposed by the party. Aroused by these practices, the leaders of Polish cultural and scientific life abandoned the policy of passive resistance. In March 1964 thirty-four of them submitted a letter of protest to Cyrankiewicz. In it they criticized the government for tightening censorship and violating constitutionally guaranteed freedom of expression. The communist leadership took a number of repressive measures against some of the signatories. Only the highly unfavourable publicity caused the government to relent. In the autumn of the same year, however, one of the protesters, Melchior Wankowicz, an outstanding author and naturalized American, was sentenced by a Warsaw court to eighteen months imprisonment. His crime – slandering the Polish state – was contained in a private letter sent to his family in the United States. Despite Wankowicz's refusal to submit an appeal to a higher court, the government did not dare to put the sentence into effect.

The protest of 'the 34', as well as the judicial action against Wankowicz, marked the beginning of a protracted struggle between Polish intellectuals and the regime. The writers especially, the party leadership held, 'were out of step with the rest of the nation'.[27] The government did not hesitate to take drastic measures, such as stiff prison sentences passed *in camera*, against its intellectual opponents. Its tactics were master-minded by Zenon Kliszko, influential Politburo member and close associate of Gomułka, who acted as chief ideologist of the party. But mobilization of communist sympathizers in writers', journalists', and students' organizations could not prevent their members, including those belonging to the PUWP, from opposing the official government policies. Of special interest was the intellectual ferment at Warsaw University, in which young students, frequently sons and daughters of leading communists and high state officials, took a prominent part. Their ideological zeal and desire for change made them, at least indirectly, allies of the silenced non-communist majority. In 1965 the regime found it necessary to arrest and try the spokesmen of this group, the two Warsaw University lecturers Karol Modzelewski and Jacek Kuron, who had circulated pamphlets accusing the party of having betrayed communist ideals.

This flagrant violation of freedom of expression contributed to the consolidation of the intellectual opposition. Undaunted by the

[27] See report of David Halberstam, *New York Times* (2 April 1965).

persecution by party and university organs, the students continued to protest against officially prescribed cultural policies. They found a natural leader in Leszek Kołakowski, the brilliant professor of philosophy at Warsaw University, whose writings on 'humanitarian socialism' fired the imagination of his young adherents.[28] Speaking at a student gathering called for the purpose of 'commemorating' the October 1956 revolt, the young professor contrasted the fervent hopes of 1956 with the sad reality of 1966. He concluded that there was nothing to celebrate in a society dominated by a ruling group of inefficient and irresponsible people who severely restricted political life and rendered truly creative work impossible. As a result of his speech Kołakowski was expelled from the party, to the consternation of the liberal writers who regarded the party action as 'an attack against humanistic socialism'. The regime's attempts to intimidate its ideological opponents ended in failure. Some communist writers responded to pressure by turning in their PUWP membership cards.

The temporary truce between the party and the representatives of the intelligentsia was interrupted by an aggressive speech from Zenon Kliszko at the 1967 plenary meeting of the Central Committee of the PUWP. Addressing himself to the problem of criticism, he emphasized that the party would not allow 'criticism which is destructive and demagogic and which blackens our reality through a one-sided concentration on negative phenomena'. For this reason, Kliszko stated, the regime must insist on 'restriction of freedom for the enemies of our system'.[29] Thus, at a time when neighbouring Czechoslovakia and Hungary continued to liberalize their cultural policies, Gomułka's Poland moved backward and limited freedom of expression in cases of 'illegitimate criticism'. Kliszko left no doubt about the prerogative of the party to decide arbitrarily on the 'legitimacy' of the written and spoken word. As the developments of 1968 were to prove, the party's restrictive policy only widened the gap separating it from the majority of Polish intellectuals.

Attempts at fundamental economic reforms, started after Gomułka's return to power, got bogged down because of the regressive policies of his regime. Despite the growth of both industrial and agricultural production, the overall improvement in the standard of living was disappointing. The newly created Economic Council, headed by the American-trained Oskar Lange, worked out the 'Polish Economic Model', which envisaged a drastic

---

[28] In his study 'Responsibility and History', which appeared in the Warsaw weekly *Nowa Kultura* in September 1957, Kołakowski emphasized the humanitarian mission of Marxism.

[29] See A. Ross Johanson, 'Warsaw: Politics and the Intellectuals', *East Europe*, vol. 16, No. 7 (July 1967), p. 12.

reorganization of the administration and management of the national economy. Its purpose was to abolish the old system of control from the top, replacing it by decentralization of economic decision-making. Each industrial enterprise was to become economically independent and financially self-supporting, and was to be administered by a state-appointed director who would perform his function in co-operation with the Workers' Councils. The fixing of wages and prices was to be determined by the real cost of production. The acceptance of the profit motive, which was to become a substitute for administrative direction, went a long way towards the introduction of some of the basic principles of a capitalist-type economy.

The political trend of post-1956 developments prevented the Economic Council from putting the major part of its reforms into effect. After the Monat incident Gomułka became apprehensive not only of the political but also of the economic tendencies of the first two years of his regime. Using the crisis of 1958 as a pretext, he accepted the advice of those who favoured a return to conservative practices. The change became even more apparent in 1959 when the conservative hard-liners Eugeniusz Szyr and Julian Tokarski were appointed deputy premiers and entrusted with economic affairs. For some time Polish economists continued to discuss and elaborate their 'model' as originally conceived by the Council. In reality, however, the reforms remained largely on paper. The practice returned to the traditionalist views of centralized administrative direction. As time passed, the Council lost all its influence and in 1963 it was officially abolished. By then the Workers' Councils had been deprived of their role as organs of workers' self-government. They merged with the trade union Works' Councils and the party committees of individual enterprises to become so-called Workers' Self-Government Conferences. The new organs came under the absolute control of the factory management and the party.

Poland continued to be plagued by the problem of an immense population growth.[30] Return to old economic policies did not make it easier for the government to create new jobs for hundreds of thousands of new workers. In fact, the continuation of economic mismanagement greatly increased the gravity of what the regime somewhat euphemistically referred to as 'over-employment' and 'over-staffing'. A solution to these ills was sought in mass dismissals of workers and officials. It was not surprising that during the early

[30] In recent years the natural increase of the population has gone down considerably, sinking from 19·5 per thousand in 1955 to 11·7 in 1963, 10·2 in 1964, and 9·4 in 1966.

sixties the country suffered from serious strikes (again declared to be illegal) and other indications of economic instability. Symbolic were the strikes and demonstrations in the two plants so closely connected with the 1956 revolt – the *Cegielski* works in Poznań and the *Zeran* enterprises in Warsaw, whose workers had stood in the forefront of the liberalization movement. Meetings of the party organs in 1964 and 1965 dealt predominantly with economic difficulties and the means by which they could be removed. The discussions revealed considerable differences among the leading economists. Only towards the end of 1965 did the conservative hard-liners recognize the arguments in favour of economic changes.

But reforms were kept to the absolute minimum. The doctrinaire leaders of the PUWP lacked the imagination and will to go any further. Fundamental changes, they feared, would undermine their hold over the life of the country. As a result, their policies were marked by deliberate delay and half-measures incapable of removing the main economic ills. Thus Poland, during 1956–58 ahead of the other Soviet Bloc states in the field of economic reform, was now more than overshadowed by Hungary and Czechoslovakia. It may well be that again the necessity for decentralization was recognized, for the principle of independent investment policies among individual enterprises was introduced. The private economic sector was also given some encouragement, especially through the so-called 'agency' system.[31] But piecemeal reforms, which left the concept of centralized planning and economic bureaucracy intact, could do little to improve matters. Such measures could hardly silence the complaints of the people about low wages, increasing prices, and, occasionally, the inadequate supply of foodstuffs.

Church-state relations also saw a fundamental withdrawal from the ideals of October 1956. Initial mutual toleration and even harmony had caused the episcopate to appeal to the electorate to participate in the voting of January 1957. The apparent desire of the regime to make peace with the Church caused people to disregard the conflict between the alleged aims and the actual policies of the government. Thus Gomułka took no action against that discredited product of Stalinism, Piasecki, abandoned by many of his adherents. However, control over the largest Catholic welfare organization, *Caritas*, which in 1950 had been taken over by the state, was never returned to the ecclesiastical authorities. Nor did the Gomułka regime abolish the Patriot-Priests movement, which allowed itself to be used in the struggle against the Church.

---

[31] By this system state or co-operative enterprises are managed by private individuals. The state retains ownership of the capital, but the enterprise is managed at the risk of a private entrepreneur.

The events of 1958 led to a hardening of the attitudes of both government and party towards the Church. The idea of peaceful co-existence, which had seemed to prevail since 1956, was gradually replaced by that of ideological competition. In this struggle the government made full use of its administrative and police powers, disregarding the provisions of its *modus vivendi* with the Roman Catholic Church reached in 1956. The conflict centred around two crucial problems, both seriously affecting the Church's spiritual mission.

The first concerned religious education. Eager to limit church influence over youth, the government first subjected religious instruction to far-reaching limitations. Later on, such teaching was forbidden on school premises. At the same time it introduced a series of troublesome and oppressive controls over classes of religion held in churches and other religious buildings. Equally vexing was the issue of the government's fiscal policies in relation to church income and that of other ecclesiastical institutions. In 1959 both were deprived of their privileged position and subjected to full taxation. Such taxes were probably not always exacted in full, being occasionally fixed at a rate lower than that prescribed by the tax laws; but the blackmail quality of this policy made it a convenient tool to keep the Church in line with the regime's intentions. It was 'a kind of Sword of Damocles, which, though normally suspended in mid-air, might descend on selected victims at any time'.[32]

The Polish episcopate headed by Cardinal Wyszyński faced the ever-increasing pressure with determination and a spirit of defiance. It refused to be cowed into submission. Characteristic of this attitude was Wyszyński's statement made after the 1961 elections, which took place in an entirely different atmosphere from those of 1957. Paying tribute to what he called 'inner' freedom, he declared :

... a political system can build streets and factories, but it cannot administer in the same way human consciences. There are moral values which have nothing to do with political systems, that exist independently of regimes and pressures....[33]

The tacit recognition of the truth of these words and the realization of their validity, especially in Poland, prevented the regime from attempting to do away with all the privileges of Polish Catholicism gained since 1956. While not reluctant to violate many provisions of the 1956 *modus vivendi*, the Polish leaders did not dare to deny its validity.

[32] Hiscocks, op. cit., p. 302.
[33] *New York Times* (19 March 1961).

For in its struggle against communist atheism the Roman Catholic Church possessed a number of overwhelming assets. Having been deprived of its property, it could no longer be branded as capitalist. The fact that it depended essentially on voluntary donations from the faithful sealed its association with the nation and became an important element of its strength. Equally effective was the Church's emphasis on its strictly spiritual mission, divorced from political issues and shunning anti-state activities. As a result, the insistence on respect for religion and its representative, the Church, while of great political significance, did not render the Catholic hierarchy vulnerable to the accusation of striving for political power.

The non-political nature of Roman Catholicism was further enhanced by its ability to assume the role of representative and protector of Polish national traditions. Whatever the regime and party might do, they could hardly compete with the almost mystical influence of the Church over the people. Symbolic of this power is Częstochowa with its monastery of *Jasna Góra*, the Mountain of Light, enclosing the legendary shrine of the Black Madonna. Irrespective of the vagueness of its historical background, the pilgrimage to the 'Mother of Częstochowa' – Mary Queen of Poland – has become a contemporary symbol and a national myth exuding a magic power over millions of Poles.[34] To them Częstochowa represents a symbiosis of religious devotion with loyalty to Polish national traditions.

The Church is blessed by a splendid organization, which makes Poland one of the few countries which do not suffer from scarcity of ecclesiastical and lay churchmen. The ascetic Stefan Wyszyński has been able to maintain his ascendancy over the Polish people, representing a force which has infiltrated into the very ranks of the Communist Party. His statesmanship has not succumbed to the temptation to use the spiritual influence of the Church for directly political purposes. Again and again, he has displayed a willingness 'to give Caesar what is Caesar's', but in the spiritual realm he has remained unassailable. At the same time the Cardinal is fully aware of the inherent weakness of the Church. Strong spiritually, politically its power is strictly limited. Coercive power is entirely in the hands of the regime. What the Polish police may lack in reliability can be supplemented – should this be necessary – by the power of the Soviet state.

[34] The shrine, the beginnings of which go back to the fourteenth century, achieved its nationwide reputation only in the nineteenth century. Its popularity is due to a large extent to the great Polish author, Henryk Sienkiewicz, who used the legend of the Black Madonna in the novel *Potop* (Deluge) describing the resistance of the Poles against the Swedes.

While unable to 'nationalize' the traditions of the people the party also possessed assets derived from Polish patriotism. Post-war developments have provided it with an important weapon. The Poles fear the emergence of a strong Germany, which might claim the return of territories which today have become an integral part of the Polish state. It is the communist state which controls the internal and external means for the defence of Polish territorial integrity.

There is another factor which seems to work in favour of the party : the immense socio-political changes, especially industrialization and urbanization, which have taken place since the end of the war. The younger generation, brought up in cities, is no longer attracted to problems relating to the combat between state and Church, 'which are still playing, as they have played for centuries, the familiar variations on the Canossa theme'.[35] The Church can rest assured that young people have little interest in the meaningless jargon of communist ideology. But it cannot be certain that this same youth is prepared to seek their concepts of freedom and justice in the teachings of Roman Catholicism.

The circumstances of the co-existence of Church and state in Poland have caused one writer to contrast the power and impotence of the Church with the power and impotence of the state.[36] The relationship of these two basic factors of Polish national life has not lacked moments of dramatic conflict during which the power of the state has been pitted against the equally formidable spiritual might of the *ecclesia*. Invariably, the two antagonists have never allowed the clash to reach the point of no return.

In 1961 conflict over control of religious education, however fierce it might have appeared, ended in a compromise. The decision of the episcopate not to interfere in the 1961 elections was readily recompensed by the government, which allowed Wyszyński and eventually thirty other bishops to participate in the Second Vatican Council. But the regime lost no opportunity to weaken its opponent. In 1963 it attempted to take advantage of the conciliatory attitude of Pope John XXIII to establish direct relations with the Vatican over the head of the Polish Primate. Despite occasional sniping relative calm reigned in Church–state relations until the preparations for the celebration of the millennium of the Polish state in the autumn of 1966. As was to be expected, this celebration, which coincided with that of Poland's conversion to Christianity, precipitated a violent new conflict.

Not illogically, the episcopate regarded the anniversary as a

[35] Stehle, op. cit., p. 99.
[36] Ibid., pp. 8–119.

religious event, emphasizing the fact that in 966 Poland had entered the community of European Christian principalities. On the other hand, the government was determined to use the celebrations for establishing its title to at least a share of the Polish national past. It combined the millennium festivities with the twenty-second anniversary of the Lublin Manifesto, which had given birth to People's Poland. As stated by *Trybuna Ludu*, 'it is the deep conviction of all patriots that this anniversary is the crowning point of our present historical process, and the custodian and heir of the great progressive traditions of our nation and state'.[37]

Inadvertently, the episcopate provided the government with ammunition against itself. In November 1965 Wyszyński and thirty-five bishops sent a letter to all German bishops inviting them to attend the Jasna Góra millennium celebration. Reviewing the eventful thousand years of Polish-German relations, the letter ended by granting and asking forgiveness for past wrongs. From January 1966, the regime started an organized campaign against the Church and its main representatives, accusing them of acting against the *raison d'être* of the Polish state. Despite a relatively mild statement from Gomułka, who criticized the bishops for laying undue emphasis on the Polish ties with the West, the party apparatus did its best to whip up hatred against the Church. All organizations were mobilized – the PUWP and the press, as well as the National Unity Front, the trade unions, and even local organs of government. Meetings were held and resolutions passed against the harmful and politically adventurous activities of the Polish episcopate.

The Cardinal was denied the right to travel to Rome and later to the United States and Canada. This ban was extended to cover the travel of all church dignitaries. The government decided to bar all foreign Catholic prelates from attending the millennium celebrations, including Pope Paul VI, whom the Polish hierarchy intended to invite to pay homage to the Black Madonna. Such a visit, the regime indicated, would be highly inopportune.

The summer of 1966 witnessed a series of confrontations between the Church and the party. About half a million people attended the ceremonies at Częstochowa, where the empty papal throne bore witness to the militancy of the clergy. In nearby Katowice the regime's colourful celebration – given full coverage by Radio Warsaw – was marked by the speech of the Head of State, Edward Ochab, who criticized the chauvinism of the Germans and their church representatives. Of the many confrontations in different

37 *Trybuna Ludu* (22 January 1966).

parts of Poland the most important took place at the beginning of May in Kraków, and resulted in a personal triumph for the Polish Primate. Despite occasional acts of overt persecution, the Catholics held their own in the struggle against the regime. In the latter part of 1966 official propaganda concentrated its attacks on Wyszyński, who was referred to as 'the Polish Mindszenty' endeavouring to destroy the unity of the nation by fomenting a campaign against the basic ideals of People's Poland. The Cardinal replied with a dignified and self-confident statement: 'I waged no political struggle against the authorities.... But I will defend the Church and its rights in Poland. I will defend freedom of conscience and the right of Catholic education for the children and the youth of this country.'[38]

After December 1966 the conflict between Church and state began to subside. A more detached discussion of the differences separating the antagonists was made possible by Kremlin overtures to the Vatican, expressed by the visit of the Soviet President, N. V. Podgorny, to the Pope. In May 1967 the Holy See made a number of ecclesiastical appointments. Karol Wojtyla, archbishop of Kraków, was appointed Cardinal and the vicars-general nominated by Wyszyński for the western dioceses were replaced by four apostolic administrators. This gesture provided the regime with a welcome opportunity to put an end to a highly embarrassing conflict, which had clearly demonstrated its inability to curb the activities of the Church as a power-political factor.

While not giving up its policy of continuous pinpricks and basic opposition towards the clergy, the regime called off the millennium campaign and took a number of measures favourable to the episcopate. The seesaw struggle between Church and state continued, however, finding its expression in a dispute over the adequacy of church facilities, complaints against state censorship, and in the violent conflict between the regime-supported Pax organization and the church hierarchy, who opposed Piasecki's theory on the priority of politics over religion. Furthermore, the regime was not entirely satisfied with the Vatican's treatment of the western dioceses.

In 1968 the Church profited, at least indirectly, from the internecine struggle within the PUWP between the Gomułka faction and that of the 'partisans'. Preoccupation with 'revisionist tendencies, neocapitalism, and the Zionist threat' prevented the regime from concentrating on its contest with the Church. The Church, too, welcomed the relaxation of tensions which alone could enable it to combat religious indifference stemming from profound social changes.

[38] Quoted *East Europe,* vol. 12, No. 12 (December 1966), pp. 52–3.

The dramatic transformation which took place within the PUWP was undoubtedly the most important departure from the reforms of the 'Polish October'. There were external reasons, such as the country's geographical position and its dependence on Soviet aid for the defence of its Western Territories, which precluded further intensification of liberal reforms. More important, when it came to the reversal of the liberalization policies, was Gomułka's own personality and intellect. Despite his tendency towards independence of judgement, his background and mentality were those of a mistrustful party functionary. His pragmatic approach to the solution of everyday problems had little effect on his adherence to the precepts of orthodox Marxism-Leninism – the only intellectual experience to which he had been exposed. Whenever he had to take an important decision, it was the communist doctrine that determined his action.

In October 1956 there had been basically four groups within the PUWP : the conservative and orthodox Natolinists, headed by Zenon Nowak, Franciszek Mazur, and Wiktor Kłosiewicz; the *Puławska* reformers, including Ochab, Cyrankiewicz, and Rapacki; the unqualified supporters of Gomułka, among whom Kliszko, Spychalski, Władysław Bieńkowski, as well as the younger and more radical communists, Jerzy Morawski and Władysław Matwin, were the most prominent; and those who, having been influential in securing Gomułka's victory, lacked representation in the party leadership and, because of their radical democratic views, had no influence on the formulation of policy. They were led by Kołakowski and Eligiusz Lasota.[39].

Seen in retrospect, Gomułka's decision in October 1956 to combine with mild reformers and even liberals was purely a tactical one. While riding the crest of the wave of liberal victory, he was forced to concede much more to the idea of democratization than he had originally intended. In reality, he remained unaffected by the complex idea of democratic and more humane communism. His essentially orthodox and pedestrian outlook and his autocratic streak prevented him from grasping the abstract concept of freedom propagated by his most effective supporters. Gomułka made use of these alien elements only in order 'to save Polish communism from its own excesses'. Having assumed the leadership, he did not associate himself with the *Puławska* group of pre-war communists, certainly not with the extreme 'left' intellectuals. Instead, he made a bid for the support of some of his former enemies in the dogmatic *Natolin* group, diplomatically striking a balance between the two factions.

In his speeches delivered immediately after October 1956 Gomułka

[39] This division has been taken from Werner Markert, ed., *Osteuropa Handbuch Polen* (Cologne, 1959), p. 259.

warned with equal emphasis against the dangers of dogmatism and revisionism. But soon his own inclinations, influenced by the clamour for the restoration of 'full democracy' by his no longer desirable leftist adherents, forced him to declare revisionism the main obstacle on the Polish road to socialism. This change of emphasis, coupled with measures taken against the liberal faction, gained Gomułka prestige both in Moscow and among his orthodox domestic opponents. Many former Stalinists, particularly among the members of the party apparatus, were allowed to retain a modicum of power and gave up their opposition, so that the Third Party Congress in 1959 brought about the consolidation of Gomułka's personal rule. His speech at the Congress was, it seemed, an extremely shrewd blending of Polish patriotism with an apparently genuine devotion to Marxism-Leninism and the 'mainstay' of the international communist movement, the CPSU.

The Monat affair and the economic failure of 1959 greatly irritated Gomułka. He attributed both these setbacks to the unreliability and incapability of the intellectuals and the reformists. For this reason in October 1959 he proceeded to a radical shift to the right. In a sudden party and government shake-up he recalled from 'exile' not only the former Natolinists Szyr and Tokarski, but also the highly compromised Stalinist Kazimierz Witaszewski, and placed them in important positions. The more liberal members of the original Gomułka team, such as the Education Minister, Bieńkowski (responsible for the *modus vivendi* with the Church), and Morawski, the young Politburo member, were relegated to insignificant posts.

To claim that this development towards an apparently more rigid regime was due to Soviet intervention would be an oversimplification of a highly complex political phenomenon. Rather it was due to Gomułka's belief that, as far as Poland was concerned, the de-Stalinization process should be regarded as terminated, and that the regime's main task was to maintain the *status quo*. In fact, until 1962 very few things seemed to indicate the return to a more severe, if not neo-Stalinist, type of regime. Yet liberal opinion continued to warn against such a contingency. The threat of political stagnation, implied in Gomułka's policies, was regarded as a danger to the liberalization movement. This sentiment was best expressed in the statement of Professor Kotarbiński, President of the Academy of Sciences, at a meeting in the Warsaw intellectuals' club, *Krzywe Koło* (Crooked Circle). 'The thaw,' he stated, 'must be accelerated and a climate created in which people can freely express their real thoughts about public affairs.'[40]

As later developments proved, Gomułka's personal rule and

40 Stehle, op. cit., p. 54.

peculiar tactics, characterized by a tendency towards unimaginative *immobilisme*, gradually led to a general hardening of the party line and a return to more rigid methods of government. The 1956 split between the orthodox Stalinists and their reform-minded opponents of the *Puławska* group lost much of its sharpness. The attempt in early 1964 of the *Natolin* extremists, led by Kazimierz Mijal and Kłosiewicz, to discredit Gomułka by accusing him of *petit-bourgeois* softness and 'right-wing nationalism' ended in dismal failure. Other former Stalinists were gained for the regime by being allowed to share both office and political responsibility.

It was the traditional division between the 'Muscovites' and the leaders of the small but militant group of wartime communist partisans, which in the sixties seemed to have assumed renewed importance. Having been brought up in the hard school of underground struggle and intrigue, these men displayed a tendency towards ruthless and high-handed methods of government. Its common background rather than carefully co-ordinated activities gave to this loose group the name of 'partisans'. They pursued similar aims and recommended similar methods. Thus they favoured a tough anti-Church policy, increased controls over intellectual life, and a more authoritarian approach to the building of Polish communism. They combined their authoritarianism with clearly nationalistic and even chauvinistic trends, insisting that Polish interests should be put before those of communist internationalism and of Moscow. The partisans found a competent leader in General Mieczysław Moczar, Deputy Minister of the Interior. Ryszard Strzelecki, a member of the party Secretariat, at least for a time also appeared to be Moczar's ally. While outwardly recognizing the authority of 'comrade Wiesław' (referring to Gomułka by his wartime pseudonym), Moczar in his pronouncements outside Warsaw endeavoured to appear a more energetic and militant defender of Polish national interests than the First Party Secretary. The group derived its main support from among the party *aparatchiki*, particularly those who were associated with the defence or security establishments.

It was not surprising that the older, less dynamic, and generally more moderate pre-war communists became the main target of the younger, ambitious, and aggressive members of the partisan group. Regarding himself as above the petty jealousies of his subordinates, Gomułka, a former wartime partisan himself, at first paid little attention to his former associates' bid for power. It seems that even the evidence of the June 1964 Fourth Congress of the PUWP, which clearly demonstrated the existence of bitter factional strife, failed to shake his self-confidence. The Congress greatly weakened the representation of the revisionists, wiped out that of the liberal elements, and seriously impaired the strength of the non-co-operative members of the former Stalinist group. The Gomułka group improved its position in all party organs. Of the twelve-member Politburo six belonged to it, four to the former *Puławska* group, and two to the former Natolinists. The fact that his leadership remained unchallenged, that his followers entrenched themselves in leading party organs, and that the Congress demonstrated an apparent party unity, made Gomułka blind to the consolidation of the partisan group, which was soon to become a threat to his own position.

Apart from the Gomułka faction only the partisans registered large gains in the Central Committee. But they did not penetrate into any of the leading organs. Ryszard Strzelecki alone became a candidate member of the Politburo. Gomułka's belief that the balance of power among the individual factions would cement party unity proved to be utterly wrong. At the end of 1964 he was forced to make concessions to the power-hungry partisans. Strzelecki became a full member of the Politburo and, more important, Moczar became Minister of the Interior. Only then did Gomułka begin to recognize the true nature of the partisans. Trying to take the wind out of the sails of their propaganda, he sought refuge in communist dogma and a return to rigid policies. The election of May 1965 revealed the PUWP's unpopularity. While the composition of the *Sejm* remained basically the same, the electoral law, which had introduced a limited degree of choice, made it possible for the voters to express their lack of confidence in the party. With the exception of Gomułka, Spychalski, and Edward Gierek, the new star on the horizon of Polish communism, the political leaders of the National Unity Front were elected by notably smaller majorities than other candidates. Further, the fact that one-half of the former deputies were not allowed to run again clearly demonstrated the lack of unity within the PUWP and its satellite parties.

Despite its lack of support, the partisan group continued to increase its influence by pushing its members into important positions in the party and state bureaucracy, as well as the security establishment. Amid increasing signs of worsening relations between the party and the rest of the nation, the regime returned to many of the oppressive methods of the past. Aware of its unpopularity, it became excessively intolerant even of mild criticism, such as that levelled against it by Adam Schaff, until then the official theoretician of Polish communism.[41] Much harsher was the treatment meted out to outright opponents, such as Kuroń and Modzelewski and their adherents.

---

[41] In his *Marxism and the Individual*, published in late 1965, Schaff placed emphasis on the importance of the individual and the necessity to reconcile his rights with the interests of the state and party.

Characteristically, this section of the opposition, whose beliefs were marked by utopian socialism and a tendency towards anarchism, were declared to be a 'serious danger' to socialist Poland.

Some of the most resented attitudes of the past, such as glorification of the police, harsh criticism of the heroes of the 1944 uprising, and bureaucratic suppression of civil rights reappeared in Polish public life. Now ten years after 1956, Gomułka, disregarding the heritage of the Glorious October, found himself surrounded by only a few of his former supporters whose enthusiasm had lost all its genuine ring and persuasiveness. Instead, most of the important positions were going to sycophants and yes-men and – what was much worse – opportunistic careerists and those bent on securing power for power's sake. Gomułka no longer tried to achieve greater independence of the Kremlin. On the contrary, he established friendly relations first with Khrushchev and later with his successors, supporting the policies dictated by Moscow.

Unwittingly, he and his associates began to succumb to the same defects which they had reproached in their predecessors. True, Gomułka did not give up his Spartan simplicity, but he failed to prevent the bureaucratic élite from developing a peculiar fondness for the niceties of life – automobiles, luxurious apartments, and generally a standard of living inaccessible to the overwhelming majority of Poles. From being the 'crusading reformer' of 1956 Gomułka had changed into a bigot incapable of seeing beyond the limited horizons of communism. By his own acts he had lost the basis of his popular support : young people turned their backs on a man who had failed them in their innermost hopes; writers, students, and other members of the intelligentsia rebelled against his inborn anti-intellectualism; and reformists turned against a man who had combined with many former dogmatists. At the same time, however, Gomułka's past made him suspected by all orthodox communists.

No wonder that political influence within the party tended to concentrate in the hands of autocratic and nationalistically-minded individuals. General discontent caused many young members unwittingly to be drawn to the ideas of Moczar. By the middle of 1966 Moczar had assumed a dominant position in the regular security organs, the Citizens' Voluntary Militia (usually referred to as ORMO), and in the Defence Ministry. Having adopted the slogan of the Hungarian communist leader, János Kádár – 'whoever is not against us is with us,' the partisans gained support both within and outside the party. Through their control of the organization of fighters for Polish independence (Union of Fighters for Freedom and Democracy; referred to by its initials as ZBOWID), Moczar and his associates were enabled to bestow various distinctions and privileges. Thus those who received decorations for real or alleged services to their country were entitled to higher pensions, priorities in employment, better housing, and many other economic advantages. Through their insistence on nationalism the partisans tried to gain at least passive support from the masses and blind them to the high-handed twisting of Marxism and return to Stalinist practices. A section of the Polish public was attracted by the unashamed anti-semitism of the partisans.

Their success alarmed the more liberal members of the party, especially writers, newspapermen, and scholars, but criticism, being carried out within the internal framework of the party, proved ineffective. The aims of the liberals – more spiritual freedom, curbing of censorship, and the readmission of Kołakowski into the party, for instance – could not influence the policies of the regime. To be successful the believers in a more humane socialism required a unified programme and determined leadership. They lacked both. They were further weakened by their inability to gain support among the non-party intellectuals and masses.

Another centre of protest was provided by the Stalinists, whose leader, Kazimierz Mijal, had in 1966 found refuge in Tirana and used the Albanian radio to attack the 'revisionist, *petit-bourgeois*, and chauvinistic' policies of the PUWP leadership. Mijal, and the handful of his associates who had joined him in Albania, occasionally shed an interesting light on internal conditions within the Polish Communist Party. In Poland, however, they had practically no following.

The crisis was most evident among the youth, whose apolitical attitude to public affairs bordered on apathy. The few who became party members tended to be critical of Gomułka, whose leadership had lost all its past lustre. The opposition group at Warsaw University greatly irritated the party and the regime. This was not because of its size, but rather because of its ideological orientation. In their criticism the students cleverly employed the tools of Marxist doctrine and dialectic. Following the example of Kuroń and Modzelewski, they argued that under Polish socialism workers were exploited. They called for a revolution in the interests of the working class, which would overthrow 'bureaucracy and the present conditions of production and take over control of its own work'.[42] Despite the exclusive nature of this movement, which was composed of a handful of young people who took their Marxism seriously, the party regarded it as a potential nest of Trotskyism and other leftist deviations.

Faced with these forces of real or imaginary opposition, the party

[42] Alexander Bregman, 'The Strange Case of Kuron and Modzelewski', *East Europe*, vol. 15, No. 12 (December 1966), p. 10

leadership resorted to unimaginative insistence on ideological uniformity and used slogans which harped on the pernicious influence of the West, the reactionary policies of the Church, and the revisionism permeating mass communications and literary circles. The June 1967 war between Israel and her Arab neighbours revealed the internal tension within the PUWP and Gomułka's inability to deal with it by his customary political practices, which closely followed the Soviet line, balancing competing factions against one another. The Arab-Israeli conflict gave impetus to an outburst of anti-semitism, fanned mainly by the more militant members of the Partisan group. The distinction between Zionism, which was declared reprehensible, and anti-semitism, which was rejected, was entirely blurred. Violent attacks against Israeli aggressors and 'Zionist cosmopolitans' filled the pages of the Polish press and became the main topic of numerous staged meetings and declarations.

In order to restrain the most rabid anti-semites, Gomułka made a statement which, perhaps inadvertently, opened the gates for a violent anti-Jewish movement. There were, he declared, 'Zionist circles of Jews who are Polish citizens' and who represented a 'fifth column'[43] undermining world peace and the security of Poland. Whatever his intentions might have been, his words gave an official stamp to the anti-Jewish campaign which started in the second half of 1967 and was directed against senior officers in the armed forces and later against well-known journalists, many of whom were communists of long standing. Together with 'Jewish cosmopolitans', those who sympathized with them were also purged as suspected 'revisionists'. The changes in personnel which followed invariably tended to benefit the orthodox and conservative party members, particularly those who belonged to the partisan group. Their growing influence gave rise to a rumour that in 1968 Gomułka – despite the far-reaching concessions he had made to his radical opponents – might be removed from his position or reduced to that of a figurehead leader.

The 1968 Crisis

The year 1968 in eastern Europe was dominated by the revolutionary events in Czechoslovakia. The temporary victory of the liberal-minded government of Alexander Dubček; the occupation of that country by the armies of the Soviet Union and her four Warsaw Pact allies; as well as the desperate efforts of the Czechs and Slovaks to save at least some of the achievements of their 'humanitarian' communism, commanded worldwide interest. This struggle for freedom overshadowed political developments in Poland.

But Poland was also experiencing radical changes. Unfortunately,

[43] See *East Europe*, vol. 16, No. 8 (August 1967), p. 29.

the Polish trend was the exact opposite to that in Czechoslovakia. The Polish scene was marked by further strangulation of intellectual life, intensification of the regime's controls over the people, and a purge of the PUWP characterized by openly anti-semitic overtones. In their relations with the communist bloc the party and its leader took an active part in the criticism of the rebellious Czech and Slovak 'revisionists' and in the repressive action against them. The internal and external policies of the Gomułka regime were interconnected and determined by two factors – the internecine struggle within the Polish party and the relationship of its leaders with the Kremlin.

During the course of 1968 it became clear that the ageing Gomułka – far from being prepared to relinquish his position and power – was determined to put up a vehement struggle against his opponents. He mobilized all the ideological and political weapons at his disposal to prove beyond the slightest doubt that his regime was immune from the contagion of revisionism and that the struggle against those 'bourgeois-capitalist, chauvinistic, or cosmopolitan elements' still remaining in Poland would be pursued with the utmost ruthlessness. With one eye Gomułka followed the moves and intrigues of his potential enemies, with the other he scrutinized the effect of his policies on the Kremlin whose full support he needed in order to survive.

This policy led to a gradual liquidation of the last remnants of the spiritual and intellectual freedoms won in the days of the Glorious October. The students especially became aware of the discrepancy between the glib promises and grim reality of Gomułka's Poland. Disgusted over the treatment of Leszek Kołakowski, tired of the outworn clichés with which they were fed by the party ideologist Kliszko, and discouraged by their professional prospects after graduation, they had come to despise the 'Gomułka establishment' which within less than eleven years had sold out to Moscow and its type of communism. These bitter feelings precipitated the student community's conflict with the regime.

A performance of Mickiewicz's *Dziady* (Forefathers' Eve) at the Warsaw National Theatre provided the regime with a welcome opportunity to assert its power. The play's anti-Tsarist character, especially the lines 'We Poles sold our souls for a couple of silver roubles' and 'The only things Moscow sends us are jackasses, idiots and spies . . .', drew demonstrative applause from the audience.[44] Allegedly prodded by the Soviet embassy, the government ordered the play to be removed from the repertoire, claiming that a part of the audience had converted it into a 'political demonstration'. After

[44] See Jonathan Randal's report to the *New York Times* of 1 February 1968.

the last performance on 30 January the first wave of student demonstrations took place, resulting in numerous arrests. At the end of February the Warsaw branch of the Writers' Union at a stormy meeting adopted a resolution demanding the reinstatement of *Dziady*; at the same time the writers clamoured for greater participation in the formulation of cultural policies, democratization of artistic life, and discontinuation of the excesses of censorship. There were strong protests at the use of 'administrative methods' against the representatives of Polish culture.

The student riots, in which other dissatisfied elements of the population also participated, reached their zenith in the period between 8 and 19 March. Massive demonstrations started first in Warsaw, then spread to other university cities, and ended in violent street disturbances in Kraków on 18 March. Struggles took place between students demanding elementary civil and political rights and the units of the regular police strengthened by the Voluntary Reserves of the Citizens' Militia (ORMO), whose answers to liberal and democratic slogans were clubs, tear-gas, and mass arrests. More than a thousand students were placed under arrest pending trial. Of special interest were the bitter encounters in Kraków, where the police were alleged to have used dogs to disperse crowds of students.[45]

The regime's response – in addition to the suppression of the orderly student demonstrations – was a whole variety of drastic measures taken against those held responsible for the outbreaks. Disciplinary measures were taken against university instructors who 'failed to prevent' the riots, as well as those writers who, it was held, inspired student opposition. The most disturbing aspect of this punitive action was the association of the 'March events' with the active anti-Zionist campaign. In fact, the 'student rebellion' was used as a pretext to invigorate the flagging efforts against 'Polish Zionists' and eventually provided the impetus for a campaign to expel the majority of Jews from important party and government positions.

Most of those expressly mentioned as 'ringleaders' of the 'uprising of the intellectuals' had Jewish names and action against them was accompanied by the dismissal of their parents from important government positions. In their commentaries on the 'March events' – as the student demonstrations were referred to in Poland – the great majority of the newspapers succumbed to expressions of anti-semitism. The same was true of a number of meetings called by the party and nonparty organizations to protest against the dangers of Zionism. The

---

[45] On 19 March the *Gazeta Krakowska* carried a report that one of Kraków's first aid stations 'treated 112 persons yesterday. In the majority of cases, patients were involved who suffered injuries at their place of work. Several of them were bitten by dogs.'

young demonstrators, as the official means of communication emphasized, were 'hooligan elements' bent on destructive and disruptive activities, and motivated by a desire to use the bogey of anti-semitism to incite world opinion against the Polish state. *Słowo Powszechne,* the Pax-controlled pro-regime daily, ascribed the student riots to an Israeli-West German conspiracy, the purpose of which was to induce Polish Zionists to stir up trouble in Poland. The paper stated that 'Zionists . . . want to turn intellectuals and youth against the primary demands of patriotic responsibility . . .' Pointed reference to student leaders bearing such names as Blumstein and Rubinstein clearly betrayed the anti-semitic tenor of the article.[46] The Partisan dominated *Kurier Polski* went even further and directly attacked the Jewish Cultural Association, allegedly for providing aid to the rebellious students. Moreover, the listing of prominent Polish intellectuals, including a relatively large number of Jews, as 'enemies of People's Poland' was a thinly veiled expression of racial hatred.

The anti-Zionist campaign, supported by the regime, did not fail to encourage anti-semitic elements within the party. This became evident at the meeting of the Moscow activists on 19 March, at which Gomułka delivered a major political speech. His remarks on the problem of Zionism called forth an outburst of wild shouting which prevented him from immediately continuing his speech. He refused wholehearted endorsement of the anti-semitic campaign, pointing out that there is a 'group of citizens who are of Jewish origin . . . to whom Poland is the only fatherland'. Members of this group, who represented a majority of all Polish Jews, had been 'a credit to People's Poland', he declared. Gomułka's statement that 'our party is fully determined to oppose any phenomena which bear traces of anti-semitism' was weakened by his equivocal attitude towards Zionism. 'It would be a misunderstanding', he stated, 'to see in Zionism a danger to socialism in Poland or to the existing social political system'. This comment might have undermined what he regarded, perhaps erroneously, as the foundation of Polish anti-semitism, had it not been accompanied by a further analysis of the problem of Zionism. In addition to 'patriotic Jews', he made a distinction between two other, allegedly less desirable, categories of Jews : the first owed its loyalty to Israel and not to Poland and should be enabled to emigrate to its fatherland; the second was of doubtful loyalty, being neither Polish nor Jewish; because of their 'cosmopolitan feelings' such people should 'avoid those fields of work where affirmation of nationality is indispensable'. Reference to Antoni Słonimski as representative of the latter group further blunted Gomułka's repudiation of 'all forms of anti-semitism'.

[46] See *Słowo Powszechne* (11 March 1968).

The main characteristics of the speech, which referred to the Jewish question only in passing, were its defence of the regime's policies during the 'March crisis' and an all-out attack against the enemies of socialism represented by 'revisionists' and 'a handful of reactionary anti-Soviet individuals'. Gomułka lashed out against members of the intelligentsia, singling out by name a number of outstanding writers and university professors, including Paweł Jasienica, Stefan Kisielewski, Leszek Kołakowski, and Zygmunt Bauman. They were accused of leading the students 'along a false road hostile to socialism'.[47]

This speech enabled Gomułka to resume the initiative in the party. But it did not immediately disarm his opponents and critics, particularly from among the more aggressive and nationalistically minded members of the party bureaucracy who tended to back the policies of Moczar. The issue of Zionism, which Gomułka tried to minimize, provided them with a potent watchword and gave the impetus to a radical purge of the party ranks. The three categories of Jews mentioned by Gomułka were in many cases telescoped into one, namely that composed of Jews who had no place in Polish public life. For many party and government functionaries this was a welcome opportunity to get rid of their competitors and to improve their professional and party standing.

One after another persons of Jewish origin disappeared from state administrative services, lost their positions in the economic life of the country, or were removed from their university posts. Men such as the economist Włodzimierz Brus and even Adam Schaff, who until recently had been regarded as one of the leading ideologists of Polish communism, were purged. As a rule, demotions were accompanied by exclusion from all party functions and more often than not by expulsion. The purge was by no means directed only against Zionists. Anti-Zionism served as a convenient cover-up for actions against 'revisionists' and 'liberals', as well as those party functionaries who were opposed to racial discrimination. While they enjoyed the benevolent support of Moczar, in most cases the purges were organized 'from below' by radically minded Young Turks in the PUWP. Typical of this approach was the shake-up carried out in the Ministry for Foreign Affairs by the younger party activists, members of the Ministry's party cell. Sitting in judgement over the loyalty of their colleagues, they demoted or even dismissed a large number of officials with many years of experience behind them. According to one estimate the changes in the Ministry involved about 40 per cent of the middle and top posts.[48] The Foreign Minister, Adam Rapacki, was

---

[47] The speech appeared in the 20 March issue of *Trybuna Ludu*.
[48] See the report of Jonathan Randal, *New York Times* (31 October 1968).

not even informed of what was going on. When, in the month of April, his deputy, Marian Naszkowski, was purged, apparently because of his Jewish background, the indignant Rapacki resigned in protest against the high-handed action of his subordinates. The Moczar group favoured the intensification of the purges in the belief that they might undermine the foundations of Gomułka's power by driving those bureaucrats whom he himself had appointed from positions of importance. While publicly paying homage to 'comrade Wiesław', his opponents hinted that he was no longer capable of dealing energetically with the revisionists.

That Gomułka managed to retain the upper hand in the struggle within the PUWP – euphemistically referred to as 'party work' – was due mainly to two factors. In the realm of internal policies he used the same tactic as in 1956, but with different allies. He decided to adopt the aims and methods of his 'would-be' opponents and use their programme, policy, and slogans for his own needs.[49] Despite his refusal to recognize Zionism as a genuine danger to Polish socialism, Gomułka did nothing to stop the continuing wave of anti-semitism from spreading into all fields of Polish life. In his May Day celebration speech he emphasized that his regime's stand against imperialism had 'touched off reckless, vicious attacks against Poland by international Zionism, and accusations of anti-semitism'. Only in a few cases, such as that of the Deputy Foreign Minister Naszkowski (who was ceremoniously installed as editor-in-chief of *Nowe Drogi*), were the anti-semitic practices corrected. Even after the plenary session of the PUWP Central Committee on 8 July, at which anti-semitic excesses were expressly condemned, the purge of Jews and more liberal members of the party continued. In fact, it was at this meeting that Gomułka indirectly sanctioned the anti-Zionist campaign by insisting that the vast majority of changes in cadres were justified. He stated, however, that Western reports about Naszkowski being of Jewish origin were inaccurate.

The July Central Committee session signalled an important success in Gomułka's efforts to restore his prestige and authority in the party. It was, however, achieved only at the price of the final abandonment of relative leniency towards the remnants of 'revisionism', especially in Polish academic life. Moczar became an alternate member of the Politburo and member of the Central Secretariat in charge of military and security affairs. These concessions gained Gomułka the support of a large part, if not the majority, of the voivodship (*województwo* : province) First Party Secretaries, whose relative youth and ambition had caused them initially to favour a policy of

[49] Jan Nowak, 'The Struggle for Party Control in Poland', *East Europe*, vol. 17, No. 6 (June 1968), p. 6.

dynamic change. Gomułka might successfully have arrested the attacks of his opponents, but in doing so he had lost his political individuality. The government changes which followed the Central Committee meeting were not of great significance, but Jerzy Albrecht, the last of Gomułka's liberal supporters from 1956, was deprived of his cabinet post.

The second factor which played into Gomułka's hands was his consistently pro-Soviet stand in the crusade against Czechoslovak heresy. As early as 20 April the Soviet ambassador to Poland, Averky Aristov, had hailed him as 'that loyal son of the Polish people'. As the conflict between the Czechoslovak reformist leadership and the Kremlin intensified, the Warsaw regime was second only to that of East Germany in approving every aspect of Soviet and CPSU policy. The fact that Gomułka placed himself and his country at the service of the Kremlin greatly strengthened his position within the PUWP. It would be unfair, however, to claim that his resolute stand against Czechoslovak reformism was nothing but a calculated move to gain Soviet aid against his domestic adversaries. Gomułka's doctrinaire and narrow-minded approach to communism and his instinctive fear of experiments caused him to distrust Dubček and his associates from the moment they took over the direction of their party and state. His anti-Czechoslovak stand was made more palatable in party circles because of strongly resented Czechoslovak criticism of the anti-semitic practices of the Warsaw regime.

Yet the propaganda barrage between the two countries and the relatively significant Polish participation in the invasion of the Czech lands stood in the way of the political ambitions of his opponents and greatly limited the scope of their political propaganda. No longer could they reproach the Polish leader's lack of action and tendency towards half-measures. Nor could they use their favourite slogan of 'patriotism' and insistence on Polish interests, which as a result of the patriotic resistance of the Czechs and Slovaks had acquired a bad reputation among the Soviet leaders.

Whatever the motivation of Gomułka's anti-Czechoslovak policies might have been, his enthusiastic and active support of the Soviet intervention was another act symbolizing the total abandonment and bankruptcy of the spirit of 1956. On 7 November 1956 the Gomułka-controlled Central Committee of the PUWP had declared itself solemnly against outside, especially military, intervention by foreign states in the internal affairs of other nations. 'For this reason,' the Central Committee had stated, 'our party regards the intervention of Soviet troops in Hungary as a colossal blunder and a serious blow to the international workers' movement...'[50] In 1968 Gomułka and

[50] Statement of the Central Committee of the PUWP of 7 November 1956.

his associates repeatedly dismissed any criticism of the Soviet, and also their own, intervention in Czechoslovakia. Explaining it in terms of the threat of German imperialism to Czechoslovakia and the danger of a counter-revolution in that country, Gomułka declared it to be 'our duty, patriotic, national, and internationalist' to prevent the dissociation of the Czechs and Slovaks from the community of socialist states. Acting as if the decision to invade was his own, he declared that 'we had more data than anyone else to determine the extent of the threat to socialism in Czechoslovakia and the danger emerging from this development to our states and peoples'.[51]

The fact that Czechoslovakia continued to dominate the political life of Poland for more than two months after the invasion betrayed considerable controversy smouldering below the official surface. It seems clear that the intelligentsia, which only recently had sympathized with Dubček and his reforms, abhorred the role played by the Warsaw regime in the Czechoslovak crisis.[52] The regime became even more uneasy as – apart from the PUWP – the majority of Poles, who had not been consulted, displayed no enthusiasm for official policies. In fact, the behaviour of the party, almost frantically trying to justify its action, provided another example of the degree of its alienation from the people.

Even after the late summer setback suffered by Moczar and other opponents of Gomułka, party infighting continued until the opening of the Fifth PUWP Congress on 11 November. Among the 1,764 delegates not only Adam Schaff, Stefan Żółkiewski, and other liberals, but also Adam Rapacki, were missing. The main characteristic of this carefully prepared gathering, in which decisions were made 'unanimously', was the great emphasis on ideology. Despite the fact that Gomułka devoted a major part of his long report to Poland's economic development, his remarks on the necessity of ideological purity and the dangers of revisionism were of special significance. His emphasis on democratic centralism (the lack of which he indirectly reproached his post-March critics for), his discussion of the Czecho-slovak crisis (made necessary by 'creeping counter-revolution'), as well as his insistence on party unity, clearly pointed to the import-ance of ideological matters. Similar views were expressed in the Congress resolution and speeches which subscribed to the Brezhnev Doctrine of 'limited sovereignty' on grounds of the overriding inter-ests of the 'socialist community' of states. Congressional approval of the anti-revisionist campaign in cultural and educational matters –

[51] *Trybuna Ludu* (9 September 1968).
[52] Three outstanding representatives of Polish cultural and artistic life, two living in the West (Slawomir Mrożek and Zygmunt Mycielski) and one living in Poland (Jerzy Andrzejewski), raised their voices in protest against Polish participation in the invasion of Czechoslovakia.

which caused the dismissal from the party and public service of a large number of outstanding Polish intellectuals – was also motivated by ideological considerations.[53] Social science studies, it was emphasized, must stress 'socialist thought' and reject all bourgeois concepts. Above all, academic freedom must not be used 'to spread political views and social theories contrary to socialism'. The Congress confirmed sharp limitations on the autonomous position of university faculties, the introduction of new admission criteria favouring candidates of worker and peasant origin, and the expansion of ideological instruction in 'political science' courses. By and large, the Congress reserved for the party an increased control over cultural institutions and activities, which were to be conducted 'in a socialist spirit'.

Strict adherence to ideology as interpreted by the Soviet Union was declared to be compulsory in the sphere of international affairs. Gomułka supplemented his adherence to the Brezhnev Doctrine by proclaiming what might be termed a principle of collective security among the socialist states :

> The international position of the socialist camp exerts direct influence on the strength and operation of each of the communist parties. Whoever, paying no attention to this fact, attacks the socialist countries, no matter what his motivations may be, weakens the position of his own party and the entire communist movement.[54]

This novel concept of collective security protected the members of the 'Socialist Commonwealth' from attack both from abroad and from within. The Congress was critical not only of the Chinese and Albanian parties, but also of Yugoslavia's policy of non-alignment.

The speeches of Gomułka and his associates confirmed the overall tendency of the Warsaw regime to continue the repressive policies introduced after the events of March 1968. At the same time, however, Gomułka seemed to be the undisputed leader of Polish communism. The degree of his victory can be measured by two important indices. First, while three members of the old Politburo were removed (the former Stalinists, Szyr and Waniołka, and the reformist Rapacki), their replacements did not boost the anti-Gomułka opposition. Moczar suffered a definite setback by remaining only a candidate member of the Politburo. Secondly, the Central Committee was cleansed of liberal elements, of whom twenty-seven lost their membership. In order to strengthen his position Gomułka promoted practic-

---

[53] Ninety-nine faculty members of Warsaw University were deprived of their posts.
[54] *Trybuna Ludu* (12 November 1968), p. 77.

ally all First Secretaries of the party voivodship organizations to the Central Committee. This move was intended to introduce younger and more dynamic members into the party bureaucracy and provide for equilibrium between central and provincial representatives.

Only in the party Secretariat did the so-called Moczar group manage to maintain its position. Four of its nine members (including Moczar himself) must be regarded as adherents of the partisan group. By and large, with the exception of the Central Committee in which the turnover of membership was considerable, the sixteen full and candidate members of the Politburo, as well as the nine members of the Central Secretariat, registered only five changes. On the other hand, with two exceptions, people of Jewish origin disappeared entirely from leading positions within the PUWP. The government reshuffle which followed the Fifth Congress further strengthened party control over all important centres of power. The Ministry for Foreign Affairs, vacated by Rapacki, was taken over by Stefan Jędrychowski, the former chief of the State Planning Commission.

The Congress confirmed the position of Gomułka and at the same time demonstrated the lack of cohesion and organization of his opponents. Yet it did not address itself to the pressing problems of PUWP internal politics, nor did it present a new programme to deal with the country's difficult economic problems. It provided evidence of the growing dependence of the PUWP, and Poland, on the Soviet Union. Surprisingly, the necessity for Soviet-Polish co-operation – grudgingly conceded in the past – came to be regarded as a *sine qua non* of Polish national existence. The acceptance of this association – a triumph for Gomułka – was made more palatable by the recognition of Poland and her party as a special partner of the Kremlin.

The apparent success of Gomułka was by no means complete. Personal rivalry, characteristic of the pre-Congress period, did not disappear. In addition to Moczar, there were other contenders for the leading position, including Edward Gierek, the chief of the Silesian PUWP district. Unfortunately for Gomułka the decisions adopted by the Congress did not include an imaginative programme of reform within the party and government organs. Instead the Congress tended to seek refuge in the obsolete and outworn clichés of Marxism-Leninism modelled, more often than not, along the lines of Soviet experience.

No doubt at least one argument may support the position of Gomułka. After what happened in Czechoslovakia the Soviet leadership may think twice before allowing 'their man' – however unpopular and ineffective he may now be – to be unseated by his untested rivals. But the lesson of the Novotny precedent is still valid.

Gomułka's inability to improve the quality of the party and to increase substantially the country's standard of living, might easily cost him his position. There is no reason to assume that the Soviet leadership – if offered an equally loyal but more efficient and imaginative alternative – would not deny Gomułka its support, as it did to a much more pliable instrument of Soviet policies in Czechoslovakia.

Chapter 10

Poland Today

'Daremne żale, próżny trud,
Bezsilne złorzeczenia ! . . .
Trzeba z żywymi naprzód iść
Po życie sięgać nowe.'

Adam Asnyk, 1877)[1]

BECAUSE OF ITS LONG HISTORY Polish communism has played an important role in the development of the international communist movement. In Poland it has never been popular. In fact, most people have regarded it as an element alien to Polish national life. Even the Polish communist leaders were painfully aware of this fact. In the inter-war period only Soviet support enabled them to maintain their existence. The ignominious dissolution of the party in 1938 and the ruthless extermination of many of its leaders, which took place at Stalin's behest, proved beyond any doubt the total dependence of Polish communism on the Kremlin.

It was not surprising that the new Polish Workers' Party, re-created in 1942, again through Soviet initiative, could not gain the support of the Polish people. The PPR was immediately recognized for what it really was – a creature of the Soviet Union, regarded by the average Pole with traditional mistrust and even hatred. To improve its standing the party made an attempt to 'Polonize' its image by leaving out the word 'communist' from its title and by recruiting allies from among the dissident members of the radical wings of the socialist and peasant parties. All these attempts proved so unsuccessful that by the end of the war the overwhelming majority of Poles had remained faithful to their national past and their traditional political orientation. Post-war developments proved that the building of a well-organized and disciplined party presented a difficult task for the Polish communist leaders.

The PPR, which at the beginning of 1945 had only 20,000 members, was worse off than other communist parties in eastern Europe.

---

[1] 'Vain laments, futile efforts, helpless curses ! . . . it is necessary to go forward with the living and to reach for a new life.' Adam Asnyk, *Wybór Wierszy* (Warsaw, 1952), pp. 26–7.

It lacked all the qualifications necessary for the assumption of power. There were only a few party cadres and practically no men capable of taking over the administration of the country. The Communist Party and its leaders could do nothing without Soviet aid and the assistance of fellow-travelling opportunists who had consciously associated themselves with the PPR, believing that it would emerge victorious after the termination of the Second World War. Members of this group welcomed the opportunity to join with communists in filling the high offices of state. The other, especially lower and intermediate, administrative jobs were occupied by a variety of people chosen at random and retained mainly because of their indispensability.

The building-up of the Communist Party was much more difficult than the organization of the government. For a long time the PPR – despite intensive recruitment – remained much smaller than the PPS. The fusion of the two parties in 1948 greatly strengthened the communists as it provided them with sorely needed organizational talent. They were thus much better equipped to fulfil their role of leadership in the state. Party membership increased to over $1\frac{1}{2}$ million.

It soon became clear that the fusion, forced upon the majority of former PPS members by their more 'progressive' leaders, could not contribute to ideological unity within the new PUWP. While the party managed to eliminate its peasant competitors, it suffered from an internal crisis so great that by 1956 its membership had gone down to little over a million. Yet the communist leadership was able to create the necessary agencies of power – the youth movement, loyal non-communist parties, and a host of non-party organizations controlled through the Front of National Unity – with the PUWP in undisputed control. The adoption of the 1952 constitution was regarded as a formal expression of the stabilization of the regime. It accelerated the adaptation of the legal and institutional structure of Poland to the concept of the dictatorship of the proletariat.

The growth and entrenchment of the party apparatus seemed to confirm the success of Polish communism. That this impression was wrong was proved by the events which followed the death of Stalin and the Twentieth CPSU Congress. The crisis of 1956 shook the very foundations of Polish communism. However far-reaching the initial reforms and promises of reform made by Gomułka might have been, the position of the party bureaucracy remained intact. It was this fact which facilitated Gomułka's post-1958 withdrawal from his liberalization and democratization programme. By the late sixties only two achievements of the Glorious October period remained –

the toleration of independent peasants and relative accommodation between the regime and the Church. In all other respects, including the bureaucratization of the party, Poland succumbed to communist orthodoxy, similar to that in the Soviet Union.

The growth of Soviet influence made itself felt even in the realm of foreign policy, which for a few years after 1956 displayed a healthy tendency towards some degree of independence. On the other hand, Gomułka and his party, which is now the third largest in the world, managed to secure for themselves a special position within the Soviet Bloc.

The PUWP – its Structure and Leadership

Two defects characterized the Polish United Workers' Party (PZPR-*Polska Zjednoczona Partia Robotnicza*). From the beginning it had lacked internal unity and was plagued, perhaps more than other communist parties of the area, by continued intrigues, factionalism, and purges. As a result, there was a considerable turnover in party membership, which since the fusion with the PPS in 1948 continued to decline. After the post-Gomułka verification campaign it sank, by March 1959, to less than 1,100,000. It took the PUWP almost sixteen years before it managed, in 1964, to exceed its 1948 membership by a little over 60,000. In November 1968, when the Fifth PUWP Congress met, the membership had risen to 2,000,030. While it is the third largest communist party in the world, its relative strength is about the same as in 1948 at the time of its foundation.[2] In the period between the Fourth and Fifth Congresses about 700,000 new members were recruited. This gain was substantially offset by the fact that during the same four years some 230,000 members had become separated from the party, many of them because of breaches of discipline. A large percentage of PUWP members are relative newcomers. Only 390,000 belonged to the party before its fusion with the PPS, while more than one-half of members and candidates joined after the Third Congress of 1959.

The second defect of the party is even more serious. It has never been able to achieve the 'correct' social composition of its membership. Not the workers or peasants, but the intelligentsia, consisting predominantly of the beneficiaries of the regime, represents the backbone of the party. A comparison of the progressive 'growth' of the party with the successive changes in its social composition provides the following, as far as Polish communism is concerned, highly unsatisfactory picture :

[2] In 1948 the PUWP had 6·2 and in 1968 6·3 per cent of the total population.

	1948	1954	1959	1964	1968
Membership (in millions)	1,503	1,297	1,023	1,568	2,030
Workers (%)	60	48	42	40	40
Peasants (%)	18	13	12	11	11
Intelligentsia (%)	17	37	42	44	49
Others (%)	5	2	4	5	—

Sources: Richard F. Staar, 'Warsaw's Quiet Congress', *East Europe*, vol. 13, No. 8 (August 1964), p. 4, and Jerzy Ptakowski, 'The Fifth Polish Party Congress', *East Europe*, vol. 18, No. 1. (January 1969), p. 5.

The slow growth of the party can be explained by its inability to attract young people. The students especially – with the exception of the short-lived period between 1956 and 1957 – adopted a negative attitude to the party. For them the 'conflict of generations' has become a convenient pretext for not joining the ranks of the PUWP.

The history of the party before 1956 was marked by the growth of the party apparatus which soon succumbed to rigid bureaucratization. Party functionaries assumed the position of a privileged class, separating themselves by both their beliefs and behaviour from the nation. At the same time the party leadership lacked the cohesion necessary to withstand the external pressures which had made themselves felt after the Twentieth CPSU Congress. This lack of solidarity, combined with a 'spark of independence, sometimes camouflaged by outward servility', was one of the factors which brought Gomułka back to power.[3] The first speech of the reinstated leader promised democratization not only of public life but also of the party. The latter was to be secured by the introduction of 'adequate control by party bodies over the party apparatus'. Gomułka's efforts to infuse Spartan simplicity and more responsibility into the party remained unsuccessful. While at first many of the Stalinist excesses were eliminated, Gomułka failed to break the mentality of the party bosses. The majority of the old secretaries retained their positions. After 1958, when Gomułka began to discard his policies of October 1956, many of the shortcomings of the party apparatus reappeared, again alienating the party from the Polish people. A tendency towards dogmatism, anti-intellectualism, and opposition to all reforms became obvious, especially after Gomułka, driven by political developments, had gradually adopted the aims and methods of his hard-line opponents. By 1968 the party functionaries, whose excesses Gomułka had promised to prevent, had become decisive elements in the party

[3] Dziewanowski, op. cit., p. 256.

struggle. The Polish leader could not afford to incur their enmity.

The PUWP's organizational structure does not differ substantially from that of other communist parties in the Soviet Bloc. The party is divided into five tiers on the basis of a combination of territorial and functional principles. The territorial organization follows closely the administrative divisions of Poland. The functional party organization is determined by the place of employment of the party member. On the all-important lowest level there are three types of primary party units : in factories, mines, governmental agencies, hospitals, etc., there are production or institutional organizations; the needs of the rural areas are served by village organizations; finally, town-dwellers who are not members of production units are also organized on the basis of the territorial principle.

Of special importance are the village organizations, which lag in membership and are generally regarded as the 'Achilles Heel' of the PUWP set-up. They are particularly important as the Agricultural Circles, originally intended to serve as Poland's substitute for collective farming, cannot be used for strictly party purposes. In recent years the voivodship party committees and two of the five municipal committees (Warsaw and Łódź) have assumed special importance in the party structure. Their First Secretaries play a role far exceeding their theoretical competence. This is particularly true of the Katowice voivodship, which has the largest number of party members (272,000) and whose First Secretary, Edward Gierek, has a special position in the party. Regarding himself more as an equal than a subordinate of Gomułka, he is generally regarded as his successor, if not competitor. The party's strength is concentrated in the richer and economically more advanced western provinces whose population is fully aware of the danger of 'German imperialism'. In the eastern, less developed, voivodships, especially in those of Warsaw and Białystok, where the memories of the Russian occupation are still strong, the party is much weaker, being exposed to the constant danger of 'revisionism' and other forms of reactionary activity.

The hub of the party organization is its central organs, which fulfil tasks similar to those of their counterparts in other communist societies. This is particularly true of the party congresses which since 1943 have met six times altogether – in 1945, 1948, 1954, 1959, 1964, and 1968. These allegedly supreme party gatherings are not dissimilar from the congresses of the CPSU, being characterized by a careful selection of delegates, well-'prepared' speeches, and unanimous decisions. This 'rubber-stamp' quality of PUWP congresses prevents internal factionalism, a characteristic of Polish communism, from appearing on the surface. As in other states of the communist bloc, so in Poland the Central Committee has been able at least in

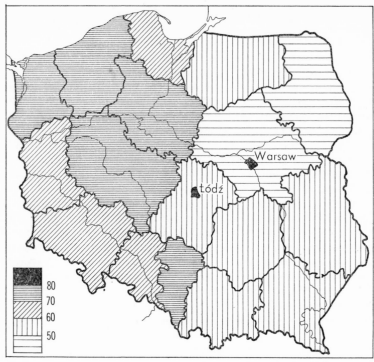

11. Comparative density of PUWP organizations

Source: Jerzy Płakowski, 'The Fifth Polish Party Congress', *East Europe*, vol. 18, No. 1 (January 1969), p. 6. Map shows number of CP members per 1,000 inhabitants.

some instances to rid itself of its subordinate role. Thus the first steps leading up to the Glorious October were taken by the members of the Central Committee, which set an example to the still divided Politburo. But the decisive role of the Central Committee was closely associated with the period of crisis caused by the onslaught of 'communist liberalism'. The abandonment of the post-1956 policies and the defeat of the reform wing within the PUWP brought about a decrease in the influence of the Central Committee as a truly independent and policy-making body. Its importance was again derived from the hard core of its members holding leading positions in party and government. This tendency has been further emphasized by the great increase in the number of party functionaries elected to the Central Committee by the 1964 Congress. Yet membership of this body is sufficiently important to serve as an indication of the relative strength of the individual party factions and as a platform for their conflict. This was proved during the crisis of 1968, relating to the issue of Zionism, and that of the struggle for the leadership of the party.

The most important political factor in Poland is the twelve-member Political Bureau of the Central Committee. Controlled by Władysław Gomułka, half of its members are his most intimate associates – men like Spychalski, Kliszko, and Ignacy Loga-Sowiński, who shared his leader's fate during the Stalinist persecution; those who rallied to him in the internal upheaval of 1956, such as Stefan Jędrychowski; and the ubiquitous former socialist Cyrankiewicz. While more independent than any other member of the Politburo, Gierek gave full support to Gomułka at the 1968 Party Congress. In fact, only the candidate Politburo member Moczar could be regarded as an outright opponent of Gomułka. The four newcomers, while in favour of a perhaps more authoritarian policy, were old party functionaries dedicated – with the possible exception of Stefan Olszowski – to Gomułka and Gierek.

In view of the lack of party unity the party apparatus has always played an important role, representing the element of continuity within the PUWP. Its approach to communist theory and practice is by no means uniform. Even in the Central Secretariat Gomułka's opponents, led by Moczar, are strongly represented. Within the broader framework of the party apparatus, including the subordinate party levels, adherents of different party factions may be found. Of these the hard-liners, both traditionally orthodox and Partisan, predominate. Strengthened by the Fifth Party Congress, this group has lent the PUWP its rigid and conservative flavour.

Until recently Gomułka's personality and tactical skill represented the most powerful unifying factor within the Polish communist movement. He has long ceased to be a mere symbol – as he was in 1956 – and become a shrewd political manipulator, keeping a balance between the competing factions of the party. Because of his doctrinaire approach to Marxism-Leninism and his tendency towards autocratic rule, he has gradually shifted to the hard-line methods of the bureaucratic elements within the party organization. Above all, he insists on internal discipline within the party, whose interests he regards as the sole criterion of all issues and actions. The past effectiveness of Gomułka's leadership has been greatly enhanced by the fact that the great majority of his deputies have possessed a number of almost identical characteristics, such as age, class background, educational standards, and, most importantly, political career and experience.[4] Since 1964 the pressure of the younger, more dynamic, generation

[4] See Richard F. Staar, *Poland 1944–1962. The Sovietization of a Captive People* (New Orleans, 1962), pp. 179–88.

has forced Gomułka to admit to positions of political importance members of the partisan group and, since the Fifth Party Congress, representatives of the provincial party organizations too. This 'changing of the guard' was more dramatic than it may appear on the surface. Gomułka, the one-time pragmatist with a genuine concern for the people, and the symbol of a better future for Poland, was forced to give up the ideas which, in 1956, brought him to power. It remains to be seen whether this turnabout will not eventually cost him his leading position. While he has lost the confidence of the 'silent majority' of the Polish people, he may not be prepared to go far enough to satisfy the demands of his hard-line supporters in the party apparatus.

That communism was unable to gain the support of the Polish nation has been best expressed by its failure to create a genuine youth movement. Before October 1956 the Union of Polish Youth had more than 2 million members. But it was this organization which was generally regarded as one of the main representatives of Stalinism. As a result, it disintegrated when the edifice of Polish Stalinism fell to pieces. The liberalization movement had its most devoted and energetic supporters among young people. The weekly *Po prostu* and numerous youth clubs, as well as the organizations of democratic and Catholic youth, which sprang up throughout the country, were their main spokesmen. At first, they demanded absolute freedom of association. Soon they were to find out that even post-1956 Poland could not afford the existence of voluntary associations, such as the two Alliances, of Democratic and of Catholic Youth. The student leaders rather grudgingly accepted the 'advice' of the party that there should be two youth organizations – 'Union of Socialist Youth' in the cities and industrial centres and 'Rural Youth Union' in the Polish countryside. Both associations were declared to be quasi-political and their aim was to wage, under the guidance of the PUWP, a constant struggle against the hostile forces of capitalism and revisionism. Youth was to become the most important factor in the building of socialism.

At the time of its Fourth Congress at the beginning of 1968 the Union of Socialist Youth had 1,056,000 members. The Rural Youth organization, which is formally associated with the United Peasant Party but is to serve the cause of socialism, is somewhat smaller. The total of organized youth still represents about one-fifth of young men and women between the ages of fifteen and twenty-five, who are eligible for membership. Even more distressing from the regime's point of view have been the constant complaints about the inability and even unwillingness of the members of the youth unions to measure up to the expectations of the party. The resolution passed at the

Fourth Socialist Union Congress emphasized the political aims of the association, criticizing the inability of its leadership to attract workers and members of the 'engineering and technical staff'.

The regime can find little encouragement in the fact that the Polish Students' Union has been able to incorporate almost 80 per cent of all students. Membership of this organization has little political significance. It can be regarded as compulsory, having become the main test of the socio-political attitudes of the students, which are decisive for the granting of scholarships and, most recently too, for the admission to study. In December 1962 a high party functionary severely criticized the behaviour of the students, many of whom had been unable to understand 'that only conformity of personal effort with national objectives can open the way for the development of their talents and abilities'.[5]

Thus the 'ideology of withdrawal' became the main characteristic of Polish youth. Many young people lost interest in public affairs and fell back into that 'internal emigration' which can be found in all modern autocratic societies. The youngest generation in particular had nothing but scorn for the hypocritical world of adults. Its main interests seemed to be entirely materialistic – possession of an apartment, refrigerator, a television set, or an automobile, all indicating symbols of success. This group of young Poles, it was stated, found its self-expression in American jazz, dances, films, and literature – in fact in everything which had a Western label.

Yet the events of 1968 proved that Polish youth had not lost its idealism. The demands for which the Polish students demonstrated and suffered indignities clearly indicated their belief in the priority of freedom. They did not ask for material advantages, but for freedom of speech, assembly, association, and scientific research, as well as guarantees of civil and political rights. While cowed into silence by ruthless persecution, the voice of youth cannot be suppressed, especially in Poland where those under thirty-five years of age represent 66 per cent of the population. Their convictions were expressed by their watchword of March 1968: 'there can be no bread without freedom, there can be no studies without freedom.'[6]

Another youth organization serving 'the construction of socialism' is the Polish Boy and Girl Scouts' Union. By the time of its October 1968 Congress, the Union, which is composed of children and teenagers, had 2 million members and 67,000 instructors. While more detached from the PUWP than the youth organizations, the Scout

[5] *Trybuna Ludu* (18 December 1962).
[6] Jan Nowak, 'Conflict of Generations in Poland', *East Europe,* vol. 17, No. 5 (May 1968), p. 15.

movement has been skilfully used as a vehicle for the regime's propaganda.

Non-Communist 'Parties' and non-Party Organizations

Those who believed that October 1956 would provide for the existence of independent voluntary associations were bitterly disappointed. Of course, in Polish society there are many political and social organizations which, in keeping with official interpretation, serve the interests of different groups of the population. They may be politically important, but none – including the non-communist political parties – are permitted independent policies of their own. They are all dominated by the Communist Party and are used as an indispensable instrument through which it rules the country. They transmit communist policies to the masses, propagandize their universal acceptance, and help to control their execution. Any other function would be incompatible with the principle of the communist monopoly of power proclaimed by Gomułka himself. These groups are organized along the lines of the PUWP and their hierarchical structure is based on the territorial divisions of the country. Each has its national headquarters and secretariat located in the Polish capital. The political parties and the most important mass organizations are grouped in the so-called Front of National Unity which has central, regional, and local committees. The Front serves a dual purpose : to symbolize the idea of national solidarity and to serve as the regime's electoral organization. It prepares one single electoral platform, selects the candidates, and lends its name to the single list which is submitted to the electorate.

Irrespective of their size, social significance, and practical aims, the members of the National Unity Front are dominated by the PUWP and operate as its auxiliaries. The two non-communist political parties – the United Peasant Party and the Democratic Party – serve the same purpose. They do not play the role of an opposition, which for all practical purposes has been forbidden. As early as the end of 1957 Gomułka repudiated the idea of geninue opposition parties and stated : 'freedom for all political parties means also freedom for the bourgeois parties'.[7] At the same time, however, Gomułka hinted that the main obstacle to the granting of such freedom was the Soviet Union. Those who favour a multi-party system, Gomułka declared, 'would perhaps suggest that we change the geographic and political situation of Poland, that it be moved to another part of the globe or to another planet'.[8] But soon Gomułka changed his opinion

---

[7] Quoted 'The Polish Election', *East Europe*, vol. 6, No. 3 (March 1957), p. 4.
[8] Ibid.

and became a genuine opponent of freedom of political association. During the post-1958 retreat from liberalization policies the non-communist parties were reduced to a position of absolute subservience to the communist regime.

Yet the Polish non-communist parties are not without political importance for the PUWP. Their size and scope of activity are definitely larger than those of their counterparts in other East-Central European states. In fact, the existence of more political parties is necessary because of the weakness of the Communist Party in certain areas of the country. Alone it would be unable to secure smooth functioning of the complicated structure of communist society. This is particularly true of the eastern provinces of Poland, in which the PUWP is relatively weak. It is forced to rely on the United Peasant Party whose 364,000 members, organized in more than 20,000 circles, play an important role in the countryside. The party provides for close ties between the peasantry and the representatives of the regime, struggles against village reactionaries, and advocates the establishment of co-operatives, particularly the so-called Agricultural Circles. The Democratic Party is much smaller and is said to represent artisans, small businessmen, as well as the members of the intelligentsia. These two parties, especially the former, have a relatively large representation in the *Sejm*, the Council of State, and particularly the local organs of government. But they cannot be considered parties in the Western sense of the term. Above all, they have to support PUWP activities in the construction of socialism. Thus they cannot offer the electorate a genuine alternative. In fact, their leaders, being more knowledgeable of peasant mentality, offer valuable services to the regime.

In addition to political parties and youth organizations, the National Unity Front includes a number of mass organizations, some with a membership of several million. Perhaps most important and definitely most numerous are the trade unions, with more than 8 million members from a labour force of almost 10 million. As in the Soviet Union, they have little in common with Western-type workers' unions. They are controlled by the party and government and their policies are determined by the PUWP leadership. There are many other organizations, such as the large Women's League, the Polish-Soviet Friendship Society, the Union of Fighters for Freedom and Democracy (headed by Mieczysław Moczar), and a host of social and professional groups. Although some may not be directly associated with the Front, they represent important factors serving the regime in the execution of its long-range programmes and immediate aims.

Another organization which emerged after 1956 was the Agricultural Circles. For some time these were regarded as the main vehicle for the regime's agricultural policies. Both in name and in their initial functions, these organizations reminded Polish agriculturalists of their traditional co-operatives going back to the pre-war period. They were to rally on a voluntary basis the peasants 'for work on development and improvement of agricultural production through the co-ordination of individual efforts by mutual aid and collaboration'.[9] Their main task was to assist the small farmers in purchasing seeds, fertilizers, coal, and building materials at lower prices. Also, the peasants hoped, the Agricultural Circles would help them to acquire private tractors. The regime, however, viewed the Circles as a new and original method of organizing agriculture, which would provide for an ultimate solution to the problem of 'socializing the countryside'.

For this reason individual peasants were refused aid in their efforts to purchase small tractors. Only the Agricultural Circles were given the right to acquire especially large tractors as the 'common property' of their members. The aim of this policy was to motorize Polish agriculture by replacing individually owned horses by tractors. The plan proved to be a failure, as the heavy tractors purchased by the Circles were of little use on tiny peasant plots. When, after 1959, the Agricultural Circles were put entirely under the control of the government and their competence limited to the mechanization and motorization of agriculture, they lost whatever appeal they might have had for the Polish agriculturalist. The fact that state aid went to the inefficient state farms and the transformed Agricultural Circles, which had nothing in common with the autonomous peasant organizations, was particularly resented. By the end of 1967 only about one-third of individual farms had become members of the Agricultural Circles, which in many cases had proved unable to cover the costs of their operation.

In this brief survey of the most important social organizations the Catholic Church – potentially the most prominent and powerful group speaking on behalf of the majority of Poles – is not included. This omission is due to the consistent refusal of the Catholic hierarchy to accept the leadership of the PUWP, especially in ideological matters. Between these two mighty competitors a balance of power emerged and the regime has so far been unable to get the upper hand. On several occasions it has attempted to weaken, or at least to neutralize, the Church's power and influence. It gave support to Piasecki's Pax and the Christian Social Association. Such efforts, as well as abortive attempts to organize pro-communist Patriot Priests, ended in dismal failure.

Ironically, the only important organization which even the regime was forced to recognize as a representative of the Catholic world

[9] *Trybuna Ludu* (2 August 1959).

outlook, is the at times militantly 'non-communist' group of Catholic intellectuals known as *Znak*. This organization, which has acquired
its name from the monthly periodical *Znak* (Sign), was admitted into
the Front of National Unity. While it does not possess the status of
a political party, it was allowed to participate in the post-1956 parliamentary elections. Its five deputies, while denied the right to form a
parliamentary club, represent an independent political 'circle' and
until recently were elected to various functions in the *Sejm*.

The policies of *Znak* are based on a peculiar blend of unreserved
Catholicism and anti-Marxism. Its representatives are convinced
about the irreconciliability of Catholic and Marxist philosophies, but
they do not believe in the necessity of a conflict. There is nothing,
they claim, which should stand in the way of co-operation between
Catholics and communists in the realm of practical day-to-day policies. For church believers cannot remain indifferent to the fate of the
Polish people. As pointed out by one observer, 'the Znak followers
believed that the *sensus catholicus* imposed on them the duty to be
concerned with the interests of their nations'.[10] Accordingly the *Znak*
group is opposed to all measures which would split the nation and
worsen Church-state relations. On the contrary, it does its best to
take a positive and constructive attitude towards the regime. In
practice, its approach is based on the combination of complete
allegiance to the Catholic Church with a pragmatic approach to
public affairs. Approving policies which favour the Polish national
interest and opposing those in conflict with Christian ethics, *Znak*
can be regarded as the sole representative of a degree of pluralism in
Polish public and political life. The fact that occasionally *Znak*
deputies have voted against bills which they have regarded as incompatible with their consciences, has lent them at least some
characteristics of a Western-type opposition.

Why is it that a communist regime has tolerated a handful of men
who courageously oppose and publicly criticize certain of its policies? The fact that *Znak* adherents claim to be representing 'millions
of people in Poland' might be a cause of concern for the regime. The
answer to this question is not easy. It may well be that it is a tacit
recognition of the importance and relevance of the Catholic point
of view in an overwhelmingly Catholic country. It may, on the other
hand, be a tactical measure by which the party tries to channel, and
indirectly control, the latent Catholic opposition. Whatever the real
reason for the regime's behaviour may be, *Znak* represents a unique
phenomenon in the communist world which 'may well be likened to
a barometer, registering the direction of political pressures in

10 Bromke, op. cit., p. 236.

Gomułka's Poland'.[11] The latter interpretation has been confirmed during the 1968 political crisis, when *Znak* and its individual members were exposed to violent attacks by the hard-liners, which eventually received Gomułka's tacit backing.

In April 1968 *Znak* parliamentary intervention opposing the 'brutal action' against the students and expressing concern over its consequences for 'democratic civil liberties' and the government's cultural policy was answered by the Prime Minister himself. By their intervention, said Cyrankiewicz, the *Znak* deputies had 'put themselves in the ranks of the inspirers of the events' and contributed to the nefarious activities of the 'ringleaders and firebrands'.[12] His attack was joined by other communist deputies and their Peasant and Democratic Party allies, who went so far as to hint at an 'alliance of certain Catholic circles with Zionism'. Kliszko commended the pro-regime behaviour of the Pax movement and the Christian Social Association and declared that the *Znak* group found itself in 'deep political isolation'.[13] Even more significant was Gomułka's violent attack, in his speech of March 1968, against Stefan Kisielewski, former *Znak* member of the *Sejm* and an outstanding fighter for the liberalization and democratization of Polish life, because of his criticism of the regime's cultural policies at the meeting of the Warsaw branch of the Writers' Union.[14] In the subsequent government changes the *Znak* deputy Jerzy Zawieyski was forced to resign from his membership of the State Council.

Thus political development since 1958 has been characterized by a consistent withdrawal from the liberal platform of 1956 and has made co-operation between *Znak* and the Communist Party increasingly difficult. The victory of the hard-liners in 1968 has further limited the possibilities for *Znak* to become a force in Polish public life.

Constitutional System and Political Reality

Until 1952 the constitutional foundation of the Polish political system consisted of a number of documents. Their mutual relationship was not clear, being open to different interpretations. The representatives of the Moscow-sponsored movement insisted – mainly for propaganda reasons – on the continued validity of the liberal-democratic constitution of March 1921. It was used with some success as a means to undermine the 'reactionary' government in London. Having crossed the Polish frontier, the communist-led Lublin government lost most of its interest in this democratic document and tended

[11] Adam Bromke, 'The "Znak" Group in Poland', *East Europe*, vol. 11, No. 2 (February 1962), p. 15.
[12] See *East Europe*, vol. 17, No. 6 (May 1968), p. 53.
[13] Report of Jonathan Randal, *New York Times* (11 April 1968).
[14] For Gomułka's speech see *Trybuna Ludu* (20 March 1968).

to minimize its importance. In the famous Manifesto of 21 July 1944, its two revolutionary organs, the National Council of the Homeland and the Committee of National Liberation, were directed to act only 'on the basis' of the 1921 constitution whose 'fundamental principles' were declared to be valid until the adoption of a new constitutional charter. But these 'principles' were never spelled out. As a result, the organs of communist revolution were enabled to take measures contrary to the fundamental assumptions and the spirit of that document. Thus the decree relating to the organization, on all administrative levels, of a net of National Councils (*Rady narodowe*) and conferring on the highly unrepresentative and essentially self-appointed National Council of the Homeland the status of the Polish parliament (the *Sejm*) was in clear conflict with the constitution. The same was true of the decree establishing within this body a Soviet-type Presidium. Last but not least, legislation introducing land reform and the nationalization of all key industries, enacted in 1944 and 1946, lacked constitutional sanction. It may well be that these two reforms – undoubtedly welcomed by the majority of the Polish people – were sanctioned by the referendum of June 1946. But popular referendum was not provided for in the constitutional charter of 1921. The abolition of the Senate, another measure 'approved' by the referendum, was an even more flagrant violation of both letter and spirit of the March constitution. Many other decrees passed in the realm of criminal and civil law suffered from the same shortcoming. Of these the so-called 'Little Criminal Code' of June 1946 was the most important. It introduced new offences, and increased penalties for existing ones, mainly in order to provide for a more adequate protection of the state and its property. Of great political importance in an overwhelmingly Catholic country was the new regulation of family law, passed as early as September 1945, which dissociated marriage from all confessional ties. In another category were the decrees of July 1944 establishing different police and state security organs.

When, in January 1947, Poland's Constituent *Sejm* was 'elected', it passed a number of legislative measures which were intended to introduce order into the legal system and a return to some of the Polish constitutional traditions. One of its first actions was the adoption of the 'Little Constitution' of 19 February 1947.[15] It re-established the traditional office of President of the Republic, determined the powers of the legislature, provided for a Supreme Auditing Board, and declared the principle of the independence of courts. This same document, however, included provisions indicating continued development towards Soviet constitutional patterns. At least

[15] The act was entitled 'The Constitutional Act Concerning the Organization and Powers of the Supreme Organs of the Republic of Poland'.

in part the communist constitutional concept of the unity of state power was adopted. This tendency was expressed by the creation of a State Council, which was nothing but a modified Soviet Presidium. The State Council was headed by the President of the Republic. While it did not act as a 'collective head' of state, its competence and organization were similar to those of its Moscow counterpart, possessing both legislative and executive functions. The most serious defect of the 'Little Constitution' was the absence of a Bill of Rights. This omission was due to the insistence of the communists, who refused to accept a list of rights and duties of citizens, similar to those in Western constitutions. The Diet adopted a mere Human Rights Declaration. While accepted unanimously, the Declaration was not legally binding.

The existence of a constitution did not prevent further introduction of Soviet-type institutions and administrative practices. The basic law has been aptly described as being little more than a 'decorative fig-leaf on Poland's developing totalitarian structure'.[16] Soon it became clear that this provisional document could be regarded at best as a 'guide to action', at worst as an instrument entirely out of touch with the new social and economic situation. Some of its 'alterations' consisted of a change of emphasis, but others were downright extra-constitutional. Typical of the latter was the practice of the State Council to arrogate to itself the power to issue executive orders (not mentioned in the constitution), thus making it the most important organ of government, especially in matters of local administration. Following the Soviet example a new institution emerged within the cabinet – the Presidium of the Council of Ministers. Most important from the political point of view was the law of March 1950 regulating the greatly increased powers of the People's Councils. Thus the last vestiges of the traditional system of provincial and local administration disappeared. The new regulation introduced the principle of dual subordination of the administrative and executive organs (the presidia) of local government. They were subjected to the control of their own People's Council and to that of the presidia of the next higher level of the local government structure, and through them to the organs of the central government, particularly the Ministry of the Interior. The provisional constitution represented the basic law of the country for almost five and a half years. In this period many legislative measures adapting the legal, economic, and cultural life of Poland to the requirements of a communist society were enacted. Typical of these was the Act of July 1950 on the new judicial organization, whereby courts were instructed 'to educate the citizens in the spirit of loyalty to People's Poland, of observance of

16 Dziewanowski, op. cit., p. 229.

the principles of people's legality, labour discipline, and concern for social property'.[17]

The main characteristic of the constitutional system was its vagueness and uncertainty, both qualities perfectly suited to a policy of gradual Sovietization. Only thus can it be explained why the Constitution of the Polish People's Republic of 22 July 1952, by which the country finally acquired the status of a 'People's Democracy', was fundamentally a summary of the previous achievements of the Warsaw regime. It reflected, too, existing circumstances in state and society during the period of Stalinism. It was similar to the other People's Democratic constitutions, but at that time it represented evident progress in the development towards socialism. Its preamble and the first article clearly expressed the class nature of the new system. Power was no longer vested in the people, but in the 'working people of town and country'. The state was given the task of securing the interests, as well as the material and cultural growth, of the working people. At the same time it was enjoined to carry on a relentless struggle against 'those classes of society which live by exploiting the workers and peasants'.[18]

The more advanced nature of the Polish constitution was best expressed in its relationship to private property and private enterprise. In the tripartite division of the Polish economic system (characteristic of all People's Democracies), the concept of private property has been very narrowly interpreted. The state, it was emphasized, recognized and protected three types of ownership: state property, especially socialized industry; individual property of land and other means of production belonging to farmers, artisans, and persons engaged in domestic handicrafts; and finally personal property. The ownership of land tilled by production co-operatives – the Polish version of Soviet-type collectives – remained at least nominally vested in the individual co-operative members. Even the protection of the individual property of peasants was not declared to be unlimited, being 'recognized and protected on the basis of existing legislation'. This provision seemed to imply that at the time of its promulgation the constitution envisaged a possible compulsory collectivization.

In keeping with the fundamental concept of communist constitutionalism the 1952 constitution recognized the principle of a unified and centralized state power, including not only legislative, but also controlling and executive, functions. The exercise of this power is the prerogative of a unicameral *Sejm* which, theoretically speaking, should be the cornerstone of all governmental activity. While similar to other parliaments, its powers include two all-important functions –

[17] Oscar Halecki, ed., *Poland*, p. 90.
[18] Art. 3 of the Polish constitution.

the passage of national economic plans and the election of the fifteen-member Council of State. The new Council is different from its predecessor. It possesses powers practically identical with those of the Soviet Presidium. In addition to acting as a collective Head of State, it controls the activities of the local People's Councils; it also has the right to issue decrees with the force of law and to legislate during the intervals between sessions of the *Sejm*; finally, it is also entrusted with judicial powers, being responsible for the universally binding interpretation of laws.

The supreme executive and administrative organ of state authority is the Council of Ministers presided over by the Prime Minister. Legally, it is the main policy-making organ whose duties include – in addition to maintaining public law and order – control of Poland's defence and foreign policies, as well as the supreme direction of the work of the presidia of the People's Councils. One of its main tasks, apart from the preparation of the budget, is the formulation of the economic plan and control over its execution. In relation to the *Sejm* the position of the premier and his cabinet is very similar to that of other parliamentary systems. The premier is chosen by the Diet, submits to it the list of Ministers, and is accountable for all his and his government's political activities.

The organization of local government has been entrusted to People's Councils, whose organizational structure is almost identical with that of the Russian Soviets. According to the principle of unified state power there is, theoretically speaking, no distinction between central and local organs of government. Having developed from the revolutionary National Councils, the People's Councils are organized territorially on four different levels: Provinces (*Wojewódstwo*), Counties (*Powiat*), Municipalities (*Miasto*), and urban and rural Communes (*Gromada*). Under the control of the Council of State and the Council of Ministers the organs of local government exercise those functions which have been expressly vested in them. As determined by the law of January 1958 the scope of their jurisdiction is very wide. The actual exercise of their executive functions is in the hands of their presidia, which are elected by the individual People's Councils and whose officials act on behalf of both local and central government. The provisions of the Polish constitution on organs of local government and administration are more elaborate than those of its Soviet counterpart, emphasizing their role as intermediaries between the regime and the broad masses of the population.

The constitution has relatively few provisions on the administration of justice. The judiciary, whose activities are supervised by the Ministry of Justice and the Supreme Court, is subordinated to the *raison d'être* of a socialist state. The judges, both lay and professional, do not enjoy any independence in the exercise of their function, being regarded as civil servants. There is no right of judicial review and the courts are also forbidden to question the validity of governmental decrees and ordinances. The approach to fundamental civil rights is based on communist constitutional theory. Thus main emphasis is laid on economic and social rights, which are considered to represent the basis of all other rights and duties of citizens. The constitution also indicates in a general manner the means by which the state is to guarantee the implementation of the Bill of Rights.

The aim of the Polish constitution was to provide as broad a framework as possible for further transformation of society – the elimination of the exploiting classes; the combating of bourgeois-capitalist practices; and the positive construction of socialism. The basic law is designed to reflect the changes in the legal superstructure resulting from changed social and economic conditions in the Polish People's Republic. In reality, however, it failed to trace even a remotely accurate picture of the governmental and political organization of the country. The PUWP and its Politburo, the actual holders of sovereign power in the Polish state, are not even mentioned. Nor does the constitution refer to the principle of democratic centralism which guides all party and state activities.

It is the party which decides on the composition, organization, and work of all governmental organs. The plenary sessions of the *Sejm* are characterized by their brevity and a general tendency towards unanimity. One can hardly say that this 'highest organ of state authority' has been able to escape the deadening effect of communist conformity. Until recently the legislative committees of the Polish *Sejm*, with their non-communist deputies, have been able to assert their influence, forcing the government to make meaningful 'concessions'.[19] Yet in all constitutional organs only those who hold important party positions can make full use of their prerogatives. The rest are experts whose activities are limited at best to the execution of policies determined by the PUWP.

The gap between law as it is written and as it is applied was best illustrated by the general provisions of the electoral law. The pre-1956 electoral law, having emulated the example of the Soviet Union, introduced a totalitarian pattern of voting. The candidates were nominated by 'mass social organizations of the working people' to run on the single list of the Front of National Unity. As only one candidate for each seat in the *Sejm* was nominated, the voting changed into a meaningless ritual. Dominated by the Communist

[19] See Vincent C. Chrypinski, 'Poland's Parliamentary Committees', *East Europe*, vol. 14, No. 1 (January 1965), pp. 17–24.

Party, the Front saw to it that only reliable Peasant Party, Democratic Party, and non-party candidates appeared on the list. No wonder that the elections – despite a mass turnout – took place in an atmosphere of gloom and general apathy.

The electoral law was changed after October 1956. At the height of general enthusiasm Gomułka promised that the new regulation would 'enable people to elect and not merely to vote'. This promise remained largely unfulfilled, but Poland introduced an electoral system unique in the Soviet Bloc states. The National Unity Front retained its monopolistic position as the only electoral ticket submitted to the voters. But the number of candidates appearing on the ballots in the individual districts was allowed to exceed by well over 50 per cent the number of seats to be filled. The electorate was given the right to express its preference for certain candidates by deleting the names of others from the ballot. Little more than one-half of the 717 candidates who ran in the January 1957 election on the National Unity Front list were members of the Communist Party. The rest belonged to the two non-communist parties, or ran as non-party candidates. As only 459 candidates could be elected, there seemed to exist at least a theoretical possibility of a communist defeat. That this did not happen was due to a number of considerations which greatly strengthened the position of the PUWP. Of these the most decisive was the popularity of Gomułka who, for some time after October 1956, was regarded as a national hero. He managed to achieve the support even of the Catholic Church. In addition, other considerations of electoral technique rendered a communist defeat practically impossible.

In the elections of 1961 and 1965 the PUWP could no longer rely on the popularity of its leader. While the right to delete names and the right of a secret ballot, secured by the availability of envelopes into which the ballots could be inserted, were preserved, the new electoral law introduced security precautions guaranteeing the position of the Communist Party. The ratio between the number of candidates and the seats to be filled was altered to 616 against 460. Moreover, of the 616 candidates 387 were PUWP members, who were thereby guaranteed a majority of two in the *Sejm*, even if the improbable happened and all non-communist candidates were elected. No wonder that by 1965 a large part of the voters made no use of the facilities for secret balloting. Yet this change alone would hardly have explained the surprising 'stability' of Polish political life. In fact, the almost identical results in the two elections tended to justify the suspicion that the distribution of the *Sejm* seats resulted rather from a quota agreement than a genuine electoral contest.[20] Only the progressive transformation of Gomułka's Poland, which shed most of its liberal characteristics, can explain how the elections lost the glamour of 1957. The Poles themselves were quick to notice the artificiality of their elections. Realizing that they were held for the purpose of registering approval of PUWP policies, they referred to them as 'consent elections'.[21] The following table presents the strength of the individual parties and members of the non-party group in the 1957, 1961, 1965, and 1969 elections :

Results of Polish Elections

	1957		1961		1965		1969	
	seats	%	seats	%	seats	%	seats	%
PUWP	239	52·1	256	55·7	255	55·4	255	55·4
United Peasant Party	118	25·7	117	25·4	117	25·4	117	25·4
Democratic Party	39	8·5	39	8·5	39	8·5	39	8·5
Non-Party members	93	13·7	48	10·4	49	10·7	49	10·7
	459	100·0	460	100·0	460	100·0	460	100·0

Sources: *Rocznik statystyczny*, 1957, p. 406; *Rocznik statystyczny*, 1962, p. 447; *Rocznik statystyczny*, 1966, p. 557; *East Europe*, vol. 18, No. 7 (July 1969), pp. 52–3.

The fact that results in the June 1969 election were identical with those of 1965 underlined the meaningless character of the electoral process. Again more candidates than seats for the *Sejm* appeared on the ballots, but this opportunity for choice was more than offset by the practice of placing 'less desirable' candidates at the very bottom of the list. Their election would have been possible, had a large number of voters dared to vote in secret and had they crossed out all the leading candidates. The political atmosphere, however, precluded any such action. On the other hand, in a number of districts names of leading party members were deleted so that they received less votes than the lower-placed candidates. Thus Cyrankiewicz dropped from the first to the last eligible spot in the Kraków electoral district. Even so he received 90 per cent of the vote.

The 'consolidation' of the regime was demonstrated by the decrease in the number of those who abstained from the election, or submitted

[20] See Jerzy Ptakowski, 'Parliamentary Elections in Poland', *East Europe*, vol. 14, No. 8 (August 1965), pp. 15–16.
[21] Jerzy J. Wiatr, 'Elections and Voting Behaviour in Poland', *International Political Science Conference* (September 1960), p. 4.

either invalid or even anti-Front votes. The following table indicates the growing conformity in Polish elections :

Protest Votes in Polish Elections

Abstentions

	1957	1961	1965	1969
Number	1,051,868	961,539	663,487	506,430
Percentage	5·86	5·17	3·38	2·39

Invalid Ballots

	1957	1961	1965	1969
Number	58,897	19,067	1,840	7,760
Percentage	0·33	0·10	0·07	0·04

Ballots Against the National Unity Front List

	1957	1961	1965	1969
Number	280,002	292,009	226,324	161,569
Percentage of valid votes	1·50	1·57	1·15	0·78

Total Number of Protest Votes

1,390,767	1,272,615	891,651	675,765

Source : *East Europe*, vol. 18, No. 7 (July 1969), pp. 52–3.

Perhaps more important than the actual electoral results was the elimination of almost 40 per cent of former members of the *Sejm*, including a number of party dignitaries, such as Ochab, Rapacki, Szyr, and Jerzy Albrecht. The extent of the turnover in the *Sejm* clearly indicated Gomułka's displeasure with the performance or political reliability of many deputies.

A similar discrepancy between constitutional promise and political reality can be found in the sphere of local government. By means of the People's Councils broader strata of the population are to be drawn into active participation in the administration of public affairs. To be successful, the still relatively small group of party members, who represent the élite, requires not only acquiescence but also some degree of genuine co-operation from the people. This is especially true in the countryside, where the majority of peasants view with utmost distrust any attempt at governmental control. There are many reasons why the regime's efforts to secure mass participation have been less than satisfactory. In order to gain more popularity the communists allowed a somewhat larger representation to the group of non-party members in the election of the 180,000-odd deputies of the various People's Councils. Even so the People's Councils do not reflect a true picture of Polish political opinion. Nor do they provide for an efficient system of public administration.

In one important respect Poland did not emulate the example of the other members of the Soviet Bloc. Article 10, section 1 of the constitution, safeguarding the 'independent farms of working peasants', was never allowed to become obsolete. The provisions of section 2 of the same Article, promising 'special support and all-round aid to the co-operative farms', did not become a starting-point for an all-out collectivization campaign. The events of 1956 led to an absolute collapse of the existing collective farms. In 1968 only 1·1 per cent of agricultural land was collectivized and 13·4 per cent was owned by the government as state farms.[22] Overall agricultural production has greatly increased, but the yields of independent farmers have by far surpassed those of state farms. The difference would have been even greater, had it not been for the policy of the government, which ever since 1959 started to support state farms at the expense of the peasant holdings. Despite the fact that they pay no taxes and receive preferential treatment in the acquisition of machinery and the allocation of fertilizers, almost one-half of state farms operate at deficit.

The unfavourable attitude of the regime towards the peasants was because Gomułka and his party never gave up the idea of 'socializing' the countryside. This aim was to be achieved by the support of state farms and through the organization of Agricultural Circles operating under the control of the government. Both proved to be unsuccessful. The state farms managed to increase their share of agricultural land, but the Agricultural Circles, especially after their reorganization in 1959, did not gain the confidence of the peasants. That the regime did not give up its socializing tendencies was proved by the provisions of the 1968 Agricultural Expropriation Act. This enabled the state to take over farms whose owners (because of old age and lack of successors) could not undertake 'intensification of production' on their own. In exchange for their property such farmers receive a state pension. The Act also made it possible for the state to force compulsory sale of farms neglected by their owners. During parliamentary discussion on the bills, which were not supported by the *Znak* deputies, it was stated that 'the way land is used ceases to be the private matter

---

[22] 0·5 per cent of land was farmed by the Agricultural Circles and the rest remained in private hands.

of its owner' but has become 'a public matter which concerns all of us'. The emphasis on the promotion of state farms was reaffirmed by Gomułka on the occasion of the 1968 Harvest Festival. State farms, he stated, will be taking over farms already neglected as well as those which are 'threatened with neglect'.[23]

Another deviation from the Soviet model concerned private enterprise, which since the post-war period has continued to exist in Poland. This violation of ideological orthodoxy was caused by the catastrophic situation in retail trade and in services. Being recognized by the constitution, allowance for small-scale private undertakings became indispensable, as the state-run enterprises failed to provide for a bearable standard of living. In its approach to private initiative in trade and services, the regime developed a curious schizophrenia. Realizing the necessity to satisfy at least the most urgent needs of consumers, the communist planners have readily taken into account the contribution of the private entrepreneur. On the other hand, as true Marxist-Leninists, they could not publicly admit the usefulness of the private economic sector. As a result, it is officially regarded as an unwelcome remnant of the bourgeois-capitalist system which has no place in a socialist society. By various means private entrepreneurs are placed at a disadvantage in comparison with the state-owned and state-run economy. In more recent years the regime has introduced the so-called 'agency system', under which different types of small-scale state and co-operative enterprises are leased to private persons who work them on their own account, taking risk and profit.

Despite the tendency of the bureaucrats to permit methods foreign to a socialist economy, the difficulties and constant harassment to which the private entrepreneurs are being exposed, set a limit to the scope of their activities. For every unscrupulous individual – who by whatever means, including bribery, manages to derive profit from his operations – there are several honest traders and artisans whose business falls victim to the vicissitudes of their ventures. Yet private enterprise has become indispensable to the state. In fact, in the sixties the attitude of the regime, especially towards certain types of services, has become one of benevolent toleration.

In the course of its existence the government of People's Poland has used law as a powerful instrument of social and political change. The representatives of the regime have adopted uncompromisingly the traditional approach to law, subordinating it to the general line and the immediate needs of the PUWP. Initial legislation was in most cases hasty measures aimed at the entrenchment of the new government and the disintegration of the 'antagonistic' classes. This was true of the new organization of public security, the administra-

[23] *Trybuna Ludu* (9 September 1968).

tion of justice, and the basic laws securing the interests of the socialist state. Thus the 'Little Criminal Code' introduced severe punishments and rigid procedural rules with regard to acts dangerous to the state.[24] Of similar significance was the post-1944 organization of the security police and the reorganization of state prosecution in 1950. The main task of the new laws and codes was to protect public property and to guard law and order 'in the broadest sense', as well as to prosecute crime. Speaking at the Third PUWP Congress, Gomułka referred to the 'struggle for the establishment of socialist justice and legality' and to the necessity of a 'further adjustment of the existing legislation to the needs of the Polish state'.[25]

The fact that this statement was made as late as 1959 is an indication of the unique characteristic of the law-making process in People's Poland. While insisting on the necessity of change, Polish legislators proceeded very cautiously with the replacement of prewar statutes and regulations. More than any other society of communist East-Central Europe, Poland tried to maintain some degree of legal continuity with the past. Codification work started as early as 1947, but only in 1956 was a Codification Commission appointed from among representatives of legal science and judicial practice to provide for a more systematic approach to legal reform. Its activities covered all fields of law. Even so, the building of socialist law took place at a comparatively slow pace and large segments of the pre-war legal system were retained. Less important statutes, as well as certain more significant statutory provisions, continued to be valid. This was true of parts of the 1932 Criminal Code and the Code of Criminal Procedure, which were applied as recently as 1968. The draft of the new Criminal Code, submitted to the *Sejm* in 1968, formally abolished the 'Little Criminal Code', which had frequently been used for the conviction of writers accused of 'slandering the People's Republic'. But the draft preserved in a somewhat different form the most important provisions of this objectionable law. The 1960 Code of Administrative Procedure, while entirely new, retained many of the characteristics of the old law. The same can be said of the 1964 Civil Code which in certain respects displays traces of conservative legal thinking.

This 'independence' of the Polish legal system can be associated with the fact that the 14,000-odd Polish lawyers managed for a long time to maintain a relatively high degree of autonomy. Only at the end of 1963 did the regime proceed to a virtual 'socialization' of the

[24] The full title of the Decree, which was passed on 13 June 1946, was 'Decree on Criminal Acts Particularly Dangerous During the Period of National Reconstruction'.

[25] Władysław Gomułka, *Przemówienia* (1959), p. 147.

legal profession, subordinating it entirely to the control of the Ministry of Justice.

Poland in International Affairs

The pattern of international relations after the Second World War favoured the status of small European nations. It enabled them to play to a greater or lesser degree a relatively important role in international politics and even to pursue independent foreign policies. The breakdown of this system in the Second World War caused a revulsion against attempts to base the future peace solely on the frail foundations of international law and the intricacies of pluralistic diplomacy. Wrongly or rightly, it was held that not only in war but also in peace power alone should play a decisive role. As a result, a reappraisal of the function of small and medium states in international politics took place. The changed international atmosphere was best expressed by Walter Lippmann. While he envisaged 'Good Neighbour relations and harmonious co-operation between the great and the small powers 'in the same area of strategic security', he wrote :

> We must not, as many do, identify the rights of small nations with their right to have an 'independent' foreign policy, that is to say one which manipulates the balance of power among great states. . . . In this century, small states are much too small in relation to the big ones to pursue any policy but that of the Good Neighbour.[26]

Written more than a year before the dropping of the atomic bomb and at least three years before the emergence of the bi-polar world, Lippmann's statement failed to take into account the realities of the post-war world. Had it come as late as 1945, however, Western realization of the true intentions of the Soviet Union would have had little effect on the power-political and ideological intentions of the Russian leaders in East-Central Europe. By then the Red Army occupied the major part of the area and prevented the Western Powers from exerting any real influence there. As pointed out by Winston Churchill in his memoirs, 'the real time' for establishing an equilibrium between East and West was '. . . before the Americans, and to a lesser extent the British, made their vast retirement on a 400-mile front to a depth in some places of 120 miles, thus giving the heart and a great mass of Germany over to the Russians'.[27] What were intended to be 'Good Neighbour' relations between a benevolent and understanding Great Power and its loyal small neighbours resulted

[26] Walter Lippmann, *U.S. War Aims* (New York, 1944), p. 170.
[27] Churchill, *Triumph and Tragedy*, p. 672.

in an absolute political and ideological subjugation of the states of East-Central Europe to the Kremlin. Stalin never succeeded in his endeavour to create a monolithic empire. But his policy of gradual Sovietization precluded internal and external independence for Russia's neighbours. They were condemned to the humiliating position of satellites.

In the case of Poland foreign policy identification with the Soviet Union was determined not only by the interests of the Kremlin. To an ever increasing extent it was influenced by considerations of Polish security. However unpopular, the new foreign policy orientation found much justification in the events which took place soon after the termination of hostilities. In keeping with the decisions made at the wartime conferences of the Big Three, Poland was to be compensated for the loss of territories east of the Curzon Line, which were taken by the Soviet Union, at the expense of Germany. At the time of the Potsdam Conference Soviet and partly Polish armies were in control of East Germany. Also, a large part of this area was put under Polish administration in the anticipation that it would become a part of future Poland. At the Potsdam Conference, however, disagreement as to the future western boundaries of Poland broke out among the three allies. Only the Soviet Union backed the proposal of the Poles who were given an official hearing by the Conference. The two powers insisted that – in addition to the southern part of East Prussia – the future Polish borders should include the city of Stettin and run along the rivers Odra and western Nysa to the borders of Czechoslovakia. The British and American representatives, peeved by the fact 'that Poland now had been assigned a zone of occupation in Germany without any consultation among the three allies', refused to give their blessing to Polish demands.[28] Both President Harry S. Truman and Churchill shoved aside the arguments of Stalin and Molotov that 'on the basis of justice the Germans should lose their territories in favour of Poland'. They held the Polish request immoderate, contrary to ethnic considerations, and imperilling the supply of food to the western zones of Germany.[29] In direct discussions with the leaders of the Polish delegation, including Mikołajczyk, the Western leaders turned a deaf ear to the Polish demand that the Polish acquisition of the German Eastern Territories be immediately legalized. Instead, they insisted that this was a matter to be settled at the peace conference. While recognizing 'the paternal interest' of President Truman, Churchill, and later Clement Attlee,

[28] Harry S. Truman, *Memoirs of Harry S. Truman* (2 vols., Garden City, 1955), vol. 1 (*Year of Decisions*), p. 372.
[29] Statement of V. Molotov at the hearing of the Provisional Government of National Unity before the three Foreign Ministers, Rozek, op. cit., p. 407.

and condemning the communist members of the delegation for making 'demands in the West in a way calculated to stir the British and Americans to dissent', Mikołajczyk also came out clearly in favour of the new boundaries. These, he said, 'would be a safeguard against the resurrection of Germany as a military aggressor. . . .'[30]

Thus the Potsdam Agreement of 30 July on the 'Western Frontier of Poland' fell short of Polish and Soviet expectations. The territories east of the rivers Odra and western Nysa were placed 'under the administration of the Polish state', pending 'the final determination of Poland's western frontier' by the peace conference. Another decision made at Potsdam, on the 'Orderly Transfer of German Populations', provided for the movement to Germany of the German population still remaining in Poland. This provision cast serious doubts on the 'temporary and provisional' character of the new German-Polish borders. Since the small German minority in pre-war Poland had retreated westwards with the defeated German army, the transfer could become meaningful only if applied to those territories which were placed under Polish administration. Irrespective of their subsequent statements, the Western leaders must have been aware of the permanency of their decision.

No wonder that the Poles regarded Potsdam as their victory. They believed that the 'final determination' of their western boundaries could not substantially alter the Odra–Nysa Line. Indeed, as far as Soviet and Polish opinion was concerned the Potsdam decisions were nothing but a preliminary peace settlement. The Polish government argued that 'administration' constituted a permanent legal situation which brought about irreversible legal effects. In consequence, it regarded the acquired territories (referred to as Recovered Territories) as being under the sovereign rule of the Polish state.

There is reason to believe that the Western Powers would have recognized the verdict of Potsdam, had it not been for the growing tension between them and the Warsaw regime. They regarded it only as one of the aspects of Stalinist imperialism which was beginning to endanger the security of the European continent. On the occasion of his famous speech of 3 March 1946 in Fulton, Missouri, Winston Churchill called for a Western alliance against the Soviet danger. Referring to Poland, he accused the Warsaw government of having made 'enormous and wrongful inroads upon Germany'. Of greater significance – because of its official character – was the declaration of the US Secretary of State, James Byrnes, who reopened the question of the German-Polish border. Speaking on 6 September 1946 to a German audience in Stuttgart, he declared that the Odra–

[30] Mikołajczyk, op. cit., pp. 153–4.

Nysa Line, being a result of Stalin's unilateral action, was by no means permanent. He emphasized that it did not enjoy the recognition of the Western Powers and that it might be revised in favour of Germany. Byrnes's statement was bound to encourage German hopes for a revision of the 'provisional' decision of Potsdam. After the creation of the German Federal Republic it provided fuel for a revisionist policy.

Thus an impression was created that the Soviet Union alone gave absolute support to the new Polish borders. It was confirmed by the statement of the Soviet Foreign Minister, Vyacheslav Molotov, who insisted that the transfer of the German population lent final validity to the Potsdam decision. Ten days after Byrnes's speech he stated :

> Who could ever have the idea that this transfer of German population was undertaken as an experiment?... The very idea of conducting such an experiment with millions of people is inconceivable, not to speak of its cruelty towards the Poles and towards the Germans themselves.[31]

The American and British policies towards Poland were used with great skill by the Warsaw regime for both internal and external purposes. They served as a useful instrument to compromise the position of the Peasant Party and its leader, Mikołajczyk, who was generally regarded as a friend of the West. In the realm of foreign affairs the Polish government was enabled to extol the Soviet Union as the sole guarantor of the political independence and territorial integrity of Poland. More importantly, political propaganda based on the latent menace of Germany to the very existence of the Polish state appealed to the Polish masses, irrespective of their political orientation. In fact, it represented perhaps the only issue on which the government enjoyed the support of the great majority of the people. This was particularly true of the several million Poles from pre-war eastern Poland, who settled in the Recovered Territories and began to regard them as their home.

The threat of German revisionism, supported passively by the Western Powers, gave substance to the obligation of common defence against the revived German *Drang nach Osten* contained in the otherwise highly unpopular Treaty of Friendship, Collaboration, and Mutual Assistance between the Soviet Union and Poland of 21 April 1945. Having concluded similar bilateral treaties with other Soviet-dominated states of East-Central Europe, Poland became an integral part of the Soviet Bloc. The unity of the bloc was further cemented, at least from the formal point of view, by Polish participation in

[31] Stehle, op. cit., p. 270.

the multilateral Warsaw Pact (WTO) of May 1955.[32] The pact, which was generally regarded as the Eastern response to NATO, pledged its members to render military aid to one another, if attacked by an outside power. It also established a unified military command. In January 1949 Poland became a member of the Council of Mutual Economic Assistance (CEMA), another organization of communist states in eastern Europe, created to consolidate their economic systems. While relatively dormant in the period of Stalinism, CEMA was intended in some respects to provide a Soviet reply to the Marshall Plan and to the foundation of the OEEC in western Europe.

These and other treaties with the Soviet Union and the East-Central European communist states resulted in the weakening of the influence of the United States and other Western Powers in Poland. The degree of dependence on the Soviet Union was demonstrated by the Polish refusal to participate in the Marshall Plan. Later, again emulating the example of her Kremlin master, Poland arranged her relationship with East Germany in a friendly manner. The new friendship was sealed by an agreement of July 1950 in which the Odra–Nysa border was declared to be a permanent 'boundary of peace'. The subsequent visits of the leaders of the two regimes manifested the difference between the 'peace-loving' Germans of East Germany and the 'unreformed crypto-Nazis' of the German Federal Republic.

Thus until 1956 Poland, whose national sovereignty was limited by the stationing of Soviet troops on her territory, had no independent foreign policy. Her external relations were dictated by the Soviet Union and its interests. The single dimension of Polish foreign policy orientation was determined not only by overwhelming Soviet power, but also by the German issue 'which became the strongest single factor which consolidated the communist regime and the Russian influence in Poland'.[33] Moreover, in intra-bloc relations the Polish communists carried no more weight than the other 'satellite' parties. The initial opposition of their leader, Gomułka, to the foundation of the Cominform was overruled. Later he was purged and the PUWP, headed by the pro-Soviet and subservient Bierut, took an active part in the Cominform's anti-Yugoslav campaign.

By 1956 Poland – despite the internecine struggle between the communists and the non-communist majority – had managed to repair much of the damage wrought by war and greatly strengthen her political and economic position. Of prime importance was the

[32] The official title of the Warsaw Pact is 'Treaty of Friendship, Co-operation, and Mutual Aid'. The pact had originally seven members, but since 1961 Albania's membership must be regarded as suspended.
[33] Oscar Halecki, 'Poland', in Stephen D. Kertesz, ed., *The Fate of East Central Europe* (Notre Dame, 1956), p. 141.

fact that she had been able to organize and develop the Western Territories so that they had become integrated with the rest of Poland. Morally and politically, the absorption of this newly acquired part of Poland added greatly to the self-confidence of the Warsaw government. Being populated by a larger percentage of younger people than the rest of the country, the western *wojewódstwa* (provinces) had a much higher birth-rate than the national average. It became clear that the total population of the Western Territories would soon exceed the population-level of the pre-war period when they had been a part of Germany.

The Population of the Western Territories, 1939–1967

1939		8,855,000
1944–45	about	10,500,000
1946		5,022,000
1950		5,936,000
1961	about	7,750,000
1967	about	8,386,000

Sources: L. Kosinski, 'Demographic Problems of the Polish Western and Northern Territories', in *Geographical Essays on Eastern Europe*, ed. Norman J. G. Pounds, Russian and East European Series, Indiana University, Bloomington, Indiana, Vol. 24 (1961), pp. 28–53; *Rocznik statystyczny*, 1962 and 1968.

The changes brought about by the 'Glorious October', followed by a relative relaxation of tension between East and West, seemed to provide the Warsaw government with a chance to reassert itself as a factor in European international relations. By the beginning of 1957 Poland had greatly extended her relations with western Europe, which saw in Gomułka's victory an opportunity to improve its relations with the Soviet Bloc. The American government also realized that the policy of containment applied to the Soviet Union and her satellites no longer fitted the changed conditions of Poland. The historic ties between the two countries and the political weight of several million Americans of Polish origin made it necessary that the 'liberalized and more independent' Warsaw regime be treated differently than the other states of East-Central Europe. This recognition was accompanied by a genuine Polish endeavour to become a recipient of economic aid from the United States. While this aid had to be given in a manner which would not arouse the suspicions of the Kremlin and while it fell short of Polish expectations, between June 1957 and February 1963 Poland received 637·7 million dollars. Of these, over 519 million were interest-free loans for the purpose of purchasing grain and other agricultural products. The debt was made repayable in Polish *zloty* to an American account in Warsaw which soon rose to over 8 billion *zloty*. If unused by the United States within ten years, it was to be repaid in instalments over a period of forty years. One can hardly imagine a loan on more favourable terms. Yet the sudden emergence of an American Fund in Warsaw of such magnitude became a source of friction in United States-Polish relations. The Polish government had no objections to the use of the fund for financing American diplomatic and consular representation in Poland. Other uses, however, such as the building of hospitals and other medical projects, as well as translations of American scientific literature into Polish, were not always favoured by the Warsaw regime. No doubt Polish objections to wholesale American expenditure were justified in so far as this could disrupt the carefully planned Polish economy. At the same time politically motivated opposition also appeared. The Polish leaders – conscious of American popularity in Poland – did not wish to increase it by allowing the United States to play the role of a 'Santa Claus' to the Polish people.[34] In addition to the $57 million of the Food for Freedom programme, Poland received a loan of $61 million at 4½ per cent interest. This debt was to be repaid in instalments over a period of twenty-five years. By the end of 1967 Poland had repaid $31·5 million.

In addition, Poland was allowed to purchase for *zloty* several million dollars' worth of books, films, newspapers, and authors' rights in the United States. Further subsidies came from private sources. Catholic and Protestant world church organizations, as well as Catholic welfare organizations in the United States, helped to improve the lot of the most underprivileged part of the Polish population. Alone among the East-Central European countries, Poland permitted the CARE welfare organization to operate on her territory.

Hand in hand with material aid, accompanied by the granting of the most-favoured-nation clause for Polish trade with the United States, came a substantial increase in travel and cultural exchanges. The US Department of State in particular, as well as the Ford and Rockefeller Foundations, extended invitations to numerous Polish scholars to visit America and carry on research there.

It was in this atmosphere that the Poles came forward with an initiative intended to establish a 'bridge' between East and West. To a considerable extent the reappearance of Poland on the world diplomatic scene – in which she attempted to play the role of broker – was due to the personality of the Foreign Minister, Adam

---

[34] The visits of Vice-President Nixon in 1959 and that of Robert Kennedy in 1964 enabled the Polish public to express their pro-American sympathies.

Rapacki. It may be true that he had given full support to the amalgamation of his party, the PPS, with the communists. At the same time he was one of those who sought the basis of the 'Polish road to socialism' in a more tolerant and humanitarian approach to communist theory and practice. The fact that he was a member of the PUWP Politburo did not prevent him from being, above all, a diplomat whose main duty was to promote the interests of Poland. Rapacki, a highly gifted negotiator, made full use of his skills – broad intellectual background, knowledge of languages, and, last but not least, personal charm. Under his guidance Polish foreign policy, carried out by professional diplomats, managed to work out a peace plan which drew the attention of both East and West.

The Polish initiative, soon to be referred to as the 'Rapacki Plan', was characterized by two distinctive features. First, it aimed at the solution of the crucial problems of contemporary international politics – relaxation of tensions, infusion of more confidence into East-West relations, and gradual disarmament, which was eventually to include a voluntary ban on nuclear weapons. Secondly, Polish endeavour did not address itself to all the issues of the divided world. It was limited to Central Europe, i.e. to the two Germanies and to Poland and Czechoslovakia. This second feature of the Rapacki Plan combined the interests of Poland with those of Europe and the world.

When launched in early 1957, the plan did not gain the support of the Kremlin. The Czechoslovak government, which at that time was still a model satellite of the Soviet Union, also remained unimpressed. Only Walter Ulbricht, the East German leader, gave the Polish initiative his full backing. He considered it an ingenious means by which his state and government might secure Western recognition. To secure Soviet support required great skill and determination on Rapacki's part. In 1957 he was able to introduce the main ideas of his 'denuclearization of Central Europe' project in the UN General Assembly. He indicated that it was supported by the other members of the Warsaw Pact. Presented as a contribution to world peace, the plan suggested that the two German states and the Republic of Poland 'impose a ban on the production of atomic and thermo-nuclear weapons' on their territories. At the same General Assembly session the Polish action was supported by Czechoslovakia.

Rapacki coined for the new policy the name of 'constructive coexistence'. It was intended to serve the interests of Poland by denying nuclear weapons to West Germany. Its scope was actually much wider. It aimed at a general *détente* in Europe, which would enable

(US Fiscal Years—Millions of Dollars)

Programme	Post-war relief period 1946–1948	Marshall Plan period 1949–1952	1953–1957	1958	1959	1960	1961	1962	1963	1964	1965	1966	1967	Total 1946–1967	Repayments and interest 1946–1967	Total less repayments and interest 1946–1967
			US Overseas Loans and Grants—Net Obligations and Loan Authorizations			Mutual Security Act period			Foreign Assistance Act period								
A.I.D. and Predecessor Agencies—Total[a]	—	—	30·0	25·0	6·0	—	—	—	—	—	—	—	—	61·0	31·5	29·5
Loans	—	—	30·0	25·0	6·0	—	—	—	—	—	—	—	—	61·0	31·5	29·5
Grants	—	—	—	—	—	—	—	—	—	—	—	—	—	—	—	—
Social Progress Trust Fund	—	—	—	—	—	—	—	—	—	—	—	—	—	—	—	—
Food for Freedom—Total	—	—	—	0·5	2·6	3·5	5·0	6·7	8·0	15·0	4·1	6·7	5·0	57·2	—	57·2
Title I—Sales Agreements:																
Payable in Foreign Currency																
(Total Sales Agreements)	{ }	{ }	(18·9)	(115·5)	(42·1)	(51·0)	(124·8)	(58·4)	(49·6)	(59·2)	{ }	{ }	{ }	(519·5)	( )	(519·5)
(Planned for U.S. Uses)	{ }	{ }	(18·9)	(115·5)	(42·1)	(51·0)	(124·8)	(58·4)	(49·6)	(59·2)	{ }	{ }	{ }	(519·5)	( )	(519·5)
Planned for Country Use	—	—	—	—	—	—	—	—	—	—	—	—	—	—	—	—
Economic Development Loans	—	—	—	—	—	—	—	—	—	—	—	—	—	—	—	—
Economic Development Grants	—	—	—	—	—	—	—	—	—	—	—	—	—	—	—	—
Common Defence Grants	—	—	—	—	—	—	—	—	—	—	—	—	—	—	—	—
Cooley Loans	—	—	—	—	—	—	—	—	—	—	—	—	—	—	—	—
Other Grants	—	—	—	—	—	—	—	—	—	—	—	—	—	—	—	—
Assistance from Other Country Agreements	—	—	—	—	—	—	—	—	—	—	—	—	—	—	—	—
Payable in US Dollars—Loans	—	—	—	—	—	—	—	—	—	—	—	—	—	—	—	—
Emergency Relief and Economic Development	—	—	—	—	—	—	—	—	—	—	—	—	—	—	—	—
Title II—Donations:																
Voluntary Relief Agencies	—	—	—	0·5	2·6	3·5	5·0	6·7	8·0	15·0	4·1	6·7	5·0	57·2	—	57·2
Export-Import Bank Long-Term Loans	40·0	—	—	—	—	—	—	—	—	—	—	—	—	40·0	45·9	—5·9
Other U.S. Economic Programmes[b]	401·7	—	—	—	—	—	—	—	—	—	—	—	—	401·7	38·4	363·3
Total Economic	441·7	—	30·0	25·5	8·6	3·5	5·0	6·7	8·0	15·0	4·1	6·7	5·0	559·9	115·8	444·1
Loans	77·7	—	30·0	25·0	6·0	—	—	—	—	—	—	—	—	138·7	115·8	22·9
Grants	364·0	—	—	0·5	2·6	3·5	5·0	6·7	8·0	15·0	4·1	6·7	5·0	421·2	—	421·2

a Excludes $10·6 million in grants to the Kraków Hospital, shown as a non-regional programme.
b Includes UNRRA, $964·0 million; and Surplus Property Credits, $37·7 million.
Source: AID Summary of US Assistance to Poland, 1968.

Poland to renew her traditional economic and cultural ties with the West. But the Polish initiative was repudiated by the Bonn government for a number of reasons: it violated the Hallstein Doctrine which precluded West German participation in any agreement to which East Germany was a partner; many West German political observers regarded it as a clever 'Soviet manoeuvre'; even more convincing seemed to be the objection that the Rapacki Plan would preserve the superiority of the Soviet bloc in conventional forces.

Undeterred by Bonn's refusal, the Polish Foreign Minister proceeded with great energy and resolve to gain Soviet agreement to what has been termed the first version of the Rapacki Plan. The result of his efforts was the Memorandum of the Polish government, of 14 February 1958, dispatched to all powers concerned. In order to remove the necessity of an East-West German contractual obligation, the Memorandum suggested an agreement based on unilateral commitments of the individual states. The establishment of a nuclear-free zone, it was stated, was to facilitate an agreement on the reduction of conventional armaments and of foreign armed forces stationed in the individual states of the zone. A general outline on the carrying-out of the agreement was also suggested.

Implied in this approach was a tacit acceptance of German unification, provided that it would result from disarmament and disengagement on the part of the Great Powers, and a substantial lessening, if not disappearance, of the East-West conflict. Speaking on 31 October 1958 at Oslo University, Rapacki stated that the Poles still feared German unity. He added, however, that 'reunification of Germany as a peaceful country' was necessary 'for a complete normalization of the situation in Europe'. Faced with continued West German concern about the inadequacy of the obligation to reduce conventional armaments, he formulated his second version of the denuclearization plan. He divided it into two stages: first, nuclear weapons would be 'frozen' at their existing levels; secondly, controlled nuclear disarmament would be accompanied by an appropriate reduction of conventional weaponry.

The Rapacki Plan was definitely a Polish idea. It was an expression of the post-1956 Polish autonomy in external affairs. The fact that subsequently the plan was adopted by the Soviet Union and substantially changed so as to serve the overall needs of the Eastern bloc does not detract from the originality of the Polish initiative. Yet Khrushchev's unwelcome intervention demonstrated the narrow limits of Polish external autonomy. Poland, which in foreign affairs was also represented by the increasingly anti-Western Gomułka, would not attempt to outbid her Kremlin master. Beginning with the sixties, the abandonment of the heritage of the 'Glorious October' made itself felt in Polish diplomacy. The Warsaw regime began to align its foreign policies with those of the Soviet Union, as expressed by the Warsaw Treaty Organization. When the third version of the Rapacki Plan was launched at the 1962 Disarmament Conference, it had undergone substantial changes. It was extended so as to cover other states which might wish to accede to it. The concession made to West Germany – that she would not have to negotiate with East Germany – was abandoned.

There is much justification in the criticism 'that the West was at least remiss in not taking up the Polish proposal as a subject for serious negotiation'.[35] Lack of action was owing mainly to the refusal of the West German government to normalize its relations with Poland or even to consider the thorny problem of Polish western boundaries. The nominal support given by President John F. Kennedy to the Rapacki Plan was widely acclaimed by the Poles. In practice, however, the West continued its policy of non-commitment. Thus the impression that the Soviet Union alone supported the Polish claims gained ground. This development enabled the Kremlin to subordinate the Rapacki Plan to its own policies aiming at an overall European settlement embodied in a non-aggression treaty between NATO and WTO. Consequently, the last Polish initiative, the so-called 'Gomułka Plan' of December 1963, aimed merely at the freezing of national armaments. It served Polish interests in so far as it prohibited West Germany from acquiring thermo-nuclear weapons. At the 1964 session of the UN General Assembly Poland proposed the convening of a conference on European security. This new initiative was taken up by the WTO at its July 1966 meeting in Bucharest. Its communiqué combined two policies – a sharp attack against the United States for her 'aggression' in Vietnam, and an offer aiming at the new organization of Europe. NATO and WTO were to be dissolved and replaced by an all-European organization based on the liquidation of foreign military forces and withdrawal of all foreign troops from other countries' territories. Recognition of the Odra–Nysa Line and of the present boundaries of the two German states was all that remained of the original Polish peace proposals.

By then Poland paid only lip-service to the Rapacki Plan. In reality, she gave full backing to the Kremlin policy which demanded the departure of the American army from Europe and a reorganization of the continental security system. This policy received an additional impetus from the new *Ostpolitik* of Bonn,

[35] Stehle, op. cit., p. 236.

which since 1966 made repeated and partly successful attempts at
gaining an economic, if not political, foothold in East-Central
Europe. Speaking of the establishment of diplomatic relations between the German Federal Republic and Romania, Gomułka referred to it as 'political diversion' aimed at the liquidation of the
(East) German Democratic Republic (GDR).[36] It was for this reason
that in the early months of 1967 the Warsaw regime – acting with
full support from the Kremlin – took a leading role in the consolidation of co-operation among those states which were believed to be
most directly affected by West German 'imperialism and revanchism'. Two treaties of March 1967 – of friendship, co-operation, and
mutual aid – were especially to serve this purpose. The agreement
with Czechoslovakia emphasized the 'inviolability of the existing
national frontiers in Europe'. The treaty with the GDR declared
the existence of an East German state 'an important factor for
maintaining peace' and expressly repudiated West German 'mili-
tarism and neo-nazism'.

One month later at the Karlovy Vary (Carlsbad) conference of
communist and workers' parties even greater emphasis was laid on
the integrity and political independence of the GDR. Other states
were requested to establish normal diplomatic relations with her.
The Karlovy Vary communiqué gave full support to the nuclear
non-proliferation treaty, but the Rapacki Plan was changed beyond recognition. It was watered down by listing five European
regions in which 'atom-free zones' could be established. Permanent
peace, Gomułka stated, could be achieved by a

> pact between all the European countries, including Germany,
> that would require them to renounce the use or threat of force
> as well as intervention in the internal affairs of other countries.
> The Pact would also include commitments concerning the in-
> violability of the boundaries of all the European countries.[37]

The degree of identification of Polish foreign policy with that of
the Soviet Union was demonstrated on the occasion of President de
Gaulle's visit to Poland in the late summer of 1967. Gomułka
definitely appreciated the anti-American aspects of France's foreign
policy, but he energetically repudiated the General's suggestion that
Poland might 'play a role outside the Soviet Bloc'. Together with
the Soviet leaders Gomułka believed that NATO – unlike WTO –
was undergoing a deep internal crisis caused by 'Washington's
economic, military and political guardianship' of Europe. The

[36] *Trybuna Ludu* (18 May 1967).
[37] *Politika* (30 November 1967).

belief in the growing consolidation of the WTO received a rude shock with the Czechoslovak events of 1968.

Enthusiastic Polish support for the Soviet invasion of Czechoslovakia must be viewed in terms of the internal struggle within the PUWP. One fundamental issue helped Gomułka to rationalize his action so that it was not opposed by the Polish people. This was the deep-seated fear and mistrust of Germany. All Germans were regarded as objects of suspicion, but the Polish relationship to the German Democratic Republic came to be viewed as a *mariage de convenance*. One could not forget that ever since 1950 Ulbricht's Germany had recognized Polish western borders and declared her willingness to defend them against the West Germans. Despite their long experience, which has demonstrated that a division of a nation can never become permanent, the Poles reserved their resentment and apprehension for the German Federal Republic. Observing her almost miraculous economic growth and increase in prestige, communists and non-communists alike sincerely believed in the possibility of a renewal of the German *Drang nach Osten*. Her first aim, they feared, would be the destruction of the Polish state. A reunited Germany, representing the most powerful NATO member in Europe, possessing nuclear weapons, and calling for the revision of her eastern boundaries had become a nightmare both for the government and people of Poland.

Despite the predominantly anti-militaristic behaviour of the West German government and public, their attitude towards Poland had not been such as to inspire the Poles with any degree of confidence. With a few exceptions,[38] the leading representatives of the Bonn regime repeatedly hinted at the unresolved problem of the German eastern territories. Even more disturbing was the continued rejection of the outstretched hand of Warsaw and the refusal of Bonn to establish normal diplomatic relations with it.

No wonder that even such representative figures of Polish political life as Prime Minister Cyrankiewicz occasionally lost their temper and expressed with unusual 'frankness' their apprehension of German revisionism. In a speech delivered in April 1968 to the *Sejm* Cyrankiewicz reminded the leaders of the German Federal Republic that they behaved 'as though Germans were a people

---

[38] One of the first groups to call for a more positive attitude towards Poland and its territorial demands was the so-called *Bensberger Kreis*, a group of Catholic laymen, which in early 1968 issued the *Memorandum of German Catholics on German-Polish Relations*. While its authors were recognized as sincere and honest, the response of the Poles was rather mixed, emphasizing that the document was unofficial and that it represented the views of only 'a small group'. See *Trybuna Ludu* (4 March 1968).

who bear no responsibility for the genocidal crimes committed by the Nazis during the Second World War'. He attacked them as

people who have not abjured their plans to wrest our lands and bury the independence of the Polish state, the same people who ... wantonly incite the overthrow of the German Democratic Republic, the same people who can see nothing ominous in the recrudescence of unabashedly nationalist, Fascist-leaning currents amid the West German community, its youth not excluded.[39]

It was this sentiment which Gomułka and other Polish leaders used in order to justify and explain Polish intervention against Czechoslovakia. The regime's propaganda made it an act of self-defence against Bonn's *Neo-Ostpolitik*. The military operations of Poland and of the other Warsaw Pact members aimed at the preservation of the *status quo* in Europe, endangered by the attempts of Bonn to wrest Czechoslovakia from the socialist community of states. This argument played on the psychology of the Polish masses, for whom fear of German imperialism had become an overriding consideration.

Ironically enough, in the course of 1969, *rapprochement* with the German Federal Republic was embraced by the Eastern bloc in general and by Poland in particular. This profound change in the German policy of the Warsaw Pact states might have been due to a number of factors.

The most important, perhaps, resulted from the lack of a firm and co-ordinated Western reaction to the Soviet-led invasion of Czechoslovakia and the placing of Soviet troops at a short distance from the Bavarian borders. The post-invasion atmosphere, it was held, caused the German Federal Republic and a number of other European powers to reappraise their Eastern policy and adopt a more favourable attitude towards the Soviet-sponsored all-European security conference, as suggested at several meetings of the Warsaw Pact, especially at the one held in Budapest in March 1969. Another analysis of the East-West *rapprochement* saw its causes in the present circumstances of the Soviet Union. It was pointed out that embarrassing difficulties in the international communist movement, as well as the growing threat in the East, were inducing the Kremlin to work for a relaxation of tensions in the West, and to go so far as to accept American and Canadian participation in the European security conference. The main aim of this meeting would be the improvement of the Soviet ideological image and the securing of the threatened border with China.

[39] *Polish Perspectives* (Warsaw), vol. XI, No. 5 (May 1968), p. 7.

Whatever its causes, the new policy evoked almost immediate response in Poland. As early as the first months of 1969 Polish experts on West German political affairs detected a 'definite differentiation' in West German political thinking on Poland. The previous stereotype clichés, used by Warsaw to single out West Germany for her 'imperialism and revanchism', were abandoned. They gave way to a more sober view of Polish-German relations, which were to be based on those political forces in West Germany which were 'more friendly to us', especially in the ranks of the Social Democratic Party.

It was Gomułka himself who on 17 May 1969 took a decisive step towards a Polish-West German *détente*. He based his declaration on the statement of the Bonn Foreign Minister, Willy Brandt, uttered on the occasion of the March 1968 Social Democratic Congress in Nuremberg. Ignoring that, at the time, the Poles had paid little attention to Brandt's words, Gomułka underlined the fact that the German Foreign Minister had expressed the desire 'to recognize or respect the Odra–Nysa Line until settlement by a peace treaty'. Gomułka declared that this Nuremberg formula was still unacceptable to the Poles, and insisted on an unconditional recognition of the post-1945 Polish western borders. But he admitted that Brandt's approach was an important 'step forward'. The solution proposed by Gomułka was an international treaty between the two states which would recognize the finality of the Odra–Nysa frontier. It seems that this agreement, as originally conceived, was to be concluded independently of the broader issue of the 'normalization' of West German-East European relations. Yet the Polish leader did not deny a close association of the two problems. 'Normalization', he stated, presupposed the fulfilment of three conditions : unconditional acceptance of the Odra–Nysa Line; recognition of the German Democratic Republic as a sovereign state; and signing of the nuclear non-proliferation treaty by the Bonn government.

Gomułka's declaration became the starting-point for a Polish-West German dialogue, marked by a mild tone and a realistic spirit. While Brandt refused to accept the idea of a bilateral settlement of the border issue, he continued to speak in favour of a reconciliation with Poland and offered Warsaw an exchange of declarations renouncing the use of force. He spoke of border questions too. This caused misgiving among the Poles but, nevertheless, they continued to discuss their relations with the German Federal Republic in a factual and unemotional manner. Many commentators went so far as to express hope that Brandt's response, while unsatisfactory, could not be regarded as the last word. The fact that Polish-West

German relations had undergone a profound change was demonstrated by a number of visits paid by leading West German personalities to Warsaw and to other Polish centres. Perhaps most important was the visit of Klaus Schütz, the governing mayor of West Berlin, whose pleadings for the 'recognition of realities' increased Polish hopes for an impending change of mind in Bonn.[40]

In the exchange of views with Bonn, the Poles tended more and more to subordinate their particular interests to those of the socialist camp as expressed by the Soviet Union. This tendency became more evident at the end of July 1969, when the Soviet leadership started direct negotiations with West Germany, paying special attention to the representatives of the Social Democrats and the Free Democratic Party, who advocated a more flexible approach to Russia and eastern Europe. Thus the Soviet Union and her policies remained the key to Polish diplomacy, which took great pains not to incur the displeasure of Moscow by proceeding unilaterally. At the same time, Gomułka and his associates realized that the new Soviet emphasis on *rapprochement* with the West served the national interests of Poland.

The West Germans also preferred to deal with the case of Poland within the broader framework of East-West relations. When Willy Brandt became Chancellor in September 1969 – an event welcomed by practically all communist states of eastern Europe – he spoke in his inaugural speech of the necessity for reconciliation and closer ties with the communist powers, mentioning expressly the Soviet Union, Poland, and East Germany. To Poland he paid particular regard by predicting the establishment of full diplomatic relations between Bonn and Warsaw.

In the execution of its *Ostpolitik* programme the Bonn government intensified its negotiations with the Kremlin, aiming at an agreement by which the two powers would renounce the use of force in the settlement of their disputes. Brandt and his Foreign Minister, Walter Scheel, reacted favourably to the Soviet proposal on the holding of a European security conference as soon as practicable in Helsinki. Less successful were Brandt's negotiations with East Germany, whose leaders feared that a genuine East-West *rapprochement* might run against their own political and economic interests. To the displeasure of Moscow and the other members of the Warsaw bloc, Ulbricht refused to be satisfied with a mere *modus vivendi*, as suggested by Brandt, and insisted on full diplo-

[40] In an article published in the West German weekly *Die Zeit* on 27 June 1969, Schütz spoke in favour of West Germany accepting the Odra–Nysa line, though not in the form of a bilateral treaty. He also expressed the opinion that 'what was important were not formulas, such as a border treaty, but that, above all, the content of a declaration is important'.

matic recognition. On this point the behaviour of Ulbricht's allies remained ambiguous.

At the end of November 1969 Brandt approached Warsaw on a diplomatic level with the suggestion that Poland and West Germany enter into 'comprehensive negotiations' with a view to improving their overall relations. Despite the fact that he refused to change his fundamentally negative stand on a Polish-West German bilateral treaty confirming the existing borders on the Odra–Nysa Line, he clearly indicated his desire to establish closer contacts with Poland.

The new Polish policy was confirmed at the December 1969 meeting of party and state leaders of the Warsaw Pact in Moscow. Stressing even more enthusiastically the necessity for a security conference, to which the United States and Canada would also be invited, the communiqué adopted in Moscow reiterated the determination of the communist states to work for the removal of European tensions, as well as for other 'peace' preliminaries expressed on different occasions by the Kremlin. Discarding the insistence on full diplomatic recognition of East Germany by Bonn, the communiqué demanded that 'all states establish equal relations with the German Democratic Republic on the basis of international law'. The Polish demand for an express acceptance of the Odra–Nysa Line was somewhat weakened. The Warsaw Pact states insisted that all countries 'recognize the existing European borders, including the border along the Odra–Nysa Line, as final and unchangeable'. The 'usual' warnings against revanchism and neo-Nazism were overshadowed by the lavish praise for the political changes taking place in Brandt's Germany, as well as the tendency of the West German public towards 'a realistic policy of co-operation', as demonstrated by the signing of the nuclear non-proliferation treaty.

Bonn welcomed the Moscow communiqué, declaring it to be 'the most conciliatory in recent years'. It was interpreted as Soviet agreement to the initiation of bilateral contacts between East European communist countries and West Germany. The United States, however, expressed concern over the 'nebulous and imprecise' agenda of the European security conference, as well as over the *Ostpolitik* of Bonn. As a result the declaration on the new moves on the European political chessboard, adopted at the NATO meeting in Brussels, represented a compromise. It welcomed the Warsaw Pact call for East-West talks, but – in deference to the United States – insisted that the conference be carefully prepared and preceded by a Soviet demonstration of good faith on at least some key problems of European security.

Not surprisingly the subsequent discussions between the West German government and the Soviet Union were viewed with scepticism, not only by the United States, but also by Great Britain and initially by France. These Moscow talks provided an extremely favourable background for the second round of Polish-West German trade talks. Amid rumours of an imminent loan of over $500 million to Warsaw, the two countries proceeded to a more systematic consideration of different aspects of their mutual trade relations. It seems that, like all East European countries, Poland was also eager to secure Western plants and machinery and to gain access to technological know-how so that she could increase her industrial efficiency.

Towards the end of 1969 Poland informed the Bonn government of her willingness to go on to more concrete political talks. These, it was understood, were to provide a security guarantee for the western borders and to take up the German offer on the conclusion of an agreement on the renunciation of force. In his New Year speech Gomułka foresaw the continuation of an official exchange of views between Warsaw and Bonn and again emphasized the importance of full recognition of the western borders, referring to it as one of the 'realities' of post-war Europe. He weakened his intransigence somewhat by stating that the issue involved in Polish-West German relations 'was not a border problem, but only a problem of peace'.

But East Germany's insistence on full diplomatic recognition, which the Soviet Union did not dare or care to deny, caused a cooling-off in Brandt's fervour to promote understanding with the Soviets and eastern Europe. Certain remarks, which crept into his Report on the State of the Nation, indicated a revision of his original views. West German participation in a European security conference, he stated, 'would make little sense, if it were not accompanied by a positive beginning in better relations between Germans'. Brandt emphasized that he was not a 'wanderer between two worlds', his policy of peace being dependent on 'the security and friendship of proven alliances' with the Western Powers. By the end of January, however, the Bonn government had returned to its quest for an understanding with the Soviets and Poland, dispatching high Foreign Service officials to Moscow and Warsaw.

It is clear that Warsaw's new approach to Germany was sincere, being based on weighty political and economic considerations. Mindful of the consequences of Locarno, which had turned German expansionism towards the East, Gomułka and his government tried to achieve as secure a diplomatic guarantee of Poland's western borders as possible. His West German overtures were in many respects a continuation of Rapacki's previous unsuccessful policies which had been watered down because of Soviet intervention. The fact that this time Soviet interests appear to be identical with those of the Poles cannot be overestimated. Indeed, all steps undertaken by Warsaw can be fitted into the general political trend of the Soviet Union and have enjoyed the Kremlin's full approval.

However inevitable, the linking of Polish foreign policy with that of the Soviet Union has certain disadvantages. For it may well be that Moscow's aim is not to bring about a relaxation of tension in Europe, but to induce West Germany to assume a more neutral role in Europe, or to lull the NATO powers into unilateral disarmament. In other words, the Kremlin European security plan might be motivated by a desire to prevent the creation of a united western Europe. In that case the Polish manoeuvre may again prove to be a failure in the long run.

It is fair to say that in the last decade Polish representatives have assumed prominent roles in the diplomacy of Europe. But an independent foreign policy initiative – as envisaged by Rapacki – has been replaced by strict alignment with the Soviet Union. It is interesting that the disappearance of an independent foreign policy has been accompanied by the growing prestige of Poland, the PUWP, and its leader in the community of socialist states. With the sixties Gomułka established closer relations with Nikita Khrushchev and became the second most important leader in the Soviet orbit. After a brief crisis caused by the unceremonial removal of Khrushchev from the CPSU leadership, Gomułka re-established his position and prestige with Kosygin and Brezhnev. However profitable from the point of view of Poland's importance within the Eastern bloc, his lofty status has been bought at the price of subservience to the external, and to some extent the internal, policies of the Kremlin.

Place Name Variations

TOWNS

Polish	English	French	German	Russian	Other
Białystok				Belostok Byelostok	
Brześć nad Bugiem	Brest Litovsk				Brześć Litewski (Polish)
Bydgoszcz Bytom			Bromberg Beuthen		
Chorzów			Königshütte		Krolewska Huta (Pol.)
Cieszyn Częstochowa			Teschen Tschenstochau	Chenstochhov	Teśin (Czech) Chenstokhov
Dbrowa Gornicza			Dombrau		
Elbląg			Elbing		
Gdańsk Gdynia Gliwice Gniezno Grudziądz	Dantzig		Danzig Gdingen Gleiwitz Gnesen Graudenz		Hnezdno (Cz.)

Inowrocław			Hohensalza		
Kalisz			Kalisch		
Kamieniec				Kamenets Podolski	
Karwina			Karwin		Karviná (Cz.)
Katowice			Kattowitz		Stalinogród (Polish temp.)
Kielce				Kel'tsy	
Kijów	Kiev	Kiev	Kiew	Kiyev	
Kłodzko			Glatz		Kladsko (Cz.)
Kołobrzeg			Kolberg		
Kowno	Kaunas		Kaven, Kaunas	Kovno	Kaunas (Lith.)
Koźle			Cosel, Kosel		
Kraków	Cracow	Cracovie	Krakau		Krakov (Cz.)
Królewiec			Königsberg	Kaliningrad	
Liegnica			Legnitz		
Łódź	Lodz		Littmanstadt	Lodz, Lodz'	
Lublin				Lyublin	
Lwów			Lemberg	L'vov, Lvov	
Malbork			Marienburg		
Morawska Ostrawa	Morawska Ostrawa		Märhisch Ostrau		Ostrava Moravská Ostrava

Polish	English	French	German	Russian	Other
Olsztyn			Allenstein		
Opole			Oppeln		Opolí (Cz.)
Orawa					Orava (Cz.)
Oświęcim			Auschwitz		Oravsky Podzámok (Slovak)
Poznań	Poznan		Posen		
Racibórz			Ratibor		Ratiboř (Cz.)
Szczecin			Stettin		
Szklarska Poręba			Schreiberhau		
Tarnowskie Góry			Tarnowitz		
Toruń			Thorn		
Trzyniec					Třinec (Cz.)
Wałbrzych			Waldenburg		
Warszawa	Warsaw	Varsovie	Warschau	Varshava	Vilnyus (Lith.)
Wilno	Vilna		Wilna	Vilno, Vilna / Vilna	Vilnius (Lith.)
Witkowice			Witkowitz		Vitkovice

Wolin	Wollin		
Wrocław	Breslau		Vratislav (Cz.)
Zabrze	Hindenberg		
Zamość		Zamost'ye	
Żary	Sorau		
Zgorzelec	Görlitz		Zhořelec (Cz.)
Zielona Góra	Grünberg		

RIVERS

Bóbr	Bober		Bobrava (Cz.)
Bug			
Bzura			
Motława	Motlau		
Narew		Ngrev	
Niemen	Memel	Neman	Nemunas (Lith.)
Noteć	Netze		
Nysa	Neisse		Nisa (Cz.)

	English	French	German	Russian	Other
Odra Olza			Oder		Odra (Cz.) Olše (Cz.)
Pregoła Prypeć	Pripet		Pregel	Pregel' Pripyat, Pripyat'	
Warta Wisła	Vistula	Vistule	Warthe Weichsel	Varta Visla	
Zbrucz				Zbruch	

REGIONAL NAMES

	English	French	German	Russian	Other
Beskidy Białoruś	Beskids Belorussia Byelorussia White Russia	Byelorussie	Beskiden Weissrussland	Byelorossiya	Beskydy (Cz.) Bílá Rus (Cz.)
Galicja	Galicia	Galicie	Galizien	Galitsiya	Halič (Cz.)
Karkonosze Kujawy	Giant Mtns. Cujavia		Riesengebirge Kujawien		Krkonoše (Cz.)
Litwa	Lithuania	Lithuanie	Litauen	Litva	Lietuva (Lith.)

(Polish)	(English)	(French)	(German)		(Latin / Czech / Hungarian)
Łysa Góra	Bald Mtn.				
Małopolska	Little Poland	Petite Pologne	Klein Polen		
Mazowsze	Masovia				Mazovia (Latin)
Mazury, Masury	Masuria		Masuren		
Podole	Podolia	Podolie			
Pomorze	Pomerania	Pomeranie	Pommern		Pomořany (Cz.)
Prusy	Prussia	Prussie	Preussen		
Śląsk, Dolny	Silesia, Lower	Basse Silésie	Niederschlesien		Slezsko (Cz.)
Śląsk, Górny	Silesia, Upper	Haute Silésie	Oberschlesien		Spiš (Cz.)
Spisz			Zips		
Świętokrzyskie Góry	Holy Cross Mtns.				
Tatry	Tatra		Tatra		Tatry (Cz.) / Tátra (Hung.)
Warmja	Warmia		Ermland		
Wielkopolska	Great(er) Poland	Grande Pologne	Gross Polen		
Wyżyna Lubelska	Lublin Uplands				
Wołyń	Volhynia			Wolyn	
Suwałki	Suvalki			Suvalki	

Bibliography

Bibliography

History

The standard English language work is *The Cambridge History of Poland*, ed. W. F. Reddaway, J. H. Penson, O. Halecki, and R. Dyboski (2 vols., Cambridge, 1950–51).

Shorter works are

O. Halecki, *A History of Poland* (2nd edn., London and New York, 1956).

H. Roos, *A History of Modern Poland* (London and New York, 1966).

L. R. Lewitter, 'Poland under the Saxon Kings', *The New Cambridge Modern History*, vol. VII, and 'The Partitions of Poland', ibid., vol. VIII.

Historia Polski (5 vols., Warsaw, Państwowe Wydawnictwo Naukowe, 1958–59), is an up-to-date social and economic history.

Geography and Resources

A survey of the economy and resources is given in Oscar Halecki (ed.), *Poland* (New York, 1957), a volume in the series *East-Central Europe under the Communists*. The geography of Poland is covered in N. J. G. Pounds, *Eastern Europe* (London, 1967), and its political aspects in the same author's *Poland Between East and West* (Princeton, N.J., 1964). Alfred Zauberman, *Industrial Progress in Poland, Czechoslovakia and East Germany 1937–1962* (London, 1964) surveys the economic growth of the post-war period. A somewhat older, but still useful, coverage of the same subject are : Thad Paul Alton, *Polish Postwar Economy* (New York, 1955), and *La Pologne* (Paris : Institut National de la Statistique et des Études Économiques, 1954). On the mining and metallurgical industries, see N. J. G. Pounds, *The Upper Silesian Industrial Region* (Bloomington, Ind., 1958). On development in the Western Territories, see Elisabeth Wiskemann, *Germany's Eastern Neighbours* (London and New York, 1956).

On more specialized aspects of Polish history, see : Pierre Francastel (ed.), *Les Origines des Villes Polonaises* (Paris, 1960);

William John Rose, *The Drama of Upper Silesia* (London, 1936); Ian F. D. Morrow, *The Peace Settlement in the German Polish Borderlands* (London, 1936).

CHAPTERS 5 TO 10

Primary sources, Memoirs, Documents, Speeches

D'Abernon, Viscount, *The Diary of an Ambassador*, 3 vols., New York, 1929–31.

Anders, Général Wladyslaw, *Mémoires* (1939–1946), traduit du polonais par J. Rzewuska, Paris, 1948.

Beck, Józef, *Final Report*, New York, 1957.

Gomułka, Władysław (Wiesław), *W walce o demokrację ludową* (In the Struggle for the People's Democracy), 2 vols., Łódź, 1947.

Gomułka, Władysław, *Przemówienia* (Speeches). Published on an annual basis, 1956–64, Książka i Wiedza, Warsaw, 1957–65.

Kurkiewicz, Władysław *et al.*, *Tysiąc lat dziejów Polski* (Thousand Years of Polish History), Warsaw, 1962.

Laroche, Jules, *La Pologne de Pilsudski.* Souvenirs d'une ambassade, 1926–1935, Paris, 1953.

Lloyd George, David, *The Truth About the Peace Treaties*, London, 1938.

Mały Słownik historii Polski (Small Encyclopedia of Polish History), Warsaw, 1964.

Mikołajczyk, Stanisław, *The Rape of Poland : The Pattern of Soviet Domination*, London and New York, 1948.

Raczynski, Edward Count, *In Allied London*, London, 1962.

Rocznik statystyczny (Statistical Yearbook), 1957, 1961, 1966.

Twenty Years of the Polish People's Republic, Państwowe wydawnictwo Ekonomiczne, Warsaw, 1964.

Witos, Wincenty, *Moje Wspomnienia* (My Memoirs), 3 vols., Instytut Literacki, Paris, 1964.

Zinner, Paul E., ed., *National Communism and Popular Revolt in Eastern Europe. A Selection of Documents on Events in Poland and Hungary*, February–November 1956, New York, 1956.

Piłsudski, Józef, *Pisma zbiorowe* (Collected Writings), 10 vols., Warsaw, 1937–38.

Ciechanowski, Jan, *Defeat in Victory*, New York, 1947.

Bliss Lane, Arthur, *I Saw Poland Betrayed*, Indianapolis, 1948.

The Polish Republic

General Historical Works
Reddaway, W. F., Penson, J. H., Halecki, O., and Dyboski, R., *Cambridge History of Poland*, 2 vols., Cambridge, 1941, 1950.
Halecki, Oscar, *A History of Poland*, London and New York, 1956.
Dyboski, Roman, *Poland in World Civilization*, New York, 1950.
Roos, Hans, *A History of Modern Poland. From the Foundation of the State in the First World War to the Present Day* (translated from the German by J. R. Foster), London and New York, 1966.

Political Histories
Wereszycki, Henryk, *Historia polityczna Polski w dobie popowstaniowej 1864–1918* (Political History of Poland in the Post-Insurrectionist Period 1864–1918), Warsaw, 1948.
Pobóg-Malinowski, Władysław, *Najnowska historia polityczna Polski 1864–1939* (Recent Political History of Poland 1864–1939), 2 vols., London, 1963, 1967.
Mackiewicz, Stanisław, *Historia Polski od 11 listopada 1918 r. do 17 września 1939 r.* (History of Poland from 11 November 1918 until 17 September 1939), London, 1941.

Politics of the Polish Republic
Buell, Raymond Leslie, *Poland : Key to Europe*, New York, 1939.
Fiala, Václav, *Soudobé Polsko* (Contemporary Poland), Prague, 1936.
Machray, Robert, *The Poland of Piłsudski*, New York, 1937.
Muhlstein, Anatole, *Le Maréchal Piłsudski 1867–1919*, Paris, 1939.
Rose, William John, *The Rise of Polish Democracy*, London, 1948.
Schmitt, Bernadotte, ed., *Poland*, Berkeley, Calif., 1945.
Seton-Watson, Hugh, *Eastern Europe Between the Wars 1918–1941*, New York, 1952.
Mackiewicz, Stanisław, *Polityka Becka* (The Politics of Beck), Paris, 1964.

Inter-War Foreign Policy and Diplomacy
Batowski, Henryk, *Kryzys dyplomatyczny w Europie, jesień 1938–wiosna 1939* (Diplomatic Crisis in Europe, Fall 1938–Spring 1939), Wydawnictwo Ministerstwa Obrony Narodowej, Warsaw, 1962.
Batowski, Henryk, *Pierwsze Tygodnie Wojny. Dyplomacja zachodnia do połowy września 1939 r.* (The First Weeks of the

War. Western Diplomacy until the middle of September 1939), Poznań, 1967.

Dębicki, Oscar, *Foreign Policy of Poland, 1919–39*, New York, 1962.

Komarnicki, Tytus, *Rebirth of the Polish Republic; A Study in the Diplomatic History of Europe, 1914–1920*, London, 1957.

Korbel, Josef, *Poland Between East and West. Soviet and German Diplomacy Towards Poland 1919–1933*, Princeton, N.J., 1963.

Roos, Hans, *Polen und Europa*, Tübingen, 1957.

Wandycz, Piotr S., *France and Her Eastern Allies 1919–1925. French–Czechoslovak–Polish Relations from the Paris Peace Conference to Locarno*, Minneapolis, 1962.

Poland During World War II

Bór-Komorowski, T., *The Secret Army*, London, 1950.

Karski, Jan, *Story of a Secret State*, London, 1941.

Korboński, Stefan, *W imieniu Rzeczypospolitej*... (In the Name of the Republic), Paris, 1954.

Rozek, Edward J., *Allied Wartime Diplomacy: A Pattern in Poland*, New York, 1958.

Stypułkowski, Z., *Invitation to Moscow*, London, 1951.

The People's Republic

Background of Polish Communism

Dziewanowski, M. K., *The Communist Party of Poland*, Cambridge, Mass., 1959.

Halecki, Oscar, ed., *Poland*, East-Central Europe under the Communists Series, New York, 1957.

Markert, Werner, ed., *Osteuropa Handbuch: Polen*, Cologne, 1959.

Morisson, James F., *The Polish People's Republic*, Baltimore, 1968.

Staar, Richard F., *Poland 1944–1962. The Sovietization of a Captive People*, New Orleans, 1962.

Ulam, Adam B., *Titoism and the Cominform*, Cambridge, Mass., 1952.

Wiskemann, Elisabeth, *Germany's Eastern Neighbours: Problems relating to the Oder–Neisse Line and the Czech Frontier Regions*, London and New York, 1956.

Post-1956 Poland

Bethell, Nicholas, *Gomułka, His Poland and His Communism*, London, 1969.

Bromke, Adam, *Poland's Politics: Idealism vs. Realism*, Cambridge, Mass., 1967.

Gibney, Frank, *The Frozen Revolution*, New York, 1959.

Hiscocks, Richard, *Poland: Bridge for the Abyss?* An Interpretation of Developments in Post-War Poland, London, 1963.

Korbónski, Stefan, *Warsaw in Exile*, New York, 1966.

Lewis, Flora, *The Polish Volcano. A Case History of Hope*, New York, 1958; London, 1959.

Montias, John M., *Central Planning in Poland*, New Haven, 1962.

Schneiderman, S. L., *The Warsaw Heresy*, New York, 1959. York, 1959.

Stehle, Hansjakob, *The Independent Satellite* (translated from the German by D. J. S. Thompson), New York, 1965.

Syrop, Konrad, *Spring in October: The Polish Revolution of 1956*, New York and London, 1957.

Index

Index

Printed in Great Britain by The Garden City Press Limited
Letchworth, Hertfordshire